LATIN AMERICAN
POLITICAL MOVEMENTS

LATIN AMERICAN POLITICAL MOVEMENTS

Edited by Ciarán Ó Maoláin

Facts On File Publications
New York, New York • Oxford, England

LATIN AMERICAN POLITICAL MOVEMENTS

Published by **Longman Group Limited**, Longman House,
Burnt Mill, Harlow, Essex CM20 2JE, UK

© Longman Group Limited 1985

First published 1985

British Library Cataloguing in Publication Data
Latin American political movements.
   1. Latin America—Politics and government
   I. Ó Maoláin, Ciarán
   320.98   JL966
   ISBN 0-582-90275-4

First published in the United States by
Facts on File, Inc., 460 Park Avenue South,
New York, NY 10016, USA
ISBN 0-8160-1410-8

Printed in Great Britain by
The Eastern Press Ltd, London and Reading
Cover design by Archetype, London SE20 8AJ

Contents

For Mary

Introduction

The aim of this work is to present in a compact and readily accessible form, basic factual information on political parties and alliances, guerrilla movements, pressure groups and other legal and illegal organizations currently active in the ever-changing political scene in the 20 Latin American republics and Puerto Rico.

Each of the 21 sections is introduced by an outline of the country's political history, constitutional framework and recent election results. Movements are then listed alphabetically according to the vernacular form of the name, each entry containing the available information on the leadership, structure, history, policies and other aspects of the movement. Finally, there is an index of personal names.

As is the case with any reference work in such a fluid field of study, this book will inevitably contain outdated information, particularly in respect of leadership names, the composition of multi-group alliances, and the existence and activities of minor or clandestine formations. The use of non-specialist secondary sources and reliance on data supplied by opponents or partisans of particular movements have their own hazards, but it is hoped that careful editing will have eliminated major inaccuracies and distortions. However, membership and publication circulation figures, where stated, are usually derived directly or indirectly from the organizations concerned and may not be realistic.

Particular acknowledgement is due of the use made of the monthly news reference service, *Keesing's Contemporary Archives*, and of its Latin American specialists, contacts and information resources. I have aspired in this volume to the standards of objectivity and accuracy which have since 1931 been the stock-in-trade of *Keesing's*. Mention should be made in this context of two earlier reference titles from the *Keesing's* stable, namely *Political Dissent: An International Guide to Dissident, Extra-Parliamentary, Guerrilla and Illegal Political Movements* (1983) and *Political Parties of the World* (2nd edition 1984), whose coverage of Latin American movements and parties provided a starting-point for the present volume.

By no means all the forces at work in Latin American political life can be covered in a work of this kind: formally-constituted political movements are important, but so are social, economic or cultural institutions and phenomena, such as the armed forces, the various tendencies within the Catholic Church, the landed oligarchy, the press, peasant squatter movements, the emerging feminist movement, shanty town associations, and so on; nor has it been thought desirable to enter into controversies about *caudillismo*, patron–client relationships, imperialism, urban–rural or highland–lowland dynamics, inter-racial and inter-ethnic tensions, or the other concerns of contemporary analysts of the Latin American reality.

Thanks for their assistance with various aspects of the research and compilation are due to Alan Day, Henry Degenhardt, Posy Hill, Rob Birsel, Sonia Ruseler and Serge Cipko, to many of the movements listed, to the Latin American Department of Portsmouth Polytechnic and to Latin American diplomats, exiles, solidarity groups and resource centres in London. Any errors or omissions which readers may detect are my responsibility and I will gratefully receive information concerning them.

October 1985   CÓM

Argentina

Capital: Buenos Aires   **Population: 30,600,000**

Argentina gained independence from Spain in 1816. The dominant political parties in the present century have been the Unión Cívica Radical (UCR), which was in power in 1916–30, and the Peronist movement, in power from 1946–55 and 1973–76. The regime of Gen. Juan Domingo Perón was overthrown by a military coup in September 1955, and elections held in 1958 gave power to the Instransigente faction of the UCR, with Dr Arturo Frondizi as President. Another coup in 1962 deposed Frondizi and in 1963 Dr Arturo Illía was elected President as the leader of the UCR del Pueblo. Yet another coup in 1966 led to seven years of military government, and a period of Peronist rule under Dr Héctor Cámpora (1973), Gen. Péron (1973–74) and his widow Isabel Martínez de Perón (1974–76), was ended by a coup in March 1976 which installed a three-man military junta.

The mid- to late 1970s were marked by a period of "dirty war" between the armed forces and left-wing and Peronist guerrilla groups, principally the Montoneros and the Ejército Revolucionario del Pueblo. Of the many thousands who "disappeared" during the successful counter-insurgency campaign, most are now known to have been executed by the military authorities or (in the early part of the campaign) by death squads including the Alianza Anticomunista Argentina (AAA or Triple A); there were frequent reports of other violations of human rights, giving rise to protest groups such as the Madres de Plaza de Mayo, representing parents of the "disappeared".

In 1981 five opposition parties representing about 80 per cent of the electorate formed an alliance, the Multipartidaria, to press for a return to civilian rule. The collapse of the junta was hastened by the defeat in 1982 of Argentina's attempt to regain control of the Islas Malvinas/Falkland Islands from the United Kingdom, which had ruled the islands since 1833. Civilian government was restored after elections in October 1983, which were won by the UCR and installed Raúl Alfonsín as President.

Constitutional background. The federal Republic of Argentina has an executive President elected for a six-year term by an electoral college which is elected by universal adult suffrage. The legislature consists of a Chamber of Deputies of 254 members elected directly, for six-year terms with half the seats up for election every three years, and a 46-member Senate elected by the legislatures of each of the 23 provinces, serving nine-year terms with one-third of the seats up for election every three years.

Recent election results. In the presidential election of Oct. 30, 1983, Raúl Alfonsín of the UCR won 51.8 per cent of the vote and 317 of the 600 seats in the electoral college and duly took office on Dec. 10. The other main candidates were Italo Luder of the (Peronist) Partido Justicialista (40.2 per cent, 259 seats) and Oscar Alende of the Partido Intransigente (2.3 per cent, 2 seats). In simultaneous general elections the UCR won 129 of the 254 seats in the Chamber of Deputies, the Partido Justicialista winning 111, the Intransigentes 3, the UCD 2, the PDC 1 and regional parties 8. Mid-term congressional elections in November 1985 were too late for inclusion in this book.

Alianza Federal
Federal Alliance
Leadership. Francisco Manrique (president)

Orientation. Right-wing

Founded. June 1983

History. This alliance was formed by four groups in order to present a joint candidate in the 1983 presidential elections. The candidate – Manrique – was unsuccessful.

Membership. The parties which formed the alliance were the Partido Federal, the Concentración Democrática, the Fuerza Federalista Popular and the Movimiento Línea Popular (see below).

Alianza Socialista
Socialist Alliance
Orientation. Socialist

History. This left-wing group was active in 1984.

Asamblea Permanente para los Derechos Humanos
Permanent Assembly for Human Rights
Leadership. Jaime Schmirgeld (secretary–co-ordinator)

Orientation. Human rights concerns

History. The Assembly is one of a number of pressure groups active on human rights issues in 1985.

Centro de Estudios Legales y Sociales (CELS)
Legal and Social Studies Centre
Leadership. Carmen Aguiar de Lapacó (general secretary)

Orientation. Human rights concerns

History. This organization is perhaps the most active of the human rights pressure groups existing in Argentina in 1985.

Associated organizations. The general secretary of the CELS is a member of the executive committee of the Madres de Plaza de Mayo (see below).

International affiliations. The CELS is affiliated to the International Commission of Jurists and to the International League for Human Rights.

Cinco de Abril
April 5 group
Orientation. Left-wing guerrilla group

History. This little-known group claimed responsibility for a bombing carried out on June 8, 1980. It has not recently been reported as active and may be extinct.

Concentración Democrática
Democratic Concentration

History. This group joined the Alianza Federal (see above) in June 1983.

Confederación Socialista Argentina

See PSP (below).

Democracia Cristiana

See PDC (below).

Democracia Social
Social Democracy

Leadership. Adml (retd) Emilio Massera (leader)

Orientation. Right-wing nationalist

Founded. 1981

History. On Nov. 3, 1982, it was announced that Adml Massera had been placed under a 20-day arrest by the Navy High Command after he had stated that Licio Gelli, the leader of the right-wing Italian masonic lodge, Propaganda Due (P-2), had rendered "unquestionably valuable service to the [Argentinian] Republic, especially in the war against terrorism" and had helped to improve Argentina's image abroad since 1976. In a statement issued later in November by the Admiral's press office it was claimed that the party was "the only force capable of creating a new stage in the national movement".

Ejército Revolucionario del Pueblo (ERP)

See PRT-ERP (below).

Familiares de Desaparecidos y Detenidos por Razones Políticas
Families of Political Prisoners and Disappeared Persons

Orientation. Human rights concerns

History. This group, like the Madres de Plaza de Mayo (see below) and other human rights pressure groups active in 1985, is primarily concerned with obtaining the release of persons arrested for political reasons by the military government, and a full account of those persons killed by the authorities during the counterinsurgency campaign of the late 1970s.

Frente Democrático de la Izquierda
Democratic Leftist Front

Leadership. Rafael Martínez Raymonda (leader)

Orientation. Centre-left

Founded. June 1983

History. This alliance of the PDP and the PSD (see below) unsuccessfully contested the 1983 presidential election with Martínez, the PDP leader, as its candidate.

Frente de Izquierda Popular
Popular Leftist Front

Leadership. Jorge Abelardo Ramos (leader)

Orientation. Socialist

History. This group opposed the 16-point agreement between the UCR, the Peronists and other parties in June 1984 (see UCR, below).

Frente Nacional Socialista Argentino (FNSA)
Argentinian National Socialist Front

Orientation. Fascist

History. This organization was active in the mid-1970s, and claimed responsibility for several bombings of synagogues in Buenos Aires. After protests from the Jewish community, the military junta on Sept. 13, 1975, banned the publication, distribution and export of anti-semitic literature, which had until then circulated freely in Argentina, mainly from the Editorial Milicia publishing house. The Front has not subsequently been reported as active.

Policies. The FNSA, in a published statement, attributed Argentina's political and economic problems to a conspiracy by a "Jewish–Bolshevist plutocracy".

Fuerza Federalista Popular
Popular Federalist Force

History. This group joined the Alianza Federal (see above) before the 1983 presidential election.

Intransigencia y Movilización Peronista
Peronist Intransigence and Mobilization

Leadership. Nilda Garres (leader)

Orientation. Peronist

History. This group is a faction of the Peronist movement (see Partido Justicialista below).

Liga Argentina por los Derechos del Hombre
Argentinian League for Human Rights

Leadership. Salvador María Losada (president)

Orientation. Human rights concerns

History. This is one of a number of human rights pressure groups active in 1985.

Madres de Plaza de Mayo
Mothers of the Plaza de Mayo

Orientation. Human rights concerns

History. This grouping, initially informal but now with an executive committee, consists principally of the mothers of persons who disappeared under the military juntas of 1976–83; it takes its name from the square in central Buenos Aires where the mothers held weekly silent demonstrations, wearing white scarves on their heads, to demand the return alive, or an official admission of the death, of their offspring. Despite being ridiculed by the military regime as the Locas (Madwomen) of the Plaza de Mayo, the women won considerable international attention and sympathy for their cause. Together with an offshoot, the Abuelas (Grandmothers) of the Plaza de Mayo, they have played a prominent role in bringing to justice some of those involved in the "dirty war" against the left; in locating the fostered children of kidnapped victims, and in supporting the establishment of similar groups in other Latin American countries.

Publications. *Madres de Plaza de Mayo*, monthly bulletin

Movimiento de Integración y Desarrollo (MID)
Movement for Integration and Development

Leadership. Rogelio Frigerio, Antonio Salonia, Arturo Frondizi (leaders)

Orientation. Centrist

Founded. 1963

History. The MID broke away from the UCR (see below) and later joined with Peronist and other parties to support the successful Peronist candidate, Dr Héctor Cámpora, in the 1973 presidential election. In 1983 its unsuccessful presidential candidate was Frigerio. The MID has one member in the Senate. In June 1984 the MID supported the 16-point agreement between the UCR, the Peronists and other parties (see UCR, below).

Policies. The MID advocates increased industrialization, the encouragement of domestic savings and foreign investment, the opening of new markets abroad and the widest possible participation in the political life of the country.

Membership. 145,000

Movimiento Línea Popular
Popular Line Movement

History. This group joined the Alianza Federal, an electoral coalition formed in 1983 (see above).

Movimiento Nacional Justicialista (MNJ)

See Partido Justicialista (below).

Movimiento Peronista Montonero (MPM)
Peronist Montonero Movement

Leadership. Mario Firmenich (last leader)

Orientation. Peronist guerrilla movement

Founded. 1970

Dissolved. December 1983

History. The Montonero movement, named after irregular cavalry forces of the 19th century, began guerrilla activities in 1970 in support of left-wing Peronist policies; after the election of a Peronist President in April 1973 it ceased its limited offensive operations. At that time it was at the height of its popularity, having the support of tens of thousands of Peronists, but it parted company with the government and resumed its campaign with a series of highly-profitable kidnappings, and attacks on industrialists and military targets, starting in September 1974. The movement suffered heavy losses in the "dirty war" of the armed forces against the left during the period of military rule. It merged with the banned Partido Peronista Auténtico (see below) in April 1977, forming a Consejo Supremo de Montoneros Peronistas (Supreme Council of Peronist Montoneros). The MPM suffered a split in 1980, leading to the creation of the Montoneros 17 de Octubre (October 17 Montoneros) under Miguel Bassano. The movement was virtually inactive in the early 1980s and was reportedly dissolved after the arrest of Firmenich in Brazil in 1983. He was extradited to Argentina in 1984.

Membership. The strength of the movement was estimated at 350 active members in 1980.

Movimiento Popular Neuquino
Neuquén Popular Movement

Orientation. Regionalist

History. This small movement, representing the province of Neuquén, won both the province's seats in the Senate in October 1983.

Movimiento al Socialismo (MAS)
Movement towards Socialism

Leadership. Silvia Dias, Luis Zamora (leaders)

Orientation. Trotskyist

History. The MAS presented Zamora as its candidate in the 1983 presidential elections, gaining some 55,000 votes.

Membership. 55,173

International affiliations. The group was reported in 1984 to have links with Trotskyist groups in other American countries, and particularly in the United States.

Pacto Liberal Autónomo
Autonomous Liberal Pact

Orientation. Regionalist

History. This party holds both Corrientes seats in the Senate elected in 1983.

Partido Bloquista de San Juan
San Juan Bloc Party

Orientation. Regionalist

History. This party holds both the seats representing San Juan province in the Senate.

Partido Comunista de Argentina (PCA)
Communist Party of Argentina

Leadership. Rubén Iscaro, Irene Rodríguez (leaders); Athos Fava (general secretary)

Orientation. Orthodox communist

Founded. Jan. 6, 1918

History. The party was founded by a Marxist faction of the Partido Socialista de Argentina (Socialist Party of Argentina). It was banned in 1966 but in 1973, following the election to parliament of two PCA members as candidates of an Alianza Popular Revolucionaria (People's Revolutionary Alliance), the party was legalized without being granted electoral rights. It held a congress in 1973 and a national conference in November 1975, when it claimed to have 145,000 members organized in 3,925 branches, and a further 68,000 supporters in its youth wing. With all other parties it was suspended by the military junta in 1976.

In 1982 it welcomed the formation of the Multipartidaria alliance; it was legalized in the following year and presented Iscaro as its (unsuccessful) presidential candidate. The party opposed the June 1984 UCR–Peronist accord (see UCR, below).

Policies. The PCA's election slogan in 1983 was "Communists and Peronists, together we will win", but there was some opposition within the party to such a strategy. It generally supports the international policy of the Communist Party of the Soviet Union.

Structure. The PCA has a central committee which is elected at party congresses and which, in turn, appoints an executive committee and a secretariat.

Membership. Estimates of its strength vary from less than 100,000 to about 300,000.

International affiliations. The PCA is recognized by the Soviet Communist Party and its allied parties.

Partido Comunista Revolucionario (PCR)
Revolutionary Communist Party

Orientation. Maoist

History. This offshoot of the PCA (see above) adopted a pro-Chinese line on its formation in the 1970s.

Partido Conservador Popular
Popular Conservative Party

Orientation. Conservative

History. This party was reportedly active in 1985.

Partido Demócrata Cristiano (PDC)
Christian Democratic Party

Leadership. Francisco Cerro, Gabriel Ponzatti (leaders)

Orientation. Christian democrat

History. This party, which was one of the constituents of the Multipartidaria alliance, nominated Cerro as its presidential candidate in 1983. It contested the general elections of October 1983, but won only one seat in the Chamber. It lent its support to the UCR–Peronist agreement of June 1984 (see UCR, below).

Membership. 68,000

International affiliations. The party has affiliated to the Christian Democratic International and to the Christian Democratic Organization of America.

Partido Demócrata Progresista (PDP)
Progressive Democratic Party

Leadership. Rafael Martínez Raymonda (leader); José de Cara

Orientation. Centrist

History. The PDP was involved in discussions with the military government's interior minister in March 1980 as part of preparations for the normalization of political activities. In August 1980 it joined the Unión del Centro Democrático (see below). For the 1983 elections the PDP joined with the PSD (see below) in the Frente Democrático de la Izquierda, with Martínez as its presidential candidate.

Membership. 53,000

Partido Federal
Federal Party

Leadership. Francisco Manrique (president)

Orientation. Right-wing

History. Manrique was present at a meeting held on June 24, 1982, by the newly-appointed head of the military regime, Gen. Reynaldo Bignone, and some 30 politicians representing 14 political parties; Bignone agreed to lift the ban on political activities and to hold general elections before March 1984. In the event, general elections were held in October 1983, when Manrique was the unsuccessful candidate of a right-wing coalition. The Partido Federal refused to support the agreement reached in June 1984 by the UCR, Peronists and other parties (see UCR, below).

Associated organizations. The party was the leading element in the Alianza Federal, formed in 1983 (see above).

Partido de Independencia
Independence Party

Leadership. 11-member collective leadership

Orientation. Centre-right nationalist

Founded. Dec. 14, 1982

History. This party put forward on its formation an "emergency plan" to avoid civil war.

Partido de Integración Demócrata (PID)
Democratic Integration Party

Orientation. Conservative

Founded. Jan. 31, 1983

History. This party received heavy television coverage on its launch, leading to suggestions – denied by the party and the government – that it enjoyed the sponsorship of the military regime.

Partido Intransigente
Intransigent Party

Leadership. Dr Oscar Alende (president); Lisandro Viale (vice-president); Mariano Lorences (secretary)

Orientation. Socialist

History. This party, which developed as a faction of the UCR, refused in 1980 to take part in talks with the military regime on the normalization of political activities. Alende was a candidate in the October 1983 presidential election, obtaining 344,434 votes (2.3 per cent of the total). The party refused to support the UCR–Peronist agreement of June 1984 (see UCR, below).

Membership. 81,000

Partido Justicialista
Justicialist Party

Leadership. Vicente L. Saadi (first vice-president); Jorge Triacca (second vice-president, representing the "62 Organizations" of Peronist trade unionism); Herminio Iglesias (secretary-general, leader of right wing)

Orientation. Peronist

History. This party has its origins in the Peronist movement founded by Lt.-Gen. Juan Domingo Perón Sosa, who as President of Argentina in 1946–55 pursued populist and ultra-nationalist policies and (particularly through his wife, Eva Perón) advocated social improvement. After his overthrow in 1955 Perón went into exile in Spain, from where he continued to direct the Peronist movement, although his party had been outlawed and had divided into various factions. In elections held in 1962, and promptly annulled by the military, Peronists gained one-third of the votes. Elections held in March 1973 were won by the Peronist party, then known as the Frente Justicialista de Liberación (Frejuli – Justicialist Liberation Front), whose leader, Dr Héctor Cámpora, became President. However, he resigned three months later to permit the election of Perón, who had returned from exile in November 1972. His third wife, María Estela Martínez de Perón (known as Isabel), became Vice-President and succeeded him as President on his death on July 1, 1974. She was overthrown in March 1976 by the military who installed a three-man junta and suspended all political and trade union activities.

In August 1980 Peronist representatives were invited to take part in discussions on the normalization of political activities, and in July 1981 the Peronists – then known as the Movimiento Nacional Justicialista (MNJ – National Justicialist Movement) – took part in the formation of the Multipartidaria alliance to press for early general elections. Peronist leaders exiled in 1976, including Martínez de Perón, were permitted from mid-April 1983 to return to Argentina.

In the elections of Oct. 30, 1983, the Partido Justicialista won 5,936,556 votes (40.2 per cent) for its candidates for the electoral college; it came second in the Chamber of Deputies, and gained half the Senate seats and half the provincial governorships. Its presidential candidate was Dr Italo Lúder.

In June 1984 the party, together with several smaller parties, reached a 16-point agreement with the UCR on the necessary measures to be taken to stabilize the internal situation in the wake of the military dictatorship (see UCR, below). The right wing of the party campaigned vociferously, but unsuccessfully, for massive abstention in the November 1984 referendum which accepted the solution agreed between Argentina and Chile concerning the Beagle Channel islands. A deepening of the party's internal divisions in the congress held in December led to the holding of two rival congresses in early February 1985, by the right-wing *oficialista* tendency and the progressive *renovador* tendency, both of which returned Martínez de Perón as president of the MNJ; on Feb. 4, however, she formally tendered her resignation from the post. The main leader of the *renovadores*, Orlando Britos, met one of the principal *oficialista* leaders, Miguel Lorenzo, in April, in an attempt to reunite the party, but the two factions engaged in legal manoeuvres and propaganda battles with the aim of establishing the legitimacy of their respective national councils. A "unitary" congress held in July appeared to give the *oficialistas* complete control over the party's name and resources.

Membership. 3,000,000

Partido Nacional del Centro
National Centre Party
Orientation. Conservative

Founded. July 1980

History. This party was active in the early 1980s.

Partido Obrero
Workers' Party
Leadership. Gregorio Flores, Catalina R. de Guagnini, Juan Carlos Venturini (leaders)

Orientation. Trotskyist

Founded. 1984

History. One of this party's leaders, Gregorio Flores, fought the 1983 presidential election without success.

Membership. 61,000

Partido Obrero Comunista Marxista–Leninista
Workers' Communist Party (Marxist–Leninist)

Orientation. Trotskyist

History. This small formation was active in 1984.

Partido Peronista Auténtico (PPA)
Authentic Peronist Party

Leadership. Dr Oscar Bidegain, Mario Firmenich, Ricardo Obregón Cano (leaders)

Orientation. Peronist

Founded. March 12, 1975

History. The PPA was formed under the leadership of Dr Bidegain, a former governor of Mendoza province who, with other founders of the PPA, was expelled on April 4 from the mainstream Peronist movement, the Frejuli (see Partido Justicialista, above). The PPA created its own national council in September, held a congress in November and was banned in December. In April 1977 it merged with the MPM guerrilla movement of Mario Firmenich (see above), creating a Consejo Supremo de Montoneros Peronistas (Supreme Council of Peronist Montoneros). Firmenich was arrested in Brazil in 1983 and extradited to Argentina in 1984. Bidegain returned from exile in December 1983 (along with Cano) in order to re-establish the PPA as a legal political party, but was arrested on charges including illegal association and verbal incitement.

Policies. On its foundation the party stated its intention to "fight monopolies, promote worker participation in the planning and control of the national economy, and denounce the compromise (of the Peronist government) with imperialism to the detriment of the people". It campaigned against the military regime which held power from 1976 to 1983.

Partido Político Obrero
Workers' Political Party

Orientation. Left-wing

History. This minor group was active in 1984.

Partido Popular Cristiano (PPC)
Popular Christian Party

Leadership. José Antonio Allende (leader)

Orientation. Social Christian

History. This group was active in 1984.

Partido Revolucionario de Trabajadores – Ejército Revolucionario del Pueblo (PRT-ERP)
Revolutionary Workers' Party – People's Revolutionary Army

Leadership. Luis Mattini (leader)

Orientation. Trotskyist

Founded. 1970

History. The ERP was formed in July 1970 by Roberto Mario Santucho as the armed wing of the PRT, and from 1972 was rather better known than the parent party. Its first major action was the kidnapping on March 21, 1972, of a Fiat executive, who was killed on April 10 after the government forbade negotiations on the payment of a ransom and other demands. Also on April 10 the ERP, in co-operation with the FRAP (see above), killed the commander of the Second Army in Rosario. A group of 29 ERP, FRAP and Montonero prisoners escaped from custody in Patagonia on Aug. 24; 10 of them, including Santucho, flew to Cuba, but 19 were recaptured, of whom 16 were killed, allegedly while trying to escape. The ERP subsequently carried out numerous kidnappings (of businessmen, army officers and newspaper publishers) and on July 4, 1973, hijacked an airliner to Cuba. It was in September declared illegal by the Peronist government, towards which it had previously maintained a neutral position.

It continued its campaign into 1974, with kidnappings, attacks on military targets (particularly in the north-western provinces of Catamarca and Tucumán), and the assassination on July 15 of a former Minister of the Interior. Faced with an effective and somewhat ruthless army counteroffensive, the ERP offered in October to negotiate a truce, but the offer was ignored. The group was less active in later years. It carried out an attack on the Córdoba police headquarters on Aug. 20, 1975, with seven people killed, and on Dec. 23–24 it mounted a major operation against military bases in the Buenos Aires district, with more than 160 people killed in fighting in which the army used heavy artillery and helicopter gunships. Another ERP attack, on a communications base at La Plata, was repulsed on Dec. 27.

Santucho and other members of the group were killed near the capital on July 19, 1976. By 1977 the ERP was suppressed in rural Tucumán, but arrests and trials of alleged supporters of the group continued in later years. The Paraguayan police alleged that ERP members were involved in the assassination in Asunción on Sept. 17, 1980, of the exiled Nicaraguan dictator, Anastasio Somoza Debayle. The PRT has remained active in exile but at present appears to have little influence in Argentina.

International affiliations. The PRT–ERP broke off relations with the Fourth International in 1973, as the latter did not approve of the ERP guerrilla strategy. In February 1974 the group set up a Junta Coordinadora Revolucionaria (JCR – Revolutionary Co-ordinating Board) linking it with the Bolivian Ejército de Liberación Nacional, the Chilean Movimiento de la Izquierda Revolucionaria and the Uruguayan Movimiento de Liberación Nacional.

Partido Socialista Auténtico
Authentic Socialist Party
Orientation. Leftist
History. This party was active in 1984.

Partido Socialista del Chaco
See PSP (below).

Partido Socialista Democrático (PSD)
Democratic Socialist Party
Address. Rivadavia 2307, 1034 Buenos Aires
Leadership. Américo Ghioldi (leader); Raúl Dellpiane
Orientation. Centre-left
History. This party, which had formed part of the Unión del Centro Democrático (see below), joined the PDP (see above) in the Frente Democrática de la Izquierda, with the PDP's leader as its candidate in the 1983 presidential election.
Membership. 39,000

11

Partido Socialista Popular (PSP)
Popular Socialist Party

Leadership.   Guillermo Estévez Boero, Edgardo Rossi (leaders)

Orientation.   Social democratic

Founded.   Oct. 15, 1982

History.   Tracing its origins from the Partido Socialista Argentino founded in the 19th century by Juan B. Justo, the PSP was formed with the co-operation of the Confederación Socialista (CS – Socialist Confederation) and the provincial Partido Socialista del Chaco. It supported the Peronist candidate in the 1983 presidential election and won 30,000 votes in the congressional contest. It has subsequently sought to merge with other small moderate socialist formations. In June 1984 it added its support to the 16-point accord reached by the Peronists and the UCR (see UCR, below).

Membership.   60,500

International affiliations.   The PSP has been a member of the Socialist International, but Argentinian membership of that organization was suspended pending the further evolution of political forces in Argentina.

Partido Socialista Unificado
Unified Socialist Party

Leadership.   Simón Lázara (leader)

Orientation.   Left-wing

History.   This party was reportedly active in 1984.

Unión del Centro Democrático
Union of the Democratic Centre

Leadership.   Alvaro Alsogaray (leader)

Orientation.   Centrist

Founded.   August 1980

History.   The Union was formed as a coalition of eight small parties of the centre and centre-left, including the Unión Cristiana Demócrata (Christian Democratic Union, led by Gerardo Ancarola), the PDP and the PSD (see below). It won two seats in the Chamber of Deputies elected in October 1983. In June 1984 it declined to support the 16-point agreement reached by the UCR, the Peronists and other parties (see UCR, below).

Policies.   On its formation, the Union described its aim as the challenging of the monopolization of political debate by populist parties.

Unión Cívica Radical (UCR)
Radical Civic Union

Telephone.   (1) 49-0036

Leadership.   Dr Raúl Alfonsín Foulkes, Dr Víctor Martínez (President and Vice-President of Argentina; leaders); Germán López (leader of populist wing)

Orientation.   Moderate radical

Founded.   1890

History.   The UCR was in power from 1916 to 1930, when it was replaced by a military regime. The party strongly opposed the rule of Gen. Perón (1946–55). In 1956 a party congress nominated Arturo Frondizi as its presidential candidate, whereupon Dr Ricardo Balbín, who had unsuccessfully contested presidential elections in 1951, broke away from the

UCR to form the Unión Cívica Radical del Pueblo (UCRP). However, Frondizi, renaming his party the Unión Cívica Radical Intransigente (UCRI), won the 1958 elections with the support of Peronists and left-wing groups.

In 1962 the armed forces deposed President Frondizi, and in 1963 Dr Arturo Umberto Illía of the UCRP was elected President, only to be ousted by another coup in 1966. In 1973 Dr Balbín, heading a reunited UCR, stood unsuccessfully in two presidential elections; he died on Sept. 9, 1981.

By 1982 the UCR consisted of three factions: a mainstream "línea nacional" group led by Dr Carlos Contín, the "renovación y cambio" group of Alfonsín and the Movimiento de Afirmación Yrigoyenista (Yrigoyenista Affirmation Movement, named after the UCR founder) led by Dr Luis León. A national committee meeting in July 1982 confirmed Contín as president of the UCR and adopted policies rejecting collaborating with the military regime and calling for a "strong popular democracy" and the reorganization of the armed forces as a purely defensive institution.

In the 1983 elections the UCR candidate, Alfonsín, won the presidency with 7,659,530 popular votes, giving him 51 per cent of the electoral college votes, and the party won an absolute majority in the Chamber of Deputies, but only 16 of the 48 Senate seats and seven of the 24 provincial governorships. In June 1984 the UCR proposed, and the Partido Justicialista, the MID, the PDC, the PSP and other parties accepted, a basic 16-point programme – the Acta de Coincidencias – outlining the measures to be adopted to stabilize the internal political situation and deal with the economic crisis inherited from the military regime.

Policies. In his reform programme announced on July 31, 1983, Alfonsín proposed the abolition of compulsory military service, the reduction of military expenditure from 10 per cent to 2 per cent of gross national product, a reform of the code of military justice to make it conform to the civil code, and the creation of a body to make available "privileged information" to human rights groups.

Membership. 1,500,000

International affiliations. The Alfonsín majority tendency of the UCR has contacts with European social democratic parties.

Unión Cristiana Demócrata

See Unión del Centro Democrático (above).

Unión Popular
Popular Union

Leadership. Antonio Cafiere (leader)

Orientation. Centre-left

Founded. September 1985

History. This movement was founded partly as a result of the divisions in the Peronist movement. Its leader was a former Minister of the Economy.

Associated organizations. The party was supported by the Grupo de los 25 (Group of 25) trade union alliance, which arose as part of the *renovador* movement in Peronism (see Partido Justicialista, above).

Bolivia

Bolivia won its independence in 1825, since when it has had a singularly volatile political history; it has a very long tradition of military coups, mainly by the right wing but occasionally by the left; many leading politicians have at one time or another been arrested or exiled by their opponents. Internal unrest has been caused by revolutionary insurrections and by peasant and labour protest movements.

Since the 1940s the dominant political forces have been the Movimiento Nacionalista Revolucionario (MNR), now divided into two large and several small factions; the right wing of the armed forces, part of which allied itself with the drugs trade; and the trade union-based left wing, which has had some military support and has sometimes been allied with the MNRI (the left wing of the MNR). In a presidential election held on June 29, 1980, Dr Hernán Siles Suazo of the UDP coalition (dominated by the MNRI) obtained the highest number of votes, but not an absolute majority; his coalition simultaneously won 57 of the 157 seats in congress. A military coup took place on July 17, and in August Siles Zuazo formed a clandestine government. On Sept. 17, 1982, the armed forces announced a return to civilian rule, and on Oct. 5 Congress, assembled on the basis of the 1980 elections, installed Siles Zuazo as President. The UDP alliance subsequently broke down and Siles Zuazo governed with the support of the MNRI. In July 1985 fresh elections were held, and although Gen. Hugo Bánzer, who had been President in 1971–78, received the largest number of votes, his closest rival, Víctor Paz Estenssoro of the other main MNR faction, was installed as President (for the third time since 1952).

Constitutional background. The Republic of Bolivia has an executive President, a 157-member House of Representatives and a 27-member Senate, all elected for four-year terms by universal and compulsory suffrage of married citizens over 18 years of age and unmarried citizens over 21. A system of proportional representation is used in congressional elections.

Recent election results. In the elections of July 14, 1985, Gen. Hugo Bánzer Suárez of the right-wing ADN gained 28.6 per cent of the presidential vote and his party gained 51 of the 157 congressional seats. Víctor Paz Estenssoro of the MNRH gained 26.4 per cent (and his party 59 seats); Jaime Paz Zamora of the MIR 8.8 per cent (16 seats); Roberto Jordán Pando of the MNRI 4.8 per cent (8 seats); Carlos Serrate Reich of the MNRV 4.2 per cent (6 seats), and the remainder was shared by several smaller parties.

Acción Cívica Popular (ACP)
Popular Civic Action

History. This small party contested election for the first time in 1985, when its presidential candidate won an insignificant share of the vote.

Acción Humanista Revolucionaria (Ahur)
Humanist Revolutionary Action

History. This party also contested the presidential election of 1985 with no success.

Alianza Democrática Nacionalista (ADN)
Democratic Nationalist Alliance

Leadership. Gen. (retd) Hugo Bánzer Suárez (leader)

Orientation. Ultra-right nationalist

Founded. 1979

History. The ADN was formed by Bánzer, who was President of Bolivia in 1971–78, in order to contest the 1979 presidential and congressional elections. He came third in 1979, with 14.9 per cent of the vote, and again in the presidential election of 1980, with 16.9 per cent. The ADN at first supported the military regime which seized power after the 1980 elections but withdrew its support in April 1981; Bánzer was deported in the following month after being accused of plotting a coup.

The ADN was one of the parties which on June 26, 1982, demanded the resignation of the military regime and the recall of Congress. On July 14, 1985, Bánzer won 493,735 votes in the presidential election (28.6 per cent), more than any other candidate, and his party won 51 seats in Congress; however an alliance of centrist and left-wing parties in Congress gave the presidency to Paz Estenssoro of the MNRH (see below) by 94 votes to 51.

Alianza de Izquierda Nacional (ALIN)
National Left Alliance

Address. Edificio Cosmos, Oficina 4, La Paz

Leadership. Rubén Sánchez Valdivia (leader)

Orientation. Left-wing

History. This minor party was active in the early 1980s.

Alianza Renovadora Nacional (Arena)
National Renewal Alliance

History. This minor party contested the 1985 presidential election, but its candidate polled insignificantly.

Alianza Revolucionaria Barrientista (ARB)
Revolutionary Barrientista Alliance

Address. Edificio Asbún Nuevo, 2°, La Paz

Leadership. Dr Jorge Burgoa Alarcón (leader)

History. This minor party was active in the early 1980s.

Bloque de la Vanguardia Revolucionaria (BVR)
Revolutionary Vanguard Bloc

Leadership. Amadeo Vargas Arce (leader)

History. This minor party was active in the early 1980s.

15

Centro Nacionalista (CEN)
Nationalist Centre

Address. Héroes del Acre 1746, Oficina La Voz del Pueblo, La Paz

Leadership. Dr Roberto Zapata de la Barra (leader)

Orientation. Ultra-right

History. This party supported the military regime imposed in 1980.

Policies. The CEN rejects both "liberal democratic bourgeois capitalism" and "Marxist scientific socialism" as historically superseded; it advocates economic nationalism to overcome class struggle and create an integrated society with equality of opportunity.

Comité Nacional para la Defensa de la Democracia (Conade)
National Committee for the Defence of Democracy

Orientation. Human rights concerns

Founded. April 1980

History. This group was formed by representatives of the Catholic Church, trade unions, political parties and newspapers after the kidnapping and killing of a Jesuit journalist by a right-wing death squad on March 21, 1980.

Falange Socialista Boliviana (FSB)
Bolivian Socialist Falange

Leadership. David Añez Pedraza (president)

Orientation. Right-wing nationalist

Founded. August 1937

History. Formed on the model of the Spanish Falange which supported the Franco regime, the FSB first gained parliamentary representation in 1946 and by 1965 had 15 deputies and eight senators. A left wing which had developed within the party broke away in 1970 to form the FSBI (see below). Following the 1971 coup which brought President Bánzer to power the FSB co-operated with the armed forces and the MNR (see below) in the Frente Nacionalista Popular (Popular Nationalist Front), but in 1974 the party split between a majority right-wing constitutionalist faction led by Dr Mario Gutiérrez and known as the FSB–Gutiérrez, and a right-wing pro-military faction led by Gastón Moreira Ostria and Dr Augusto Mendizabal, known as the FSB–Moreira.

The FSB–Gutiérrez withdrew its presidential candidate, Col. José Patiño Ayaroa, before the 1978 elections, opposed the subsequent coup by Gen. Padilla and in 1979 joined the MARC (see below) and the Unión Demócrata Cristiana (UDC – Christian Democratic Union) in the Alianza para la Integración Nacional (APIN – Alliance for National Integration) which backed Gen. René Bernal Escalante in the inconclusive presidential election of July (in which Gutiérrez was the APIN vice-presidential candidate). The APIN team obtained 4.1 per cent of the vote. The FSB–Moreira supported Bánzer's nominee, Gen. Pereda, in the 1978 presidential election, and in 1979 supported Bánzer himself as the (unsuccessful) candidate of the ADN (see above).

The FSB remained in existence in 1985 but appeared to have lost most of its support to the ADN and other right-wing formations. Its presidential candidate in July, the party leader, obtained only 19,985 votes (1.2 per cent), and the party won three seats in Congress.

Falange Socialista Boliviana de Izquierda (FSBI)
Bolivian Socialist Falange of the Left

Address. Casilla 1649, La Paz

Leadership. Dr Enrique Riveros Aliaga (leader)

Orientation. Left nationalist

Founded. March 1970

History. The FSBI broke away from the FSB (see above) and opposed the Bánzer coup of 1971. In December of that year it formed the Frente de Izquierda Nacional (National Left Front) together with the Movimiento Nacionalista de Izquierda (MNI – National Left Movement) and the Movimiento Campesino Tupaj Catari (MCTC – Tupaj Catari Peasant Movement). Under the Bánzer dictatorship its leaders were persecuted, imprisoned and exiled. In 1978 Riveros was its candidate in presidential elections annulled by the military. The FSBI has since remained independent of all other parties.

Policies. The FSBI advocates a social, political and economic restructuring of Bolivia along revolutionary nationalist lines, uninfluenced by other countries.

Structure. The party has a national central committee and departmental, provincial and cantonal committees.

Membership. 150,000

Federación Unica de Trabajadores Campesinos
Single Federation of Peasant Workers

Orientation. Peasant union

History. This left-wing group was active in land occupations and other operations, mainly in the department of Oruro, in the early 1980s.

Frente Pueblo Unido (FPU)
United People's Front

Leadership. Antonio Araníbar Quiroga (leader)

Orientation. Marxist

Founded. 1985

History. This left-wing alliance was formed to contest the 1985 elections, in which its leader (a former general secretary of the MIR and now the leader of MIR–Bolivia Libre) as presidential candidate, won 38,124 votes (2.2 per cent); the alliance won four seats in Congress.

Membership. The constituent parties of the FPU are the PRIN, the PCB, the MIR–Masas and the MIR–Bolivia Libre (see below).

Frente Revolucionario de Izquierda (FRI)
Left Revolutionary Front

Address. Calle Mercado 996, 2° piso, Oficina 2, La Paz

Leadership. Dr Manuel Morales Dávila

Orientation. Very left-wing

History. The FRI's unsuccessful candidate in the 1978 presidential election was supported by groups including the Partido Obrero Revolucionario (POR – Workers' Revolutionary Party), the PCB–ML and the PRIN (see below).

Fuerza Progresista Nacional (FPN)
National Progressive Force

History. This small movement contested the July 1985 presidential elections but secured less than 1 per cent of the vote.

Izquierda Unida (IU)
United Left

Orientation. Socialist

History. This grouping contested the 1985 presidential elections but secured an insignificant percentage of the vote.

Mandato de Acción y Unidad Nacional (MAN)
Mandate for Action and National Unity

Address. Casilla 2169, La Paz

Leadership. Dr Gonzalo Romero Alvarez García (leader); Dr Fernando Oblitas Mendoza (secretary)

Orientation. Nationalist

Founded. January 1972

History. The MAN was formed under the Bánzer regime; although currently in opposition, some of its members have served as ministers or under-secretaries.

Policies. The MAN stands for the development of Bolivia's potential, national unity, social justice, the defence of human rights and of the family, self-determination and the restoration of Bolivia's access to the sea.

Structure. The leadership alternates between two members who together constitute the national leadership council. There are also a national consultative council, a national secretariat and regional structures throughout the country.

Membership. 2,000

Movimiento Agrario Revolucionario del Campesinado Boliviano (MARC)
Revolutionary Agrarian Movement of the Bolivian Peasantry

Address. Calle Yanacocha 448, Oficina 17, La Paz

Leadership. Gen. (retd) René Bernal Escalante (president); Dr José Zegarra Cerruto (executive secretary)

Orientation. Nationalist

Founded. June 1978

History. This party was formed among peasants in Punata province, in Cochabamba. It was part of the APIN (see FSB, above) and contested the July 1979 general election.

Policies. The MARC described itself as nationalist and Christian, with the main aim of liberating the peasantry through a land reform whereby the land would belong to those who worked it with the most advanced technology.

Structure. The movement has a national convention, a national council with an executive committee, and departmental and other committees.

Movimiento Indio Tupac Katari (MITKA)
Tupac Katari Indian Movement

Address. Avenida Eduardo Avaroa 1091, La Paz

Leadership. Luciano Tapia Quisbert (leader)

History. The MITKA leader was an unsuccessful candidate in the 1978 presidential elections (subsequently annulled) and again in 1979, when he gained 1.9 per cent of the vote.

Movimiento de la Izquierda Revolucionaria (MIR)
Movement of the Revolutionary Left

Address. Avenida América 119, 2° piso, La Paz

Leadership. Jaime Paz Zamora (leader)

Orientation. Socialist

Founded. September 1971

History. The MIR arose out of various left-wing groups which participated in the resistance to the right-wing coup which overthrew President Juan José Torres in 1971. Due to its opposition to the Bánzer regime it repeatedly lost its leaders between 1971 and 1978. In the 1978, 1979 and 1980 presidential elections it supported Dr Hernán Siles Zuazo of the UDP alliance (see MNRI, below).

The MIR strongly opposed the military regime in power in 1980–82 and Paz went into exile in Panama, from whence he returned in July 1982. In October he was elected Vice-President under Siles Zuazo and six MIR members joined a UDP Cabinet dominated by President Siles Zuazo's MNRI. In January 1983 the MIR withdrew from the Cabinet (while retaining the vice-presidency), but in April 1984 it resumed participation after certain concessions had been made concerning economic policy. In December Paz Zamora resigned the vice-presidency in order to contest the 1985 presidential election; the other MIR members in the Cabinet resigned immediately afterwards, although one MIR member was reappointed in a reshuffle in January 1985. The question of the attitude of the MIR to the government resulted in the formation of two dissident factions (see below), to one of which the then general secretary of the MIR, Antonio Aranibar, defected early in 1985.

In the July 1985 elections Paz Zamora won 153,143 votes (8.8 per cent) for the presidency, and the party won 16 seats in Congress. A MIR deputy, Gastón Encinas Valverde, was chosen as president of the Chamber.

Policies. The MIR is a non-communist Marxist party which seeks to create a single revolutionary social bloc uniting the middle classes, the working class and the peasantry to achieve "the national and social liberation of the Bolivian people".

Movimiento de la Izquierda Revolucionaria – Bolivia Libre (MIR–Bolivia Libre)
Revolutionary Left Movement – Free Bolivia

Leadership. Antonio Aranibar Quiroga (leader)

Orientation. Socialist

Founded. January 1985

History. Aranibar, formerly the general secretary of the MIR (see above), led a substantial proportion of the MIR membership out of the party and into an alliance – the FPU (see above) which stood against the MIR in the July 1985 elections with Aranibar as its presidential candidate.

Movimiento de la Izquierda Revolucionaria – Masas (MIR–Masas)
Revolutionary Left Movement – Masses

Leadership. Walter Delgadillo (leader)

Orientation. Socialist

Founded. 1984

History. This dissident faction of the MIR (see above) joined the left-wing FUP alliance (see above) to contest the 1985 presidential and congressional elections.

Associated organizations. Delgadillo is the general secretary of the main trade union organization, the Central Obrera Boliviana, in which the PCB and the PRIN (see below) are also influential.

Movimiento Nacional Tupaj Katari (MNTK)
Tupaj Katari National Movement

Address. Calle Montaño 420, Figueroa 680, La Paz

Leadership. José Ticona (leader)

History. This minor party was active in the early 1980s.

Movimiento Nacionalista Revolucionario Histórico (MNRH)
Nationalist Revolutionary Movement – Historic

Address. Jenaro Sanjines 541, Pasaje Kuljis, La Paz

Leadership. Dr Víctor Paz Estenssoro (President of the Republic, leader); Edwin Rodríguez Aguirre (executive secretary)

Orientation. Centre-right

Founded. June 1941, as Movimiento Nacionalista Revolucionario (MNR, Nationalist Revolutionary Movement)

History. The MNR participated in the government of President Gualberto Villaroel, which took power in December 1943 and was overthrown in July 1946. In the May 1951 presidential elections the exiled Paz, as the candidate of the MNR, received the largest number of votes, but not the required absolute majority; a military junta then took power, but was overthrown by the MNR in April 1952, enabling Paz to return and assume the presidency.

The MNR government introduced land reform, universal adult suffrage (including the previously unenfranchised illiterate majority), the nationalization of the mining sector and other reforms. President Paz was overthrown by his Vice-President, Gen. René Barrientos, in November 1964.

The MNR participated until November 1973 in the Bánzer regime installed by a coup in 1971, but later accused Bánzer of corruption and dictatorship. In 1979 its left wing broke away to form the MNRI (see below), and the Paz faction, known since 1965 as the MNR del Pueblo, later became the MNRH. It came second to the MNRI in the 1979 and 1980 elections; its presidential candidate was Paz, who secured 20.1 per cent of the vote in 1980. In June 1982 the MNRH joined with other parties to demand the resignation of the military regime and the recall of Congress on the basis of the 1980 elections.

In the July 1985 elections Paz Estenssoro won 456,704 votes (26.84 per cent), some 40,000 fewer than the ADN leader Hugo Bánzer; as no candidate had secured more than 50 per cent, the presidency was the subject of a congressional vote, and the centrist and left-wing parties combined to declare Paz Estenssoro President for the third time. His Vice-President was Julio Garret Ayllón. The party won 59 seats in Congress, making it the largest single bloc; a member, Gonzalo Sánchez de Lozada, was elected president of the Senate (and thus of Congress).

Policies. The MNRH is for a strong and independent national state and an alliance of social classes.

Membership. 700,000

Movimiento Nacionalista Revolucionario de la Izquierda (MNRI)
Nationalist Revolutionary Movement of the Left

Leadership. Roberto Jordán Pando, Dr Hernán Siles Zuazo (leaders); Federico Alvarez Plata (general secretary)

Orientation. Centre-left

Founded. July 1979

History. The MNRI developed as a left-wing faction of the Movimiento Nacionalista Revolucionario, founded in 1941, and broke away from what became the MNRH (see above) in 1979. It was the leading force in the Unidad Democrática Popular (UDP – Popular Democratic Unity), an alliance founded by Siles Zuazo in April 1978 and also incorporating the MIR (see above) and the PCB (see below). In successive presidential elections Siles Zuazo narrowly defeated the MNRH candidate, winning 36 per cent in 1979 and 38.7 per cent in 1980, but failed to obtain the 50 per cent required for election.

During the 1980–82 military regime Siles Zuazo was in exile in Peru, but he returned on Oct. 8, 1982, after the validation of the 1980 elections, and on Oct. 10 was confirmed as President by 113 votes in the 153-member Congress. He formed a UDP coalition government dominated by MNRI members; he lost the support of the MIR from January 1983 to April 1984, and again from December 1984, and of the PCB from November 1984. In early 1985 he was left with a Cabinet consisting almost entirely of MNRI members and opposed by the left, the trade unions, the army and the peasantry.

In June 1985 presidential elections were held, Siles Zuazo having decided to step down one year earlier than necessary. The extent of his government's unpopularity was revealed by the reduction of its share of the presidential vote to 4.8 per cent (82,418 votes), while the MNRI's congressional bloc was reduced to eight members.

Policies. The MNRI came to power aiming to establish "a truly representative government of a people who are mainly workers and peasants", to end "fratricidal struggles", to renegotiate the country's foreign debt "without accepting impositions which may affect our sovereignty", and to take joint action with Peru and Colombia to suppress drug trafficking.

Movimiento Nacionalista Revolucionario de la Izquierda – Uno (MNRI-1)
Nationalist Revolutionary Movement of the Left – One

Founded. 1985

History. This breakaway faction of the MNRI contested the 1985 elections with no success.

Movimiento Nacionalista Revolucionario de Vanguardia (MNRV)
Vanguard Nationalist Revolutionary Movement

Leadership. Carlos Serrate Reich (leader)

Founded. 1985

History. This group established itself as the fifth largest party in the June 1985 elections, winning 72,197 votes (4.2 per cent) for Serrate's presidential candidature and also securing six seats in Congress.

21

Publications. Serrate is the editor of an important daily newspaper, *Hoy* (circulation 25,000).

Movimiento Popular de Liberación Nacional (MPLN)
People's National Liberation Movement

Leadership. Ramiro Velasco Romero (leader)

History. This minor party was active in the early 1980s.

Movimiento Revolucionario Espártaco (MRE)
Spartacist Revolutionary Movement

Address. Villa Fatima, Calle 17 n° 1774, La Paz

Leadership. Dulfredo Rúa (leader)

Orientation. Ultra-left

History. This minor party merged with the PS-1 in 1984.

Movimiento Revolucionario Tupaj Katari (MRTK)
Tupaj Katari Revolutionary Movement

Address. Casilla 3636, La Paz

Leadership. Juan Condori Uruchi, Dr Clemente Ramos Flores, Daniel Calle M. (leaders)

Orientation. Left-wing and *indigenista* (i.e. represents the interests of the Indian peasantry)

Founded. May 1978

History. The MRTK traces its origins to the independence movements started in the late 18th century by Tupaj Katari in Bolivia (and Tupaj Amaru in Peru), and more directly to the peasant movements of the late 1940s and early '50s. A Confederación Tupaj Katari was founded in 1971. Partido de la Izquierda Revolucionaria (see below). In the 1978 and Democrática y Popular (People's Democratic Unity Front), and in 1979 it supported Víctor Paz of the MNRH in the presidential election. In early 1985 it split, its then leader, Genaro Flores, departing to form the MRTK-L (see below); the rump of the MRTK contested the July elections but did very much worse than the Flores group.

Policies. The MRTK was constituted as a left-wing national democratic organization for all classes, based mainly on the peasants and other exploited strata, with the object of establishing a just society, majority rule and self-determination of the people.

Structure. The movement has a national executive committee and other committees at departmental, provincial and cantonal level.

Membership. 80,000

Publications. *Tupaj Katari*, monthly, circulation 15,000

Movimiento Revolucionario Tupaj Katari – Liberación (MRTK-L)
Tupaj Katari Revolutionary Movement – Liberation

Leadership. Genaro Flores Santos (leader)

Orientation. Left-wing *indigenista*

Founded. 1985

History. This faction split from the MRTK (see above) in 1985 and performed rather better than the parent party in the June elections, winning 31,678 votes (1.8 per cent) for Flores as presidential candidate and securing two seats in Congress.

Associated organizations. Flores is president of the Confederación Sindical Unica de Trabajadores Campesinos de Bolivia (CSUTCB – Single Confederation of Peasant Labour Unions of Bolivia), a major trade union formation.

Ofensiva de la Izquierda Democrática (OID)
Offensive of the Democratic Left

Address. Plaza Venezuela 1440, Edificio Hermann, 11° piso, La Paz

Leadership. Luis Adolfo Siles Salinas (leader)

Orientation. Social democratic

Founded. 1979

History. Siles Salinas had, as leader of the Partido Social Democrático, been President of Bolivia in April–September 1969. After supporting the UDP alliance led by his half-brother Hernán Siles Zuazo (see MNRI, above), he established the OID shortly before the 1979 elections. As the OID candidate in the 1980 presidential election he secured 2.6 per cent of the vote.

Organización Socialista de los Trabajadores (OST)
Workers' Socialist Organization

Address. General Lanza 1866, La Paz

Leadership. Sonia Montaño (leader)

Orientation. Socialist

History. This minor party was active in the early 1980s.

Partido Barrientista Auténtico (PBA)
Authentic Barrientista Party

Leadership. René Alvarez Puente (leader)

History. This minor party was active in the early 1980s.

Partido Comunista de Bolivia (PCB)
Communist Party of Bolivia

Leadership. Simón Reyes Rivera (first secretary)

Orientation. Orthodox communist

Founded. January 1950

History. The PCB was formed by Marxist–Leninist members of the Partido de la Izquierda Recolucionaria (see below). In 1965 a pro-Chinese faction broke away to become the PCB–ML (see below). In the 1978 and 1979 elections the PCB, although illegal, supported Hernán Siles Zuazo and the UDP coalition (see MNRI, above); in 1982, when Siles Zuazo came to power, the PCB was legalized and was given two portfolios in the UDP Cabinet.

At the party's fifth congress in February 1985 Reyes Rivera, a leader of the miners' union, was elected to the main leadership post in succession to Jorge Kolle Cueto. The party contested the July 1985 elections as part of the left-wing FPU alliance (see above).

Policies. The party is committed to the democratic process. Its foreign policies are broadly in line with those of the Communist Party of the Soviet Union.

Structure. The party is based on cells of three or more members; elected district committees appoint secretariats and working commissions. The supreme organ of the party is the national congress, which elects a central committee, which in turn elects a political committee and a first secretary.

Membership. 300

International affiliations. The PCB is recognized by the Communist Party of the Soviet Union and its allied parties.

Partido Comunista de Bolivia – Marxista–Leninista (PCB–ML)
Communist Party of Bolivia (Marxist–Leninist)

Leadership. Oscar Zamora Mendinacelli (first secretary)

Orientation. Maoist

Founded. April 1965

History. The party arose out of a split in the PCB (see above) and supported the Chinese Communist Party in its ideological dispute with the Soviet party. Illegal and clandestine from its inception, the party waged an intensive struggle against the military regimes of Barrientos (1964–69), Ovando (1969–70) and Bánzer (1971–78). In the 1978 elections it supported the presidential candidate of the FRI (see above); in 1979 it supported Paz Estenssoro of the MNRH, and in 1980, with the FRI, it again supported the MNRH candidate.

Policies. Its aim is the national liberation of the Bolivian people and the construction of socialism in accordance with the particular needs and traditions of Bolivia. It stands for the self-determination of all peoples and a new international economic order, and is opposed to hegemonic superpowers.

Partido Comunista Marxista–Leninista Disidente
Dissident Communist Party – Marxist–Leninist

Orientation. Left-wing communist

History. This party was formed after a split in the PCB (see above) and was active in the early 1980s.

Partido Demócrata Cristiana (PDC)
Christian Democratic Party

Address. Casilla 4345, La Paz

Leadership. Benjamín Miguel (leader); Dr Luis Ossio Sanjines, Miguel Rochas

Orientation. Left-wing Christian democratic

Founded. February 1954, as Partido Social Cristiano (Social Christian Party)

History. The party, which adopted its present name at a congress in November 1964, arose from socio-political study groups of the Catholic laity. In partial elections in 1962 it gained one seat (for Miguel) in the Chamber of Deputies. In 1966 it was given one ministerial post, but from 1969 it opposed successive military governments; under Bánzer (1971–78) it fought for human rights, civil liberties and the holding of elections, and Miguel and the PDC organizing secretary, Félix Vargas, were exiled from 1974.

In the elections of 1979 the PDC (together with the MRTK and the FRI – see above – and the PRA – see below) allied itself with the MNRH (see above), gaining nine seats in the Chamber and three in the Senate. Following the restoration of democratic government in late 1982, the party was given on Jan. 31, 1983, a single seat in the Siles Zuazo Cabinet.

In 1985 its presidential candidate was Luis Ossio, who won 24,079 votes (1.4 per cent), while the party gained three seats in Congress.

Policies. The PDC is a democratic centre-left party with progressive social and economic policies.

Structure. The party elects a national consultative council and a national committee, and departmental, provincial and regional committees.

Membership. 50,000

International affiliations. Christian Democratic International; Christian Democratic Organization of America

Partido de la Izquierda Revolucionaria (PIR)
Revolutionary Left Party

Leadership. Dr Ricardo Anaya Arce (leader)

Orientation. Socialist

Founded. 1940

History. This minor party, which went into decline after the breakaway in 1950 of the PCB (see above), was active in the early 1980s.

Partido Liberal
Liberal Party

Address. Venancio Burgoa 947, La Paz

Leadership. Dr Eduardo Montes y Montes (leader)

History. This minor party was active in the early 1980s.

Partido Nacionalista del Pueblo (PNP)
People's Nationalist Party

Address. Avenida del Ejército 1068, La Paz

Leadership. Guillermo Mendoza Riglos (leader)

History. This minor party was active in the early 1980s.

Partido Obrero Revolucionario (POR)
Workers' Revolutionary Party

Leadership. Guillermo Lora (leader)

Orientation. Trotskyist

History. Although outlawed in 1967, the POR supported the candidate of the FRI (see above) in the 1978 presidential elections (which were subsequently annulled).

Partido Obrero Revolucionario – Combate (PORC)
Workers' Revolutionary Party – Combat

Leadership. Hugo González Moscoso (leader)

Orientation. Trotskyist

History. The PORC was formed by a dissident faction of the POR (see above).

Partido Obrero Revolucionario Trotskista Posadista (PORTP)
Posadist Trotskyist Workers' Revolutionary Party

Address. Calle Coitia 13, La Paz

Leadership. Carlos Flores Bedregal (leader)

Orientation. Trotskyist

History. This minor party, a splinter group of the POR (see above), was active in the early 1980s.

International affiliations. Posadist Fourth International

Partido Revolucionario Auténtico (PRA)
Authentic Revolutionary Party

Address. Calle Yanacocha 448, Oficina 2, La Paz

Leadership. Dr Walter Guevara Arce (leader)

Founded. 1960

History. The PRA was established as a faction of the MNR and Guevara stood as its candidate against Paz Estenssoro of the MNR in the 1960 presidential election. In 1974 Guevara was sent into exile by the Bánzer regime. In 1978 and 1979 the PRA supported Paz Estenssoro's candidature for the presidency; the election of 1979 being inconclusive, Guevara, as president of the Senate, was appointed to head an interim government and held office from August to November. In the presidential election of June 1980 he gained only 2.6 per cent of the vote.

Partido Revolucionario Auténtico Ríos (PRAR)
Ríos Authentic Revolutionary Party

Address. Edificio Conavi, 11° piso, Oficina 3, La Paz

Leadership. Jorge Ríos Gamarra (leader)

History. This faction broke away from the PRA (see above) in the early 1980s.

Partido Revolucionario de la Izquierda Nacional (PRIN)
Revolutionary Party of the National Left

Address. Colón 693, La Paz

Leadership. Juan Lechín Oquendo (leader)

Orientation. Left-wing

Founded. 1964

History. The PRIN was established by Lechín, then head of the miners' union and Vice-President of Bolivia, after his expulsion from President Paz Estenssoro's MNR. Lechín spent many years in exile between 1965 and 1978. The PRIN did not take part in the 1966 presidential election, and in that of 1978 it supported the candidate of the FIR (see above). In 1985 it supported the FPU (see above).

Associated organizations. The leader of the PRIN is the executive secretary of the largest trade union organization, the Central Obrera Boliviana (COB – Bolivian Workers' Confederation), and president of the Federación Sindical de Trabajadores Mineros Bolivianos (FSTMB – Bolivian Mineworkers' Trade Union Federation).

Partido Revolucionario de la Izquierda Nacional Gueiler (PRIN–G)
Revolutionary Party of the National Left – Gueiler

Address. Calle Mercado 996, 2° piso, La Paz

Leadership. Lidia Gueiler Tejada (leader)

History. Gueiler was on Aug. 4, 1979, chosen as president of the newly-elected Chamber of Deputies, and on Nov. 16 was appointed by Congress as interim Head of State pending the 1980 elections. She formed a coalition government composed mainly of the Paz Estenssoro wing of the MNR and its allies; in July 1980 her regime was overthrown by a coup led by Gen. Luis García Meza, who denounced Gueiler as having permitted "communism, Castroism and anarchy".

Partido Revolucionario de la Izquierda Nacional Laboral (PRIN–L)
Revolutionary Party of the National Labour Left

Address. Casilla 1657, La Paz

Leadership. Edwin Moller (representative of collective leadership)

Orientation. Socialist

History. This minor party was active in the early 1980s.

Partido Revolucionario de Trabajadores Bolivianos (PRTB)
Bolivian Workers' Revolutionary Party

Leadership. Antonio Peredo (leader)

Orientation. Marxist

Founded. 1972

History. The PRTB was founded as the political wing of the Ejército de Liberación Nacional (ELN – National Liberation Army), a guerrilla organization formed by Dr Ernesto (Che) Guevara in 1967. The ELN was militarily defeated, and Guevara killed, in October 1967, although it carried out a few other actions in 1970–73. The PRTB was created with the aim of forming "a broad resistance movement combining legal, semi-legal and clandestine organizations". In 1985 the party contested the presidential election but polled insignificantly.

Partido Revolucionario de los Trabajadores de Bolivia – Romero (PRTBR)
Romero Revolutionary Workers' Party of Bolivia

Address. Calle Pisagua 385, La Paz

Leadership. Rubén Romero Equino (leader)

Orientation. Socialist

History. This minor party was founded after a split in the PRTB (see above).

Partido Social Cristiano (PSC)
Social Christian Party

Address. Casilla 8152, La Paz

Leadership. Jaime Húmerez Seleme (leader)

Orientation. Christian democratic

History. This minor party was active in the early 1980s.

Publications. Húmerez is the editor of a La Paz daily newspaper, *Meridiano* (circulation 6,500).

Partido Social Demócrata (PSD)
Social Democratic Party

Address. Edificio Barrosquira, 6° piso, La Paz

Leadership. Dr Antonio Chiquie Dipp (leader)

Orientation. Social democratic

Founded. 1945

History. The PSD was founded by middle-class intellectuals.

Partido Socialista Aponte (PSA)
Aponte Socialist Party

Leadership. Dr Orlando Capriles Villazón (leader)

Orientation. Socialist

History. This minor party was active in the early 1980s.

Partido Socialista Tito Atahuichi (PSTA)
Tito Atahuichi Socialist Party

Address. Edificio Terrazas, Calle Yanacocha 448, La Paz

Leadership. Dr Sabino Tito Atahuichi (leader)

Orientation. Socialist

History. This minor party was active in the early 1980s.

Partido Socialista – Uno (PS-1)
Socialist Party – One

Leadership. Walter Vázquez (leader); Ramiro Velasco

Orientation. Socialist

History. The PS-1 leader, Marcelo Quiroga Santa Cruz, unsuccessfully contested the 1978 and 1979 presidential elections, gaining 4.8 per cent of the vote in 1979. He obtained 8 per cent in the June 1980 election, but was assassinated in the following month. The PS-1 joined other parties on June 26, 1982, in demanding the restoration of a civilian government.

In July 1985 the PS-1 presidential candidate, Ramiro Velasco, won 2.2 per cent of the vote (38,782 votes) and came sixth. The party simultaneously won five seats in Congress.

Partido Unión Boliviana (PUB)
Bolivian Unity Party

Address. Pichincha 729, esq. Indaburo, La Paz

Leadership. Walter González Valda (leader)

History. In the 1979 presidential election González obtained 1.3 per cent of the vote as the candidate of the PUB.

Partido de Vanguardia Obrero (VO)
Workers' Vanguard Party

Address. Plaza Venezuela 1452, La Paz

Leadership. Filemón Escobar (leader)

History. In the 1979 presidential election the VO candidate came last, with 1.1 per cent of the vote.

Unión Democrática Cristiana (UDC)
Christian Democratic Union

Address. Calle Yanacocha 448, Oficina 20, La Paz

Leadership. Freddy Vargas Méndez (leader)

Orientation. Christian Democratic

History. This minor party was active in the early 1980s.

Vanguardia Comunista del Partido Obrero Revolucionario (VCPOR)
Communist Vanguard of the Revolutionary Workers' Party

Address. Manuel Loza 2004, La Paz

Leadership. Víctor Sosa (leader)

History. This minor party was active in the early 1980s.

Vanguardia Obrera (VO)

See Partido de Vanguardia Obrera (above).

Brazil

Capital: Brasília   **Population: 135,000,000**

Brazil became independent from Portugal in 1821, and a federal republic in 1891. The country's fifth President in the post-war era, the leftist João Goulart, was deposed by a right-wing military coup which on April 1, 1964, installed a government under Gen. Humberto Castelo Branco. Brazil remained under effective military rule for the next two decades, and from 1965 to 1969 only two, government-created, entities were permitted to function as political parties: the pro-military Aliança Renovadora Nacional (Arena), and the opposition Movimento Democrático Brasileiro (MDB).

The Castelo Branco regime and succeeding military governments kept a tight grip on the country and met with little effective opposition from political or guerrilla movements. Among left-wing organizations which did engage in limited guerrilla warfare in the late 1960s and early '70s were the Aliança Libertadora Nacional (ALN, led by Carlos Marighella); the Vanguarda Popular Revolucionária (VPR, led by Carlos Lamarca); the Movimento Revolucionário 8 de Outubro (MR-8); the Movimento Revolucionário Tiradentes (MRT, led by Dimas António Cassemiro), and the Vanguarda Armada Revolucionária Palmares. The far right organized a number of death squads, some of which (see below) remained active into the 1980s. The military government has been accused of many breaches of human rights, involving inter alia the disappearance of hundreds of left-wingers and the use of torture and political detention.

Political opposition to the government revived with the dissolution in 1979 by Congress of the two official parties and the organization of new parties. Arena was replaced by the Partido Democrático Social, the MDB gave rise to various movements including the Partido do Movimento Democrático Brasileiro (PMDB), and other organizations including an independent labour party, the Partido dos Trabalhadores, developed but were in the main unable to satisfy the stringent conditions laid down for recognition as a political party.

Congressional elections took place in 1982 and, after a widespread but unsuccessful campaign for a return to direct election of the President, a civilian President was indirectly elected in early 1985. Tancredo de Almeida Neves, a liberal, died before he could succeed Gen. João Baptista de Figueiredo, who had been in power since 1978;

Neves' running mate, José Sarney, was installed on March 15 as acting President and on April 22 as President.

Constitutional background. The Federative Republic of Brazil consists of 24 states, one federal district – Brasília – and two territories. According to the 1969 Constitution, which was created and occasionally altered by the military government and is to be replaced altogether by a forthcoming constituent assembly, legislative power is exercised by a National Congress consisting of (i) a Chamber of Deputies of variable size, directly elected every four years, and (ii) a 69-member Federal Senate directly elected for eight-year terms with elections at four-year intervals for, alternately, one-third and two-thirds of the members. Congressional elections are by universal and compulsory suffrage of literate adults (although a clause of the Constitution has been interpreted as disenfranchising indigenous peoples).

Executive power is exercised by the President, assisted by an appointed cabinet; the Constitution originally specified that the President and Vice-President were chosen for a five-year term by an electoral college comprised of Congress and delegates of the state legislatures, but the military regime later increased the term to six years. The new civilian administration has promised direct elections.

Under measures introduced in 1979, political parties may be formed provided that they gain the support of at least 10 per cent of the members of each chamber of Congress, or 5 per cent of the vote at the next elections, spread over at least nine states, and that they meet other conditions banning parties with foreign links or which promoted "racial, religious or class bias". Later measures restricted participation in the local and general elections of 1982 to those parties which had branches in at least 20 per cent of the townships of each of at least nine states, and which presented a candidate for every vacancy in each such state.

Recent election results. The indirect presidential election held in January 1985 would have resulted in the appointment on March 15 of a liberal, Tancredo Neves, who secured 480 of the 677 votes; there were 180 votes for Paulo Salim Maluf of the PDS and 17 abstentions. (Neves' terminal illness meant that his vice-presidential candidate, José Sarney, was installed in his place.) In congressional elections on Nov. 15, 1982 – the first multi-party contest since 1962 – the PDS won 235 seats in the Chamber of Deputies, the PMDB 200, the PDT 24, the PTB 14 and the PT 6, the total of seats being 479. In the Senate, where only one-third of the membership was up for election, the distribution of seats was PDS 46, PMDB 21, PDT 1 and PTB 1.

Aliança Democrática
See PFL and PMDB (below).

Centro Democrático Brasileiro
See Movimento Nacional Constituyente (below).

Esquadrão da Morte
Death Squad

Orientation. Ultra-right

Founded. 1964

History. This group was founded secretly by policemen who sought revenge for the killing of a colleague; it openly claimed responsibility for its activities after 1968, and by 1970 its members were believed to have killed more than 1,000 "undesirables", generally marking their victims with a skull and crossbones. A number of serving and former policemen were convicted of death squad killings in 1972–76. In 1979 the suspected head of the organization, Police Commissioner Sergio Paranhos Fleury, who had been taken into custody on several previous occasions, was formally charged with involvement in the killings but died on May 1 after an accident.

The Esquadrão continued its activities into the 1980s, with at least 250 deaths attributed to it in 1980.

Falange Patria Nova (FPN)
New Homeland Falange

Orientation. Ultra-right

Founded. 1980

History. This group was responsible for a number of bomb attacks, including one on a news stand selling progressive periodicals in Brasília on Aug. 11, 1980, and three in Rio de Janeiro on Aug. 27, killing one person and injuring seven.

Frente Progressista
Progressive Front

Orientation. Left-wing

Founded. December 1984

History. The front was formed by left-wing members of the PMDB, the PDT and the PT, with the aim of "acting as a brake on the conservative tendencies of the next government".

Liberdade e Luta (Libelu)
Freedom and Struggle

Leadership. Clara Ant (leader)

Orientation. Trotskyist

History. Libelu operates as a Trotskyist tendency within the non-socialist Partido dos Trabalhadores (see below).

Movimento Nacional Constituyente
National Constituent Movement

Orientation. Democratic

Founded. January 1985

History. This movement was launched by the Centro Democrático Brasileiro (Brazilian Democratic Centre) in early January 1985. Its first public meeting, on Jan. 26, was attended by representatives of the Catholic Church, the PMDB, the PDT, the PT, student and trade unions.

Policies. The objective of the movement is to secure the early enactment of a democratic constitution guaranteeing civil liberties and representative government.

31

Movimento Revolucionário 8 de Outubro (MR-8)
October 8 Revolutionary Movement

Orientation.   Left-wing guerrilla group

Founded.   Late 1960s

History.   The MR-8, named after the date of Che Guevara's death in Bolivia in 1967, was active in the late 1960s and early '70s, and was responsible for the kidnapping for three days in early September 1969 of the US ambassador to Brazil; the ambassador was freed after the government conceded the group's demand for the release into exile of 15 political prisoners, including Gregorio Becerra (76), a PCB member sentenced to 19 years' imprisonment in 1964, and two persons who had killed a US officer in São Paulo in 1968. Some 26 members of the MR-8 were among the 70 prisoners released into exile in January 1971 in order to secure the release of the Swiss ambassador to Brazil, who had been kidnapped by Carlos Marighella's Aliança Libertadora Nacional group. The MR-8 was inactive in the later 1970s but its banner was among those flown at political rallies in 1984.

Partido Comunista do Brasil (PC do B)
Communist Party of Brazil

Leadership.   João Amazonas (general secretary)

Orientation.   Maoist

Founded.   1961

History.   The PC do B was formed after a split in the orthodox communist PCB (see below). It has been illegal since its foundation. During a raid by security forces in São Paulo on Dec. 16, 1976, three members of the party's central committee, including the founder, Pedro de Araujo Pomar, were killed and six others were arrested. Some exiled members of the PC do B were allowed to return to Brazil under a presidential amnesty in August 1979. The party has subsequently supported the campaign for democratization and civilian government.

Policies.   Originally pro-Chinese, the party now identifies with the ideology and foreign policies of the Albanian Party of Labour. During 1985 it sought legal recognition as a party, which would enable it to participate in elections.

Publications.   *Tribuna da Luta Operária*

Partido Comunista Brasileiro (PCB)
Brazilian Communist Party

Leadership.   Giaconda Dias (general secretary)

Orientation.   Communist

Founded.   March 25, 1922, as Partido Comunista do Brasil (PC do B – Communist Party of Brazil)

History.   The PC do B was banned shortly after its formation. In November 1935 it took part in an unsuccessful insurrection, following which Luis Carlos Prestes, its leader and until May 1980 its general secretary, was imprisoned. The party was legalized at the end of the Second World War, and in the 1945 elections it gained 10 per cent of the vote and 17 seats in the Chamber of Deputies. It was banned again in 1947.

In 1960 the party was again permitted to function, and assumed the present form of its name. During the period of military rule initiated by the coup of 1964 it operated clandestinely; a number of its members were arrested in 1973–74 when the party was supporting the MDB in its calls for a return to democracy. On March 23, 1975, 23 people were imprisoned for terms ranging from seven months to five years for attempting to reorganize the party. Despite police raids on its printing presses in Rio de Janeiro and São Paulo in January 1975, the party's newspaper, *Voz Operária*, reappeared in April and August 1976; it claimed that half the party's leaders had been killed and others had been imprisoned and tortured in the past two years, and denounced the government as a dictatorship. Early in August 1976 another 17 communists were imprisoned for two to three years, eight of them losing their civil rights for five to eight years.

Prestes and several other party members returned from exile under a presidential amnesty signed in August 1979. *Voz Operária* resumed publication on Oct. 2, 1980, but the party as such was not accorded legal status. In the November 1982 elections it gave unofficial support to democratic parties including the PMDB and the PT (see below). The entire central committee and about 80 members of the party were arrested during a party congress in São Paulo on Dec. 13, 1982. All but seven were released on the following day.

The PCB held another congress in São Paulo on Jan. 10, 1984, and, confirming the leadership's policy of campaigning for a nationalist and democratic government, expelled Prestes, who maintained that the party should press instead for a revolutionary government. The PCP's printing works in Brasília was closed down, and two members arrested, on Oct. 15, 1984.

Policies. The PCB gravitated towards the Eurocommunist tendency espoused by the communist parties of Italy and Spain in the 1970s. It supported the campaign for liberalization and democratization, in particular by working within the PMDB (see below). During 1984 the party drew up a manifesto calling for "national emancipation, a representative and democratic regime based on a multi-party system, and respect for human rights"; it attributed Brazil's problems to "the implementation of a dependent capitalist development model [and] an extremely unstable and anti-democratic political situation". The party is engaged in a campaign to win legal recognition and the right to participate in elections.

Publications. *Voz Operária*

International affiliations. The party is recognized by the Communist Party of the Soviet Union.

Partido Democrático Social (PDS)
Social Democratic Party

Leadership. Aloysio Chaves, Nelso Marchezan (leaders); Amaral Peixoto (president)

Orientation. Conservative

Founded. 1980

History. The PDS was established by the military government as a successor to Arena (see introduction). It was built on Arena's organization, giving it an electoral advantage compounded by extensive revisions of the voting procedure. By the end of 1980 it had 3,066 branches and the support of 213 of the 420 deputies and 37 of the 60 senators, marginally less than the support enjoyed by Arena. In the 1982 elections it remained the largest party in Congress, with 235 of the 479 deputies and 46 of the 69 senators; it also won 12 of the 23 state governorships. The last of the military presidents, João Figueiredo, continued to rule by decree until in May 1983 the PDS formed a pro-government alliance with the PTB, together controlling 248 seats in the Chamber and a majority in the presidential electoral college. The PTB support was, however, withdrawn in August after disagreements on economic policy.

The party divided in 1984, mainly over the question of the presidential succession, some of its more liberal members leaving to form what became the Partido Frente Liberal (see below). The remainder of the PDS nominated Paulo Salim Maluf, formerly governor of São Paulo, for the presidency, but lost to the PFL. Maluf served briefly as party president before being replaced on Jan. 23, 1985, by Peixoto, who announced his hopes of reuniting the party.

Policies. The PDS is Christian democratic and conservative, favouring economic development and the attraction of foreign capital.

Partido Democrático Trabalhista (PDT)
Democratic Labour Party

Address. Rua Sete de Setembro 141, 4°, 20.050 Rio de Janeiro, RJ

Leadership. Leonel da Moura Brizola (leader); Doutel de Andrade (acting president); Mateus Schmidt (general secretary)

Orientation. Social democratic

Founded. June 26, 1980

History. The founders of the PDT regarded it as the continuation of the pre-1965 Partido Trabalhista Brasileiro, but adopted its present name after a controversial court case in 1980 awarded rights over the name of the PTB to what appeared to be a minority faction of the party (see PTB, below). It initially had the support of 10 deputies, but in 1982 it gained 24 seats in the Chamber to become the largest of the three labour blocs. It simultaneously won the governorship of Rio de Janeiro, the party's stronghold.

Policies. The PDT has called for full employment, redistribution of income, land reform, and the planning of industrial and agricultural production around the people's needs.

Partido da Frente Liberal (PFL)
Liberal Front Party

Leadership. José Sarney (President of the Republic, effective leader); Dr António Aureliano Chaves de Mendonça (honorary president); Marco Maciel (executive president)

Orientation. Liberal

Founded. December 1984

History. The Front developed in June 1984 as a liberal faction within the PDS (see above), allied itself with the PMDB (see below) in August as the Aliança Democrática, and was in December constituted as a party, its members including the former PDS president José Sarney and the then Vice-President of the Republic, Chaves de Mendonça. The initial objective was to support the centrist PMDB candidate in the January 1985 indirect presidential election. The candidate, Neves, won a large majority, but died before he could take office; Sarney, as Vice-President, was sworn in in his place. The first convention of the PFL took place in Brasília on Jan. 23, and was supported by 72 federal deputies and 12 senators, making it the third largest parliamentary party (after the PMDB and the PDS). Maciel, a former governor of Pernambuco, was elected executive president. Portfolios in the Cabinet installed in March were divided among PFL and PMDB members and independents.

Policies. The PFL advocates constitutional reforms, including the direct election of the President. It opposes authoritarianism, centralization and state involvement in the economy.

Partido do Movimento Democratico Brasileiro (PMDB)
Party of the Brazilian Democratic Movement

Leadership. Ulysses Guimarães (president); Miguel Arrais (first vice-president); Alfonso Camargo (general secretary); José Freitas Nobre, Humberto Lucena (other leaders)

Orientation. Centrist

Founded. 1980

History. The PMDB was founded by centrist members of the opposition MDB when the latter was dissolved by Congress (see introduction); it was supported by about 100 deputies and 20 senators, and had received the unofficial support of left-wing forces including the PCB in its calls for democratization. By the end of 1980 the party had 2,127 branches, mostly inherited from the MDB.

The party co-operated from February 1981 with the Partido Popular (PP – People's Party), formed in January 1980 by centrist former members of the pro-government Arena (see introduction) and led by Tancredo Neves. By 1981 the PP had 869 branches and the support of 66 deputies and 10 senators. In view of a ban on electoral alliances the PP leadership agreed on Dec. 20, 1981, to merge their party with the PMDB, although at a PP conference more than one-third of the delegates had opposed the suggestion. The merger took place and was approved by the Supreme Electoral Tribunal on March 2, 1982.

In the 1982 elections the enlarged PMDB won 200 seats in the Chamber and 21 in the Senate, as well as nine of the 23 governorships. It subsequently allied with the Frente Liberal (see PFL, above) as the Aliança Democrática (Democratic Alliance) to support Tancredo Neves in the 1985 presidential election, and was allocated a number of portfolios in the resulting Cabinet.

Policies. The party is essentially Christian democratic but covers a wide spectrum of opinion from liberal conservatism to orthodox communism.

Associated organizations. The PMDB has substantial influence in the trade union movement through the Coordenação Nacional das Classes Trabalhadores (CNCT – National Co-ordinating Body of the Working Classes).

Partido Popular (PP)

See PMDB (above).

Partido Republicano Brasileiro (PRB)
Brazilian Republican Party

Orientation. Centrist

Founded. Jan. 31, 1985

Policies. The PRB supports the decentralization of the federal government, a stronger role for Congress, an open economy, human rights and representative democracy.

Partido Revolucionário Comunista (PRC)
Communist Revolutionary Party

Leadership. Genuíno Neto (leader)

Orientation. Revolutionary communist

Founded. June 21, 1984

History. This organization, launched in 1984, was apparently not connected with the Partido Comunista Revolucionário do Brasil, a Maoist offshoot of the PCB formed in March 1967 by Carlos Marighella and others and inactive since 1970.

Policies. The PRC's objectives in 1984 included "the revolutionary overthrow of the military dictatorship, carrying down the bourgeois state with it, and the construction of a workers' and peoples' democracy". It rejected "alliances with the bourgeoisie" and international links.

Structure. The PRC is organized as a network of committees and cells.

Partido dos Trabalhadores (PT)
Workers' Party

Telephone. São Paulo 223–2740

Leadership. Airton Soares (leader); Luís Inácio da Silva (known as Lula; president); Jaco Bitar (vice-president)

Orientation. Leftist

Founded. 1978

History. The PT was formed as Brazil's first national labour party, having its roots in the independent trade union movement which developed in the late 1970s in the industries around São Paulo. It acquired legal status in 1980. Both Soares and the PT's founder, da Silva, were members of the original Partido Trabalhista Brasileiro (PTB – Brazilian Labour Party), which was formed in 1945 and was in government under João Goulart in 1961–64. Early in 1981, 10 PT members were imprisoned for from two to 3½ years and disqualified from political activities for five years. Da Silva and four other leaders of the union movement were acquitted on March 1, 1984, of incitement to murder, the charges arising out of their speeches in 1980 protesting at the murder of a peasant leader whose murderer was subsequently killed by peasants.

Policies. The party has called for a more equitable distribution of income, the creation of jobs, effective land reform and the guaranteeing of democratic freedoms. It does not describe itself as socialist or revolutionary but calls for "a society without exploiters and exploited".

Structure. The PT is organized in cells. By the end of 1980 it had branches in 625 (out of 3,959) municipalities and in 13 (of 23) states.

Membership. 276,000

Associated organizations. The PT has close but informal relations with the independent or "autêntico" trade union movement, now represented by the Central Unica dos Trabalhadores (CUT – United Confederation of Workers), of which Lula is the leader. It has also been supported by left-wing elements of the Catholic Church.

Partido Trabalhista Brasileiro (PTB)
Brazilian Labour Party

Leadership. Celso Peçanha (leader); Ricardo Ribeiro (president)

Orientation. Democratic

Founded. 1980

History. The present-day PTB is one of two parties claiming direct descent from the original party of that name, the other being the PDT (see above). A minority faction of the PTB won a court case in 1980 which gave it the use of the party name; most of the members, however, regrouped as the PDT. By the end of 1980 the PTB had 334 branches; it emerged from the elections of 1982 with 14 seats in the Chamber and one in the Senate, and (under its previous leader, Ivete Cue de Vargas) entered into a short-lived coalition with the PDS during 1983.

Policies. The party has called for a new constitution providing for a democratic multi-party system and political representation and rights for workers and students.

Tenente Mendes
Lieutenant Mendes

Orientation. Ultra-right

History. This group was responsible for an attempt in January 1980 to assassinate Leonel Brizola, a leftist politician who went on to found the PDT (see above). Its other attacks were mainly directed against progressive newspapers.

Vanguarda do Comando de Caça aos Comunistas (CCC)
Vanguard of the Commando for Hunting Communists

Orientation. Ultra-right

History. In 1980 this group, together with the Esquadrão da Morte (see above), was held responsible for killing up to 100 people a month. On Aug. 28 it bombed a school in Rio de Janeiro, causing no injuries.

Chile

Capital: Santiago   **Population: 12,000,000**

The Republic of Chile won its independence in 1818, and was ruled for the rest of the 19th century by an agrarian oligarchy. In the present century the political parties of the oligarchy – and in particular the Partido Nacional (PN) – have contended for power with the mainly middle class Christian democratic movement and the labour-based left-wing forces, the leading elements of which have been the Partido Socialista de Chile (PSCh) and the Partido Comunista de Chile (PCCh). In 1970 Dr Salvador Allende Gossens, the candidate of the Unidad Popular coalition (including both main leftist parties), was constitutionally elected President of Chile in succession to Eduardo Frei Montalva of the Partido Demócrata Cristiano (PDC).

The Allende administration attempted to carry out a programme of radical social and economic reforms, but it was confronted with a rapidly deteriorating economic situation and a concerted effort by internal and external forces to destabilize the government. This opposition culminated in a right-wing military coup, led by Gen. Augusto Pinochet Ugarte, on Sept. 11, 1973. The coup installed a four-man junta of the commanders of the army, the air force, the navy and the paramilitary police; Congress was dissolved, Marxist parties were banned and other parties were at first placed in "indefinite recess" and, from March 1977, also banned. Many left-wing and centrist activists were killed, arrested, tortured, exiled or "disappeared", but most parties continued to operate in exile and more or less clandestinely inside Chile; some on the left adopted a strategy of armed resistance to the junta, especially from 1983. The continued existence of the parties was acknowledged by members of the regime from 1981, and in 1984 the regime announced that parties were to be allowed to function under certain conditions, notably that they accepted the "fundamental law" of 1981 (see below). The main political parties have formed a number of coalitions and alliances to press for a rapid return to democracy. The military regime has frequently been criticized at home and abroad for violations of human rights, and the international movement in solidarity with the Chilean people has gained the support of parties of the centre and left in most Latin American and European countries.

Human rights issues. The UN Commission on Human Rights stated in 1976 that the junta had systematically extended its suppression of human rights from the political to other sectors of the population including the Church, trade unions, academics and professional groups. Other governments were urged to exert economic pressure on Chile to cease arbitrary arrests, torture and deportations, and the Commission proposed the trial of a named "leading torturer" by the international community. The UN General Assembly has repeatedly condemned "constant and flagrant violations of human rights and fundamental freedoms" in Chile and censured the Pinochet regime for refusing to co-operate with the Human Rights Commission.

A 1977 report by Amnesty International (rejected by the junta) stated that at least 1,500 political prisoners had disappeared since 1973; that secret prison camps existed in remote areas; and that it had complete documentation on 500 prisoners whom the Chilean authorities claimed not to have arrested. UN reports stated that 582 persons were arrested for political or "national security" reasons in 1976, 346 in 1977 and 378 from January to October 1978. Amnesty and UN reports in the early 1980s indicated a decline in the number of "disappearances" and deaths under torture, but stated that torture, arbitrary detention and other abuses continued on a routine basis.

After a further condemnation of the Chilean regime by the UN Commission for Human Rights on March 13, 1985, the (independent) Comisión Chilena de Derechos Humanos stated that between the reimposition in November 1984 of a "state of siege" and the end of April 1985 there had been 33,798 recorded cases of political arrest. Death squad activities had increased in 1984–85, but protests by church leaders and others led to the arrest or sacking of more than 50 members of the *carabineros* – the paramilitary police – in connection with death squad killings and kidnappings.

Church opposition. The Catholic Church in Chile has been active in human rights work and other anti-junta activity, notably in 1973–75 through the Comité de Cooperación para la Paz en Chile (in which other churches were also represented) and subsequently through the Vicaría de Solidaridad. In November 1975 the junta accused the Church of protecting "Marxist elements" and arrested nine members of the Comité, which was closed down at the end of December. The Vicaría, established in January 1976, has called for judicial investigations of "disappearances", has helped individuals who have come into conflict with the state security apparatus and has denounced cases of torture and death squad executions.

Trade union opposition. The Central Unica de Trabajadores de Chile (CUT) was banned as a "communist front" in September 1973, and subsequent decrees placed severe restrictions on the right to organize, the right to strike, and other trade union activities. In late 1977 seven trade union leaders were exiled to remote mountain villages and in 1978 their unions were outlawed. National trade union federations and co-ordinating bodies have nevertheless continued to exist, and from 1981 have become increasingly involved in opposition activities. Christian democratic union leaders established a national committee – the Grupo de los Diez – and a national federation – the Unión Democrática de los Trabajadores (UDT) – in 1981. Tucapel Jiménez, the leader of the public employees' union, was killed in February 1982 after proposing the establishment of an opposition union movement. In 1983 five unions, including that of the copper miners, established the Comando Nacional de Trabajadores and began a campaign for a return to democracy. Unions have subsequently played a major role in the organization of days of protest.

Constitutional background. Until the 1973 coup Chile was a parliamentary democracy with an executive President and a National Congress elected by universal adult suffrage. After the coup, absolute power rested with the military junta, and increasingly with its leader, Gen. Pinochet. In June 1974 Pinochet was designated Supreme Chief of State, and in December, President of the Republic (although he did not formally assume that title until March 1981). The junta proclaimed various "constitutional acts" in 1976 purporting to establish an "authoritarian democracy", and in 1981 a "fundamental law", separating the presidency from the junta, provided for a bicameral legislature which would not, however, be elected until 1989. The country has been under "state of siege" and "state of exception" regulations, suspending most civil liberties, since the coup.

Recent election results. No elections have taken place since March 1973, when congressional elections gave no party a clear majority; a presidential election in 1970 had been won by Dr Allende for Unidad Popular. Following the right-wing military coup of September 1973, the junta has held two referendums, one in 1978 to provide a general endorsement of the regime's policies and another in 1980 to approve the proposed "fundamental law"; according to the official results, both were won by the junta with substantial majorities. There are to be no legislative or presidential elections until 1989.

Acuerdo Democrático Nacional (Adena)
National Democratic Accord

Leadership. Juan de Dios Carmona (president)

Orientation. Conservative

Founded. 1984

History. The Adena was formed as an alliance of centre-right and right-wing parties including the MAN (see below).

Acuerdo Nacional para la Evolución Pacífica hacia la Democracia Plena y Auténtica
National Accord for Peaceful Evolution towards Complete and Genuine Democracy

Not an organization, but a document expressing five demands for a restoration of democracy and civil liberties, launched in August 1985 by 11 parties meeting at the request of the Primate of Chile; see Alianza Democrática (below).

Ad Mapu

Leadership. José Santos Millao (president); Rosamel Millamán (general secretary)

Orientation. *Indigenista*

History. This group, formed by indigenous Mapuche communities in southern Chile, was suppressed by the security forces, and its leaders sent into internal exile, in April 1984. A leader of the group had been assassinated by the Acha (see below) in January.

International affiliations. Ad Mapu is linked with the Consejo Indio Sudamericano (CISA – South American Indian Council), of which Millamán was treasurer in 1984.

Alianza Chilena Anticomunista (Acha)
Chilean Anti-Communist Alliance

Orientation. Ultra-right death squad

History. This group claimed responsibility for a number of attacks on centrist and left-wing activists in 1984, including the killing in January of a leader of Ad Mapu (see above) and an assault in March on Jorge Lavandero of the Proden (see below).

Alianza Democrática (AD)
Democratic Alliance

Leadership. Gabriel Valdés Subercaseaux (president); Raúl Troncoso C. (general secretary); Enrique Silva Cimma, Marcial Mora, Ricardo Lagos, Armando Jaramillo (other members of executive committee)

Orientation. Centre-left

Founded. Aug. 6, 1983

History. The AD was formed by the principal non-communist progressive formations to work for the restoration of democracy and stability. Following mass anti-government demonstrations early in August

1983, the group called for the resignation of the Pinochet regime and the holding of elections to a constituent assembly which would reform the Constitution and act as a legislature during a transitional period. An AD delegation had talks with the Minister of the Interior, Sergio Onofre Jarpa, on Aug. 25 and Sept. 5, but made no apparent progress. The executive committee of the AD was formed in October and Valdés became president in March 1984. The group has supported the days of protest called by the CNT (see below), and on Nov. 18, 1983, held a rally which it estimated was attended by 1,000,000 people; official spokesmen put the attendance at 95,000. Several AD leaders were temporarily detained in October 1984.

Policies. On its foundation the AD issued a 10-point manifesto covering the economic situation, human rights and civil liberties, the role of the armed forces, the nature of the democracy which it sought to establish, the internal regulation of the AD, new labour legislation and university autonomy. The AD expressed its opposition to any form of one-party government which exercised control of the media and which used violence against political opponents. The AD parties met with the PN, the UN and other parties on Aug. 25, 1985, at the initiative of the Cardinal Archbishop of Santiago, and issued a joint statement on a "national accord for transition to full democracy", calling for the lifting of the state of emergency, the restoration of all civil liberties, and the introduction of new electoral legislation; the statement included an undertaking that there would be no prosecutions for violations of human rights committed by servants of the military regime. Among national figures who added their endorsement to the proposal was Gen. Gustavo Leigh, one of the original members of the four-man junta installed in 1973; the regime responded with a speech by Pinochet on Sept. 11 – the anniversary of the coup – in which he rejected the proposal as a "political manouevre" which could be taken advantage of by the agents of "totalitarian communism".

Structure. The AD has a national committee consisting of the leaders of its constituent parties; the presidency of the alliance, held in 1984 by Ricardo Lagos and in 1985 by Valdés (the leader of the PDC), was subsequently to rotate at six-monthly intervals among the party leaders.

Membership. The founding members of the AD were the Bloque Socialista Chileno, the PDC, the Partido Radical (then engaged in a reunification process), the Partido Republicano and the Partido Social Demócrata (see below).

Asociación de Familiares de Detenidos Desaparecidos (AFDD)
Association of Relatives of Disappeared Prisoners

Leadership. Sola Sierra (president)

Orientation. Human rights concerns

History. The AFDD represents the families of political prisoners who have been "disappeared" by the authorities. It has documented many individual cases, organized a number of demonstrations and co-ordinated various legal appeals.

Avanzada Nacional
National Advance

Orientation. Right-wing

History. This small grouping declined in August 1985 to support the call for a "national accord" on a restoration of democracy (see Alianza Democrática, above).

Bloque Socialista Chileno (BSCh)
Chilean Socialist Bloc

Leadership. Ricardo Núñez (president)

Orientation. Socialist

Founded. September 1983

History. Preceded by the Convergencia Socialista (Socialist Convergence), this alliance was created by parties which had belonged to the Unidad Popular coalition. It has supported the days of protest against the Pinochet regime, held irregularly in 1983–85. Leading members of the group were arrested in November 1984.

Membership. Organizations represented in the Bloc were majority sections of the PSCh (the major participant), MAPU, MAPU-OC and Izquierda Cristiana (see below).

Associated organizations. Together with other parties the Bloc has been active in the broader-based Alianza Democrática (see above) in the campaign for the return of democracy. Of these parties, the Bloc is closest to the Partido Radical.

Comando Nacional de Trabajadores (CNT)
Workers' National Command

Leadership. Rodolfo Seguel (president); Manuel Bustos (vice-president); Arturo Martínez (general secretary)

Orientation. Democratic labour movement

Founded. May 1983

History. The CNT was formed by five trade unions, the most important of which was the Confederación de Trabajadores del Cubre (CTC – Copper Workers' Confederation), led by Seguel. It has been the main instigator of the days of protest called periodically since May 1983. Many such demonstrations have met with a violent response from the authorities, 11 people being killed in confrontations with the police during two days of protest in September 1985. Seguel was arrested shortly thereafter and charged with various offences against the security of the state.

Policies. The CNT advocates the ending of military rule and a return to representative democracy; it has associated itself with the August 1985 "national accord" proposal (see Alianza Democrática, above).

Structure. The CNT is led by an executive committee consisting of the leaders of the member unions. It directs a network of support groups through a Consejo de Federaciones, Asociaciones y Sindicatos Nacionales (Confasin – Council of National Federations, Associations and Trade Unions).

Membership. In August 1985 the CNT had 14 affiliates, all national trade union federations.

Comando de Resistencia Popular Javier Carrera (CRP)
Javier Carrera Popular Resistance Commando

Orientation. Left-wing guerrilla group

Founded. April 1980

History. This group, which carried out two guerrilla operations in 1980, was thought to be an offshoot of the MIR (see below).

Comando Vengador de Mártires (Covema)
Martyrs' Avengers Commando

Orientation. Right-wing guerrilla group

Founded. 1980

History. This group claimed responsibility for a number of attacks made from July 1980 onwards, including the temporary kidnapping of journalists connected with church radio stations and of six students, one of whom died of wounds inflicted by the kidnappers.

Comisión Chilena de Derechos Humanos
Chilean Human Rights Commission

Leadership. Jaime Castillo Velasco (president); Omar Rosales (vice-president)

Orientation. Human rights concerns

History. This commission has frequently denounced the Pinochet regime's use of arbitrary detention, torture, deportation and other deprivations of human rights against those suspected of opposing the regime. As a result it has frequently come into conflict with the regime and in August 1985 its vice-president was sent into internal exile.

Comisión Permanente de Libertad de Expresión
Permanent Committee for the Freedom of Expression

Address. Almirante Simpson 7, Santiago

Orientation. Democratic

Founded. 1984

History. The Commission was founded by journalists and opposition figures to document and protest against governmental violations of freedom of expression. It has campaigned in particular against the closure and prior censorship of a number of periodicals and radio stations in 1984–85.

Comisión contra la Tortura
Commission against Torture

Leadership. Dr Pedro Castillo (president)

Orientation. Human rights concerns

History. This body, like the Human Rights Commission, has denounced abuses of human rights under the military regime. It has concentrated on documenting and protesting cases of torture by the security forces. Its president was sent into internal exile in August 1985.

Comité de Derechos del Pueblo (Codepu)
People's Rights Committee

Leadership. Fabiola Letelier (president)

Orientation. Human rights concerns

History. This small human rights group was active in early 1985 in a campaign to save the lives of five political prisoners who were subjected to a military trial.

Coordinadora Nacional Sindical (CNS)
Nation Trade Union Co-ordinating Body

Leadership. Juan Manuel Sepúlveda Malbrán, Manuel Bustos (leaders)

Orientation. Democratic trade union group

Founded. 1978

History. The CNS was established as a national alliance of left-wing trade unions. It continued to exist after its affiliates were banned as "Marxist" in 1978. After petitioning the government for basic changes in social and economic policies, trade union liberties and wage increases, 11 leading members of the CNS were arrested in July 1981 and Sepúlveda, who had earlier left the country, was on Aug. 13 prohibited from returning to Chile. The CNS continued to operate in 1984, its main spokesperson inside Chile being Arturo Martínez.

Membership. Among the founding organizations were five textile, construction, engineering and mineworkers' confederations, a peasant union and a group called Unidad Obrera Campesina (UOC – Peasant–Worker Unity). All the groups were declared illegal on Oct. 19, 1978.

Democracia Cristiana (DC)

See PDC (below).

Derecha Republicana

See Partido Republicano (below).

Federación Socialista Democrática
Democratic Socialist Federation

Orientation. Social democratic

Founded. April 1984

History. This alliance was founded at the initiative of the Partido Radical as part of its efforts to strengthen the social democratic presence on the Chilean left.

Membership. The founding members of the Federation were the Partido Radical, the Partido Social Demócrata and the Unión Popular Socialista (see below).

Federación de Trabajadores Demócrata Cristiana (FTDC)
Christian Democratic Workers' Federation

Leadership. Ernesto Fogel (president); Luis Sepúlveda (general secretary)

Orientation. Christian democratic

History. This union federation was active in 1985.

Frente Cívico

See PSCh, Briones faction (below).

Frente Patriótico Manuel Rodríguez (FPMR)
Manual Rodríguez Patriotic Front

Leadership. Daniel Huerta (presumed commander)

Orientation. Left-wing guerrilla movement

Founded. 1984

History. This movement, named after a guerrilla leader of the independence era and also known as the Milicias Rodriguistas (Rodríguez Militia), is thought to be linked to the PCCh. It made itself known by occupying a radio station on March 7–8, 1984, to broadcast an anti-government statement. It has carried out a series of bombings, initially of electrical installations, beginning in April 1984; during 1985 its targets included local government offices (two people were killed in a bombing on

May 14) and US transnational corporations. Its activities have been mainly in the capital, with some attacks in Valparaíso and elsewhere.

Policies. In a manifesto issued in December 1984 the FPMR offered its support to the demands of political parties for a return to democracy, and to those of trade union organizations for extensive economic reforms. It called for widespread actions of sabotage and "armed propaganda" in an effort to hasten the fall of the Pinochet regime.

Associated organizations. It is regarded by the regime as the military wing of the PCCh (see below); the communist leadership, while pursuing a political strategy, has consistently refused to denounce the guerrilla struggle of the FPMR.

Fuerzas Armadas de la Resistencia Popular (FARP)
Popular Resistance Armed Forces

Orientation. Left-wing guerrilla group

Founded. November 1984

History. The formation of the FARP was announced by the MIR (see below) following the killing of four policemen in an attack in central Valparaíso on Nov. 2, 1984.

Grupo Antimarxista (GRAPA)
Anti-Marxist Group

Orientation. Ultra-right paramilitary group

History. This organization carried out attacks in 1984.

Grupo de los Diez
Group of Ten

Leadership. Hernol Flores (leader)

Orientation. Christian democratic

Founded. 1981

History. This group of trade union leaders was established to oversee the creation of a national federation of Christian democratic unions.

Associated organizations. See UDT (below).

Grupo de Estudios Constitucionales (Grupo de los 24)

See Intransigencia Democrática (below).

Intransigencia Democrática
Democratic Intransigence

Leadership. Manuel Sanheuza Cruz (president)

Orientation. Democratic

Founded. 1985

History. This group was founded by the leader of the Grupo de Estudios Constitucionales (Constitutional Studies Group), better known as the Grupo de los 24 (Group of 24), a non-partisan committee of lawyers and others established in 1978 to work for the return of democracy. Sanhueza has called for a campaign of civil disobedience to bring down the military regime and replace it with a pluralistic democracy. His group maintains that the armed forces have no right to any political role and that consequently the opposition has no duty to enter into negotiations with the military regime; on that point it differs with other opposition groups, notably the PDC.

Izquierda Cristiana (IC)
Christian Left

Leadership. Raúl Reyes Susarte (leader); Luis Maira (general secretary); Roberto Celedón (spokesperson)

Orientation. Progressive Christian

History. This small group was formed by elements of the PDC (see below) which, influenced by liberation theology, supported the Unidad Popular alliance. It was banned by the military regime in 1973, since when it has participated in anti-junta activities and has in particular acted as a bridge between the Unidad Popular parties and the left wing of the PDC.

Policies. The IC leadership has given a guarded welcome to the 1985 proposal for a "national accord" on the restoration of democracy (see Alianza Democrática, above).

Associated organizations. See Alianza Democrática, BSCh (above) and MDP (below).

Movimiento de Acción Nacional (MAN)
National Action Movement

Leadership. Federico Willoughby (president); Pablo Rodríguez (leader)

Orientation. Nationalist

History. This small party was active in 1985.

Policies. The MAN offers support to the military regime and opposes a return to democracy.

Associated organizations. The party is a member of the Adena (see above).

Movimiento de Acción Popular Unitaria (MAPU)
United Popular Action Movement

Leadership. Oscar Garretón (leader)

Orientation. Leftist

History. The MAPU was one of the members of the Unidad Popular alliance in power under President Allende in 1970–73. It was banned after the September 1973 military coup and subsequently engaged in underground activities.

Associated organizations. See AD, BSCh (above); MDP (below).

Movimiento de Acción Popular Unitaria – Obrero Campesino (MAPU-OC or MOC)
Worker and Peasant United Popular Action Movement

Leadership. Sr Gazmuri (leader, in exile); Marcelo Contreras (general secretary in Chile)

Orientation. Leftist

History. This faction of the MAPU (see above) has also operated clandestinely since the 1973 coup. Its then leader, Jaime Anselmo Cuevas Hormazábal, was arrested in April 1980.

Associated organizations. See BSCh, Alianza Democrática (above).

Movimiento Contra el Cáncer Marxista (MCCM)
Movement against the Cancer of Marxism

Orientation. Ultra-right paramilitary group

History. This group was active in 1984.

46

Movimiento Democrático Popular
Popular Democratic Movement

Leadership. Dr Manuel Almeyda (president); José Sanfuentes Palma (general secretary); Jaime Insunza (past general secretary, in exile)

Orientation. Socialist

Founded. Sept. 3, 1983

History. The MDP was set up as an alliance of communist and socialist parties declared illegal after the 1973 coup. It has organized rallies and days of protest against the regime's economic policies, the first taking place in Santiago in December 1983. Almeyda was imprisoned for two months, and Insunza expelled from Chile, in early 1984, for "engaging in communist activities". Other MDP leaders were arrested in October and November, 1984, but subsequently released, and the alliance was declared illegal on Feb. 1, 1985.

Policies. The MDP is divided between parties which support the "national accord" proposed in August 1985 by 11 democratic parties (see Alianza Democrática, above) and others which oppose the terms of the accord. The Movement demands the immediate restoration of representative democracy and of civil liberties, and also advocates the formulation of a new economic strategy designed in particular to relieve unemployment.

Structure. The MDP is directed by a national council comprised of delegates of the members parties.

Membership. The parties represented in the MDP are the Communist Party (to which Insunza belonged), the Clodomiro Almeyda faction of the PSCh, and the MIR (see below); and the Izquierda Cristiana and MAPU (see above). The first three opposed the "national accord", while the last two, as members of the AD, supported it.

Movimiento de Izquierda Revolucionaria (MIR)
Movement of the Revolutionary Left

Leadership.   Andrés Pascal Allende (general secretary); Fr Rafael Maroto (delegate to MDP)

Orientation. Revolutionary socialist

Founded. 1965

History. The MIR was established as an illegal guerrilla movement. It gave critical support to the Unidad Popular government installed in 1970, repeatedly calling for an acceleration of the transformation of the economy and society. Its leader in 1971, Miguel Enríquez, called for the replacement of Congress by a "people's assembly" and for the takeover without compensation of farms and factories.

The organization resumed its guerrilla activities following the September 1973 military coup. A truce, said to have been offered by the Armed Forces Intelligence Service, was publicly rejected by the MIR on Sept. 10, 1974; on Oct. 5, Enríquez was killed in a clash with troops in Santiago. On Jan. 8, 1975, 12 army officers were given prison sentences of up to 15 years for collaborating with the MIR. On Nov. 10, the military authorities announced the arrest of 15 MIR members and the discovery of a plot to infiltrate 1,200 activists into southern Chile from Argentina, with the co-operation of the Argentinian ERP guerrilla movement; the organizers of the plan were said to include Andrés Pascal Allende, who had been involved in a gunfight with police on Oct. 15 in which another MIR leader was killed.

47

Allende and three others were given safe conduct out of Chile in January 1976; on his arrival in Costa Rica in February, Allende stated that since 1973 40,000 people had been killed by the military regime and a further 110,000 had been held as political prisoners.

In October 1977 the MIR carried out bombings in Santiago, including attacks on government buildings on Oct. 14–16, reportedly in revenge for the death of Beatriz Allende, a daughter of the late President, who had committed suicide while exiled in Cuba. The organization claimed to have carried out more than 100 attacks during 1980, including the assassination on July 15 of the head of the army intelligence school which led to mass arrests and numerous kidnappings by right-wing groups.

Seven alleged members of the MIR were killed in late 1981 near the residence in Valdivia province (500 miles south of the capital) of the Foreign Minister. On Nov. 18 three policemen were killed in a gunfight outside the house of the presidential chief of staff. Two alleged members of the MIR were killed in incidents on May 9 and July 17; an agent of the secret police was killed by the MIR on July 6, and three alleged *miristas* were expelled from Chile on Nov. 22. Another member of the MIR was killed on Jan. 16, 1982, and the group's second-in-command, Dagoberto Cortes Guajardo, was killed in a shootout in Santiago on Nov. 27. Four *miristas* took refuge in the Apostolic Nunciature in Santiago in January 1984, and were eventually allowed out of Chile on safe conducts. They had been accused, with five other members of the MIR, of involvement in the assassination in August 1983 of the military commander of the Santiago area. The MIR announced the establishment of a guerrilla arm, the FARP (see above), in late 1984.

Policies. The MIR has moderated its stance in recent years from one of opposition to the established parties of the left to a broad front strategy; in mid-January 1981 the MIR leadership joined with exiled leaders of the Unidad Popular parties in a declaration of unity providing for a joint struggle against the Pinochet regime. The MIR has stated that its ultimate objective is the creation of a single revolutionary party (Partido Unico de la Revolución) embracing all existing left-wing and popular parties and movements. The MIR opposes the terms of the "national accord" proposed in 1985 (see Alianza Democrática, above).

Associated organizations. See MDP (above).

Movimiento Liberal
Liberal Movement

Orientation. Right-wing democratic

History. This small party (also known as the Partido Liberal) was in August 1985 one of 11 to sign the proposal for a "national accord" on the return of democracy (see Alianza Democrática, above).

Movimiento Nacionalista Popular (MNP)
Popular Nationalist Movement

Leadership. Roberto Thieme (leader)

Orientation. Ultra-nationalist

Founded. 1980

History. The leader of the MNP, a former military oficer, had as general secretary of the neo-fascist Patria y Libertad (Homeland and Liberty) group been involved in efforts to subvert the Unidad Popular government in 1970–73. Initially a supporter of the 1973 coup, Thieme later broke with Pinochet and established the MNP in Temuco, in the south, where it received some support from dissident farmers.

In October 1982 Thieme mounted an unsuccessful coup attempt, and subsequently left Chile to live in Argentina. There have been no recent reports of MNP activities in Chile.

Policies. The MNP leader claimed in 1982 that the Pinochet regime had betrayed the "nationalist revolution" by encouraging US and other foreign interests to increase their influence over Chile's affairs. He later declared his admiration for the achievements of the military regime of Gen. Juan Velasco which held power in Peru after 1968.

Movimiento Sindical Unitario (MSU)
Movement for Trade Union Unity

Leadership. Carlos Frez (leader)

Orientation. Democratic

History. This body was one of several trade union organizations active in the democratic opposition in 1984–85.

Movimiento Social Cristiano
Social Christian Movement

Leadership. Juan de Dios Carmona (president)

Orientation. Centre-right

Founded. 1984

History. This group, which drew its support from the right wing of the PDC, was reported to be active in 1985.

Movimiento Unión Nacional (MUN)
National Union Movement

Orientation. Right-wing democratic

History. The MUN was one of the original 11 signatories of the "national accord" proposal of August 1985 (see Alianza Democrática, above).

Multipartidaria
Multi-party Alliance

Orientation. Democratic broad front

Founded. March 14, 1983

History. The Multipartidaria alliance was launched with the publication of a manifesto signed by leading figures of non-communist opposition parties. It attracted the support of various prominent politicians and trade union leaders. The alliance presented proposals for constitutional reforms to the Pinochet regime. As a political force it has been superseded by the Alianza Democrática (see above).

Policies. The alliance has called for a return to democratic government, the lifting of restrictions on political and trade union activities, and other political reforms.

Membership. The 1983 manifesto was signed on behalf of the PDC (by Gabriel Valdés), the Partido Radical (Enrique Silva and Luis Fernando Luengo), the Partido Republicano (Hugo Zepeda and Julio Subercaseaux), the Partido Social Demócrata (Luis Bossay), and various factions of the PSCh (Hernán Vodavonic, Julio Stuardo and Ramón Silva).

Associated organizations. The Proden (see below) was constituted as the information and publicity wing of the Multipartidaria.

Partido Comunista Chileno (PCCh)
Chilean Communist Party

Leadership. Jaime Insunza (leader); Luis Corvalán Lepe (secretary general)

Orientation. Orthodox communist

Founded. 1912, as Partido Socialista de los Trabajadores (PST – Socialist Workers' Party)

History. The PST decided at its fourth congress, held in Rancagua in January 1922, to affiliate with the Third International and adopt its present name. By 1970 the PCCh was the third largest communist party in a non-communist country (after those of France and Italy).

In the congressional elections of 1969 the PCCh gained 22 of the 150 seats in the Chamber of Deputies; in the presidential election of 1970 it was part of the Unidad Popular (see below), whose candidate, Salvador Allende, was elected with 36.3 per cent of the votes cast. The PCCh was given ministerial posts in the Allende government. In December 1971 the party (which then claimed 150,000 members) set up a Frente Revolucionario de los Trabajadores (Revolutionary Workers' Front) which established "anti-fascist brigades" in the factories.

In 1970–73 the party advocated a strategy of gradual progress towards socialism, at a rate acceptable to progressive sectors of the middle class, and in particular to the left wing of the PDC (see below). This it contrasted with the rapid and revolutionary change demanded by "sectarian" groups further to the left, such as the MIR (see above). In the congressional elections of 1973 the Unidad Popular parties won 43.4 per cent of the votes, to 54.7 per cent for the (opposition) Federación de Partidos Democráticos; the left alliance consequently gained only 63 of the 150 seats in the Chamber, of which the PCCh gained 25.

After the coup of September 1973, Corvalán and many other party members were imprisoned and the PCCh banned. It has since operated clandestinely within Chile and, in exile, has coordinated its activities with the other Unidad Popular parties and has repeatedly called for the unity of all democratic forces to defeat the Pinochet regime. Corvalán was released into exile in 1976 in exchange for a Soviet opposition figure, and currently leads the party from Cuba; a similar deal in 1977 freed Jorge Montes, a PCCh leader imprisoned in 1974, in exchange for a number of East German prisoners.

In October 1983 Gen. Fernando Matthei, the Air Force commander and a member of the ruling junta, stated his willingness to negotiate with the PCCh because "the Marxists are a reality in this country and I prefer to face reality". The party is currently pursuing a mainly political campaign, but it has not rejected the use of military tactics, and has itself been the target of right-wing guerrillas; three prominent members of the party were killed in March 1985 by a death squad apparently controlled by members of the paramilitary police.

Policies. Domestically, the PCCh advocates a broad front of the left and the Christian Democrats against military rule, while maintaining its belief in the basic communist principles of the dictatorship of the proletariat and proletarian internationalism. It has supported guerrilla warfare as one element of the wider struggle against the Pinochet regime. It has indicated its opposition to the proposed terms of the "national accord" as announced in mid-1985 (see Alianza Democrática, above). Internationally, its policies are in broad agreement with those of the Soviet Union.

Structure. The supreme organ of the party is the congress, which now meets infrequently; the party organized a clandestine conference in Chile in June 1984. The congress – or conference – determines policy and appoints a central committee and a political commission, which in turn appoints a secretariat. Much of the leadership of the party is currently in exile. The youth wing of the PCCh is the Juventudes Comunistas (Communist Youth).

Associated organizations. See FPMR and MDP (above).

International affiliations. The PCCh is recognized by the communist parties of the Soviet Union and its allies.

Partido Demócrata Cristiano (PDC)
Christian Democratic Party

Leadership. Gabriel Valdés Subercaseaux (president); Jaime Castillo Velasco, Claudio Huepe, José Ruiz di Giorgio, Juan Hamilton, Gutemberg Martínez (first to fifth vice-presidents); Eugenio Ortega (secretary general); Miguel Salazar (president of youth wing)

Orientation. Centre-right

Founded. 1957

History. The PDC (often known as the Democracia Cristiana, DC) was created as the successor to a Falange Nacional (National Falange) founded in 1934. As a democratic reformist party, it advocated a doctrine based on Christian humanism to overcome Chile's poverty; differing interpretations of its basic philosophy have meant that there have traditionally been left- and right-wing tendencies within the party.

Dr Eduardo Frei Montalva, then leader of the PDC, was President of the Republic from 1964 to 1970, when he was succeeded by Salvador Allende of the Unidad Popular coalition. The PDC strongly opposed the Allende government and at first gave tacit support to the military regime which seized power in September 1973; from 1974, the party was divided between a right wing willing to co-operate with the junta, and what appeared to be the main body of the party which maintained unofficial contact outside Chile with the Unidad Popular parties.

A secret congress of the PDC in March 1975 issued a declaration describing the ruling junta as "a right-wing dictatorship with fascist manifestations", and its policies as "erroneous, unjust and incompatible with our principles regarding human rights, the economy and the situation of the workers"; on the other hand, the congress rejected any liaison with "clandestine organizations". Later in the month the Christian Democratic radio station was closed temporarily by the junta. Frei refused to participate in a "Council of State" established by the junta at the end of 1975, and in January 1976 called for a "democratic alternative" to military rule. The party's weekly paper was suspended in March 1976 (its daily having been forced to close in September 1973); the radio station was closed indefinitely in January 1977.

On March 2, 1977, two PDC leaders called for a peaceful, gradual transition to democracy. On the same day the junta announced the discovery of a Christian Democratic plot to overthrow the government, and banned all the remaining political parties – the PDC, the Partido Nacional, the Radical Democrats and the Radical Left. The PDC continued to operate in exile and clandestinely within Chile, where a number of its supporters were imprisoned or sentenced to internal exile. The party called for a "no" vote in the January 1978 plebiscite (see introduction).

51

On Oct. 16, 1980, the then president of the PDC, Andrés Zaldívar, was prohibited from returning to Chile unless he accepted the official result of the constitutional plebiscite of September (see introduction). He was succeeded as president by Valdés. Frei died on Jan. 22, 1982, when Pinochet declared three days of official mourning; the government memorial service on Jan. 25 was boycotted by the family, who held an alternative service attended by thousands and addressed by the Cardinal Archbishop of Santiago.

Under Valdés the PDC has advocated co-operation among a wide range of democratic parties (but not the PCCh) to secure an end to military rule. It has given complete support to the "national accord" proposed in August 1985 (see Alianza Democrática, above). The leadership of the party is subject to re-election at national meetings (Juntas Nacionales), that of May 1985 resulting in the re-election to the presidency of Valdés in preference to Juan Hamilton (a *"freista"*).

Structure. The PDC is directed by a political commission elected by a national congress. It has a youth wing, the Juventud de la Democracia Cristiana (JDC – Christian Democratic Youth).

Associated organizations. The PDC was a founder member of both the Multipartidaria and the Alianza Democrática opposition alliances (see above), formed respectively in March and August 1983.

International affiliations. The party is a member of the Christian Democratic International, of which Andrés Zaldívar Larraín is president, and of the Christian Democratic Organization of America.

Partido Democrático Nacional (Padena)
National Democratic Party

Leadership. Luis Minchell (leader)

Orientation. Right-wing

History. In late 1985 this party was divided into two tendencies, one of which was very close politically to the Partido Nacional (see below).

Partido Liberal

See Movimiento Liberal (above).

Partido Nacional
National Party

Leadership. Carmen Sáenz de Phillips (leader); Fernando Ochagavia (vice-president)

Orientation. Right-wing

History. The Partido Nacional, a traditional right-wing party, remained active in Chile in 1985 despite having been banned on March 12, 1977, together with all other parties. It lost most of its support to the anti-military Partido Republicano (see below) which was formed in 1984.

Policies. The party was involved in the August 1985 discussions leading to the formulation of a "national accord" on a return to democracy (see Alianza Democrática, above). It has nevertheless been associated with attempts to form a more restricted coalition with right-wing parties, and in particular the Partido Democrático Nacional, with a section of which it joined in October 1984 to publish a call for a "democratic consensus" and a liberalization of the regime.

Partido Radical
Radical Party

Address. Pitágoras 344, 03020 México DF, Mexico

Leadership. Enrique Silva Cimma (president, leader of right wing); Anselmo Sule (vice-president); Carlos González Márquez (general secretary); Aníbal Palma (leader of left wing)

Orientation. Social democratic

Founded. 1863

History. The Radical Party became Chile's main progressive formation in the early 20th century and held the presidency in 1938–52. Strongly anti-communist in the 1940s and 1950s, it later moved to the left and in 1969 joined the Unidad Popular alliance (see below) which won the presidency for Salvador Allende in 1970. Radicals held ministerial posts throughout the period of Unidad Popular government, although the party was weakened by the breakaway of elements opposed to its espousal of Marxism in 1971. The party has subsequently found its support mainly among white-collar workers and teachers.

As part of the Unidad Popular, the party was banned by the military regime which seized power in 1973, and was forced to operate clandestinely or from exile. Thereafter it has aimed at the formation of broad fronts, both among Chilean parties and internationally, in opposition to the junta. Since 1980 the party has experienced divisions between the exiled leadership (in Mexico), which favoured armed struggle and closer relations with Marxist–Leninist groups, and the internal leadership which presented social democratic policies. This led in 1983 to the replacement of Anselmo Sule as internal leader by Enrique Silva, a former president of the constitutional tribunal. The party then initiated a reunification process with the elements which left in the early 1970s, with the aim of building a strong social democratic presence on the Chilean left. There are still marked right- and left-wing tendencies in the party.

Associated organizations. The party joined the Multipartidaria opposition alliance, formed in 1983, and subsequently the Alianza Democrática (see above). As part of its effort to strengthen the non-Marxist left, the party joined the Federación Socialista Democrática (see above) in April 1984.

International affiliations. The Party is the Chilean member of the Socialist International, of which Sule is a vice-president.

Partido Republicano
Republican Party

Leadership. Hugo Zepeda (president); Julio Subercaseaux, Armando Jaramillo (leaders)

Orientation. Centre-right

Founded. 1983

History. This party was established by a majority faction of the Partido Nacional (see above). It is itself divided into factions, the right of the party (known as the Derecha Republicana) being led by Jaramillo.

Policies. It has called for an end to military rule and a rapid return to constitutional government.

Associated organizations. The party was a founding member of both the Alianza Democrática and the Multipartidaria opposition alliances (see above).

Partido Social Demócrata
Social Democratic Party

Leadership. Mario Sharpe (president); René Abeliuk (vice-president)

Orientation. Centre-left

History. This small group was active in 1984–85

Associated organizations. The party was a founding member of the Multipartidaria opposition alliance and subsequently of the Alianza Democrática (see above). In April 1984 it joined the Federación Socialista Democrática (see above).

Partido Socialista de Chile (PSCh)
Socialist Party of Chile (Almeyda faction)

Leadership. Dr Clodomiro Almeyda Medina (leader)

Orientation. Marxist

History. This (minority) faction of the Socialist Party emerged in the early 1980s (Almeyda having been expelled from Chile in 1975) to challenge the leadership of Carlos Altamirano, then general secretary of what is now the Briones faction (see below).

Policies. In contrast to the majority faction of the PSCh, the Almeyda faction has close links with the communist party; it advocates increased co-operation among the left parties, while agreeing with the majority leadership that there should be collaboration with non-socialist democratic parties. The faction has nevertheless refused to endorse the 1985 proposal for a "national accord" on a transition to democracy (see Alianza Democrática, above).

Associated organizations. The Almeyda PSCh is allied with the PCCh in the MDP (see above); it is also part of the broader Multipartidaria alliance (see above).

Partido Socialista de Chile (PSCh)
Socialist Party of Chile (Briones faction)

Leadership. Carlos Briones (general secretary)

Orientation. Marxist

Founded. 1940s

History. The PSCh leader, Dr Salvador Allende Gossens, was elected President of Chile in 1970 as the candidate of the Unidad Popular alliance (see below). The party programme at the time of the election included the replacement of Congress with an "assembly of the people", the nationalization of banks and foreign-owned businesses and the development of close ties with socialist countries.

The government was overthrown, and Allende died, in a military coup on Sept. 11, 1973. The Unidad Popular parties were banned and many PSCh members were exiled or imprisoned (including a group of 56 sentenced to up to 30 years in mid-1974 for "treason and sedition").

The exiled PSCh leadership split in 1977 with the departure of a former economics minister, Pedro Vuskovic, who claimed that the Unidad Popular strategy of co-operation with the "bourgeois democrats" of the PDC was unrealistic and compromised the socialist principles of the PSCh. At a meeting in Algeria in March 1978, leaders in exile and from within Chile agreed on a united leadership (under Carlos Altamirano) and increased collaboration with the PDC, but in the early 1980s two smaller factions, including that of Clodomiro Almeyda (see above), emerged. In 1984

Altamirano was succeeded as general secretary of the majority faction by Carlos Briones, a former minister in the Allende government.

The Briones faction has stated its willingness to reunite the PSCh, but has major theoretical, strategic and tactical differences with the Almeyda faction; there are fewer differences between it and the Mandujano group (see below).

Policies. The Briones faction pursues a united front policy aimed at grouping the largest possible range of progressive formations – not excluding the PCCh – in opposition to the Pinochet regime. To that end it has welcomed, with certain reservations, the "national accord" proposed in August 1985 by 11 democratic parties (see Alianza Democrática, above). Within the AD it proposes the creation of a Frente Cívico (Civic Front) which would include the AD parties, non-AD democratic parties and other "social organizations", largely as a means of associating communists with the AD platform without the formal integration of the PCCh in the Alliance.

Associated organizations. This faction of the PSCh was in September 1983 the main founder of the Bloque Socialista Chileno (see above), though it has participated in the Alianza Democrática. Together with other sections of the PSCh it joined the Multipartidaria opposition alliance (see above).

Partido Socialista de Chile (PSCh)
Socialist Party of Chile (Mandujano faction)

Leadership. Sr Mandujano (leader)

Orientation. Marxist

History. This group was in late 1985 the smallest of three factions of the PSCh. It is fairly close in theory and practice to the majority (Briones) faction, and has had discussions with it on the possible reunification of the party.

Policies. The group was involved in the preparation of the "national accord" document of August 1985 (see Alianza Democrática, above) but did not immediately add its signature to the proposal pending internal discussions.

Proyecto para el Desarrollo Nacional (Proden)
Project for National Development

Leadership. Jorge Lavanderos (leader)

Orientation. Democratic opposition

Founded. 1982

History. The Proden was formed by a group of centrist and right-wing politicians and trade union leaders as the information and publicity arm of the Multipartidaria alliance (see above). In February 1983 it called for the transfer of power from Pinochet to the four-man military junta "as a preliminary step to democracy". A rally organized by Proden in October 1983 attracted 40,000 people. In March 1984 it was reported that Lavanderos had been attacked and beaten up by a small right-wing group, the Acha (see above).

Unidad Popular
Popular Unity

Leadership. Dr Clodomiro Almeyda Medina (first secretary)

Orientation. Left-wing

Founded. 1969

History. Set up as an electoral alliance of left-wing parties, the Unidad Popular in 1970 secured the election of a Socialist, Dr Salvador Allende Gossens, as President of the Republic, winning 36.3 per cent of the votes. The Unidad Popular government came into increasing conflict with domestic and foreign right-wing groups, and on Sept. 11, 1973, a violent military coup overthrew the government. President Allende either committed suicide or was killed during the fighting.

The military regime, under Gen. Augusto Pinochet Ugarte, declared Unidad Popular and its constituent parties illegal, and many of its supporters were killed, imprisoned or exiled. The Unidad Popular parties have subsequently co-operated outside Chile and clandestinely inside the country.

On May 1, 1974, the Unidad Popular parties jointly called for the formation of an "anti-fascist front" and for an end to "illegal detention, tortures and summary executions". The parties met, together with left-wingers in the PDC, in Venezuela in July 1975, and decided to work together for the restoration of "a just and socialist democracy in Chile"; they issued a joint programme in August, aimed at resisting the military regime and restoring democratic freedoms; and in September 1976 they again called for a broad front including the Christian Democrats. In January 1981 the Unidad Popular parties, together with the MIR (see above), issued a similar statement to the press in Santiago. Anti-government demonstrators in Santiago in March 1983 used the Unidad Popular slogan "Bread, Justice, Work and Liberty", although the alliance as such has largely been superseded by new coalitions such as the Multipartidaria, Alianza Democrática, the MDP and so on.

Membership. The parties which combined to create the Unidad Popular were the PSCh, the PCCh, the Partido Radical, the Izquierda Cristiana, the MAPU and the MAPU-OC (see above).

Unión Democrática Independiente (UDI)
Independent Democratic Union

Leadership. Jaime Guzmán (president)

Orientation. Right-wing

History. The UDI was formed as a right-wing pressure group; it has given qualified support to the Pinochet regime. It has attempted to establish links with right-wing elements in the PDC and the smaller centrist parties.

Policies. The UDI has called for the creation of a nominated parliament in order to deflect popular pressure for the restoration of democracy. It declined to sign the August 1985 appeal for a transition to democracy (see Alianza Democrática, above).

Unión Democrática de Trabajadores (UDT)
Democratic Workers' Union

Leadership. Hernol Flores (leader)

Orientation. Christian democratic

Founded. 1981

History. This national federation was established by the Grupo de los Diez (see above) to co-ordinate the activities and policies of Christian democratic trade unions. Its leader is also the leader of a private employees' union.

Policies. The UDT has signed the "national accord" proposal put forward in August 1985 (see Alianza Democrática, above).

Membership. 49 unions, 780,000 individuals

Unión Nacional
See MUN (above).

Unión Popular Socialista (UPS)
People's Socialist Union
Leadership. Ramón Silva Ulloa (leader)
Orientation. Social democratic
History. This small group was active in 1984–85.

Associated organizations. In April 1984, together with two other social democratic groups, it formed the Federación Socialista Democrática (see above). It was one of 11 parties to call in August 1985 for a transition to democracy (see Alianza Democrática, above).

Colombia

Capital: Bogotá   **Population: 31,000,000**

After liberation by Simón Bolívar's forces, Colombia became a republic in 1819, although its borders have been redrawn several times since then – most recently with the secession of Panama in 1903. By the 1840s two main political parties, the Partido Liberal and the Partido Conservador, had emerged, and they have been the main forces in Colombian politics ever since.

Despite its violent political history, Colombia has retained a strong attachment to representative democracy and an aversion to dictatorships, which have never had any measure of success. The last military government was replaced in 1958 with a liberal–conservative coalition government, which remained in power, the presidency alternating between the parties and each being allocated an equal representation in Congress, until 1974; the parties continue to share power on a less formal basis, although by 1985 the liberals – albeit divided into two factions – have established a definite electoral lead over the conservatives. The most recent governments have been those of Dr Alfonso López Michelsen (liberal, 1974–78); Dr Julio César Turbay Ayala (liberal, 1978–82), and Dr Belisario Betancur Cuartas (conservative, elected 1982).

Political violence. Colombia's long tradition of political violence goes back to 1840, when revolts by local *caudillos* against central government power gave rise to a two-year civil war. Another, inter-provincial, civil war occurred in the early 1860s; dozens of localized conflicts were recorded in the rest of the century, and a civil war costing about 100,000 lives took place in 1899–1902. From the late 1940s to the mid-'50s – the period known as *La Violencia* – about 180,000 Colombians were killed in acts of violence due partly to banditry and local disputes but mainly to a civil war between conservative and liberal factions. In the 1960s and '70s thousands more lost their lives as a result of left-wing guerrilla warfare and official and unofficial counterinsurgency activities, including killings by drug industry death squads.

For the year 1977, police statistics showed 133 political killings and 87 kidnappings. On Oct. 22, 1980, the Minister of Defence stated that in the past three years guerrillas had killed 128 members of the security forces and 417 peasants; had attacked 83 military bases and 152 banks; and had obtained US$4,000,000 through 88 kidnappings and 10 cases of extortion. He also said that 1,830 guerrillas were still at large while 1,027 were in prison. In 1981, the police reported 100 kidnappings, 63 by guerrillas and 37 by common criminals; 44 of the victims had been freed during the year, nine had been killed and 47 remained in the hands of their abductors at the year's end. A Peace Commission was established by the main parties in October 1981 and worked for the introduction of a general amnesty. The guerrillas suffered severe losses in the early part of 1982.

Shortly before he relinquished office, President Turbay Ayala on June 20, 1982, lifted the state of siege which had been in force almost continuously for 34 years and at the same time cancelled over 30 emergency decrees. His successor as President, Dr Betancur, undertook at his inauguration on Aug. 7 to continue efforts to achieve a truce with the guerrilla groups. An amnesty was declared in November and accepted by about 2,000 guerrillas; direct negotiations between the government and the guerrilla leaders took place in1983–84, a ceasefire was declared in May 1984, and (despite the assassination of the Minister of Justice in May) most of the guerrilla groups had come to an agreement with the government by August which permitted them to engage in electoral politics without disbanding or disarming their forces. Sporadic violence continued, some of it related to the drug trade rather than to politics, and 215 kidnappings were recorded in 1984, 132 of which were attributed to guerrilla movements. An amnesty law passed by Congress in May 1985 allowed for the reintegration into civilian life of guerrillas accused of political offences other than kidnapping, extortion and murder outside armed combat, but in June the M-19 movement announced that the truce was at an end; together with smaller groups it resumed armed activities, while the larger FARC maintained its support for the peace process. Official statistics recorded the deaths of 605 guerrillas, 272 peasants, 168 policemen and 72 soldiers in fighting during the year to mid-July 1985.

Constitutional background. Under the 1886 Constitution, as amended, The Republic of Colombia has an executive President and a Congress consisting of a 114-member Senate and a 199-member

House of Representatives, the President and Congress being elected for four-year terms by universal adult suffrage. The President is elected by a simple majority and Congress by a system of proportional representation. Competing lists may be presented by factions of any party but the votes gained by lists which do not obtain an electoral quota are credited to the most successful list of the same party.

Recent election results. In elections held on March 14, 1982, there was a 45 per cent turnout of eligible voters and seats in the House were won as follows: Partido Liberal 114, Partido Conservador 84, UDI (left-wing) 1. The Senate seats were distributed as follows: liberals 62, conservatives 51, UDI 1. In a presidential election on May 30, the liberal vote was split by the emergence of the Nuevo Liberalismo faction, with the result that the conservative candidate, Dr Belisario Betancur Cuartas (standing for the Movimiento Nacional centre-right alliance), was elected with 46.8 per cent of the vote, against 41 per cent for the liberal candidate, 10.9 per cent for Nuevo Liberalismo and 1.2 per cent for the UDI. The elections were also contested by the far-left MOIR, whose presidential candidate, however, withdrew from the contest.

Alianza Nacional Popular (ANAPO)
National Popular Alliance

Leadership.   Joaquín Mejía (leader)

Orientation.   Centre-right

Founded.   1960

History.   The ANAPO was formed as the political vehicle of ex-dictator Gustavo Rojas Pinilla (in power in 1953–57) and his daughter María Eugenia Rojas de Moreno Díaz. Although not recognized as a political party, ANAPO candidates stood as conservatives or liberals in the 1962 congressional elections and gained several seats. The group also took part in the 1966 elections, as one of three groups constituting the opposition, gaining 36 of the 180 seats in the House; in 1968 it obtained six of the 102 seats allotted to the liberals, and 36 of the 102 conservative seats. The ANAPO presidential candidate, José Jaramillo Giraldo, gained 28 per cent of the vote.

In 1970 the ANAPO made further gains, obtaining 72 of the 210 seats to become the strongest opposition party, Rojas Pinilla lost the presidential election amid accusations of electoral fraud. In 1971 the Alliance constituted itself as a political party. In 1974 it was reduced to 15 out of 199 seats; in the same year, Rojas de Moreno, as the first woman to stand for the Colombian presidency, secured about 10 per cent of the total vote.

The 1978 presidential and congressional elections were contested by an alliance of the ANAPO, the Unión Opositora Nacional (National Opposition Union) and the Movimiento Liberal Indpendiente (Independent Liberal Movement), which together gained four seats in the House. The ANAPO did not take part at all in the 1982 elections.

Policies.   The ANAPO proposes a "Colombian socialism" based on Christian social doctrine. It advocates the unification of all trade unions; discouragement of birth control; limitation of foreign investment; free education for all and free health services for the poor; and the allocation of a house with a hectare of land to each homeless peasant family.

Structure. The party is organized on a hierarchical basis.

Brigada Pedro León Arboleda (PLA)
Pedro León Arboleda Brigade

Orientation. Left-wing guerrilla group

History. This group, an element of the EPL (see below), claimed responsibility for numerous acts of violence, including the occupation of the Partido Liberal headquarters in Medellín on Jan. 23, 1980. One of its leaders, María Isabel Ramírez de Montano, was arrested on May 12, 1980. It subsequently declined but remained active in 1984.

Membership. The PLA was officially stated to have 309 active guerrillas in September 1980; however in 1982 the Peace Commission reduced the estimate to 100 members.

Comando Quintin Lame
Quintin Lame Commando

Orientation. *Indigenista* land rights group

Founded. 1984

History. This group, which takes its name from the indigenous leader Manuel Quintin Lame (who died in October 1967), consists mainly of Paez Indians from the south of the country, around Cauca. Its first action was an armed raid on factory premises in reprisal for the forcible eviction of 150 indigenous families from the company's lands. The group has a significant following and claims to control many barrios. It has co-operated in 1985 with the Frente Ricardo Franco (see below).

Comando Ricardo Franco – Frente Sur
Ricardo Franco Commando – Southern Front

Leadership. Gustavo Arías Londoño (known as Boris; leader)

Founded. 1984

Orientation. Leftist guerrilla movement

History. In 1984, when the major guerrilla movements including M-19 and FARC concluded a ceasefire agreement with the government, some of their members who opposed any compromise combined forces to create the Comando Ricardo Franco, which remains active. Its leader, "comandante Boris", was formerly a member of the M-19 high command. It is linked with the FARC defectors of the Frente Ricardo Franco (see below).

Democracia Cristiana (DC)
Christian Democrats

Address. Avenida 42, 18-08, Apartado 25867, Bogotá

Leadership. José Agustín Linares (president); José Albendea (general secretary)

Orientation. Christian democrat

Founded. August 1964

History. The Colombian Christian democratic movement has made little electoral impact, although it has had a notable intellectual influence in the country's political life. The party took part in the Frente Unido (United Front) of Fr Camilo Torres, but withdrew from it when it came to be dominated by Marxists (with Fr Torres joining the guerrilla struggle in 1965).

In the presidential elections of 1970 and 1978 the DC supported the (unsuccessful) moderate conservative candidate, Belisario Betancur, while in 1974 its own presidential candidate polled less than 7,000 votes and came fifth. In the 1978 congressional elections the DC and other groups supported Betancur, on this occasion the candidate of the conservative-dominated Movimiento Nacional, and he was elected as a result of divisions in the liberal camp.

Policies. The DC is neither of the right nor of the left, is opposed to the traditional Colombian constitutional system and seeks to establish a just society characterized by solidarity and political democracy.

Structure. The party has a national assembly, a national council (of regional executive secretaries and former presidents), a national political committee, a general secretariat and regional and local committees. The party has a youth wing (affiliated to the Christian Democratic Youth of America).

Membership. 10,000

Publications. *Pensamiento Político*, theoretical journal, circulation 3,000; *Reto*, party bulletin, 5,000

International affiliations. Christian Democratic International; Christian Democratic Organization of America

Ejército de Liberación Nacional (ELN)
National Liberation Army

Leadership. Nicolás Rodríguez Bautista (leader)

Founded. 1965

Orientation. Guevarist guerrilla movement

History. The ELN at first operated in the north-eastern department of Santander under the leadership of Fabio Vásquez Castaño and with the support of a Maoist (pro-Chinese) Movimiento Obrero, Estudiantil y Campesino (Worker, Student and Peasant Movement). On Jan. 7, 1966, Fr Camilo Torres Restrepo – a former Dominican priest who advocated a "Christian revolution" to overthrow the existing social order – disclosed that he had joined the ELN, stating that as all legal means of redress were barred to the people he would pursue the armed struggle until the people gained power; on Feb. 15 he was killed in a clash with an army unit. On Aug. 1, 1967, the ELN condemned a statement by the orthodox communist PCC rejecting guerrilla warfare as "an erroneous form of revolution".

The ELN carried out a number of kidnappings, including that of Dr Fernando Londoño y Londoño, a former Minister of the Interior, on July 9, 1970; he was released on payment of a ransom equivalent to US$100,000, and claimed that his captors had tortured him. During 1970, the security forces reported that they had killed 134 guerrillas and captured 201.

In June 1975 the ELN was active in a number of departments, including Bolívar in the north, where they ambushed an army patrol and occupied three towns, leading to a major military operation against them. On Sept. 8 the ELN assassinated the Inspector-General of the Army, who had led major anti-guerrilla operations; over 50 people, including 12 university teachers, were then arrested and on Jan. 20, 1976, four ELN members were sentenced to from 24 to 28 years' imprisonment for the killing. The ELN retaliated with the killing of a policeman in the bombing of the Spanish embassy in Bogotá on the following night.

In September 1976 Vásquez was succeeded as leader by Rodríguez. During the 1978 election campaign ELN units attacked a police station in Bogotá on June 2, killing one and wounding eight policemen. By September 1980 the ELN was officially estimated to have fewer than 40 active members. However, notwithstanding President Turbay Ayala's offer of an amnesty in March 1981, the group intensified its activities near the Venezuelan border in mid-1981 and by September 1982 it was estimated to have 180 guerrillas.

In response to President Betancur's amnesty offer, effective from November 1982, one ELN leader – Fr Diego Uribe Escobar – was reported to have declared that the ELN "would not surrender arms nor accept a sham amnesty" but would "continue fighting with our people to end all forms of exploitation and oppression". Despite this, within a few days of the enactment of the amnesty law 25 ELN guerrillas surrendered, and others followed despite the assassination by the MAS (see below) of one amnestied ELN man.

In November 1983 the group kidnapped Dr Jaime Betancur Cuartas, the President's brother, but released him two weeks later. In August 1984, when the major guerrilla movements concluded a ceasefire agreement with the government, the ELN decided to remain active and has since tried to persuade the other guerrilla groups to resume the struggle and present a united front; it has formed an alliance with other active guerrilla groups. The ELN reportedly occupied the airport at Otu, in the north-east, for two hours on Aug. 26, 1985.

Policies. The ELN is a left-wing revolutionary group influenced by the Cuban revolution and by liberation theology; it aims to represent the poorest sections of the Colombian people and to create an egalitarian socialist society.

International affiliations. The Colombian security forces have claimed that the ELN has links with foreign guerrilla groups and in particular with the Bandera Roja group (Venezuela), Sendero Luminoso (Peru) and the FMLN (El Salvador).

Ejército Popular de Liberación (EPL)
People's Liberation Army

Leadership. Oscar William Calvo, Ernesto Rojas (leaders)

Orientation. Maoist guerrilla movement

Founded. January 1968

History. The EPL was formed as the military wing of the pro-Chinese PCC–ML (see below), which had broken away from the orthodox communists of the PCC in July 1965. The EPL, initially based in the department of Córdoba, suffered severe setbacks in the counterinsurgency campaigns of the 1960s and 1970s.

Early in July 1977 it tried unsuccessfully to assassinate the Air Force Chief of Staff. One of its members was in December 1978 sentenced to 14 years in prison for attacks carried out in 1977. The EPL was still active in 1980, and on March 17 of that year 14 of its members were sentenced to a total of 400 years in prison. By September its strength was officially estimated at 60 active guerrilllas, but by 1982 it was thought to number about 250 and was regarded as the third-largest guerrilla group. A clash between an EPL commando and security forces was reported from Antioquia department in November 1982, and a similar incident occurred in January 1983.

In March 1984 the EPL carried out an attack in the northern El Crucero region, killing two policemen. It also claimed responsibility for an attack on police in Bogotá in July, in which five people died. During 1984 it held discussions with government representatives and concluded a ceasefire agreement, effective for one year from Sept. 1; the truce broke down in 1985 and the EPL was a party to the declaration of unity made by various guerrilla forces in May 1985.

Escuadrones de la Muerte
Death Squads

Orientation. Right-wing guerrilla groups

History. These numerous and apparently unco-ordinated groups have been held responsible for numerous killings of left-wing militants. According to a police report of Sept. 14, 1980, the squads had killed 560 persons in Pereira (Risaraldas department) alone in January–August 1980. On Oct. 27 courts in Medellín reported that the groups had carried out 60 killings. On Nov. 24 a further 11 victims were found in Medellín. A secret service officer who had denounced the existence of death squads sought asylum at the British embassy in Bogotá on Feb. 22, 1980.

Associated organizations. See MAS (below).

Firmes
Standing Firm

Leadership. Geraldo Molina (leader)

Orientation. Democratic left-wing

Founded. 1976

History. This small group was founded by intellectuals with the intention of increasing the presence of the left in Colombian politics. The Firmes joined the Unidad Democrática de la Izquierda coalition (see below) in 1982.

Frente Ricardo Franco
Ricardo Franco Front

Leadership. Javier Delgado (leader)

Orientation. Left-wing guerrilla group

Founded. 1984

History. This group broke away from the FARC (see below) in 1984 in order to continue the guerrilla struggle, claiming that the ceasefire agreement was in any case being broken by the army. On May 22, 1984, it claimed responsibility for nine bombs which went off in the capital, killing two people. It has engaged in joint activities with other guerrilla groups. In early 1985 the FARC offered the government a list of members who had deserted after the truce agreement, and in May it declared war on the Front. A few weeks later Delgado offered ceasefire negotiations, but the group remained active; it attempted to assassinate a leader of the PCC (see below) on June 4. Most of the Front's activities have been directed at police stations and army bases in the south-western Cauca region.

Associated organizations. See Comando Ricardo Franco – Frente Sur (above).

Frente por la Unidad del Pueblo (FUP)
Front for Popular Unity

Orientation. Very left-wing

History. This coalition of Maoists and socialists was active in 1984.

Fuerzas Armadas Revolucionarias de Colombia (FARC)
Revolutionary Armed Forces of Colombia

Leadership. Manuel Marulanda Vélez (formerly known as Pedro Antonio Marín, or "Tiro Fijo", Sure Shot; leader)

Orientation. Orthodox communist guerrilla movement

Founded. April 1966

History. Among several zones taken over by local guerrilla forces and declared to be independent republics during the period of *La Violencia* was that of Gaitania (later called Marquetalia), in the department of Tolima. It was founded in 1949 by Fermin Charry Rincón (also known as Jacobo Frias Alape), a member of the central committee of the PCC (see below), who was killed in Janaury 1960 and was succeeded by Marulanda. Marquetalia was occupied by the Colombian army in May 1964, but its guerrillas decided to continue their struggle and in April 1966 established the FARC under the command of Marulanda and other members of the PCC central committee. On Sept 14, 1970, Marulanda was wrongly reported to have died. Around that time the FARC extended its guerrilla activities in the departments of Huila, Tolima, Quindio and Valle.

In July 1976 the FARC was reported to be active in the departments of Chocó and Córdoba, and on July 16 some 40 FARC guerrillas temporarily seized the town of Sabane Grande, in Sucre. A US Peace Corps worker kidnapped by the FARC on Feb. 14, 1977, was released on Feb. 11, 1980, after payment of a ransom of US$250,000. In an offensive against the FARC in December 1978–January 1979 the army claimed to have killed more than 200 guerrillas, mainly in the department of Santander. On Jan. 20, 1980, 50 FARC members attacked a police station in Huila department, killing three policemen; throughout the rest of the year the movement was involved in numerous other clashes with the security forces, suffering and inflicting many casualties, and significant numbers of its members were arrested and brought to trial. The FARC carried out other kidnappings for large ransoms.

The group on June 17, 1980, rejected the amnesty offered by President Turbay Ayala. In September it was officially stated to be the strongest of the guerrilla organizations, with about 770 active members; that estimate was revised by the national intelligence service to 5,000 members in 1983, and in 1985 left-wing press sources stated that the group had 12,000 members in 27 rural "fronts". The army uncovered FARC arsenals on two occasions late in 1982. A group of 120 FARC guerrillas attacked the town of Toribio (in Valle) and killed two officials in January 1983, and on Feb. 5 the movement ambushed an army patrol, killing eight troops and an officer.

Although the group had indicated its willingness to suspend armed activities in return for an unconditional amnesty, it stated in March 1983 that it still held 56 people who had been kidnapped, and in June it commenced joint armed actions with the M-19 (see below). By the beginning of November the FARC, the M-19 and the ELN had reached agreement on a political alliance.

In January 1984 the FARC attacked a military base at Cerro Grande (Antioquia), killing 14 soldiers, but in March it announced that it had reached a ceasefire agreement with the government whereby rural areas would be demilitarized and the FARC would be permitted to organize politically. Before the truce came into effect, the FARC and M-19 jointly attacked Corinto (Cauca), reportedly losing 30 guerrillas for two policemen and one soldier killed. The truce came into effect on May 28 and was monitored by an all-party peace commission, but the army accused the FARC of 15 violations in the first month, while the FARC made similar accusations against the army. The Defence Minister also claimed that the FARC had carried out 29 kidnappings between May 10 and June 12. (Several of the accusations probably related to the activities of a breakaway group, the Frente Ricardo Franco – see above.) The FARC acknowledged its participation in the raid on Yumbo in August in retaliation for the assassination of Carlos Toledo (see M-19, below), but in November it offered to extend the truce for seven months, bringing it up to Dec. 31, 1985. The process of reintegrating FARC guerrillas in civilian life began on Dec. 1, 1984, and in May 1985 it founded a political party, the Unión Patriótica (see below).

Policies. The FARC, while maintaining a revolutionary stance, has announced its adoption of a parliamentary strategy in pursuance of a programme including the nationalization of foreign enterprises and the introduction of free education for all Colombians.

Juventudes Inconformes de Colombia (JIC)
Non-Conformist Youth of Colombia

Orientation. Guerrilla movement

Founded. 1984

History. The JIC announced in late December 1984 that it had carried out two bombings in Cali and proposed to eliminate all drug dealers, kidnappers and thieves.

Legión Aguilas Blancas
White Eagles Legion

Orientation. Right-wing death squad

History. This group was first reported active in 1984.

Movimiento de Autodefensa Obrera (MAO)
Workers' Self-Defence Movement

Leadership. Adelaida Abadia Rey (leader)

Orientation. Left-wing guerrilla movement

History. A unit of this organization, the Comando 14 de Septiembre, was responsible for the killing on Sept. 12, 1978, of Dr Rafael Pardo Buelvas, who had been Minister of the Interior at the time of a 24-hour general strike on Sept. 14, 1974, which led to widespread clashes and the deaths of about 18 people. In May 1980 the founder of the MAO, Armando López Suárez (known as "Coleta"), and its leader, Oscar Mateus Puerto ("Julián"), were arrested, and in November eight members of the MAO were given lengthy prison sentences for the killing of Pardo.

In September 1980 it was officially estimated that the MAO had only 20 active members, but it was still active in rural areas in mid-1981. It rejected an amnesty offer in November 1982, but from Sept. 1, 1984, had a ceasefire agreement with the government.

Policies. Despite the connotations of the acronym, MAO is a Trotskyist revolutionary movement.

Movimiento Cívico Nacional
National Civic Movement

Orientation. Left-wing

History. This movement represents popular organizations throughout

Colombia; it was involved with groups including the CSTC (see PCC, below) in the organization of the general strike of June 20, 1985.

Movimiento 19 de Abril (M-19)
April 19 Movement

Leadership. Alvaro Fayad Delgado (leader); Madrid Evereth Bustamente (international secretary); Andrés Almarales Manga, Carlos Pizarro León Gómez, Antonio José Navarro Walls

Orientation. New Left urban guerrilla movement

Founded. January 1974

History. The M-19 took its name from the date of the defeat of Rojas Pinilla in the presidential election of 1970 (see ANAPO, above). Although it initially claimed to be the armed wing of the ANAPO, that party denied any connection, and by the end of the 1970s the M-19 was regarded, unlike the ANAPO, as left-wing and Marxist; it declared its aim to be the achievement of a democratic and ultimately socialist state by political means.

The first operation of the group was the theft from a museum of the sword and spurs of Simón Bolívar, the liberator of Spanish America, in January 1974. Its later actions included the kidnapping on Feb. 15, 1976, of José Raquel Mercado, president of the Confederación de Trabajadores de Colombia (CTC – Colombian Confederation of Workers), whom the M-19 accused of betraying the working class; it killed him on April 19 after failing to secure the release of political prisoners and the reinstatement of dismissed workers in return for his life.

On Aug. 28, 1978, the M-19 declared war on the right-wing Turbay Ayala government. In January 1979 it seized 5,000 firearms from an army arsenal, most of which were, according to the army, later recovered; about 150 suspected members of the group, including Argentinians, Uruguayans and West Germans, were arrested in the following weeks. Major M-19 operations in 1980 included a two-month occupation (Feb. 27 to April 27) of the embassy of the Dominican Republic, in which a team led by Rosemberg Pabón Pabón secured a ransom of US$2,500,000, an accelerated trial for imprisoned colleagues, and safe conduct to Cuba in return for the release of 57 hostages including 15 ambassadors. The group also carried out bombings at the Costa Rican and Uruguayan consulates in Cali on March 30 and of the US consulate on May 11 (when two M-19 members were killed by the premature explosion); the temporary occupation of the US cultural centre in Medellín on May 8, of a naval vessel in Cartagena on June 29, and of a radio station in Cali on Dec. 15; the interruption of television broadcasts on Sept. 14, and the hijacking to Cuba of an aircraft with 65 passengers on Dec. 15. By September it was officially regarded as the second strongest of the guerrilla groups, with about 530 active members.

By early 1981 the group was divided into two factions, one of which, led by Jaime Bateman Cayón, was willing to accept a more extensive version of an amnesty offered by the government and to contest elections; a smaller intransigent faction, the Coordinadora Nacional de Bases (CNB – National Co-ordinating Board of Local Units), favoured the continuation of the armed struggle. The abduction on Jan. 19 and subsequent killing of a US citizen accused of being a CIA agent was attributed to the latter faction. After an M-19 attack on the southern town of Mocoa on March 11, in which 11 people were killed, the army launched a counter-offensive in which 19 guerrillas were killed, 29 captured and about 50 arrested and extradited after fleeing to Ecuador; the latter number included Pabón and another M-19 leader, Dr Carlos Toledo Plata. The government broke off diplomatic relations with Cuba, alleging that the Cuban authorities had assisted the guerrillas, 15 of whom were in June sentenced by a military court to a total of 330 years in prison. The government's limited amnesty offer expired in July, and the M-19 intensified its operations, partly in collaboration with the FARC (see above). It attacked the presidential palace and a police station in Bogotá on July 19, killing one policeman; it was accused in October of planning an insurrection; on Nov. 14 a ship allegedly carrying guns for it was sunk by the navy, with four deaths; and on Jan. 27, 1982, it hijacked an airliner to Cuba.

The limited amnesty was reintroduced, but again rejected by most guerrillas, in February; it expired in June but a more extensive amnesty offer in November led to the first direct talks between the government and the seven members of the M-19 political command. In August a leading member of the group, Camilo Restrepo Valencia, was assassinated, possibly by the MAS (see below), shortly after his release from prison. Pabón, Toledo and 23 other M-19 leaders were released in November.

Although negotiations on an amnesty agreement continued, the movement's guerrillas, estimated to number 800, were engaged in various acts of violence in 1983, including the kidnapping in January of a banker's daughter, for whom a US$15,000,000 ransom was demanded. In April Bateman was reported to have died in an air crash (although there was some speculation that he was alive and in hiding); shortly afterwards the M-19 reached agreement on a political alliance with the FARC and the ELN (see above). Talks were held in Spain in October between President Betancur and Iván Marino Ospina, then leader of the M-19, and Alvaro Fayad, his deputy.

Progress towards a peaceful settlement was disrupted by an armed attack on the prison at Florencia (Caquetá) by 200 M-19 members in March 1984; 158 prisoners were freed after fighting in which 140 hostages were taken and four civilians, one prison guard and 26 guerrillas were killed. Ospina and Fayad denounced the attack and expelled its leaders from the M-19, while the government declared a state of siege in the area. In August Toledo Plata was assassinated, probably by the MAS, and Pabón led 200 M-19 and FARC guerrillas in a retaliatory raid on the town of Yumbo; three policemen, two civilians and 12 guerrillas were killed and 18 prisoners were freed. The M-19 leadership announced that a truce would not be signed until the government had guaranteed the safety of former guerrillas.

A one-year ceasefire agreement was signed on Aug. 24, 1984, although five guerrilla leaders were wounded in clashes with police on the way to the ceremony. Under the terms of the agreement the M-19 was enabled to organize openly, and launched a recruitment drive in which it claimed to have added 3,000 members in one day. Three M-19 leaders were arrested for possession of arms, leading to the withdrawal of the movement from the Peace Commission discussions, but the acquittal of the three in November, and a meeting between Betancur, Marino Ospina and Fayad in Mexico in December, prevented the total breakdown of the peace process, although there continued to be occasional clashes between M-19 and government forces, including one protracted outbreak of fighting in the Corinto mountain region in December–January.

In February 1985 a congress of the movement elected Fayad as leader in place of Marino Ospina, who remained in the five-member command. A young man putting up M-19 posters in a Cali slum was shot by police in April 1985, and heavy fighting occurred later in the month between troops and a column led by Pabón in Pradera, in the south-west. A meeting in Mexico between Fayad and government officials re-established the ceasefire, but after two death squad attempts to assassinate Antonio Navarro Wolf and other members of the M-19 command the group withdrew from the peace talks and resumed armed activities in June. On June 28, about 200 guerrillas launched an attack on the central town of Génova, in which 19 people were killed; it attacked other towns, in Quindio and Tolima departments, and on July 11 occupied Ríofrío, 60 km south-west of the capital. On Aug. 14 the military high command announced a total war on M-19, and on Aug. 28 Marino Ospina and three others were killed in an army raid in Cali. On Sept. 3 it was reported that Pabón had also been killed, and on Oct. 2, 28 guerrillas and 12 soldiers were reportedly killed in two incidents.

Policies. M-19 is a left-wing socialist movement committed to social and economic reform, including land reform; Bateman described it as "nationalist, ideologically pluralist and 80 per cent Catholic".

International affiliations. The armed forces alleged in September 1985 that evidence had been found of links between the M-19, the Peruvian Sendero Luminoso movement and the Ecuadorian Alfaro Vive group. An M-19 spokesperson confirmed that contacts existed with unspecified Venezuelan, Panamanian, Salvadorean and Nicaraguan organizations, and that individuals from other Latin American countries were serving in M-19 units.

Movimiento Nacional

See Partido Conservador (below).

Movimiento Obrero Independiente Revolucionario (MOIR)
Independent Revolutionary Workers' Movement

Address. Apartado Aéreo 19042, Bogotá

Leadership. Diego Betancur Alvarez (leader)

Orientation. Maoist

History. This movement took part in the 1974 and 1978 presidential elections as part of the communist-led UNO (see PCC, below), which in 1978 was allied with the ANAPO (see above) and a Movimiento Liberal Independiente (Independent Liberal Movement). The MOIR contested the congressional elections of 1982 on its own, with the President's son, Diego Betancur, as its leader in Bogotá; as a result of its poor showing in those elections its presidential candidate, Consuela de Montejo, withdrew from the contest.

Publications. *Tribuna Roja*, quarterly, claimed circulation 300,000

Movimiento de Renovación Nacional (MRN)
National Renewal Movement

Address. Apartado Aéreo 91175, Bogotá

Leadership. Gen. (retd) Alvaro Valencia Tovar (leader); Enrique Umaña (general secretary)

Orientation. Right-wing

Founded. November 1977

History. The MRN was established in order to contest the 1978 presidential election, in which its leader – who had been commander of the army in 1974–75, but had been dismissed after rumours of a coup – obtained some 66,000 votes. It did not take part in later elections and may now be defunct.

Policies. The party described itself as democratic right-wing, advocating more active participation in political life by ordinary citizens; it emphasized moral issues.

Publications. Renovación

Movimiento Revolucionario Estudiantil
Student Revolutionary Movement

Orientation. Guerrilla group

Founded. 1985

History. The first recorded action of this group was the assassination in June 1985 of an official of the state oil company, Ecopetrol.

Muerte a Secuestradores (MAS)
Death to Kidnappers

Orientation. Right-wing death squad

Founded. 1981

History. The MAS was formed in the city of Medellín and while its avowed aim is to act against guerrilla groups which carried out abductions, it is also thought to be linked to the drug trade. In October 1981 pamphlets dropped on Cali stated that over 200 major drug dealers had agreed to contribute over US$2,000,000 to arm a 2,000-man MAS force which would publicly execute kidnappers and take action against "their companions in prison or their closest relatives".

Of more than 500 killings attributed to the MAS, some have been of suspected guerrillas, some of trade union leaders and most of peasants. In March 1982 it killed a left-wing lawyer; in the same year it killed Henry Castro, the amnestied leader of the ELN (see above), and Camilo Restrepo of the M-19 (see above) shortly after his release from prison. It was held responsible for the killing in August 1984 of Carlos Toledo Plata, the founder of the M-19.

The left-wing guerrilla groups have consistently maintained that the MAS is closely linked with the armed forces, and evidence of this emerged in a murder trial in January 1983. After an inquiry ordered by President Betancur, a list was published in February 1983 containing the names of 163 people allegedly involved in the MAS, including 59 serving members of the armed forces, the most senior being Col. Hernando Darío Velandia Hurtado and Col. Emilio Gil Bermúdez; none of those named have so far been convicted. Every soldier was reportedly obliged to contribute a day's pay to the defence of the 59 military men. On Nov. 11, 1984, the MAS or a similar group killed the only Colombian Catholic priest of indigenous descent, Fr Alvaro Orcue, a well-known campaigner for peasant rights. Seven peasants abducted by the MAS on July 28, 1985, were found decapitated in the northern Magdalena river.

Nuevo Liberalismo
New Liberalism

Leadership. Dr Luis Carlos Galán Sarmiento (leader)

Orientation. Centre-left

Founded. 1982

History. The Nuevo Liberalismo group is a radical faction of the Partido Liberal (see below) and was set up with the support of Dr Carlos Lleras Restrepo, who had been President in 1966–70, with the aim of opposing the official liberal candidate, Dr Alfonso López Michelsen, in the 1982 presidential election. Senator Galán ~~won 10.9 per cent~~ of the vote, giving victory to the conservative candidate.

Policies. The group campaigned for the abolition of the existing two-party system and of the constitutional provision allowing former Presidents to seek re-election after a period out of office. It proposed a broad alliance of the Partido Liberal and other centrist and left-wing parties.

Publications. Nuevo Liberalismo is supported by the country's largest-selling daily paper, *El Espectador* (circulation 215,000).

Organización Revolucionaria del Pueblo (ORP)
People's Revolutionary Organization

Orientation. Guerrilla group

History. In November 1982 a group using this name claimed responsibility for the killing of Gloria Lara de Echeverry (the wife of a former president of Congress), who had been kidnapped on June 23.

Partido Comunista de Colombia (PCC)
Communist Party of Colombia

Address. Carrera 34, no. 9-28, Bogotá

Leadership. Gilberto Vieira (general secretary); Hernando Hurtado, Jaime Caicedo

Orientation. Orthodox communist

Founded. July 1930

History. The PCC was illegal for many years but acquired semi-legal status in 1957. In the 1960s it became involved in the guerrilla struggle through the FARC (see above). In the 1974 presidential election it was the leading force in the Unión Nacional de Oposición (UNO – National Opposition Union), whose candidate came fourth with over 130,000 votes (out of nearly 4,770,000). It joined the Unidad Democrática de la Izquierda coalition (see below) in 1982. A left-wing guerrilla group opposed to the PCC's parliamentary strategy, the Frente Ricardo Franco (see above), attempted to kill Hernando Hurtado on June 4, 1985.

Structure. The PCC is based on cells and has as its highest authority a congress convened every four years. The congress elects a central committee which in turn elects a central executive committee and a secretariat.

Publications. *Voz Proletaria*, weekly, circulation 45,000; *Documentos Políticos*, theoretical monthly

Associated organizations. The Confederación Sindical de Trabajadores de Colombia (CSTC – Colombian Workers' Trade Union Confederation) is communist-led; it held an illegal general strike on June 20, 1985, to protest against government economic policies and the state of siege.

International affiliations. The Party is recognized by the Soviet Communist Party and its allied parties.

Partido Comunista de Colombia – Marxista–Leninista
Communist Party of Colombia (Marxist–Leninist)

Orientation. Maoist

Founded. July 1965

History. This group broke away from the orthodox (pro-Soviet) PCC and initially adopted a strong pro-Chinese line. It became involved in the guerrilla struggle in the 1960s through the EPL (see above). The main Maoist party is now the MOIR (see above).

Partido Conservador
Conservative Party

Address. Calle 36, no. 16-56, Bogotá

Telephone. 328127

Leadership. Dr Belisario Betancur Cuartas (President of Colombia, effective leader); Misael Pastrano Borrero (party leader); Elvira Cuervo de Jaramillo, Hernando Barjuch Martínez (general secretaries); Alvaro Gómez

Orientation. Centre-right

Founded. October 1849

History. The Partido Conservador is one of the two parties which have dominated political life in Colombia since the mid-19th century, the other being the Partido Liberal. The party developed from the faction supporting Dr José Ignacio Márquez, who became President of Colombia in 1837 and was succeeded by two other conservatives. From 1848 the conservatives were supported by a newspaper, *El Nacional*. In 1851 there was an unsuccessful conservative revolt against a radical liberal presidency, but the party returned to power with the election of Mariano Ospina Rodríguez in 1857. A liberal revolt developed into a civil war, which returned the liberals to power in 1862.

After two decades of liberal rule, the independent liberal President Rafael Núñez turned in the 1880s to the conservatives for support against the radical liberals, and a Partido Nacional (National Party) was launched. The conservatives came to dominate the party and the government and in 1886 introduced a centralist constitution. Despite liberal revolts, which again led to civil war at the turn of the century, the conservatives remained in power until 1930, when a split in the movement gave victory to the liberal presidential candidate. The Partido Conservador boycotted the 1934 elections, but in 1939 gained the balance of power between two liberal factions in Congress and in 1946 won the presidency for Mariano Ospina Pérez. This was followed by the years of *La Violencia*.

When liberal leader Jorge Gaitán was murdered in Bogotá in 1948, his followers attacked conservatives in riots which became known as the *bogotazo*. A state of siege was imposed in 1949, but political killings continued; a conservative, Laureano Gómez, was elected unopposed and became President in 1950, but was overthrown in 1953 by a military coup led by Gen. Gustavo Rojas Pinilla. During the Rojas Pinilla dictatorship the liberals and conservatives agreed to work together for the restoration of democracy; under a power-sharing arrangement approved by referendum the two parties, forming a Frente Nacional (National Front), alternated in the presidency and had equal representation in the Cabinet and in the national and provincial legislatures from 1958 to 1974, and, on a less formal basis, they shared power thereafter.

After 1974 the conservatives were divided between the Alvarista faction, supporting Alvaro Gómez Hurtado (the unsuccessful candidate in the 1974 presidential election), and the Ospina-Pastranistas, led by Dr Pastrana Borrero (President in 1970–74); the factions reunited in November 1981 and, with the other members of a centre-right alliance, the Movimiento Nacional, presented a single conservative candidate, Dr Betancur, in the 1982 election.

The Betancur administration introduced various social reforms and secured agreement for a year-long ceasefire with the country's guerrilla forces. The agreement partly broke down after nine months, following attacks by right-wingers on amnestied guerrillas. The administration has

71

also restored relations with Cuba and has brought Colombia into the Non-Aligned Movement.

Policies. The Partido Conservador is a democratic conservative party advocating the rule of law, the maintenance of the separation between the executive, judicial and legislative powers, social justice on a Christian basis, and defence of the dignity of the individual.

Structure. The party has a national directorate of 18 members.

Membership. 2,500,000

Publications. *El Colombiano*, circulation 100,000; *El País*, 60,000; *La República*, 50,000; *El Siglo*, 50,000; *Occidente*, 30,000

Partido Liberal
Liberal Party

Address. Avenida Jiménez 8-56, Bogotá

Leadership. Dr Alfonso López Michelsen, Julio César Turbay (leaders)

Orientation. Reformist

Founded. 1840s

History. A liberal faction emerged in the 1820s supporting Francisco de Paula Santander against Simón Bolívar; by the 1840s liberalism was firmly established as a political force to rival the conservatives. The liberal President José Hilario López introduced reforms such as freedom of the press and the abolition of slavery. Under his rule the party divided between a radical Golgota tendency and the Democrática tendency which, together with the army, supported the installation of President José María Obando in 1853. A coup in 1854 led to a coalition government; in 1857 the conservatives took power, and after a civil war ex-President Mosquera returned to power in 1862 with liberal backing.

Twenty years of liberal rule, punctuated by 40 armed conflicts in various parts of the country, ended when the leader of the party's right wing, President Rafael Núñez, allied himself with the conservatives against the radical liberals during his second term in office, beginning in 1884. The Partido Liberal was suppressed after a revolt in 1895, but another uprising in 1899 led to a bloody civil war ended by the creation of a national assembly which made constitutional amendments giving the liberals a share in government, although the conservatives remained in power until 1930.

A liberal, Enrique Olaya Herrera, became President in 1930, and after the conservatives boycotted the 1934 elections he was succeeded by his colleague Alfonso López. The division within the party resurfaced and the next president was the moderate liberal Eduardo Santos; López, a radical, returned to power in 1942, but resigned in 1945 after a deterioration in the security situation (the President himself being temporarily kidnapped by army officers in 1944). A conservative was elected President in 1946, and the murder in 1948 of the left-wing liberal leader, Jorge Eliécer Gaitán, led to increased disorders and a virtual civil war with fighting throughout the country, mainly between conservatives and liberals.

The Partido Liberal did not take part in the 1950 elections, but made peace with the conservatives after the 1953 coup by Col. Rojas Pinilla (see ANAPO, above); from 1958 the two parties shared power, with alternating control of the presidency and equal representation in the cabinet and the legislature. This agreement – the Frente Nacional (National Front) – was not applied to Congress after 1960, leaving the liberals with a majority, but the executive coalition was continued after the expiry of the initial agreement in

1974. The liberals retained the presidency in 1974 and 1978, together with their congressional majority.

In March 1982 the liberals won 114 of the 199 seats in the House of Representatives and 62 of the 114 Senate seats, but the inability of the radical (Nuevo Liberalismo) and moderate (legitimista) factions to agree on a presidential candidate for May gave victory to the conservative candidate, Dr Betancur, although the official liberal candidate, López Michelsen, gained 41 per cent of the vote and the candidate of Nuevo Liberalismo (see above), Dr Galán, won 10.9 per cent.

Policies. The PL stands for free enterprise and moderate economic and social reforms; it is seen as representing urban industrial society rather than rural interests, although it has a strong following in some areas of the countryside.

Partido Revolucionario de los Trabajadores (PRT)
Workers' Revolutionary Party

Leadership. Valentín González (leader)

Orientation. Revolutionary

History. This group claims to have operated clandestinely for a number of years, organizing strikes, peasant land rights struggles, student protests and actions in defence of indigenous rights; in July 1984 a PRT commando reportedly led by Adriana Garces and Carlos Mario García kidnapped a wealthy industrialist and secured a very substantial ransom.

The group publicly announced its existence and objectives with the issue of a periodical, *El Combatiente*, in June 1985. The group has not adhered to the 1984 ceasefire agreement and encourages the formation of a united front of left-wing guerrilla groups.

The PRT has been accused of having links with the drugs trade, but has vehemently denied it.

Policies. The PRT describes itself as a revolutionary anti-imperialist Marxist organization opposed to the power of the Colombian oligarchy.

Publications. *El Combatiente*, quarterly

International affiliations. The PRT distributes its publications from an address in Sweden.

Partido Socialista de los Trabajadores (PST)
Socialist Workers' Party

Leadership. María Socorro Ramírez (leader)

Orientation. Socialist

History. The PST leader unsuccessfully contested the 1978 presidential election. The party joined the Unidad Democrática de la Izquierda coalition (see below) in 1982.

Patria Libre
Free Homeland

Orientation. Left-wing guerrilla group

History. This group joined the M-19, the EPL, the FARC–UP, the ELN and the PRT in 1985 in a united front opposed to ceasefire agreements.

Unidad Democrática de la Izquierda (UDI)
Democratic Unity of the Left

Leadership. Dr Gerardo Molina (leader)

Orientation. Socialist

Founded. 1982

History. The Unidad alliance was formed to fight the 1982 presidential election, in which Dr Molina was its candidate. It secured 83,000 votes, or 1.2 per cent of the total. It has one seat in each chamber of Congress.

Membership. The member parties are the Firmes, the PCC and the PST (see above).

Unión Patriótica (UP or FARC–UP)
Patriotic Union

Orientation. Left-wing

Founded. 1985

History. This party was founded as the political wing of the FARC guerrilla movement (see above). It began its operations in Florencia (in Caquetá) in August 1985.

Costa Rica

Capital: San José   **Population: 2,400,000**

Costa Rica achieved independence in 1821 since when almost every change of government has occurred peacefully and constitutionally. The only exception was in 1948, when a civil war arising from a disputed election result brought to power a revolutionary junta headed by José Figueres Ferrer. The Ferrer government abolished the armed forces, and, despite border incidents in recent years involving in particular Nicaragua, the country still has no standing army, relying on a paramilitary guard force totalling 7,000 men. In 1949 a Constitution was enacted and since then power has alternated between the Partido de Liberación Nacional (PLN), a social democratic party founded by Ferrer, and conservative or centre-right movements, currently represented by the Partido Unidad Social Cristiana (PUSC). The PLN was in power in 1985. The country has experienced considerable economic difficulties and consequent industrial unrest in the 1980s due mainly to depressed market conditions for its principal agricultural commodities.

Constitutional background. The Constitution of 1949, still in force, establishes Costa Rica as a democratic state with an exective President elected for a four-year term by universal adult suffrage. The President appoints, and presides over, a Cabinet. Legislative power is held by a unicameral Legislative Assembly similarly elected by universal adult suffrage, using a form of proportional representation. The state subsidizes campaign expenses, on a basis related to the share of the vote, for each party obtaining more than 5 per cent of the vote.

Recent election results. A legislative election on Feb. 7, 1982, produced a 77 per cent turnout and the following distribution of seats in the Assembly: PLN 33, Unidad (now the PUSC) 18, Pueblo Unido 4, Movimiento Nacional 1, Partido Democrático Alajuelense 1. A presidential election held simultaneously was won by the PLN candidate, Luis Alberto Monge Alvarez, with 57.3 per cent of the vote, compared with 32.7 per cent for the candidate of the Unidad coalition, Rafael Angel Calderón Fournier. There were three minor candidates.

Acción Democrática Alajuelense
Alajuela Democratic Action

Leadership. Francisco Alfaro Fernández (president); Juan Bautista Chacón Soto (secretary)

Orientation. Regionalist

History. The party operates only in Alajuela, which with 431,000 inhabitants is the second largest of the seven provinces. In the 1982 elections it gained one seat in the Legislative Assembly.

Acción del Pueblo
People's Action

Leadership. Angel Ruíz Zúñiga (president); Henry Mora Jiménez (secretary)

Orientation. Leftist

History. This party was reportedly active in the early 1980s.

Acción Socialista
Socialist Action

Leadership. Marcial Aguiluz Orellana (last president); Arnaldo Ferreto Segura (last secretary)

Orientation. Communist

History. Acción Socialista (also known as the Partido de Acción Socialista, PAS) was formed after the Partido Vanguardia Popular (the communist party – see below) had been declared illegal in 1949. Largely supported by communists, it unsuccessfully contested the 1970 presidential election, won two seats in the 1974 legislative election and was part of the Pueblo Unido coalition (see below) in the 1978 elections. The activities of Acción Socialista have been suspended and its members are now working legally in the Partido Vanguardia Popular and in Pueblo Unido.

Alianza Nacional Cristiana
National Christian Alliance

Leadership. Víctor Hugo González Montero (president); Juan Rodríguez Venegas (secretary)

Orientation. Christian democrat

History. This party was reported as active in the early 1980s.

Brigada Internacional Simón Bolívar
Simón Bolívar International Brigade

Orientation. Left-wing

History. Two members of this group, named after the leading figure in the 19th century Latin American independence struggle, were reportedly arrested on March 2, 1980.

75

Coalición Pueblo Unido
See Pueblo Unido (below).

Coalición Unidad (CU)
See Partido Unidad Social Cristiana (below).

Comando Carlos Argüero Echeverría
Carlos Argüero Echeverría Commando
Orientation. Left-wing guerrilla movement

History. This group, named after a Costa Rican who died in the revolution against the Somoza regime in Nicaragua, claimed responsibility for a rocket-propelled grenade attack, in which three US marines were injured, in San José on March 17, 1981.

Comité Patriótico Nacional
National Patriotic Committee
Orientation. Left-wing

Founded. 1985

History. This non-traditional leftist group was reportedly close to the policies of the PVP (see below).

Concordia Costarricense
See Partido Concordia Costarricense (below).

Defensa Nacional
National Defence
Leadership. José Francisco Herrera Romero (president); María E. Hidalgo Brenes (secretary)

Orientation. Conservative

History. This group was reportedly active in 1984.

Ejército del Pueblo Costarricense (EPC)
Costa Rican People's Army
Orientation. Right-wing guerrilla group

Founded. 1984

History. This group was reportedly active in 1985.

Foro Patriótico para la Paz y la Soberanía
Patriotic Forum for Peace and Sovereignty
Leadership. José Figueres Ferrer (leader)

Orientation. Neutralist and pacificist

Founded. May 26, 1985

History. This group was formed by a former President of Costa Rica following indications that the PLN government was expanding and improving the country's limited defence forces, and specifically in response to the arrival in Costa Rica of a group of US military advisers.

Policies. The group seeks to protect Costa Rican neutrality in the region's conflicts and to prevent the recreation of a permanent army.

Movimiento Nacional (MN)
National Movement
Leadership. Mario Echandi Jiménez (president); Rodrigo Sancho Robles (secretary)

Orientation. Conservative

History. In the 1982 elections this party gained one seat in the Legislative Assembly, and its president, who contested the presidential election, obtained 3.7 per cent of the total valid votes.

Movimiento Revolucionario del Pueblo (MRP)

See Partido de los Trabajadores (below).

Organización Socialista de los Trabajadores (OST)
Socialist Workers' Organization

Address. Apartado 949, San José

Leadership. Marta Trejos Montero (president); Rosendo Fujol Mesalles (secretary)

Orientation. Trotskyist

Founded. May 1976

History. The OST was founded by a group of militant Marxists "in order to open up a workers' political perspective clearly distinguished from the opportunism of those Latin American communist parties dependent on the leadership of the USSR, and also from the adventurism of guerrilla groups". It was legally recognized in May 1977 and took part in the general and presidential elections of February 1978, claiming to present "the first working-class presidential candidate in the country's history".

Policies. The OST describes itself as a Marxist revolutionary party advocating "the seizure of power by workers' and peasants' councils as an integral part of the world revolutionary process".

Publications. Que Hacer, official organ, every two weeks, circulation 4,000

International affiliations. The OST is the Costa Rican section of the Fourth International.

Partido Alajuelista Nueva
New Alajuela Party

Leadership. Annie Badilla Calderón (president); Carlos Alberto Retana R. (secretary)

Orientation. Regionalist

History. This party was reportedly active in 1984 in the city of Alajuela (population 34,000).

Partido Auténtico Limonense
Authentic Party of Limón

Leadership. Marvin Wrigth Lindo (president); Guillermo Joseph Wignall (secretary)

Orientation. Regionalist

History. The party operated in 1984 only in Limón, which has 187,000 inhabitants and is the smallest of the seven provinces.

Partido Comunista Costarricense
Costa Rican Communist Party

Leadership. Miguel Enrique Delgado Cascante (president)

Orientation. Marxist

Founded. 1984

History. This party was permitted to register in September 1984 after the electoral tribunal overruled an earlier decision of the civil registry not to process its application.

Partido Concordia Costarricense
Costa Rican Concord Party

Address. Calles 2 y 4, Avenida 10, San José

Telephone. 232497

Leadership. Emilio Piedra Jiménez (president); Roberto Francisco Salazar Madriz (secretary)

Orientation. Centrist

History. This party (also known as Concordia Costarricense) was active in 1984.

Partido Demócrata (PD)
Democratic Party

Leadership. Edwina Retana Chávez (president); Alvaro González Espinoza (secretary)

History. The PD is a minor party whose candidates unsuccessfully contested the 1974 and 1982 presidential elections.

Partido Demócrata Cristiano (PDC)

See Partido Unidad Social Cristiana (below).

Partido Ecológico Costarricense
Costa Rican Ecology Party

Leadership. Alexander Bonilla (leader)

Orientation. Ecologist

Founded. June 30, 1984

History. This party has indicated its intention to contest the elections due in 1986.

Partido Independiente
Independent Party

Leadership. Eugenio Jiménez Sancho (president); Gonzalo Jiménez Chaves (secretary)

History. This party was active in the early 1980s.

Partido Laborista
Labour Party

Leadership. Miguel Angel Mendoza Hernández (president); Jorge Pacheco Alvarado (secretary)

History. This party was reportedly active in 1985.

Partido de Liberación Nacional (PLN)
National Liberation Party

Address. Calle 28, Avenidas Central y 2, Apartado 2919, San José

Telephone. 323225

Leadership. Luis Alberto Monge Alvarez (President of Costa Rica, effective leader); José Figueres Ferrer (president); Daniel Odúber (national director); Rolando Araya Monge (general secretary); Edgar Ugalde (international secretary)

Orientation. Social democratic

Founded. October 1951

History. The founders of the PLN included members of the Partido Demócrata Social (PDS – Social Democratic Party), which was founded in 1948. In the 1953 elections the PLN leader, José Figueres Ferrer, was elected President of the Republic and instituted many reforms in the economic and social fields. The party lost the presidency in 1958, despite winning a majority in the Legislative Assembly, but in 1962 it retained its control of the Assembly and its favoured candidate won the presidency. The PLN lost the presidential election of 1966, but won that of 1970, with Figueres again the candidate, and retained it in 1974 with Daniel Odúber Quirós, while maintaining its majority in congress. In 1978, however, the PLN lost both the presidential and the congressional elections to the conservative Unidad Opositora (Opposition Unity) alliance.

After the 1982 elections it returned to power with 33 of the 57 assembly seats and Monge, formerly the general secretary of the party, became President, having won 53.7 per cent of the vote. On Jan. 28, 1985, it selected Oscar Arias Sánchez as its presidential candidate for 1986.

Policies. The PLN has as its objective "the peaceful transformation of the social system into democratic socialism, eliminating the rift between the classes". In the 1982 campaign Monge called for "a return to the land", promised to stimulate agricultural production, and said that economic recovery was necessary to save Costa Rica from being "swept away in a whirlwind of violence". He supported proposals for a negotiated settlement of the conflict in El Salvador and criticized the Sandinista government of Nicaragua as leaning towards the Soviet Union and Cuba. The economic policies of the current PLN regime have been conservative.

Structure. The PLN's supreme organ is a national assembly of 70 delegates. The party has a three-member national executive committee, a seven-member national political committee, seven provincial committees (appointed by provincial assemblies), 80 cantonal committees (appointed by cantonal assemblies) and 410 district assemblies.

Membership. It claims 367,000 members; the turnout in its 1985 presidential primary election was 250,000.

Publications. *Combate*, monthly, circulation 15,000

International affiliations. The PLN is a member of the Socialist International, of which Odúber is a vice-president.

Partido Nacional Costarricense
Costa Rican National Party

Leadership. Carlos Rodríguez Quirós (president); Mario Rodríguez Matamoros (secretary)

History. This minor party was reportedly active in 1984.

Partido Nacional Democrático (PND)
National Democratic Party

Leadership. Rodolfo Cerdas Cruz (president); Elodio Jara Jiménez (secretary)

Founded. Oct. 4, 1980

History. The PND was founded by Cerdas Cruz, who had previously been president of the Frente Popular Costarricense (FPC – Costa Rican Popular Front), a minor grouping which contested the 1978 elections.

Partido Nacional Independiente (PNI)
National Independent Party

Address. Calles 18 y 20, Avenida Central, San José

Telephone. 580644

Leadership. Jorge González Martén (president); Alberto Pinto Gutiérrez (secretary)

Orientation. Right-wing

Founded. 1974

History. The PNI was formed to contest the 1974 elections, in which it gained six seats in the Legislative Assembly and its presidential candidate came third. By 1978 it had declined considerably and it gained no seats in that year's Assembly elections. It was subsequently declared in suspension.

Policies. The PNI is strongly anti-communist.

Partido Obrero Campesino
Workers' and Peasants' Party

Leadership. Juan Diego Castro Fernández (president); Priscilla Quesada Rojas (secretary)

Orientation. Leftist

History. This minor party was reported as active in early 1985.

Partido Progreso Nacional (PPN)
National Progress Party

Leadership. Miguel Barzuna Sauma (president); Carlos Manuel Brenes Méndez (secretary)

Orientation. Centrist

History. This minor party was active in 1984.

Partido Radical Demócrata
Radical Democratic Party

Leadership. Juan José Echeverría Brealey (president); Rodrigo Esquivel Rodríguez (secretary)

Orientation. Left-wing

Founded. 1982

History. This party was founded by former supporters of the left-wing tendency in the Carazo administration (the conservative government of 1978–82).

Policies. The party advocates a moderate form of socialism.

Partido de Renovación Democrática (PRD)

See Partido Unidad Social Cristiana (below).

Partido Republicano Calderonista (PRC)

See Partido Unidad Social Cristiana (below).

Partido Republicano Nacional
National Republican Party

Leadership. Rolando Rodríguez Varela (president); Fernando Peña Herrera (secretary)

History. This party was reportedly active in 1984.

Partido Social Cristiano

See Partido Unidad Social Cristiano (below).

Partido Socialista Costarricense
Costa Rican Socialist Party

Leadership. Alvaro Montero Mejía (president); Alberto Salom Echeverría (secretary)

Orientation. Socialist

History. The Party fought the 1982 elections as part of the Pueblo Unido coalition (see below).

Partido de los Trabajadores
Workers' Party

Leadership. Johnny Francisco Araya Monge (president); Ilse Acosta Polonio (secretary)

Orientation. Maoist

History. The Party developed as the political wing of the Movimiento Revolucionario del Pueblo (MRP – People's Revolutionary Movement), formed to support the Nicaraguan revolutionary struggle in the late 1970s. It contested the 1978 and 1982 elections as a member of the Pueblo Unido coalition (see below).

Partido Unidad Social Cristiana (PUSC)
Social Christian Unity Party

Leadership. Cristián Tattembach Yglesias (president); Roberto Tovar Faja (secretary)

Orientation. Christian democratic

Founded. Dec. 17, 1983

History. This party (also known as Unidad Social Cristiana and as the Partido Social Cristiano) was formed by the merger of the four parties which had formed the Unidad Opositora (Opposition Unity) in 1978, and which in 1982 became the Unidad (Unity) coalition – namely the Partido Demócrata Cristiano (PDC – Christian Democratic Party), the Partido de Renovación Democrática (PRD – Democratic Renewal Party), the Partido Republicano Calderonista (PRC – Calderonist Republican Party) and the Unión Popular (UP – Popular Union).

The PDC was the largest of the constituent parties. It was founded in 1962, had unsuccessfully contested the 1970 and 1974 presidential elections, and had gained few seats in the Legislative Assembly. In 1978 it became part of the Unidad Opositora which won the presidency and the largest number of seats, though not an absolute majority, in the Assembly. In the 1982 elections the PDC was part of the losing Unidad alliance, which came second in the presidential election with 32.7 per cent of the votes and which gained 18 seats in the Assembly. The PDC had been the Costa Rican member of the Christian Democratic International and of the Christian Democratic Organization of America. The PDC was largely responsible for the ideological orientation of the new PUSC and brought with it the material and human resources of its affiliate, the Instituto de Estudios Políticos (INDEP – Institute of Political Studies), a political education and organization agency. The president of the PDC when it joined the PSC was Rafael Alberto Grillo Rivera.

The PRD had been founded in 1947 by Rodrigo Carazo Odio, who came fourth in that year's presidential election. In 1978, with the PRD as part of the Unidad Opositora, Carazo Odio was elected President of Costa Rica. The president of the PRD at the time of the formation of the PSC was Oscar Aguilar Bulgarelli.

The PRC was founded in August 1976 after a split in the PUN (see below). Its founder was Rafael Angel Calderón and its leader at the time of the formation of the PSC was Alvaro Cubillo Aguilar.

The UP was a minor conservative party led until its merger in the PUSC in 1983 by Manuel Jiménez de la Guardia.

The PUSC adopted its first president, Rafael Angel Calderón Fournier, as its candidate for the 1986 presidential elections; he had represented the Unidad coalition in the 1982 poll (see introduction).

Policies. The PUSC has called during 1984–85 for the implementation of an economic austerity programme, harsh legal action against strikers, the breaking of diplomatic relations with Nicaragua, and other right-wing policy measures.

Partido Unificación Nacional (PUN)
National Unification Party

Address. Avenida 9, Calle 29, San José

Leadership. Guillermo Villalobos Arce (president); Rogelio Ramos Valverde (secretary)

Orientation. Conservative

History. The PUN was declared in suspension after losing most of its members to a split resulting in the formation of the PRC (see PUSC, above).

Partido Unión Generaleña
Masses' Unity Party

Leadership. Carlos A. Fernández Vega (president); Hugo Sáenz Marín (secretary)

History. This minor party was reportedly functioning in 1984.

Partido Unión Nacional
National Union Party

Leadership. Olga Marta Ulate Rojas (president); Rodrigo González Saborío (secretary)

History. This group was reported to be active in early 1985.

Partido Unión Republicana
Republican Unity Party

Address. Apartado 5307, San José

Leadership. Sigurd Koberg van Patten (president); Marino Donato Magurno (secretary)

Orientation. Centrist

Founded. July 1975

History. Formed by dissident members of the PUN (see above), the party obtained official recognition in August 1975. In the elections of 1978 it obtained only 8,700 votes, or 1 per cent of the total, and lost the single seat which it had held from 1975 to 1978.

Policies. The party advocates a "republican democratic form of government".

Partido Vanguardia Popular (PVP)
Popular Vanguard Party

Address. Avenida 12, no. 1420, San José

Telephone. 232138

Leadership. Humberto Elías Vargas Carbonell (president); Arnaldo Ferreto Segura (secretary)

Orientation. Communist

Founded. 1931, as Partido Comunista (PC – Communist Party)

History. The PVP adopted its present name in 1943, and was instrumental in forming the country's main labour confederation. It was outlawed under the 1949 Constitution and did not regain legal status until May 1975. In the elections of the early 1970s its members worked for Acción Socialista (see above); in the 1978 and 1982 elections it formed part of the Pueblo Unido electoral coalition (see below). The party divided in early 1984 between factions led by Vargas, then the party secretary and regarded as pro-Soviet, and Manuel Mora Valverde, then party president and regarded as pro-Cuban. Mora, a party activist since the 1930s, was expelled on the grounds of "opportunism".

Policies. The party programme adopted in 1971 called for "a democratic, popular, agrarian and anti-imperialist revolution followed by a socialist revolution as a single, uninterrupted process".

Structure. The PVP is organized in accordance with the principle of democratic centralism; its supreme body is the congress, and between congresses its central committee plenum. The party is led by the central committee's political commission and secretariat.

Publications. *Libertad*, official organ, weekly, circulation 21,500

Associated organizations. See Pueblo Unido (below).

International affiliations. The PVP is recognized by the Communist Party of the Soviet Union and its allied parties.

Patria y Verdad
Homeland and Truth

Orientation. Right-wing guerrilla group

Founded. 1985

History. This previously unknown group was suspected of having bombed a power line near the Nicaraguan border on June 11, 1985.

Pueblo Unido (PU)
People United

Address. Calle 4, Avenidas 7 y 9, San José

Telephone. 230032

Leadership. Alberto Gutiérrez Sáenz (president); Arnaldo Ferreto Segura (secretary)

Orientation. Socialist

Founded. 1978

History. The PU coalition gained three seats in the 1978 elections to the Legislative Assembly. In 1982 it gained four seats and its presidential candidate, Rodrigo Roberto Gutiérrez, obtained 3.2 per cent of the votes.

Membership. The parties forming the coalition are the Partido Socialista Costarricense, the Partido de los Trabajadores and the PVP (see above).

Associated organizations. The PU has a significant influence in the trade union movement through the Confederación Unitaria de Trabajadores (CUT – United Confederation of Workers), which was founded in 1980 and has more than 50 affiliates.

Unidad

See PUSC (above).

Unidad Opositora

See PUSC (above).

Unidad Social Cristiana (USC)

See PUSC (above).

Unión Agrícola Cartaginés
Cartago Farmers' Union

Leadership. Guillermo Brenes Castillo (president); Rodrigo Fallas Bonilla (secretary)

Orientation. Regionalist

History. The party operates only in Cartago, which has 270,000 inhabitants and is the fourth largest of the seven provinces. It nominated its own candidates in the 1978 legislative and presidential elections, and gained one seat in the Assembly. In 1982 it did not present a presidential candidate and it lost its Assembly seat.

Unión Parlamentaria de Cartago
Cartago Parliamentary Union

Leadership. Héctor Mata Navarro (president); Antonio Morales Brenes (secretary)

Orientation. Regionalist

History. This party also operates only in the province of Cartago. It was reported as active in 1984.

Unión Popular (UP)

See PSC (above).

Cuba

Capital: Havana   **Population: 10,000,000**

Cuba was ruled by Spain until 1898 and by the USA until 1902, when it became an independent republic, although the USA retained the power to intervene in its affairs until 1934. A military coup in 1933 gave power to Fulgencio Batista Zaldivar, who headed or controlled the government until 1944; he returned to power after another coup in 1952, and initiated a dictatorship which was challenged in 1953 by a radical nationalist revolt. The leader of the revolt, Dr Fidel Castro Ruz, was later released into exile, and formed another revolutionary group which launched an attack on the Batista regime in December 1956.

The small group fomented a popular uprising which led to the defeat of Batista on Jan. 1, 1959, and the installation of a revolutionary government led by Castro. This government carried out wide-ranging reforms in the social and economic spheres, including the expropriation of businesses and lands, and in December 1961 – having defeated a US-sponsored counter-revolutionary invasion – declared the Marxist–Leninist nature of the revolution. A single party was established, and in 1965 became the Partido Comunista Cubano. The country has subsequently been allied with the Soviet Union and has given considerable support to revolutionary governments and movements elsewhere in the Third World. A new Constitution was adopted in 1976 and an indirectly-elected parliament was established late in 1976 and renewed late in 1981. Political and paramilitary opposition to the Castro government has mainly come from right-wing elements among the several hundred thousand Cubans living in the United States.

Emigré activities. Since the abortive Bay of Pigs invasion (planned by the US Central Intelligence Agency and approved by President Kennedy) in April 1961, various other landings by small groups of Cuban emigrés have been reported from time to time, as have plots to assassinate Castro; the CIA devised several such plots, mostly without the knowledge of the US government, between 1961 and 1965.

Castro stated on Sept. 28, 1968, that counter-revolutionaries were active in Cuba; two men convicted of sabotage were executed on Oct. 7. Of a group of emigrés who landed near the US base at Guantánamo on May 7, 1969, three were killed in fighting, four were captured and executed and three were sentenced to life imprisonment. Another group landed in eastern Cuba in September 1970, and were captured soon afterwards; five were sentenced to death and two to 30 years in prison in March 1971.

Cuban exile groups were also held responsible for a machine-gun attack on two Cuban fishing-boats off Florida on April 6, 1976; the bombing of the Cuban embassy in Lisbon on April 22, when two persons were killed; the bombing of the Cuban mission at the United Nations on July 5; the bombing of the representative offices of the Cubana airline in Barbados on July 10; the kidnapping of two Cuban embassy officials in Buenos Aires on Aug. 9, and the bombing of the Cubana office in Panama on Aug. 18.

After the arrival of some 260,000 Cubans in the USA between 1965 and 1973, the pace of emigration slowed down until in 1978 a new influx began with the decision of the Castro government to permit the departure of several thousand people, mainly former political prisoners. By Nov. 14, 1979, the government claimed to have freed 3,600 political prisoners, including one sentenced to 25 years in prison in 1966 for conspiring to kill Castro, and another – Huber Matos – who had been prominent in the anti-Batista struggle but had in 1959 been sentenced to 20 years in prison for treason. Most of these departed for the United States, with their families, and they were followed in April–June 1980 by about 114,000 disaffected Cubans encouraged to leave in a "sea bridge" established from the small port of Mariel. By the end of the year another 9,000 or so had left, with up to 100,000 (according to US sources) awaiting permission to leave.

In October 1980 a conference of counter-revolutionary groups was held in Caracas under the chairmanship of Huber Matos. It approved a plan designed to create the conditions for a popular uprising against the Cuban government. In the United States, anti-Castro groups were reported from 1982 onwards to be organizing training in guerrilla warfare in camps in Florida, without hindrance from the US authorities. Reports in December 1984 stated that Matos was organizing a Cuban emigré detachment to fight alongside the Nicaraguan *contra* forces, partly out of solidarity with their cause and partly in order to obtain practical experience of modern guerrilla warfare.

Constitutional background. The Republic of Cuba was defined in a Constitution approved by referendum in 1976 as "a socialist state of . . . manual and intellectual workers". The Constitution recognized the leading role of the communist party and the "fraternal friendship, aid and co-operation of the Soviet Union and other socialist countries". A 500-member National Assembly of People's Power is elected for a five-year term by delegates to municipal assemblies (the basic organs of "people's power"); the delegates are themselves elected by a simple majority of votes (with a run-off election between the leading candidates, if necessary) by secret and voluntary universal suffrage of citizens over 16 years of age. The National Assembly has constituent and legislative functions and elects the President, five Vice-Presidents, a secretary and 23 other members of the Council of State, the country's highest representative body. The President is head of state and government, and presides over a Council of Ministers appointed by the National Assembly on the President's proposal.

Recent election results. The current term of the National Assembly began in December 1981, after the election of 9,763 delegates on Oct. 11 and 10,725 delegates on Oct. 18 to the 169 municipal assemblies. Most of the candidates were members of the PCC. The Assembly has, by unanimously appointing Castro as President of the Council of State, confirmed his position as head of state and government and commander-in-chief of the Revolutionary Armed Forces.

Alpha-66

Leadership. Andrés Nazario Sargen (general secretary); Humberto Pérez Alvarado (chief of military operations)

Orientation. Right-wing guerrilla group

Founded. 1962

History. Alpha-66 is one of a number of anti-communist guerrilla groups to emerge among the substantial Cuban emigré population in the USA, and particularly in Florida. It was established by 66 such exiles and was involved in several attacks on Cuba and on Cuban property and citizens.

On April 17, 1970, 13 members of the group, led by "Colonel" Vicente Méndez, landed in eastern Cuba and killed five Cuban soldiers before nine of the group were captured and the others killed. In mid-May Alpha-66 sank two Cuban fishing boats and held 11 fishermen captive in an unsuccessful attempt to ransom them for the release of the nine prisoners.

In 1981 the group attempted a landing in Matanzas province with the object of killing Castro and sabotaging industrial installations, but Havana radio announced on July 11 that five of those involved in the venture had been arrested.

Policies. Alpha-66 seeks the overthrow of the Cuban communist system. Its activities are directed towards inspiring a popular uprising against the Castro government.

Comité de 75
Committee of 75

Orientation. Moderate emigré group

History. The Committee was founded by Cuban emigrés living in the United States and wishing to see an easing of tensions between the two countries, mainly in order to permit greater contact between the domestic and expatriate communities.

Policies. The Committee advocates negotiations on the reunification of families, the lifting of restriction on Cubans wishing to enter or leave Cuba, and the release of political prisoners.

El Condor
The Eagle

Orientation. Right-wing guerrilla group

History. This group claimed responsibility for the destruction of a Cuban airliner by a bomb on Oct. 6, 1976. The explosion, which occurred in flight off Barbados, killed 73 people, including 57 Cubans. Orlando Bosch, an anti-communist exile thought to be linked with Omega 7 and the CORU (see below), was one of four men acquitted of involvement in the bombing by a Venezuelan court in September 1980.

Coordinación de la Organización Revolucionaria Unida (CORU)
United Revolutionary Organization Co-ordination

Leadership. Orlando Bosch (leader)

Orientation. Right-wing guerrilla group

Founded. 1975

History. The CORU was founded by Bosch in Chile with the object of undermining all links between Cuba and other American states. It was held responsible for a number of acts of violence, including two bombings of the Cuban embassy in Caracas, Venezuela, in 1974, and one at Kingston airport, Jamaica, on July 9, 1976.

Cubanos Unidos
Cubans United

Leadership. Wilfredo Navarra (general secretary)

Orientation. Right-wing guerrilla group

History. This group, based in the United States, sent several boats to the US base of Guantánamo, on Cuba, in late August 1981, with the intention of setting up a "government in exile". The attempt was frustrated by a tropical storm as a result of which about 60 members of the expedition were shipwrecked while about 16 others were rescued by US coastguards.

Movimiento Nacional Cristiano
National Christian Movement

Leadership. Orlando Lorenzo (general secretary)

Orientation. Right-wing guerrilla group

History. This group, based in Florida, claimed on May 8, 1970, that raiders led by "Captain" Lorenzo had landed in Cuba without encountering opposition.

Movimiento Nacionalista Cubano (MNC)
Cuban Nationalist Movement

Orientation. Right-wing guerrilla group

History. Three members of the US-based MNC were convicted on March 23, 1979, of complicity in the murder on Sept. 26, 1976, of Orlando Letelier, a prominent Chilean politician and diplomat exiled in the United States.

Omega 7

Leadership. Eduardo Arocena (leader)

Orientation. Right-wing guerrilla group

History. Omega 7, which is based in the Cuban exile community in the United States, claimed responsibility for bombings at the Cuban mission to the United Nations in New York on Sept. 9, 1978, and at the office of a moderate Cuban emigré newspaper, also in New York, on Oct. 21. On March 25, 1979, it bombed Cuban-linked premises in New Jersey and at Kennedy Airport, New York; on April 28 it killed a Cuban travel agent, who specialized in organizing tours to Cuba for emigrés, in Puerto Rico. Also in 1978 it attacked a member of the Comité de 75 (see above).

On Sept. 11, 1980, Omega 7 killed a Cuban diplomat at the UN mission. Following the assumption of office by President Ronald Reagan in the

United States in January 1981, Omega 7 announced a "truce"; on Sept. 21 it announced the end of the truce and subsequently bombed Mexican consular premises in Miami to protest at Mexico's cordial relations with the Cuban government. Soviet and Venezuelan consular offices were also bombed by the group.

Arocena was on Nov. 9, 1984, sentenced to life imprisonment for the murder of the Cuban diplomat and various other bombing and shooting attacks; he was also sentenced in Miami in May 1985 to 20 years' imprisonment after having been convicted of most of the bombings of diplomatic premises.

Policies. Omega 7 has stated its opposition to any negotiations between the Castro government and Cuban exiles.

Associated organizations. Omega 7 is widely believed to have been involved in the 1976 bombing of a Cuban airliner (see El Condor, above) and to have links with the CORU (see above).

Organización para la Liberación de Cuba (OPLC)
Organization for the Liberation of Cuba

Leadership. Héctor Fabián (spokesman)

Orientation. Right-wing guerrilla group

History. This US-based group claimed in January 1982 that it had the backing of wealthy members of the Miami Cuban community and that its activities were not being interfered with by the Reagan administration, which was said to tolerate the existence of camps for clandestine training in guerrilla warfare.

Partido Comunista Cubano (PCC)
Cuban Communist Party

Leadership. Dr Fidel Castro Ruz (first secretary); Gen. Raúl Castro Ruz (second secretary); Carlos Aldama Escalante, José Ramón Balaguer, José Ramón Machado Ventura, Pedro Miret Prieto, Jesús Montane Oropesa, Jorge Risquet Valdés, Julián Rizo, Lionel Soto Prieto (other members of secretariat)

Orientation. Communist

Founded. 1961, as Organizaciones Revolucionarias Integradas (ORI – Integrated Revolutionary Organizations)

History. The PCC, as noted above, was founded as the ORI, a coalition of the political and military organizations which had defeated the Batista dictatorship in the revolution of 1956–59 – mainly Castro's rural guerrilla movement, the Movimento 26 de Julio (July 26 Movement), and the urban communist Partido Socialista Popular (PSP – Popular Socialist Party). (The PSP, which was formed in 1943 from an earlier communist party founded secretly in 1925, traces its origins to the anti-colonial Partido Revolucionario Cubano – Cuban Revolutionary Party – formed in 1892 by José Martí and Carlos Balino.)

Castro's guerrilla movement was named after the date of his unsuccessful uprising against the Batista regime in 1953. Sentenced to a lengthy prison term, Castro was later amnestied and exiled to Mexico, where he gathered resources and supporters. In early December 1956 Castro and a small group including Dr Ernesto "Che" Guevara landed in Cuba from the yacht *Granma* and, after initial difficulties, established a guerrilla base in the Sierra Maestra mountains, which became the centre of a growing popular movement for the restoration of democratic liberties and social justice. Batista's position steadily crumbled and Castro's final offensive in mid-1958 met with little resistance, the victory of the revolution being proclaimed on Jan. 1, 1959.

The new regime, with Castro as Prime Minister, carried out a series of nationalization measures and a radical land reform. Many of those opposed to his policies went into exile in the United States, which severed diplomatic relations with Cuba in January 1961. Isolated diplomatically and economically by the Organization of American States, the Castro government established close relations with the Soviet Union and other communist states and internally increased co-operation with the PSP, which had played only a minor part in the revolution. The abortive Bay of Pigs invasion by US-sponsored Cuban exiles in April 1961 accelerated this rapprochement and in mid-1961 the 26th of July Movement was integrated with the PSP and the Revolutionary Directorate to create the ORI. In December 1961 Castro for the first time stated the Marxist–Leninist orientation of the revolutionary movement and shortly afterwards ousted the communist "old guard" led by Aníbal Escalante.

No political parties other than the ORI were permitted to function after 1961. The ORI became in 1962 the Partido Unido de la Revolución Socialista (PURS – United Party of the Socialist Revolution), and on Oct. 4, 1965, adopted its present name. The PCC held its first congress in December 1975 when it adopted a party constitution and programme. The special status of the government party was enshrined in the 1976 constitution which defined it as "the leading force of society and the state".

Various changes in the structure and membership of the secretariat, and other high party offices, were announced in January 1985; these were widely interpreted as the replacement of veterans of the revolutionary era with younger elements.

Policies. The PCC is a Marxist–Leninist party committed to the establishment of a socialist economy and social structure. Although in the early years of the Castro regime the Cubans remained neutral in the ideological conflict between Chinese and Soviet communism, the party has since 1963 been closely allied with that of the Soviet Union and adopts a similar position to that of the Soviet Union on most foreign policy issues. The Cuban party has been particularly active in providing vocal and practical support for revolutionary movements in Latin America, Africa and elsewhere in the Third World, and has become increasingly involved in the Non-Aligned Movement.

Structure. The constitution of the PCC defines its organizing principle as democratic centralism. The supreme organ of the PCC is the congress, which elects a 148-member central committee. The central committee appoints a 14-member political bureau and a nine-member secretariat, membership of the two bodies overlapping to a large extent. The central committee also appoints the members of five commissions responsible for various areas of party policy. There are 14 provincial, 169 municipal and about 20,000 local branches.

Membership. 450,000

Publications. Granma, daily and weekly in Spanish and weekly in English and French; daily circulation 600,000; *Juventud Rebelde*, youth daily, circulation 300,000; *El Militante Comunista*, internal party monthly, circulation 180,000; various other internal, national and international periodicals

90

Associated organizations. The party has a youth organization and a women's organization. It effectively controls the trade unions, which have 2,680,000 members and are grouped in the Central de Trabajadores de Cuba (CTC – Workers' Confederation of Cuba), and many other social and political institutions.

International affiliations. The PCC enjoys close relations with the Soviet Communist Party and other communist and workers' parties.

Dominican Republic

Capital: Santo Domingo   **Population: 6,200,000**

The Dominican Republic gained its independence from Spain in 1844, but was occupied by the United States in 1916–24. A pro-US dictator, Rafael Trujillo Molina, ruled the country directly or indirectly from 1930 until his assassination in 1961. A presidential election was held in 1962 and was won by Juan Bosch Gaviño of the centre-left Partido Revolucionario Dominicano (PRD); Bosch was overthrown by the military in September 1963, and a bloody struggle which broke out in April 1965 between his followers and the military was suppressed by a US military intervention. Fresh elections in 1966 installed as President the candidate of the Partido Reformista (PR), Dr Joaquín Balaguer, formerly a close associate of Trujillo. Balaguer was re-elected in 1970 and again, having defeated an insurgency, in 1974. Following another revolt in 1975 Balaguer was defeated in the 1978 elections by Silvestre Antonio Guzmán Fernández of the PRD, leading (after an aborted military coup) to the first peaceful and constitutional transfer of power in the country's history.

In September 1979 the government claimed to have uncovered a coup plot and arrested over 100 army officers and civilians, most of whom had been connected with the Balaguer regime. In 1982 the candidate chosen by the left wing of the PRD, Dr Salvador Jorge Blanco, won the presidency, and the party gained control of Congress. The Blanco government pursued conservative economic and foreign policies and was faced from 1983 with demonstrations, strikes and political violence, some of which it blamed on Cuban and Nicaraguan subversives. At least 55 people were killed in rioting in April 1984. Large numbers of left-wing activists were arrested in 1984 and 1985, most being released shortly afterwards.

Constitutional background. Under the 1966 Constitution the Republic has an executive President and a Congress consisting of a 120-member Chamber of Deputies and a 27-member Senate, President and Congress being elected for four-year terms by universal and compulsory suffrage of married citizens and of single citizens over 18 years of age. Elections to the Chamber take place under a proportional representation system in each of the 26 provinces and the national capital district, with multi-member electoral districts, while election to the Senate is by simple plurality in single-member constituencies. The president appoints and presides over a Cabinet.

Recent election results. In elections on May 16, 1982, Salvador Jorge Blanco of the PRD was elected President with 46.6 per cent of the votes cast. Balaguer of the PR won 36.5 per cent and Bosch of the PLD 9.8 per cent. Blanco's party won a majority of seats in the Chamber – 62, compared with 50 for the PR, 7 for the PLD and 1 for the PAC – and in the Senate, with 17 seats to the PR's 10. The elections were also contested by the PQD, the ASD, the FNP, the PPC, the PCD/MAS, and the IU (for explanation of acronyms, see below).

Acción Social Cristiana (ASC)

See Movimiento de Acción Social Cristiana (below).

Alianza Social Demócrata (ASD)
Social Democratic Alliance

Leadership. Dr José Rafael Abinader (leader)

Orientation. Social democratic

History. This party unsuccessfully contested the 1982 elections with Abinader as its presidential candidate. It subsequently allied itself with the PRD and Abinader was appointed to a cabinet post.

Comités de Lucha Popular
Popular Struggle Committees

Orientation. Anti-government

Founded. 1984

History. This network of autonomous local groups, mostly organized by active members of left-wing parties, was created in order to co-ordinate the protest movement against the government's economic policies. It was responsible for the organization of strikes and demonstrations in 1984 and 1985, including a particularly successful general strike on Feb. 11, 1985.

La Estructura

See PRD (below).

Frente de Izquierda Dominicana (FID)
Dominican Left Front

Leadership. Damian Jiménez (one of leaders)

Orientation. Socialist

History. This group of 10 left-wing parties and 43 other organizations was the main force behind the strikes and demonstrations held in 1984–85 to protest against the government's austerity programme and its failure to control inflation. Many of its activists, including Jiménez, were among the groups of socialist politicians arrested in late 1984 and early 1985. It planned demonstrations in April 1985 to mark the 20th anniversary of the US intervention, giving rise to accusations by the government that it was involved in efforts to "destabilize" the country.

Policies. The Front has called for the breaking off of negotiations with the International Monetary Fund, the declaration of a moratorium on foreign debt payments until a renegotiation adjusts the terms in the Republic's favour, general wage increases, the nationalization of the financial sector, import and exchange controls and other radical economic measures.

Fuerza Nacional Progresista (FNP)
National Progressive Force

Leadership. Dr Marino Vinicio Castillo (leader)

History. This party unsuccessfully contested the 1982 elections with its leader as presidential candidate.

Grupo Armado Nacionalista Revolucionario
Revolutionary Armed Nationalist Group

Orientation. Right-wing guerrilla group

History. This hitherto unknown group claimed responsibility for a grenade attack carried out on June 18, 1982, on the premises of the central electoral tribunal, where five people were killed and at least 20 injured. Three former colonels and a number of civilians were subsequently arrested in connection with the incident.

Izquierda Unida
United Left

Leadership. Rafael Taveras (leader)

Orientation. Marxist

History. The alliance of six small Marxist parties and the Unión Patriótica Antiimperialista (UPA – Anti-Imperialist Union, led by Franklin Franco) unsuccessfully contested the 1982 elections. Taveras, its presidential candidate and the leader of the NTC (see below), was among a large number of prominent leftists arrested in August 1984.

Movimiento de Acción Social Cristiana (ASC)
Social Christian Action Movement

History. This group was reportedly active in the early 1980s.

Movimiento de Conciliación Nacional (MCN)
National Conciliation Movement

Address. Pina 207, Santo Domingo, DN

Leadership. Dr Jaime Manuel Fernández G. (president); Víctor Mena (organizing secretary)

Orientation. Centrist

Founded. February 1969

History. The MCN was formed by Dr Héctor García Godoy, who had been provisional President of the Republic in 1965–66, with the object of healing the divisions caused by the 1965 civil war. Godoy died in April 1970 and was succeeded as leader by Fernández. The MCN supported the Reformista governments elected in 1970 and 1974 but later withdrew its support. In the 1978 elections it was allied with the MID (see below), the (right-wing) PQD (see below) and other groups.

Policies. The MCN seeks to unify the progressive right and the moderate left in joint action for the benefit of the country.

Structure. The MCN has a national executive directorate and directorates in the capital, provinces and municipalities.

Membership. 659,000

Movimiento de Integración Democrática (MID)
Democratic Integration Movement

Address. Las Mercedes 607, Santo Domingo, DN

Telephone. 687-8895

Leadership. Dr Francisco Augusto Lora (leader)

Orientation. Centre-right

History. Lora contested the 1970 presidential election for the MID and the 1978 election for the MID–MCN–PQD alliance.

Movimiento Nacional de Salvación (MNS)
National Salvation Movement

Leadership. Luis Julián Pérez (leader)

Orientation. Right-wing

Founded. 1976

History. Pérez had been a close associate of Dr Balaguer, the leader of the Partido Reformista (see below) and President of the Republic from 1966–78. However, shortly after the formation of the MNS, the general secretary of the Partido Reformista said that government officials who sympathized with the new party would be dismissed as "traitors" on suspicion of seeking to oust President Balaguer.

Movimiento Popular Dominicano (MPD)
Dominican Popular Movement

Leadership. Julio de Peña Valdés (leader)

Orientation. Maoist

Founded. 1956, in Cuba

History. The founders of the MPD included many former members of the Partido Comunista (see below). Although it was refused legal status because of alleged involvement in political violence, the MPD was one of the parties which constituted a 1974 opposition electoral alliance.

Movimiento al Socialismo (MAS)
Movement towards Socialism

Orientation. Marxist

History. This party contested the 1982 elections in the Unidad Socialista alliance with the PCD, but failed to secure congressional representation.

Movimiento Socialista de los Trabajadores (MST)
Workers' Socialist Movement

Orientation. Marxist

History. The MST, derived from the same 1960s guerrilla movement as the PS (see below), contested the 1982 elections as part of the Izquerda Unida (see above).

Núcleo de Trabajadores Comunistas (NTC)
Nucleus of Communist Workers

Leadership. Rafael Taveras (leader)

Orientation. Maoist

History. This small party contested the 1982 elections in the Izquierda Unida (see above). Its leader was arrested in August 1984.

Partido Acción Constitucionalista (PAC)
Constitutionalist Action Party

History. This minor party gained one seat in the Chamber of Deputies in the elections of May 1982.

Partido de Acción Nacional
National Action Party

Orientation. Right-wing

History. This party was active in the early 1980s.

Partido Alianza Social Demócrata (ASD)

See Alianza Social Demócrata (above).

Partido Comunista Dominicano (PCD)
Dominican Communist Party

Address. Avenida Independencia 89, Santo Domingo, DN

Telephone. 685-3540

Leadership. José Israel Cuello (leader); Narciso Isa Conde (general secretary)

Orientation. Communist

Founded. 1944, as Partido Revolucionario Democrático Dominicano (Dominican Revolutionary Democratic Party)

History. The party was founded secretly during the Trujillo dictatorship. It was known as the Partido Popular Socialista Dominicano (Dominican People's Socialist Party) in 1946–65. In 1947 most leaders of the party were arrested and deported. In 1962 the party proclaimed as its short-term objective "a national liberation, anti-imperialist and anti-feudal revolution", and, after a period of semi-legal operation, the party was banned in October 1963. It took an active part in the 1965 civil war. The party was permitted to reorganize in November 1977. It contested the 1982 elections, in the Unidad Socialista (Socialist Unity) alliance with the MAS (see above), without success; its general secretary was the alliance's presidential candidate.

Policies. The PCD is an orthodox communist party with a foreign policy substantially in line with that of the Soviet Communist Party.

Structure. The PCD is based on the principle of democratic centralism; its highest authority is the congress, and between congresses the central committee, which appoints a secretariat.

Publications. Hablan los Comunistas

International affiliations. The PCD is recognized by the communist parties of the Soviet Union and its allies.

Partido Demócrata Popular (PDP)
People's Democratic Party

Address. Arzobispo Meriño 259, Santo Domingo, DN

Telephone. 685-2920

Leadership. Admiral Luis Homero Lájara Burgos (leader)

Orientation. Opposition

History. The PDP joined the 1974 Santiago agreement which established an alliance of opposition parties. Although the other five parties abstained in the 1974 presidential election, the PDP presented its own, unsuccessful, candidate.

Partido de la Liberación Dominicana (PLD)
Dominican Liberation Party

Address.   Avenida Independencia 69, Santo Domingo, DN

Telephone.   685-3540

Leadership.   Dr Juan Bosch Gaviño, Jesús Antonio Pichardo (leaders); Lidio Cadet (general secretary)

Orientation.   Left-wing

Founded.   1973

History.   The PLD was formed by Bosch as a result of a split in the PRD (see below), which he had founded and as whose candidate he had served as President of the Republic in 1963. Bosch broke with the PRD in 1973 after a guerrilla invasion by his supporters had failed to unseat the Balaguer government. His new party unsuccessfully contested the presidential and congressional election of 1978, and in 1982 won seven seats in the Chamber of Deputies while securing 179,849 votes and third place for Bosch's presidential candidature. Bosch was placed under house arrest in early 1985 for "insulting" criticism of the government.

Partido Popular Cristiano (PPC)
Popular Christian Party

Leadership.   Rogelio Delgado Bogaert (leader)

History.   This party contested the elections of 1982 without success. Delgado was its candidate for the presidency.

Partido Quisqueyano Demócrata (PQD)
Quisqueyan Democratic Party

Address.   27 de Febrero 206 altos, Santo Domingo, DN

Telephone.   567–7970

Leadership.   Gen. Elías Wessin y Wessin (president); Juan Manuel Taveras Rodríguez (general secretary)

Orientation.   Right-wing opposition

Founded.   June 1968

History.   The party has been in opposition since its formation. In May 1970 Wessin unsuccessfully contested the presidential election. In 1973 he was deported for his alleged role in a 1971 plot against the government.

In May 1974, together with most of the other members of the opposition coalition, the PQD withdrew from the election after failing to secure a postponement. In May 1978 it supported the unsuccessful MID presidential candidate but did not take part in the legislative elections. Later in the month Wessin returned from exile. The PQD failed to gain parliamentary representation in the 1982 elections, when Wessin again stood for the presidency, and is currently in a loose alliance with the Partido Reformista (see below).

Policies.   The PQD advocates representative democracy, law and order, and equality of justice and opportunity for all Dominicans.

Membership.   600,000

Publications.   *Quisqueyano*, fortnightly, circulation about 15,000

Partido Reformista (PR)
Reformist Party

Address. Avenida San Cristóbal, Ensanche La Fe, Apartado 1332, Santo Domingo, DN

Telephone. 566-7089

Leadership. Dr Joaquín Balaguer (leader); Joaquín A. Ricardo (general secretary)

Orientation. Centre-right

Founded. June 1964

History. The party (also known as the Partido Reformista Social Cristiano, PRSC) was founded by followers of Balaguer, who was President of the Republic in 1960–62 and again following elections held in 1966 (after the US military intervention of 1965); he served three consecutive terms until 1978. Since 1978 the PR has been the largest party opposing the ruling PRD (see below). Its presidential candidate in 1982 was once again Balaguer, who obtained 669,176 votes, coming second to the 854,868 votes for the PRD candidate. The party simultaneously won 10 seats in the Senate and 50 in the Chamber.

Policies. The PR defines itself as a nationalist, land-based party advocating the reform of the state through the creation of a large and powerful middle class and the uplifting of the peasant majority by a land reform freeing it from "the decadent structure of neo-feudalism". The PR is opposed to the internationalism of Marxist groups.

Structure. The supreme body of the PR is the national assembly, consisting of delegates of municipal and district directorates and the 100 members of the central executive directorate. There are also 28-member provincial directorates overseeing both urban and rural branches. There are 20 national secretariats for various interest groups – women, youth, students, peasants, workers and so on.

Publications. The party's official organ is *Orientación Reformista*, a radio programme broadcast by 35 stations.

Partido Revolucionario Dominicano (PRD)
Dominican Revolutionary Party

Address. Padre Montesinos 2, Santo Domingo, DN

Telephone. 532-9442

Leadership. Dr Salvador Jorge Blanco (President of the Republic, majority faction leader); Jacobo Majluta Azar (president); Dr José Francisco Peña Gómez (party leader); Winston Arnaud (general secretary)

Orientation. Social democratic

Founded. 1939

History. The PRD was founded in Cuba as an organization of anti-Trujillo exiles, and was established in the Dominican Republic on July 5, 1961, after the assassination of the dictator. In December 1962 the founder and leader of the PRD, Dr Juan Bosch, won the presidential election, but was overthrown in a military coup seven months later.

In April 1965 the PRD led a civilian and military insurrection with the object of reinstating the constitutional government. The United States government landed 42,000 marines in the country on April 28, with the declared object of restoring order and preventing a communist takeover. The intervention was retrospectively supported by the Organization of

American States, and troops from other countries participated. A provisional government was installed and called a new presidential election for 1966. This was won by Dr Joaquín Balaguer of the US-backed Partido Reformista (see above), and for the following 12 years the PRD was in opposition; a split in the party led to the formation by Bosch of the PLD (see above).

In May 1978 the PRD had an overwhelming victory in the elections and Antonio Guzmán Fernández became President. It won again in May 1982, Blanco being elected President and Peña Gómez mayor of the capital. (Blanco did not take office until August, following Guzmán's suicide in July and an interim presidency under Majluta.) The party is currently divided between a tendency loyal to the Blanco government and a centre-right faction led by Majluta and Peña Gómez. Although efforts were being made throughout 1985 to maintain the PRD as a single party, supporters of Majluta have registered their faction, known as La Estructura (Structure), as a political party in its own right.

Policies. The PRD has traditionally been a left-of-centre democratic socialist party; however, the Blanco government has followed policies of extreme fiscal conservatism, despite widespread discontent and outbreaks of rioting, and has been a severe critic of Cuba, Nicaragua and other socialist states.

Structure. The supreme organ of the party is the national congress, and between its sessions, the national executive committee.

Membership. 400,000

International affiliations. The party is a member of the Socialist International, of which Peña Gómez is a vice-president.

Partido Revolucionario Social Cristiano (PRSC)
Social Christian Revolutionary Party

Address. Las Mercedes 141, Apartado 2571, Santo Domingo, DN

Telephone. 688-3511

Leadership. Dr Claudio Isidoro Acosta (president); Dr Alfonso Lockward (general secretary)

Orientation. Left-wing Christian democrat

Founded. Nov. 29, 1961

History. In the 1974 elections the PRSC was a party to the Santiago agreement (allying it with the UCN, the PRD, the PQD, the MPD and the MID).

Policies. The PRSC defines its position as democratic leftist, rejecting both capitalism and communism.

International affiliations. The party belongs to the Christian Democratic International and to the Christian Democratic Organization of America.

Partido Revolucionario de los Trabajadores (PRT)
Workers' Revolutionary Party

Orientation. Marxist–Leninist

History. The PRT was a member of Izquierda Unida (see above) in the 1982 election campaign.

Partido Socialista
Socialist Party

Orientation. Marxist

Founded. 1960s, as Comité Revolucionario Camilo Torres (Camilo Torres Revolutionary Committee)

History. Founded as a guerrilla movement, the party later contested elections, in 1982 as part of the Izquierda Unida (see above).

Partido de los Trabajadores Dominicanos
Dominican Workers' Party

Address. Avenida Duarte 69 altos, Santo Domingo, DN

Telephone. 685–7705

Leadership. Rafael Chaljub Mejía (general secretary)

Orientation. Pro-Albanian communist

Founded. 1979

History. The party contested the 1982 elections as part of the Izquierda Unida (see above). It later merged with the Partido Obrero Comunista (POC – Communist Labour Party).

Partido Unión Patriótica (PUP)
Patriotic Union Party

Leadership. Roberto Santana (leader)

History. The party was active in the early 1980s.

Partido de Veteranos Civiles (PVC)
Civilian Veterans' Party

History. The PVC was reportedly active in the early 1980s.

Unión Cívica Nacional (UCN)
National Civic Union

Orientation. Centrist

Founded. 1961

History. The UCN emerged in 1961 as the largest and most influential opposition party, under the leadership of Dr Viriato Alberto Fiallo and Dr Rafael F. Bonnelly, who was President of the Republic in 1962–63. In the 1963 elections the UCN came second to the PRD (see above); in 1974 it was a member of the Santiago alliance and did not contest the elections.

Unión Patriótica Antiimperialista (UPA)

See Izquierda Unida (above).

Ecuador

Capital: Quito   **Population: 9,500,000**

The Republic of Ecuador achieved separate independence in 1830. Its first 12 decades were marked by frequent changes of government and by the development of two strong political forces – the highland-based conservatives and the coastal liberals. The Partido Liberal held the presidency throughout the latter half of that period, but in 1956 a minority Partido Conservador government was installed. In 1960 a liberal, Dr José María Velasco Ibarra, became President for the fourth time, but he was deposed in 1961 by his Vice-President, Dr Carlos Julio Arosemana Monroy. A military junta took over in 1963 and, after two provisional presidencies, Velasco was restored to power by elections in 1968. Faced with an economic crisis, Velasco suspended the Constitution and Congress in 1970 and assumed dictatorial powers. He was ousted by the military in 1972, and democratic rule was not restored until 1979, when Jaime Roldós Aguilera, of the Concentración de Fuerzas Populares (CFP), was elected President and a new Congress and Constitution were inaugurated.

President Roldós pursued reformist economic and social policies until his death in an air crash in May 1981, when he was succeeded by the Vice-President, Dr Osvaldo Hurtado Larrea. The CFP had by then developed two wings, the more radical of which became the Pueblo, Cambio y Democracia party, which withdrew its support from the more conservative Hurtado government in January 1982; Hurtado formed a new coalition with centre-right parties. Industrial and student unrest in 1980–83 led to repeated declarations of a temporary state of emergency and also to some deaths in clashes between demonstrators and the security forces.

Presidential and legislative elections in 1984 installed a conservative government under President León Febres Cordero of the Partido Social Cristiano (PSC), then part of the Frente de Reconstrucción Nacional. The opposition, which initially held a majority in the Congress, was led by the Izquierda Democrática (ID) coalition, whose presidential candidate had been Rodrigo Borja Cevallos. The austerity measures imposed by the government, and subsequent restrictions on press freedom, led to renewed public disorder and strikes in 1984–85. A dispute between the executive and the legislature concerning judicial appointments led to a constitutional crisis in late 1984, the eventual victor being the legislature. In June 1985 several opposition deputies transferred their allegiance to the government bloc, giving it a congressional majority.

Constitutional background. Under the 1979 Constitution the Republic has an executive President elected, together with a Vice-President, for a single four-year term by universal and (nominally) compulsory adult suffrage. There is a unicameral Congress, similarly elected for a four-year term, with 57 members elected on a provincial basis, in single- or multi-seat constituencies, and 12 on a national basis; a second chamber may be introduced in the near future. There is a Cabinet presided over by the President. The President is elected by an absolute majority; if no candidate gains it in the first round of voting, there follows a run-off election between the two best-placed candidates.

In order to qualify for participation in elections, parties (other than alliances formed less than six months before the election) must be recognized by the Supreme Electoral Tribunal, which requires proof that the party has members comprising at least 1.5 per cent of the electorate in at least 10 provinces, including Guayaquil and Quito. Parties securing less than 5 per cent of the vote in two successive elections lose their registration. Financial assistance may be provided by the state to the largest political parties: in 1980, the CFP received the equivalent of US$340,000, and the ID about US$180,000.

Recent election results. Nine parties contested the first-round presidential election of Jan. 29, 1984. The two leading candidates went through to a second round on May 6, when León Febres Cordero, of the PSC, won election with 52.2 per cent of the vote, while Rodrigo Borja, of the ID, received 47.8 per cent. President Cordero was sworn in on Aug. 10. In the congressional elections of Jan. 29, the 71 seats were distributed as follows (for explanation of acronyms, see below): ID 24, PSC 9, CFP 8, FRA 5, PLR 4, DP 3, MPD 3, PRE 3, FADI 2, Partido Conservador 2, PD 2, PNR 1, Partido Socialista 1, non-aligned candidates 4.

Acción Política Progresista (APP)
Progressive Political Action
Leadership. Gen. Richelieu Levoyer Artieda (leader)
Founded. December 1982
History. This minor party has failed to gain significant popular support.

¡Alfaro Vive, Carajo!
See Fuerzas Armadas Populares Eloy Alfaro (below).

Alianza Popular Revolucionaria Ecuatoriana (APRE)
Ecuadorian Popular Revolutionary Alliance
Orientation. Centrist
History. The APRE failed to secure legal registration in 1978, but remained in existence, and in 1984 became a member of the Frente de Reconstrucción Nacional (see below).

Bloque Progresista
See Frente Progresista Democrático (below).

Coalición Institucionalista Demócrata (CID)
Democratic Institutionalist Coalition

Leadership. Gil Barragán Romero (leader)

Orientation. Right-wing traditionalist

History. The CID obtained three seats in the congressional elections of April 1979. It subsequently co-operated with the Roldós government, and supported the Febres government formed in 1984. A member of the party was arrested on May 18, 1985, on suspicion of having killed the deputy leader of the PRE (see below) on April 10 and a high-ranking policeman in October 1984.

Associated organizations. See Frente de Reconstrucción Nacional (below).

Concentración de Fuerzas Populares (CFP)
Concentration of Popular Forces

Leadership. Galo Vayas (leader); Dr Averroes Bucaram Saxida (director)

Orientation. Centre-left reformist

Founded. 1946

History. The CFP first contested presidential elections in 1946, when its candidate came third. In September 1970 the then leader of the party, Assad Bucaram (who had twice been elected mayor of Guayaquil, and later prefect of the province of Guayas), was deported by the Velasco regime to Panama, where he remained until 1972. Following the suspension of all political parties by the Rodríguez regime in July 1974, a dialogue between the military government and the parties was restored in 1976, with the CFP calling for immediate elections.

In March 1978 it formed an alliance with the Christian Democrats. In the first-round presidential election on July 16, 1978, the CFP candidate, Jaime Roldós Aguilera, came first with 31 per cent of the votes, and he won the presidency in the second round on April 29, 1979. The CFP was by then divided between a faction supporting Roldós (later to become the PCD-PRR – see below) and this faction supporting Assad Bucaram; the divided party was relegated to third place in the 1980 local and provincial elections. Assad Bucaram died in May 1981.

The Bucaram faction of the party joined the DP-UDC government (see below) in January 1982. In the congressional elections of Jan. 29, 1984, the CFP won eight seats and supported the Febres government. In June 1985 Averroes Bucaram was elected president of Congress. (His bodyguard was on May 7, 1985, shot dead in Congress by a former CFP deputy who had joined the DP.)

Convergencia Democrática

See Frente Progresista Democrática (below).

Democracia Popular – Unión Demócrata Cristiana (DP or DP-UDC)
People's Democracy – Christian Democratic Union

Address. Calle Vargas 727 y Santa Prisca, Apartado 2300, Quito

Leadership. Wilfrido Lucero Bolaños (director)

Orientation. Christian democratic

Founded. April 1978

History. A Partido Demócrata Cristiano (PDC – Christian Democratic

Party) had been formed in November 1964 and had participated in the government installed in 1970. In December 1977 the PDC, led by Dr Osvaldo Hurtado Larrea, formed the Coalición Popular Democrática (CPD – Popular Democratic Coalition) in alliance with (i) Dr Julio César Trujillo's Progressive Conservative grouping, which had broken away from the PC (see below) in April 1977; (ii) the Frente Social Progresista (FSP–Progressive Social Front) led by José Corsino Cárdenas, and (iii) the Unión Nacional Democrática (UNADE – National Democratic Union) led by Luis Gómez Izquierdo. In April 1978, however, the supreme electoral tribunal barred the CPD from taking part in the forthcoming elections; the PDC and the Progressive Conservatives then united as the DP-UDC, and allied themselves with the CFP (see above). Hurtado was adopted as the vice-presidential running mate of the CFP presidential candidate, Jaime Roldós, and the team was victorious in the two-stage election conducted in July 1978 and April 1979. In congressional elections in April 1979 the DP-UDC gained five of the 31 seats obtained by the CFP bloc.

In the congressional elections of Jan. 29, 1984, it secured three seats.

Policies. The DP-UDC espouses a typical Christian democratic ideology favouring freedom, democracy, individual rights and social reforms.

Structure. The supreme organ of the party is its national congress, a gathering of national and provincial leaders. There is a national leadership council, provincial leadership councils and cantonal leadership committees.

Membership. 45,000

International affiliations. The party belongs to the Christian Democratic International and to the Christian Democratic Organization of America.

Frente Amplio de la Izquierda (FADI)
Broad Left Front

Leadership. Dr René Maugé Mosquera (director)

Orientation. Socialist

Founded. 1977

History. The FADI was established as an alliance of communist and left-wing parties. The director of the alliance, who is also the general secretary of the PCE, came sixth in the first round of the presidential election on July 16, 1978, gaining 5 per cent of the votes cast. In the congressional elections of Jan. 29, 1984, it gained only two seats.

Membership. The founding members of the FADI were the Movimiento Revolucionario de la Izquierda Cristiana (MRIC – Revolutionary Movement of the Christian Left), the Movimiento para la Unidad de la Izquierda (MUI – Left Unity Movement), the PCE (see below), the Partido Socialista Revolucionario (PSR – Revolutionary Socialist Party), the Comité del Pueblo and the MSI (for last two see URPE, below).

Associated organizations. The FADI has joined the Frente Progresista Democrática, a leftist alliance established in 1984 (see below).

Frente de Liberación de los Pobres (FLP)
Liberation Front of the Poor

Orientation. Left-wing direct-action group

Founded. 1980

History. Members of this group occupied a convent in Santo Domingo

103

on July 7–11, 1980, in support of a demand for the repeal of a national security law.

Frente Progresista Democrático
Progressive Democratic Front

Founded. July 10, 1984

History. This body (also known as the Bloque Progresista – Progressive Bloc) was founded as a coalition of leftist and centre-left parties, succeeding the Convergencia Democrática (Democratic Convergence) formed in 1980. The new bloc held 42 seats in Congress, but only 37 of its members voted consistently for opposition motions in late 1984.

Membership. Members of the Frente in 1985 included the FADI (see above), the ID, the MPD, the PD, the Partido Socialista, the PCD and the UDP (see below).

Frente Radical Alfarista (FRA)
Alfarista Radical Front

Leadership. Cecilia Calderón de Castro (leader)

Orientation. Left-wing liberal

Founded. 1972

History. The FRA took part in the first-round presidential election of July 1978, its leader gaining fifth place with 9 per cent of the votes cast; however, in January 1979 the electoral tribunal deprived it of its official recognition and in the second round, in July, it supported the successful candidate of the CFP (see above). Although the CFP gained no seats in the 1979 congressional elections, it did well in the 1980 local and provincial elections, winning 20 per cent of the total vote and over 50 per cent in the department of Guayas. In the congressional elections of Jan. 29, 1984, the FRA secured five seats, which were initially part of the opposition bloc; however, in early June 1985 the party decided to support the Febres government. Iván Castro of the FRA was then elected vice-president of Congress.

Frente de Reconstrucción Nacional
National Reconstruction Front

Orientation. Centre-right

History. The Front was formed as an electoral alliance of centrist and conservative parties, largely in succession to an earlier Frente Nacional Constitucionalista (National Constitutionalist Front), the leading component being the PSC (see below). Its candidate in the 1984 presidential election, the PSC leader León Febres Cordero, won with 52.2 per cent of the valid votes.

Membership. The parties which formed the Front were the PSC, the PLR, the PC, the PNR, the CID, the PNV and the APRE (see separate entries).

Fuerzas Armadas Populares Eloy Alfaro
Eloy Alfaro Popular Armed Forces

Leadership. Rosa Mireya Cárdenas (last known leader)

Orientation. Left-wing guerrilla group

Founded. Late 1970s

History. This organization is also known as ¡Alfaro Vive! (Alfaro Lives!)

and as ¡Alfaro Vive, Carajo! (Alfaro Lives, [expletive]!), the names being derived from Eloy Alfaro, a liberal leader who died in 1912 after leading a rebellion against a conservative government. The group originated in the 1970s, attracting former student sympathizers of the PCE, but did not begin its armed campaign until 1984. The leader of the group was arrested in Costa Rica in mid-August 1984, and taken to Ecuador on Aug. 29. Members of the organization attacked the premises of a major newspaper in Quito on Nov. 2, forcing the publication of a proclamation; a radio station in Quito was seized on June 5, 1985, and forced to make an anti-government broadcast. On Jan. 10, 1985, what appeared to be the accidental explosion of a bomb killed two alleged members of the group, also in Quito. On March 13, in a raid on the Quito police arsenal, 26 guerrillas stole about 400 firearms. On June 6 the group mounted an attack on the offices of the PLR (see below). It co-operated with the Colombian M-19 guerrilla group in the kidnapping on Aug. 7 of a leading Ecuadorean banker who was killed, together with five members of the group, in a rescue attempt in September.

Membership. 3,000

Izquierda Democrática (ID)
Democratic Left

Address. Juan León Mera 268 y Jorge Washington, Quito

Telephone. 547648

Leadership. Rodrigo Borja Cevallos (leader); Xavier Ledesma Ginatta (director); Gustavo Darquea (deputy director); Raúl Baca Carbo (general secretary); Gonzalo Córdova (international secretary)

Orientation. Leftist

Founded. November 1977

History. The ID (also known as the Partido Izquierda Democrática) held the mayoralty of Guayaquil for some months in 1978 before losing it to the CFP (see above). It gained fourth place for its leader in the 1978 first-round presidential election, with 11 per cent of the votes cast. It gave its support to the successful CFP candidate in the second and final round in April 1979. In the congressional elections of the same month the ID gained 16.6 per cent of the vote and 15 of the 69 seats, and claimed to have become the second-largest political party after the CFP.

On Aug. 10, 1980, Baca Carbo was elected president of Congress with the support of the CFP; following the emergence of two tendencies in the CFP, the ID, together with the the DP-UDC (see above), allied itself with the *roldosista* faction (which became the PDC-PRR – see below). From January 1982 the ID supported a new congressional majority alignment including the DP-UDC, the PD, the UDP and seven independent representatives. At that time the ID held 12 seats in Congress and claimed to be the largest party in the country.

In the 1984 presidential election Borja led in the first round (on Jan. 29) but lost the second round (on May 6) to the candidate of the PSC (see below). His share of the vote in the second round was 47.8 per cent. In the congressional election of Jan. 29 the ID won 24 of the 71 seats, making it by far the largest parliamentary bloc; as the main opposition grouping, it created some difficulties for the Febres government, but in June 1985 two ID members and five of the FAR (see above) decided to join the government bloc, giving Febres a narrow majority.

Policies. The ID's objectives include free parliamentary, political and economic democracy, a radical redistribution of wealth and a reduction of Ecuador's dependence on other countries.

Membership. 250,000

Associated organizations. The ID has joined the Frente Progresista Democrático, a leftist alliance established in 1984 (see above).

International affiliations. The party is a member of the Socialist International.

Movimiento 18 de Octubre de Acción Revolucionaria Astra (M-18-X)
Astra Revolutionary Action Movement of October 18
Orientation. Left-wing direct-action group

Founded. 1980

History. This movement first came to public attention when on April 18, 1980, it temporarily occupied the Columbian consulate in Quito.

Movimiento de Integración Nacional (MIN)
National Integration Movement
Leadership. Julio Ayala Serra (leader)

Founded. January 1983

History. This small organization was active in 1983.

Movimiento Popular Democrático (MPD)
Popular Democratic Movement
Leadership. Dr Jaime Hurtado González (leader)

Orientation. Maoist

History. The MPD was formed as the electoral vehicle of the (Maoist) Partido Comunista Ecuatoriano Marxista–Leninista (PCE-ML – Ecuadorian Communist Party, Marxist–Leninist). It gained one seat in the 1979 congressional elections, but did not win much support in the December 1980 local and provincial elections.

In the congressional elections of Jan. 29, 1984, it secured three seats.

Policies. The MPD's policies are broadly in line with those of the Chinese Communist Party.

Associated organizations. The MPD has joined the Frente Progresista Democrática, a leftist alliance established in 1984 (see above).

Movimiento Revolucionario de la Izquierda Cristiana (MRIC)
See FADI (above).

Movimiento para la Unidad de la Izquierda (MUI)
See FADI (above).

Partido Comunista Ecuatoriano (PCE)
Ecuadorian Communist Party
Leadership. René Maugé Mosquera (general secretary)

Orientation. Orthodox communist

Founded. 1926, as Partido Socialista del Ecuador (Socialist Party of Ecuador)

History. The party, under its original name, joined the Third (Communist) International in 1926. It assumed its present name in 1931.

The party was involved in an insurrection in 1944 and in a Constituent Assembly which drew up the 1945 Contitution. It was illegal in 1963–66, when many of its leaders were imprisoned.

In the April 1979 congressional elections the PCE led the UDP coalition (see below), which failed to win any seats. Its support declined further in the December 1980 provincial elections.

Policies.   At a congress in 1968 it adopted a programme for "national liberation in the framework of the anti-imperialist, anti-feudal, democratic revolution, with a subsequent transition to socialist revolution".

Structure.   The party is organized on the principle of democratic centralism; its supreme authority is the congress, and between congress sessions the central committee.

Publications.   *El Pueblo*, daily

Associated organizations.   The PCE is a member of the FADI coalition (see above). It has links with the Confederación de Trabajadores del Ecuador (CTE – Ecuadorean Workers' Confederation), which has about 200 affiliated unions representing about 55,000 workers.

International affiliations.   The PCE is recognized by the Soviet Communist Party and its allied parties.

Partido Conservador (PC)
Conservative Party

Leadership.   José Terán Varea (director)

Orientation.   Traditionalist conservative

Founded.   1855

History.   As the country's oldest political party, the PC is based on a traditional alliance of church and state and has its roots in the Andean highlands. After participating in government from 1956 to 1960, the PC joined the Frente Nacional Constitucionalista (FNC – National Constitutionalist Front) formed to contest the July 1978 presidential election, but left the Front in March 1978. The PC vote declined in the December 1980 local and provincial elections. In the congressional elections of Jan. 29, 1984, it gained only two seats, with which it supported the Febres government. The party was given one seat in the Febres Cabinet formed on Aug. 10, 1984.

Associated organizations.   See Frente de Reconstrucción Nacional (above).

Partido Demócrata (PD)
Democratic Party

Leadership.   Dr Francisco Huerta Montalvo (leader)

Orientation.   Left liberal

History.   The PD was formed by Huerta Montalva and Heinz Moeller, previously active in the Partido Liberal (Liberal Party – see PLR, below). The party had four members in the Chamber of Representatives until the congressional elections of Jan. 29, 1984, when it held only two seats.

Associated organizations. It has joined the Frente Progresista Democrático, a leftist alliance established in 1984 – see separate entry.

Partido Izquierda Democrática

See Izquierda Democrática (above).

Partido de Liberación Popular
People's Liberation Party

Orientation. Leftist

Founded. July 25, 1983

History. This party did not participate in the 1984 elections and has made little impact.

Partido Liberal Radical (PLR)
Radical Liberal Party

Leadership. Blasco Peña Herrera (leader); Carlos Julio Plaza A. (director)

Orientation. Traditional liberal

Founded. 1895, as Partido Liberal (Liberal Party)

History. The PLR is the direct descendent of the Liberal Party which held power continuously from 1895 to 1944, and subsequently broke up into a number of factions. It had its historical base on the coastal plain.

During the preparations for a return to civilian rule in 1976–77 the PLR withdrew from constitutional committees in protest against restrictions imposed by the government on political freedoms. In the first-round presidential election of 1978 the PLR candidate, Raúl Clemente Huerta Rendón, won 21 per cent of the vote and third place; a PLR candidate won the post of mayor of Quito at the same time. The party won four seats in the 1979 congressional elections, but did less well in the 1980 local and provincial elections. In the congressional elections of Jan. 29, 1984, it secured four seats, which it used to support the Febres government; it was given one cabinet post. The party's offices in Quito were attacked on June 6, 1985, by guerrillas of the Fuerzas Armadas Populares Eloy Alfaro (see above).

Associated organizations. See Frente de Reconstrucción Nacional (above).

Partido Nacional Republicano
National Republican Party

Orientation. Conservative

Founded. July 1984

History. This small party was formed by the merger of two groups, the Partido Nacional Ecuatoriano (Ecuadorian National Party) and the Movimiento Republicano (Republican Movement), neither of which had any congressional representation.

Partido Nacional Revolucionario (PNR)
National Revolutionary Party

Orientation. Centrist

History. This small group joined the Frente de Reconstrucción Nacional (see above) in 1984.

Partido Nacional Velasquista (PNV)
National Velasquista Party

Leadership. Alfonso Arroyo Robelly (leader)

Orientation. Centre-right

Founded. 1952

History. The PNV was founded as the personal vehicle of President José María Velasco Ibarra, who was in power for five terms, most recently in 1968–77. In July 1977 Velasco transferred his support to Acción

Democrática Ecuatoriana (Ecuadorian Democratic Action), a party formed by his nephew, Jaime Acosta Velasco. Velasco Ibarra died shortly thereafter and the PNV entered a decline. In the 1978–79 elections the major part of the PNV supported a centre-right alliance, the 11-party Frente Nacional Constitucionalista (FNC – National Constitutionalist Front). The party had little success in the December 1980 local and provincial elections, but supported the winning Frente de Reconstrucción Nacional (see above) – a successor to the FNC – in the 1984 elections.

Partido Nacionalista Revolucionario (PNR)
Nationalist Revolutionary Party

Address. Pazmiño 245, Oficina 500, Quito

Leadership. Dr Mauricio Gándara (director)

Orientation. Nationalist

Founded. 1969

History. The PNR has its origins in the Movimiento Nacional Arosemanista (National *Arosemanista* Movement) established by supporters of Dr Carlos Julio Arosemana Monroy, who as Vice-President had staged a coup in November 1961. Arosemana was in turn ousted by the army in July 1963. The movement reappeared as the Movimento Nacionalista Revolucionario, which was represented in the Constituent Assembly elected in October 1966. The PNR was officially recognized as a part in 1969. Apart from temporary support for President José María Velasco Ibarra in 1970–71, the PNR has been in opposition.

The PNR opposed the holding of a referendum on a new Constitution in January 1978, and was one of several parties claiming responsibility for the 400,000 ballot papers spoilt by voters. It also called for abstention during the second-round presidential election of April 1979, but took part in the simultaneous congressional elections, gaining one seat (for Arosemana). It retained its single seat in the congressional elections of Jan. 29, 1984.

Policies. The PNR advocates a nationalist revolution and a free and sovereign Ecuador.

Structure. It has a national convention, a co-ordinating committee and two regional and 20 provincial directors. It is organized at the levels of provinces, cantons, parishes and wards.

Membership. The party claims 50,000 active members and 20,000 registered sympathizers.

Publications. *Ecuador Primero*

Partido Roldosista Ecuatoriano
Roldosista Party of Ecuador

Address. Quito

Leadership. Abdalá Bucaram Ortiz (director)

Founded. 1980

History. The party was established by the brother-in-law of the late Dr Jaime Roldós Aguilera, who, as leader of the CFP (see above) – became President of Ecuador in 1979; Roldós died in 1981. The party obtained official recognition in December 1982. In the congressional elections of Jan. 29, 1984, it secured three seats. The deputy leader of the party, Germán Zambrano Santana, was murdered on April 10, 1985 (see CID, above).

Partido Social Cristiano (PSC)
Social Christian Party

Leadership. Sixto Durán Ballén, León Febres Cordero R. (leaders)

Orientation. Conservative

Founded. 1951

History. The PSC was formed to support Camilo Ponce Enríquez, who was President of Ecuador in 1956–60. In the congressional elections of Jan. 29, 1984, the PSC won nine seats. On May 6, Febres Cordero was elected President with 52.2 per cent of the vote in the second round, having received the backing of other centre-right parties.

Associated organizations. See Frente de Reconstrucción Nacional (above).

Partido Socialista
Socialist Party

Address. Edificio Bolívar, Apartado 103, Quito

Leadership. Héctor Soria (secretary)

Orientation. Socialist

Founded. 1933

History. The Partido Socialista gained one seat in the congressional elections of Jan. 29, 1984.

Membership. 50,000

Associated organizations. The party has joined the Frente Progresista Democrática, a leftist alliance established in 1984 (see above).

Partido Socialista Revolucionario Ecuatoriano (PSRE)
Revolutionary Socialist Party of Ecuador

Leadership. Jorge Chiriboga Guerrero (general secretary)

Orientation. Left-wing socialist

Founded. 1926, as Partido Socialista Ecuatoriano (Socialist Party of Ecuador)

History. The party assumed power, together with other revolutionary parties, in 1944, and installed the nominee of the Alianza Democrática Ecuatoriana (Ecuadorian Democratic Alliance) as President. The party subsequently lost influence.

In May 1961 it adopted its present name, adding the word "revolutionary" to emphasize its perception of "the new political dynamics of Latin America". The party supported the Cuban revolution and national liberation movements throughout the Third World. Together with other parties of the left it opposed the military regime in Ecuador and aspired to a new type of democracy.

In 1979 Chiriboga was elected to the Chamber of Representatives.

Policies. The PSRE is revolutionary and anti-imperialist, with the object of assuming power to enable the masses of Ecuador to build a free and sovereign people's democracy.

Structure. The party has a central committee which appoints a political bureau and a secretariat. There are committees at provincial, regional and sectional levels, and "basic units" or local branches.

Membership. 20,000

Associated organizations. See UDP (below).

Publications. *Tiempos de Lucha*

Pueblo, Cambio y Democracia – Partido Roldosista Popular (PCD or PCD-PRP)
Popular Roldosista Party for People, Change and Democracy

Leadership. León Roldós Aguilera (director); Ernesto Buenaño Cabrera (general secretary)

Orientation. Centre-left

Founded. 1980

History. The estalishment of Pueblo, Cambio y Democracia, as it was originally called, had been planned by President Jaime Roldós, who died in May 1981, and was implemented by his brother, Léon Roldós. It initially attracted the support of 12 of the 24 members of Congress elected in 1979 as candidates of the CFP (see above). It obtained official recognition in 1981. In January 1982 it withdrew its support from the Hurtado government. The party adopted its present name on Nov. 17, 1982.

Policies. The party pursues the reformist, approximately social democratic, policies advocated by the late President Roldós.

Associated organizations. The *roldosista* members of the CFP joined the Convergencia Democrática alliance of centrist and left-wing parties during 1980; the PCD-PRP has joined the alliance's successor, the Frente Progresista Democrática, established in 1984 (see above).

Unión Democrática Popular (UDP)
Popular Democratic Union

Leadership. Jorge Chiriboga Guerrero (leader)

Orientation. Leftist

History. The UDP was established as a left-wing electoral alliance in 1979, under the leadership of the PCE (see above). It failed to win any seats in the 1979 congressional election, but has since joined with the PSRE (see above) which gained one seat in 1979. It is not recognized officially as a political party.

Associated organizations. The UDP has affiliated to the Frente Progresista Democrática, a leftist alliance established in 1984 (see above).

Unión Revolucionaria Popular Ecuatoriana (URPE)
Ecuadorean Popular Revolutionary Union

Leadership. Jaime Galarza, Carlos Rodríguez (leaders)

Orientation. Very left-wing

Founded. 1980

History. The URPE was formed by a merger of the Movimiento Segunda Independencia (MSI – Second Independence Movement), led by Galarza, with the Comité del Pueblo (People's Committee), led by Rodríguez; the latter Maoist movement was a splinter group of the Partido Comunista Marxista Leninista (Communist Party – Marxist–Leninist). Both groups had formed part of the FADI (see above).

El Salvador

Capital: San Salvador   **Population: 4,850,000**

El Salvador gained separate independence in 1839. A densely-populated country which currently has the highest annual population growth rate in Central America (3.5 per cent), it has spent much of the present century under military rule, particularly after the suppression of a peasant rebellion in 1932 at a cost of 30,000 lives (including that of the rebel leader, Farabundo Martí). Elections in 1972 and 1977, which the mainly Christian democratic opposition denounced as fraudulent, installed successive governments of the conservative Partido de Conciliación Nacional (PCN). Following a coup against President Carlos Humberto Romero in October 1979, left-wing opposition to the new civilian–military junta developed in 1980 into a concerted military and diplomatic campaign to overthrow the regime; the unified guerrilla command, the FMLN, was supported by a political broad front grouping, the FDR.

A "government of national unity" was set up in May 1982 with the participation of the PCN, the Christian democratic PDC, the very right-wing Arena and others. The guerrilla campaign intensified late in 1982, and the armed forces and right-wing death squads embarked on counter-offensives. By the end of 1982 it was estimated that 36,000 civilians had been killed in the three-year war. Presidential elections in 1984 (boycotted by the left) were won by the PDC's José Napoleón Duarte, and his government held inconclusive negotiations with the FDR–FMLN alliance in October–November. The guerrilla war continued, with the number of civilian deaths by late 1985 approaching 50,000. Almost 20 per cent of the population had been displaced as a result of the conflict, either within El Salvador or to neighbouring countries.

Constitutional background. Under the Constitution of December 1983, the Republic has an executive President elected by universal adult suffrage (in two rounds of voting if no candidate secures an absolute majority in the first round). The Constituent Assembly elected in 1982 was redesignated as the country's Legislative Assembly and currently has 60 seats in a single chamber.

Recent election results. Elections to the Legislative Assembly took place on March 31, 1985. The PDC won 33 seats – an absolute majority – while an alliance of the Arena and the PCN took 25 seats. The PAISA and the AD each won a single seat. The presidency remained with José Napoleón Duarte, who was elected in two rounds in March and May 1984; in the second round he had obtained 53.6 per cent of the votes cast, against 46.4 per cent for Roberto d'Aubuisson of the Arena.

Acción Democrática (AD)

See Partido Acción Democrática (below).

Alianza Anticomunista Maximiliano Hernández Martínez
Maximiliano Hernández Martínez Anti-Communist Alliance

Orientation. Ultra-right death squad

History. This group (also known as the Brigada Anticomunista Maximiliano Hernández Martínez) was named after President Hernández who was in power in 1931–44 and under whose regime the peasant rebellion of 1932 was suppressed. It claimed responsibility for the killing of six leaders of the left-wing FDR alliance in November 1980. It was also reported to have delivered to a radio station in March 1982 a "death list" of 34 (mainly foreign) journalists alleged to have contacts with left-wing guerrillas.

In November 1984, after a period of inactivity, the group announced its revival to take part in a joint campaign with the Comando Domingo Monterrosa (see below).

Alianza Nacional de la Empresa Privada (ANEP)
National Alliance of Private Enterprise

Leadership. Juan Maldonado (president)

Orientation. Right-wing business association

History. The ANEP and its political organ, the Alianza Productiva (Producers' Alliance), has consistently opposed negotiations with the country's left-wing guerrilla forces, preferring a military strategy to defeat the guerrillas.

Alianza Republicana Nacional (Arena)
National Republican Alliance

Leadership. Alfredo Cristiani (leader); Mario Repdaelli (general secretary)

Founded. 1981

Orientation. Very right-wing

History. The founder and, until late 1985, the leader of the Arena was Roberto d'Aubuisson Arrieta, a former major in the National Guard's intelligence section who has been accused of involvement in the murder in March 1980 of Monsignor Oscar Arnulfo Romero y Galdames, the popular Archbishop of San Salvador, and of directing other death-squad activities around that time. As leader of the Frente Amplio Nacional (FAN – Broad National Front), he was temporarily arrested in May 1980 on suspicion of planning a right-wing coup against the junta which he had decried as "communist". On March 3, 1981, he publicly called for such a coup. After a period of exile in Guatemala, he returned to El Salvador in late 1981 and established the Arena.

In the March 1982 elections to the Constituent Assembly the party came second with 29.1 per cent of the vote and 19 seats; it held four ministerial posts in the subsequent Government of National Unity, and d'Aubuisson was elected president of the Assembly. On June 28, 1983, an Arena deputy, René Barrios Amaya, was assassinated by the FMLN after being accused of working for the US Central Intelligence Agency. In 1984 d'Aubuisson secured 29.8 per cent of the first-round presidential election, but lost the second round by a margin of 100,000 votes (7 per cent). An Arena deputy, Ricardo Arnoldo Pohl, was assassinated by the Frente Clara Elizabeth Ramírez (see below) on Jan. 27, 1984.

113

The Arena formed a coalition in late 1984 with the PCN (see below) – for the legislative elections of March 1985, in which the two parties gained 13 and 12 seats respectively in the 60-seat Legislative Assembly. The coalition won control of 105 of the 262 municipal councils elected at the same time. The Arena later called for the elections to be annulled on the grounds that the armed forces had interfered in favour of the PDC (see below), but the electoral commission ruled that the process was fair and proper.

The Arena suffered a split in 1984 leading to the formation of the Patria Libre party (see below). In September 1985 a party congress accepted d'Aubuisson's resignation as party leader, but elected him as honorary president.

Policies. The Arena stands for nationalism, law and order and uncompromising opposition to the left-wing guerrillas. It has accused the Christian democrats of destroying the country's economic and social foundations and of aiding international communism.

Bloque Antiguerrillero del Oriente (BAGO)
Eastern Anti-Guerrilla Bloc

Orientation. Ultra-right death squad

Founded. 1980

History. This group has been responsible for a number of killings and bomb attacks, including the killing of 14 alleged left-wing guerrillas on Sept. 24, 1980.

Bloque Popular Revolucionario – Fuerzas Populares de Liberación Farabundo Martí (BPR-FPL)
Popular Revolutionary Bloc – Farabundo Martí Popular Liberation Forces

Leadership. Leonel González (first secretary, commander-in-chief); Dimas Rodríguez (second secretary, alternate commander)

Orientation. Marxist–Leninist political/guerrilla movement

Founded. 1975 (BPR); 1977 (FPL)

History. The BPR opposition coalition, and its military wing, the FPL, are based in Chalatenango. The BPR was formed as a revolutionary socialist organization with the support of a large proportion of the country's teachers and members of the lower middle class, students, workers and peasants. Although initially a non-violent movement, it became allied with the FPL, formed as an offshoot of the PCS (see below) and led by Salvador Cayetano Carpio (Comandante Marcial), who had been leader of the PCS for 30 years.

The first action of the FPL was the kidnapping on April 19, 1977, and subsequent assassination of the Salvadorean Foreign Minister, in an unsuccessful attempt to secure the release of 37 political prisoners as "part of the prolonged war which the FPL is pursuing until it achieves the ultimate popular revolution towards socialism". On July 12 the FPL killed Col. (retd) Osmín Aguirre y Salinas, President of El Salvador in 1944–45, who as chief of police had in 1932 suppressed the peasant rebellion (see introduction). On Sept. 16 it killed the government-appointed rector of the University of El Salvador. On Nov. 10–12 demonstrators led by the BPR occupied the Ministry of Labour in San Salvador, holding at least 86 hostages, including two government ministers, in support of textile and agricultural workers' wage demands; the occupation ended when the government agreed to consider the demands.

In 1978 the FPL called for a boycott of the March general and municipal elections, and carried out several bomb attacks. On April 11–13, some 150 BPR members (belonging to the FECCAS and the UTC – see below) occupied the embassies of Costa Rica, Panama, Switzerland and Venezuela and the cathedral of San Salvador to demand an end to rural repression; the occupations ended peacefully on April 19.

In May 1979 the BPR occupied the Costa Rican and French embassies, securing only safe conduct out of the country for those involved, and another BPR group occupied the cathedral, leading to demonstrations in which the police killed 23 people on May 8. On May 11 two BPR leaders were released from prison; on the same day, nine BPR members seized the Venezuelan embassy, being granted safe passage out of the country after a demonstration supporting them had ended with 14 deaths. On May 23 the FPL killed the Minister of Education, and on Nov. 28 it kidnapped, and later killed, the South African ambassador in an unsuccessful attempt to secure the release of prisoners and other demands. The BPR declared after the October 1979 coup that it would not accept any truce with the "counter-revolutionary" junta. It occupied the cathedral and two ministries, taking hostages including two Cabinet members, and – after four BPR members were killed by the police – the government conceded some of its demands including food price reductions and the dissolution of the right-wing Orden militia (see POP, below).

On Jan. 8, 1980, the FPL was joined by Salvador Samayo, who had six days earlier resigned as Minister of Education. On Jan. 10 the BPR–FPL formed an alliance – the Coordinación Revolucionaria de la Masas (CRM – Revolutionary Co-ordination of the Masses) – with the LP-28–EPL, the FAPU–FARN, the PCS and the UDN (see below). In April the BPR and the other political organizations in the CRM joined the FDR and the FPL and its counterparts joined the FMLN; Carpio became the FMLN's commander. He was reported to have killed himself in Nicaragua on April 12, 1983, after the death of the FPL second-in-command, Ana Melida Montes (Comandante Ana María), in what appeared to be a factional dispute; after a period of crisis a new leadership consisting of González and Rodríguez was installed in September.

Napoleón Romero, a member of the FPL directorate, was captured by security forces on April 11, 1985, and accepted a government amnesty.

Splits in the FPL have resulted in the formation of other organizations including the Frente Clara Elizabeth Ramírez, the Movimiento Popular Roberto Sibrían and the Movimiento Laborista Cayetano Carpio (see below).

Policies. The BPR–FPL advocate a strategy of "prolonged people's war" against the established order, and until the formation of the FDR the leadership rejected alliances with "non-proletarian" parties.

Membership. Organizations belonging to the BPR by mid-1979 were the FECCAS and the UCT, the FUR-30 and the MERS (see below), the Comité de Coordinación Sindical (CCS – Trade Union Co-ordinating Committee) and other student, labour and popular movements.

Publications. The main organ of the BPR–FPL is the clandestine *Radio Farabundo Martí.*

Associated organizations. See FDR–FMLN (below).

Brigada Anticomunista Maximiliano Hernández Martínez

See Alianza Anticomunista Maximiliano Hernández Martínez (above).

Comando Domingo Monterrosa
Domingo Monterrosa Commando

Orientation. Ultra-right death squad

Founded. Late November 1984

History. This group, named after a commander of the army's counterinsurgency campaign in Morazán (who was killed in a helicopter crash in October 1984), issued a statement on Dec. 15, 1984, in which it threatened to "demolish all communist elements" in the government. The group is also known as the Frente Patriótico (Patriotic Front).

Associated organizations. See Alianza Anticomunista Maximiliano Hernández Martínez (above).

Comandos Suicidas Salvadoreños (CSS)
Salvadorean Suicide Commandos

Orientation. Guerrilla group

Founded. Oct. 18, 1984

History. The group threatened action against extreme right-wing politicians and said that it would kill the commander of the death squads; it also demanded the withdrawal of US diplomats and military advisers from El Salvador. Although ostensibly a left-wing group, it may have been formed by right-wing elements to create confusion.

Comité de Presos Políticos de El Salvador (COPPES)
El Salvador Political Prisoners' Committee

Orientation. Human rights concerns

History. The COPPES was founded by political prisoners in Salvadorean jails to publicize and attempt to prevent abuses of their rights. Three of its members were among the 13 political and 136 common prisoners who escaped from Mariona prison, near the capital, during a guerrilla attack on July 13, 1985.

Dirección Revolucionaria Unida (DRU)

See FDR–FMLN (below).

Ejército Popular de Liberación (EPL)
People's Liberation Army

Orientation. Left-wing guerrilla group

Founded. November 1979

History. This minor group was established as an offshoot of the FPL guerrilla movement (see BPR–FPL, above). Its leader, Humberto Mendoza, was killed in November 1980 and reports of its activities dwindled; it may now be defunct.

Ejército Revolucionario Popular (ERP)

See LP-28–ERP (below).

Ejército Secreto Anticomunista (ESA)

See PLN–ESA (below).

Escuadrón de la Muerte Nuevo (EMN)
New Death Squad

Orientation. Ultra-right death squad

Founded. 1980

History. This anti-communist execution squad has claimed a membership of 3,000 and has carried out numerous bombings and killings since September 1980.

Federación Campesina Cristiana de El Salvador – Unión de Trabajadores del Campo (FECCAS–UTC)

Christian Peasant Federation of El Salvador – Union of Rural Workers

Orientation. Left-wing Christian peasant unions

History. The UTC and the FECCAS were involved in demonstrations on May 1, 1977, calling for the release of political prisoners, when security forces shot dead 10 people. The UTC general secretary, Apolinario Serrano, was one of four peasant leaders killed by government forces after their arrest on Sept. 29, 1979. In the late 1970s the UTC and the FECCAS increased their co-operation, partly through the BPR (see above), and by the early 1980s they were regarded as allies of the FDR–FMLN opposition coalition.

Policies. The FECCAS and the UTC campaign for "fair wages, the right to organize, and the radical transformation of [Salvadorean] society to construct a new society where there is no poverty, hunger, repression or exploitation of one group by another".

Federación de Trabajadores Revolucionarios (FTR)

Revolutionary Workers' Federation

Orientation. Left-wing trade union group

Founded. December 1980

History. This organization was formed to provide a revolutionary leadership for the Salvadorean labour movement, and in particular to support general strikes called by the FDR.

Frente de Acción Popular Unificada – Fuerzas Armadas de la Resistencia Nacional (FAPU–FARN)

Unified Popular Action Front – Armed Forces of National Resistance

Leadership. Fermán Cienfuegos, Saúl Villalta (leaders)

Orientation. Marxist political/guerrilla movement

Founded. 1975

History. The FARN was formed as an offshoot of the ERP guerrilla group (see LP-28–ERP, below) and the FAPU as an offshoot of the PCS (see below). On Jan. 16, 1979, some 60 FAPU members occupied the Mexican embassy and the San Salvador office of the Organization of American States, taking more than 150 hostages, and demanded the release of political prisoners; the government denied that there were any such prisoners and conceded only the safe conduct to Mexico of the FAPU members. In 1978–79 the FARN kidnapped a number of important foreign businessmen, seeking cash ransoms, the release of prisoners and the publication of statements. The kidnappings, and related killings, caused a general exodus of foreign businessmen from the country.

On Jan. 10, 1980, the FAPU–FARN joined other political and military groupings on the left to form the CRM (see BPR–FPL, above). In July 1980 some 300 FARN members temporarily occupied San Miguel, El Salvador's third-largest town. The FARN leader, Ernesto Jovel, was killed in September and was succeeded by Cienfuegos. Since mid-1980 the FARN's forces have operated under the unified command of the FMLN.

Membership. The guerrilla forces of the FARN were estimated at 800 people in mid-1980.

Associated organizations. See FDR–FMLN (below).

Frente Clara Elizabeth Ramírez
Clara Elizabeth Ramírez Front

Orientation. Marxist guerrilla group

Founded. 1983

History. The Front broke away from the BPR–FPL (see above) to pursue an urban guerrilla campaign, complementing the rural struggle of the main guerrilla groups. It carried out several killings in 1984, including that on Jan. 27 of a Legislative Assembly deputy belonging to the Arena (see above) and of a PCN (see below) deputy on March 14. It claimed responsibility for the assassination on March 7, 1985, of the director of the Armed Forces Press Committee.

Policies. The Front has condemned elections under the present system as "staged by the native criminal bourgeoisie . . . to legitimize a government which will permit a greater degree of intervention by Yankee imperialism".

Frente Democrático Revolucionaro – Frente Farabundo Martí de Liberación Nacional (FDR–FMLN)
Democratic Revolutionary Front – Farabundo Martí National Liberation Front

Leadership. Guillermo Ungo (president of FDR); Eduardo Calles (vice-president of FDR); Rubén Zamora, David Mena, Juan José Martell, Jorge Billacorta (other FDR leaders); Roberto Roca, Jorge Schafik Handal, Fermán Cienfuegos, Joaquín Villalobos, Leonel González (FMLN general command); Dagoberto Gutiérrez, Marisol Galindo (other FMLN leaders)

Orientation. Left-wing political/guerrilla coalition

Founded. 1980

History. The FDR–FMLN was founded as a broad left-wing front opposed to the PDC/military government and to the social, economic and political system existing in El Salvador. The first leader of the guerrilla section of the front, the FMLN (which is named after the 1930s rebel leader – see introduction), was Salvador Cayetano Carpio, a former leader of the PCS (see below), while the first general secretary of the political section, the FDR, was Enrique Alvarez Córdova of the MPSC (see below).

The FDR organized a general strike on Aug. 13–15, 1980, which met with limited support and was accompanied by clashes with government forces in which at least 40 people were killed. On Nov. 27 six FDR members, including Alvarez and Juan Chacón of the BPR–FPL (see above), were kidnapped and killed by the Alianza Anticomunista (see above).

On Jan. 5, 1981, Guillermo Ungo of the MNR (see below) was elected president of the FDR. The guerrilla organizations in the FMLN launched a general offensive on Jan. 10–11, 1981, with heavy fighting breaking out in many parts of the country. The FDR called a general strike in support of the offensive, but the response was limited. Martial law was declared and by Jan. 19 the government claimed to have complete control; it stated that 980 guerrillas and 142 soldiers had been killed (although the Red Cross stated that most of the dead were civilians). The fighting nevertheless continued, especially north of San Salvador. In mid-January the FDR established in Mexico a seven-member diplomatic–political commission with the aim of forming a "democratic revolutionary government"; it unsuccessfully sought direct negotiations with the US government. By late May the FMLN claimed to have control of four provinces and was launching attacks against police and army positions in the capital. It claimed to have inflicted 900 casualties on the army during June alone, and on Aug. 15 established a short-lived "revolutionary government" in the eastern town of Perquín, soon recaptured by the army. The FMLN also conducted an extensive campaign of economic sabotage, with one quarter of the country's electricity pylons being blown up, and 11 bombs exploding within 10 minutes in San Salvador on Aug. 27.

International attempts to mediate between the warring parties were made during 1981, in particular by members of the Socialist International and by Panama, but were rejected by the government and by the US administration. The FDR–FMLN gained varying degrees of recognition and support from the governments of France, Mexico, the Netherlands, Yugoslavia, Cuba, Panama and Nicaragua during the year, but was condemned by Argentina, Bolivia, Chile, Colombia, the Dominican Republic, Guatemala, Honduras, Paraguay, Venezuela and Brazil. From October onwards the FMLN, then thought to have 4,000–6,000 full-time fighters, consolidated its positions in the north and north-east of the country. By the end of the year it claimed to have blown up 25 major bridges and to have killed 2,000 members of the security forces since June, for the loss of just 160 of its own members, but those figures, and most other accounts of guerrilla and government losses, were disputed between the two sides.

There was particularly heavy fighting in the area of Morazán in early 1982. On Jan. 27 the FMLN attacked the Ilopango airbase near San Salvador and destroyed 28 military aircraft. In February President López Portillo of Mexico offered to mediate in the conflict; the FDR–FMLN accepted the offer but the government refused it. The fighting continued during and after the March elections to the Constituent Assembly, especially in northern and central areas; the FDR boycotted the elections on the grounds that military pressures meant that they could not be conducted democratically, and that participation in the electoral process would allow opposition members to be identified and eliminated. In June the FMLN temporarily regained control of Perquín. From June 23 the FMLN declared a ban on road traffic. A renewed offer of dialogue was rejected by the government in October and a new FMLN offensive began in early 1983.

During 1983 the Salvadorean armed forces received almost $80,000,000 in US aid, but the guerrillas maintained their advantage and killed or wounded more than 7,000 soldiers; agricultural production was severely disrupted. The total number of deaths resulting from the conflict, including massacres attributed by most observers to the army, was put by government sources at 3,329 in 1983, and by the FDR–FMLN at 7,169.

Both sides agreed that the number of deaths fell in 1984 (government figure: 2,469; FDR–FMLN: 5,286), but there were outbreaks of very heavy fighting, particularly in the early part of the year when the armed forces mounted an assault on the guerrilla bases of Morazán and San Vicente (north-eastern, and central, El Salvador). The guerrilla movements boycotted and disrupted the March and May two-stage presidential election, but following the election of the Christian democrat, José Napoleón Duarte, the FDR repeated its offer of ceasefire discussions, and meetings took place between the FDR–FMLN leadership and government representatives, including Duarte, in October and November. The discussions produced no permanent solution, but temporary ceasefires were agreed over Christmas and the New Year and again on various occasions during a mass vaccination exercise in 1985.

The FDR–FMLN considered participation in the March 1985 elections to the Legislative Assembly while the dialogue with the government continued, but abandoned the idea after the breakdown of the dialogue, and dismissed the elections as "a farce". The armed forces, reportedly opposed to peace negotiations, mounted operations against the FMLN in Chalatenango, Morazán and elsewhere in late 1984 and early 1985, and were reported to have forced the guerrillas to rely on smaller, more mobile units rather than fixed bases in "liberated zones".

Policies. The guerrilla groups in the FMLN follow the Marxist–Leninist strategy of a "prolonged popular war" from which there would arise a "proletarian unity party" which would form the basis of a "people's state". The FDR–FMLN leadership has repeatedly stated its willingness to enter into negotiations with the Salvadorean government, while stressing that the guerrilla war would continue until a return to full democracy had been achieved. Its interim proposals have included the creation of a "national forum" supplanting the Legislative Assembly, and the merger of the guerrilla forces with the regular army.

Structure. There are two wings to the movement – the FDR, which co-ordinates opposition political activities, and the FMLN, which formulates and implements the opposition's military strategy through a Dirección Revolucionaria Unida (DRU – United Revolutionary Directorate), established in May 1980, on which are represented numerous guerrilla groups of various ideological orientations. Since mid-1981 the FMLN has been setting up an alternative government structure, which it calls Poder Popular Local (PPL – Local People's Power) in areas under its control, each PPL unit of about 1,000 people having an elected junta responsible for administration, social services, education, production and defence. (Elections to the PPL juntas were organized by the FMLN in Feburary 1985.) The forces of the FMLN in these areas consisted of front-line fighters with special training and improved weapons, guerrilla units operating almost exclusively in the controlled areas and along main roads, and defensive militias. In August 1985 the FMLN announced plans to merge its five guerrilla armies into a single organization.

Membership. The FDR–FMLN bloc consists of about 20 groups, including the BPR–FPL and the FAPU–FARN (see above), the LP-28–ERP, the MOR, the PCS–FAL, the PRTC and the UND (see below). It also succeeded the Frente Salvadoreño Democrático (FSD – Salvadorean Democratic Front), which was established in April 1980 and included the MNR and the MPSC (see below) and various trade union, student and professional organizations. The guerrilla forces comprising the FMLN have been variously estimated at from 6,500 to 14,000 people.

Publications. The FMLN has operated clandestine radio transmitters using the name *Radio Venceremos*. The FDR and its foreign support groups produce a great many bulletins and newsletters.

International affiliations. The FDR–FMLN is supported by solidarity groups in many countries. The US government has repeatedly asserted that the guerrilla movement was funded and armed by Cuba and/or the Soviet Union, through Nicaragua, and has used this argument to justify extensive military and financial support for the Salvadorean government and for the *contra* forces fighting the Nicaraguan government; the guerrillas have maintained that most of their supplies were captured or bought on the black market, and the Cuban and Nicaraguan governments have denied the provision of material, as distinct from moral, support.

Frente Farabundo Martí de Liberación Nacional (FMLN)

See FDR–FMLN (above).

Frente Patriótico

See Comando Domingo Monterrosa (above).

Frente Pedro Pablo Castillo
Pedro Pablo Castillo Front

Orientation.   Guerrilla group

Founded.   July 1985

History.   This hitherto unknown group, claiming to represent left-wing political prisoners but disowned by the FDR–FMLN, claimed responsibility for the kidnapping of President Duarte's daughter in September 1985. She was released in October in return for the freeing of several left-wing prisoners. The group is named after a hero of the independence movement.

Frente Político Anticomunista (FPA)
Anti-Communist Political Front

Orientation.   Ultra-right death squad

Founded.   May 1979

History.   Like other organizations of the kind, the FPA has carried out attacks on alleged left-wing leaders.

Frente Universitario Revolucionario (FUR-30)
University Revolutionary Front

Orientation.   Marxist student group

Founded.   1980

History.   This group – a component of the BPR (see above) – occupied the Jesuit-run University of Central America in San Salvador on Feb. 15, 1980, and seized 60 hostages including the chancellor; all were released on Feb. 18. A total of 14 members of the FUR-30 were killed on Jan. 19, 1984, by right-wing death squad members.

Fuerzas Armadas de Liberación (FAL)

See PCS–FAL (below).

Fuerzas Armadas de la Resistencia Nacional (FARN)

See FAPU–FARN (above).

Fuerzas Populares de Liberación (FPL)

See BPR–FPL (above).

Fuerzas Revolucionarias Armadas del Pueblo (FRAP)

See ORT–FRAP (below).

Guerrilleros Urbanos Mardoqueo Cruz

See PRTC (below).

Ligas de Liberación (LL)

See PRTC (below).

Ligas Populares del 28 de Febrero – Ejército Revolucionario del Pueblo (LP-28–ERP)

Popular Leagues of February 28 – People's Revolutionary Army

Leadership.   Joaquín Villalobos, Ana Guadelupe Martínez (leaders)

Orientation.   Left-wing political/guerrilla movement

Founded.   1972 (ERP); 1977 (LP-28)

History.   The LP-28, named after the date of post-electoral disturbances in 1977, is a direct-action political organization, and the ERP, founded as an independent guerrilla movement, now forms its military wing. Much of the membership of the LP-28 came from the Unión Nacional de la Oposición (UNO – National Opposition Union), which, according to the disputed official count, lost the 1977 elections. The ERP carried out several kidnappings, securing US$1,000,000 ransom for one industrialist kidnapped on Jan. 27, 1977, although he died of wounds received during his abduction. Bombs planted by the ERP in February 1977, in retaliation for the killing of a priest and four youths by security forces on Jan. 20, resulted in the deaths of 14 National Guards and in 20 injuries.

In September 1979 LP-28 supporters occupied the Ministry of Labour for a week in an attempt to secure the release of imprisoned leaders of the organization, and the group was held responsible for bomb attacks at the presidential palace and elsewhere on Sept. 25. In October 1979 the LP-28 and the ERP led an unsuccessful revolt in three townships near San Salvador, and on Oct. 19 the LP-28 announced that it would no longer take part in violent actions but would continue to "organize the masses". On Oct. 31 the ERP kidnapped Jaime Hill, a member of El Salvador's most powerful "14 Families"; he was released in March 1980 in return for the publication of manifestoes in foreign newspapers.

The LP-28 occupied the Panamanian embassy on Jan. 11–15 and Feb. 13–14, and the Spanish embassy on Feb. 5–18, 1980, securing the release of several prisoners and a promise to investigate the whereabouts of others; as a result of these incidents a number of countries withdrew their diplomatic representation – the UK in late January, the Federal Republic of Germany on Feb. 7 and Israel on Feb. 14 (all of which have since restored their representation, the UK at the level of chargé d'affaires). In May 1980 the LP-28–ERP grouping, already part of the CRM alliance (see BPR–FPL, above), became part of the wider FDR–FMLN alliance, although it has retained some operational independence. In September 1980 it carried out an attack on the US embassy, and in the following month an army offensive was launched against its bases in eastern El Salvador.

The then commander of the ERP, Alejandro Montenegro, was arrested in Honduras in September 1982 and handed over to Salvadorean security forces. He subsequently denounced the ERP and revealed details of the FMLN's operations; the FMLN stated in March 1983 that he had been tortured. A member of the ERP central committee, Yanet Samour Hasbún (Comandante Filomena), was captured by government forces on Dec. 30, 1984. The army reported on April 9, 1985, that the ERP commander, Villalobos – an influential figure in the FMLN – had been killed, but the government later acknowledged that he was alive and specifically requested his participation in renewed peace talks.

Membership.   The ERP was estimated to have 800 fighters in mid-1980.

Associated organizations.   See FDR–FMLN (below).

Movimiento Estable Republicano Centrista (Merecen)
Stable Republican Centrist Movement

Leadership. Juan Ramón Rosales y Rosales (general secretary)

Orientation. Right-wing

Founded. 1982

History. The Merecen general secretary gained 0.5 per cent of the vote in the March 1984 first-round presidential election. In the 1985 legislative elections it formed a coalition with the POP (see below), but failed to win any seats.

Movimiento de Estudiantes Revolucionarios Salvadoreños (MERS)
Salvadorean Revolutionary Students' Movement

Orientation. Marxist student group

History. Members of the MERS (a component of the BPR – see above) occupied the Ministry of Education on Feb. 5, 1980, seizing about 400 hostages in support of various demands for educational reforms; the occupation ended peacefully on Feb. 12 with agreements being signed by the ministry.

Movimiento de Liberación Popular (MLP)
People's Liberation Movement

Leadership. Fabio Castillo (leader)

Orientation. Left-wing

History. This small group, led by a former rector of the University of El Salvador, joined the FDR (see above) in 1980.

Movimento Nacional Revolucionario (MNR)
National Revolutionary Movement

Address. Apartado 5-660, CP 06500 México DF, Mexico

Telephone. Mexico City 525 6417

Telex. Mexico 1761209 GMUME

Leadership. Guillermo Manuel Ungo (leader); Francisco Marroquín (organizing secretary); Héctor Oqueli (international secretary)

Orientation. Social democratic

History. The MNR leader became a member of the civilian-military junta formed after the overthrow of President Romero in October 1979, but resigned in early January 1980 in protest at the government's "swing to the right". In April 1980 the MNR became part of a Frente Salvadoreño Democrático (FSD – Salvadorean Democratic Front), and then of the FDR (see above) of which Ungo became president. In that capacity Ungo has been the main political spokesman of the various forces seeking to overthrow the present regime.

Policies. The MNR advocates radical social reforms and a modernized capitalist economy.

Associated organizations. See FDR–FMLN (below).

International affiliations. The MNR is a full member of the Socialist International, of which Ungo is a vice-president; it has close relations with the Acción Democrática party of Venezuela and the PLN of Costa Rica. All its leaders are in exile in Mexico, Costa Rica, Venezuela or the United States.

Movimento Obrero Revolucionario Salvador Cayetano Carpio (MOR)
Salvador Cayetano Carpio Workers' Revolutionary Movement

Orientation. Left-wing

History. The MOR is named after the late left-wing leader Salvador Cayetano Carpio (see FMLN, above, and PCS, below). It broke away from the BPR–FPL (see above) in 1983.

Policies. An FPL statement condemning the formation of the movement declared that it "maintained the sectarian, anti-unity positions of the past as upheld by Marcial [i.e. Carpio], denying the FMLN's role as vanguard of the revolution and proclaiming itself the sole representative of the working class".

Movimiento Popular Revolucionario Roberto Sibrián
Roberto Sibrián People's Revolutionary Movement

Orientation. Marxist–Leninist guerrilla group

Founded. Oct. 29, 1984

History. This movement – named after a deceased member of the FPL leadership, and assumed to be a splinter group of the FPL – announced in October 1984 that it had joined the "revolutionary struggle in El Salvador, advocating a strategy with a Central American perspective".

Movimento Popular Social Cristiano (MPSC)
Social Christian People's Movement

Leadership. Roberto Lara Velado (leader); Rubén Zamora, Jorge Villacorta

Orientation. Left-wing Christian democrat

Founded. 1980

History. The MPSC (the name of which is also rendered as Movimiento Popular Socialcristiano) was formed by members of the PDC (see below) who were opposed to the participation of the PDC leader, Duarte, in the junta which took power in October 1979. The MPSC is a member of the FDR (see above).

Policies. The MPSC stands for social justice, respect for human life and an equitable distribution of wealth.

Organización Democrática Nacional (Orden)

See POP (below).

Organización para la Liberación del Comunismo (OLC)
Organization for Liberation from Communism

Orientation. Ultra-right guerrilla group

Founded. 1979

History. This group killed four members of the BPR (see above) on Jan. 29, 1980, and was held responsible for the bombing of a Catholic radio station and a university publishing office on Feb. 18.

Organización Revolucionaria de Trabajadores – Fuerzas Revolucionarias Armadas del Pueblo (ORT–FRAP)

Workers' Revolutionary Organization – People's Revolutionary Armed Forces

Orientation. Left-wing political/guerrilla movement

Founded. 1975 (FRAP); 1979 (ORT)

History. This minor element of the illegal opposition arose from a split in the ERP (see LP-28-ERP, above) in 1975; the formation of the ORT in 1979 gave the grouping a dual political–military structure.

Partido Acción Democrática (PAD)
Democratic Action Party

Leadership. René Fortín Magaña (leader)

Orientation. Centre-right

Founded. November 1981

History. The leader of the PAD (which is also known as Acción Democrática – AD) had briefly been a member of the military junta in 1960. In the March 1982 Constituent Assembly elections the PAD gained 7.7 per cent of the vote and two seats. Fortín won 3.5 per cent of the vote in the March 1984 first-round presidential election.

In 1985 the party contested elections to the Legislative Assembly, winning just one of the 60 seats. Its decision to support the PDC government led to a split in the party, with four departmental directors being expelled in April 1985.

Policies. The PAD advocates private ownership of property and opposes communists, socialists, Christian democrats and what it perceives as Soviet, Cuban and Venezuelan intervention in El Salvador.

Partido Acción Renovadora (PAR)
Renewal Action Party

Leadership. Ernesto Oyarbide (leader)

Orientation. Left-wing

Founded. 1944

History. The PAR was founded by Gen. José Asebcio Menéndez. It was suspended in 1968 but regained registration in 1981; it boycotted the March 1982 Constituent Assembly elections, along with other leftist parties, but contested the March 1985 Legislative Assembly elections, without success.

Policies. The party has advocated land reform, social justice, pluralism, the nationalization of banks and the transfer of the ownership of private enterprises to their workers.

Partido Auténtico Institucional Salvadoreño (PAISA)
Authentic Institutional Party of El Salvador

Leadership. Dr Roberto Escobar García (general secretary)

Orientation. Right-wing conservative

Founded. October 1982

History. The PAISA was founded by members of the right-wing majority of the PCN (see below) who were dissatisfied with what they perceived to be the undue moderation of the leadership. It recruited nine of the PCN's 14 representatives in the Constituent Assembly, and allied itself with the Arena (see above).

Two PAISA members of the Assembly were assassinated by unidentified gunmen in February and March 1984. Escobar, a retired army colonel, received 1.2 per cent of the vote as the party's candidate in the 1984 presidential election. In March 1985 the PAISA was reduced to a single seat in elections to what had become the Legislative Assembly, the Arena having allied itself formally with the PCN and only informally, for the simultaneous San Salvador municipal elections, with the PAISA. The party won control of one municipality (out of 262).

Policies. The PAISA is opposed to any accommodation with the country's left-wing guerrillas.

Partido Centrista Salvadoreño (PACES)
Salvadorean Centrist Party

Leadership. Tomás Chafoya Martínez (leader)

Orientation. Centrist

Founded. January 1985

History. This party was formed with the support of student groups in the University of El Salvador.

Partido Comunista Salvadoreño – Fuerzas Armadas de Liberación (PCS–FAL)
Salvadorean Communist Party – Armed Forces of Liberation

Leadership. Jorge Schafik Handal (leader); Américo Mauro Araujo (deputy leader)

Orientation. Orthodox communist political/guerrilla movement

Founded. 1930

History. The PCS has been illegal for most of the time since its formation. The general secretary of the PCS from 1940 to 1969 was Salvador Cayetano Carpio, who left the party in 1969 and went on to lead the FMLN (see above). One of its members was briefly Minister of Labour and Social Welfare in the Cabinet formed on Oct. 22, 1979, after the overthrow of President Romero, but the party was not itself legalized. In January 1980 it joined the CRM opposition coalition (see BPR–FPL, above), and it later became an influential force in the broader FDR–FMLN alliance formed in April 1980.

Structure. The PCS is an illegal political party and the FAL is its military wing.

International affiliations. The PCS is recognized by the Communist Party of the Soviet Union and its allied parties.

Partido de Conciliación Nacional (PCN)
National Conciliation Party

Address. Calle Arce 1128, San Salvador

Leadership. Dr Francisco José Guerrero (leader); Raúl Molina Martínez (general secretary)

Orientation. Centre-right

Founded. 1961

History. The PCN was in power from December 1961, when it won all 54 seats in a Constituent Assembly; the latter transformed itself into a Legislative Assembly, which the PCN dominated until the coup of October 1979. It also won all presidential elections held in the 1960s and 1970s, although the opposition consistently alleged that this was achieved by fraud.

In the Constituent Assembly elections of March 1982 the PCN came third with 18.6 per cent of the vote and 14 seats; it was given four ministries in the subsequent Government of National Unity. It suffered a split in October 1982, when many of its members – including nine of its Assembly representatives – left to form the more right-wing PAISA (see above).

A PCN deputy in the Legislative Assembly, Héctor Flores Larín, was assassinated on March 14, 1984, by the Frente Clara Elizabeth Ramírez (see above). The PCN candidate in the 1984 presidential election, Guerrero, came third in the first (March) round, with 19.3 per cent of the vote, and declared himself neutral in the second round (won by the PDC). With the support of the Arena he was elected president of the Supreme Court with effect from July 1, 1984.

In 1985 the party allied itself with Arena and won 12 seats in the Legislative Assembly (and the Arena 13); the alliance also won control of 105 of the 262 municipal councils. The PCN general secretary backed an unsuccessful attempt by the Arena to have the legislative elections annulled, but the party's executive committee disavowed the move.

Policies. A right-of-centre and strongly anti-communist party, the PCN has received the support of the Church, the military and a large section of the peasantry, and has advocated substantial social and economic reforms.

Partido Demócrata Cristiano (PDC)
Christian Democratic Party

Address. 3a Calle Poniente 836, San Salvador

Leadership. José Napoleón Duarte (President of the Republic; leader); Dr José Antonio Morales Erlich (Mayor of San Salvador; general secretary)

Orientation. Centrist

Founded. 1960

History. The PDC contested the 1961 Constituent Assembly elections in alliance with the centrist Partido Acción Revolucionaria (Revolutionary Action Party) and the right-wing Partido Social Demócrata (Social Democratic Party) as the Partido Unido Democrático (United Democratic Party), but gained no seats. With other opposition parties, it boycotted the 1962 presidential election, but in that of 1967 its candidate came second. In the elections of 1972 and 1979 it was the leading party in the Unión Nacional de la Oposición (UNO – National Opposition Union). Duarte returned from exile to join the government junta established after the overthrow of the Romero regime in 1979, and on Dec. 13, 1980, he was appointed President of El Salvador.

In the Constituent Assembly elections of March 1982 the PDC gained 40.7 per cent of the vote and 24 of the 60 seats; although the right-wing parties had a majority in the Assembly, the PDC took part in the Government of National Unity from May onwards.

The PDC leader came first (with 43.4 per cent) in the March 1984 first-round presidential election, and gained an absolute majority in the May second round. Duarte then formed his own Cabinet, although he lacked a majority in the Assembly until the legislative elections of March 1985, which gave the PDC 33 seats. The party simultaneously won control of 156 of the 262 municipalities. PDC members were elected as president and vice-president of the Legislative Assembly.

Policies. The PDC is a progressive centrist party with mainly middle-class support. It has called for land reform, for the reduction of unemployment and for social justice. Its main aim has been the creation of a legitimate government excluding extremists of left and right.

Publications. *Militante DC*

International affiliations. Christian Democratic International; Christian Democratic Organization of America

Partido de Empresarios, Campesinos y Obreros (ECO)
Businesspeople's, Peasants' and Workers' Party

Leadership. Dr Luis Rolando López (leader)

History. The ECO was in 1984 awaiting official recognition as a political party.

Partido Independiente Democrático (PID)
Independent Democratic Party

Leadership. Eduardo García Tobar (leader)

History. The PID was in early 1985 awaiting official recognition as a political party.

Partido de Liberación Nacional – Ejército Secreto Anticomunista (PLN–ESA)
National Liberation Party – Anti-Communist Secret Army

Leadership. Aquiles Baires (general secretary of the PLN and commander-in-chief of the ESA)

History. The ESA (also known as the Ejército Salvadoreño Anticomunista) was held responsible in 1980 for numerous actions directed particularly against teachers, priests, monks and nuns. On June 29, 1980, it was reported to have bombed the print shop of the University of El Salvador.

The PLN announced its existence and its relationship with the ESA in December 1983. The ESA issued death threats on Oct. 5, 1984, against union leaders, and on Oct. 15 against President Duarte (then engaged in ceasefire negotiations with the guerrillas).

Structure. The PLN is a political movement with extreme right-wing policies; the ESA is a death squad attached to the PLN.

Partido de Orientación Popular (POP)
Popular Orientation Party

Orientation. Very right-wing

Founded. 1981

History. The founder and first leader of the POP, Gen. (retd) José Alberto Medrano, had in 1968 founded the paramilitary Organización Democrática Nacional (Orden – National Democratic Order), which co-operated with the security forces until its dissolution after the October 1979 coup against President Romero (although the name of Orden was later used by death squads). Medrano had also founded the Salvadorean National Intelligence Agency and had been the leader of the Frente Unido Democrático Independiente (FUDI – Independent United Democratic Front), as whose presidential candidate in 1972 he obtained about 10 per cent of the vote. The FUDI was represented in the Legislative Assembly from 1974 to 1976.

In the March 1982 Constituent Assembly elections the POP gained 0.9 per cent of the vote and no seat; in March 1984 its presidential candidate, Guillermo Trujillo, secured only 0.4 per cent of the vote. Medrano was assassinated on March 23, 1985, by unidentified gunmen.

Policies. The POP stands for a "representative democracy" excluding political parties, private property, an end to land reform, the compensation of expropriated landowners and the privatization of the financial sector.

Partido Popular Salvadoreño (PPS)
Salvadorean People's Party

Address. Apartado (01) 425, San Salvador

Telephone. 23-2265

Leadership. Francisco Quiñónes Avila (general secretary)

Orientation. Conservative

Founded. 1966

History. The PPS was founded by right-wing defectors from the PAR (see above) and was joined by some leaders of the PCN (see above). In the 1967 presidential election its candidate came third, and in that of 1972 it won 3 per cent of the vote. In 1974 it gained four seats in the Legislative Assembly, and after 1978 it was the only opposition party represented there.

In March 1982 it gained 3 per cent of the vote and one seat in the Constituent Assembly. In 1984 its general secretary won 1.9 per cent of the vote in the first round of the presidential election. It lost its representation in the legislature as a result of the elections of March 1985.

Policies. The PPS is identified with the commercial and industrial sector.

Partido Revolucionario de los Trabajadores Centroamericanos (PRTC)
Central American Revolutionary Workers' Party

Leadership. Roberto Roca (leader)

Orientation. Left-wing political/guerrilla movement

History. The PRTC, which is also known as the Guerrilleros Urbanos Mardoqueo Cruz (Mardoqueo Cruz Urban Guerrillas) and as the Ligas de Liberación (Liberation Leagues) was responsible for the kidnapping on Sept. 21, 1979, of two businessmen, whom it released on Nov. 7 after their US employers had paid for the publication in US, Central American and European newspapers of a PRTC manifesto. The PRTC has operated since 1980 within the FDR–FMLN (see above). In June 1985 it claimed responsibility for the killing of four US marines and nine bystanders in a San Salvador café.

International affiliations. The PRTC is associated with similarly-named parties in Guatemala and Honduras.

Partido Unionista Centroamericana (PUCA)
Central American Unionist Party

Leadership. Dr Gabriel Pilopa Araújo (president)

Orientation. Supra-nationalist

History. The PUCA was active as a legally-recognized political party in 1985.

Policies. The party favours rapid regional integration and the eventual reunification of the Central American states.

Patria Libre
Free Homeland

Leadership. Hugo Barrera (leader)

Orientation. Very right-wing

Founded. May 1985

History. The founder and leader of this party had in 1984 been the vice-presidential candidate of the Arena (see above), but broke with that party after criticizing the leadership of Roberto d'Aubuisson, the 1984 presidential candidate.

Unidad Popular Democrática (UPD)
Popular Democratic Unity

Leadership. Samuel Maldonado (leader)

Orientation. Centrist trade union federation

Founded. 1980

History. The UPD is a trade union organization – the largest in the country – which has in recent years been active in advocating a ceasefire and peace negotiations between the government and guerrilla forces, in order to facilitate the reconstruction of the national economy. It supported Duarte in the 1984 presidential election.

Structure. The UPD is led by a 10-member executive committee.

Membership. 500,000

International affiliations. The organization reportedly receives substantial funding from the USA.

Unión Democrática Nacional (UDN)
National Democratic Union

Leadership. Mario Aguiñada Carranza (leader)

Orientation. Communist

History. The UDN draws its support from workers, trade unionists, teachers, students and peasants. In 1980 the party joined the CRM (see BPR, above) and later became a founding member of the FDR (see above). In January 1981 its leader went into hiding after an attempt on his life.

Policies. The UDN is a socialist and popular democratic party standing for the modernization of the national economy and extensive socio-political reforms.

Associated organizations. The UDN is in alliance with the PCS (see above). See also FDR–FMLN (above).

Unión de Guerreros Blancos (UGB)
White Warriors' Union

Orientation. Ultra-right death squad

History. This group was responsible for numerous attacks on allegedly left-wing priests and in particular against Jesuits linked to peasant organizations. In revenge for the killing of an industrialist by the FPL in April 1977, the UGB killed a Jesuit priest and in June it threatened to kill any of the 47 Jesuits then in the country who did not leave by July 20. The priests concerned were provided with police guards. The UGB killed other priests in late June and on Aug. 4, 1979, and killed 16 garage mechanics in San Salvador on Aug. 16, 1979.

Unión de Trabajadores del Campo (UTC)

See FECCAS (above).

Guatemala

Capital: Guatemala City   **Population: 8,400,000**

Guatemala gained separate independence in 1838, since when its history has been one of periods of dictatorship and occasional democratic government, interspersed with revolutionary upheavals. A period of reformist rule, 1944–1954, was ended with the overthrow of President Jacobo Arbenz Guzmán by a US-supported invasion and coup. Following the assassination of the coup leader in July 1957, successive right-wing Presidents were elected (usually with allegations of fraud) in 1958, 1966, 1970, 1974, 1978 and 1982, and right-wing military coups occurred in 1963, 1982 and 1983.

On March 7, 1982, presidential and congressional elections in which left-wing parties did not participate were, according to the widely-disputed official results, won by parties of the centre-right and right. On March 23 a coup was staged by military officers close to the very right-wing Movimiento de Liberación Nacional (MLN). The new regime suspended the 1966 Constitution and the existing political parties, and declared the elections null and void. On June 9 Gen. Efraín Ríos Montt was named by the military as President and assumed sole executive and legislative functions.

The political parties, initially favourable to the military regime, gradually came to oppose it, and left-wing guerrilla movements stepped up their activities. On Aug. 8, 1983, after several unsuccessful coup attempts, Ríos Montt was replaced by a Military Commanders' Council led by Brig.-Gen. (now Gen.) Oscar Humberto Mejía Victores. The new President announced the Council's commitment to "democratic and essentially nationalistic" ideas, and its intention "to fight by all means available to eradicate the Marxist–Leninist subversion which threatens our freedom and sovereignty". The regime held elections to a constituent assembly in July 1984, the resulting constitution, and a civilian government, to be in place by the start of 1986; a presidential election, originally proposed for July 1985, was later postponed to Oct. 27 and again to Nov. 3 (and was too late for inclusion in this book). By the closure of nominations at the beginning of August eight presidential candidates, and 15 political parties, had been registered. The country experienced economic difficulties leading to severe price rises in late 1985; consequent riots in September led to the military occupation of the university.

Guerrilla campaign and counter-measures. The country's four principal left-wing guerrilla groups have been active since the 1960s

131

in both rural and urban areas, their strategy including the assassination of government officials, judges and members of the armed forces. In February 1982 they established a unified military command and called for a boycott of the March elections. Their campaign continued after the March 23 coup; they rejected an amnesty and an offer of negotiations made by the Ríos Montt regime, which then declared certain areas of the country to be "zones of exception", and anti-guerrilla operations were intensified with the assistance of 25,000 newly-recruited peasant militiamen.

The US embassy in Guatemala City estimated the number of deaths of guerrillas and security force personnel at 1,168 in 1983 and 428 in 1984, fairly evenly divided between the two sides. The guerrilla campaign continues in 1985, with the emphasis since mid-1983 on attacking economic targets rather than seeking confrontations with the government forces; the authorities, meanwhile, are pursuing a "pacification" strategy based on the peasant militias, now numbering 700,000, fortified villages, rural economic development programmes and amnesty offers.

The leftist guerrilla campaign has given rise to numerous right-wing organizations, some of which appeared to have government support or to work in close association with the security forces. These groups have engaged in attacks on left-wing and centrist party leaders, trade unionists, journalists and lawyers. Their activities, together with those of the guerrillas, have cost tens of thousands of lives in recent years.

Amnesty International stated on Dec. 11, 1976, that since 1966 over 20,000 people, many of them political dissidents, had been killed or had disappeared without trace in Guatemala as a result of action by government or semi-official forces. According to a conservative Guatemalan newspaper there were in the first 10 months of 1980 a total of 3,617 violent deaths, including those of 389 university students, 311 peasant leaders, 326 schoolteachers, 86 university teachers and 12 journalists. A further Amnesty report on Feb. 18, 1981, said that the murders were being carried out by the police and the army and that secret detentions and summary executions had become "part of a clearly defined programme of government" and reflected "a pattern of selective and considered official action". Guatemalan church sources estimated that more than 11,000 people were killed in political violence in 1981. By 1984–85 the level of violence was fairly unchanged at 100–200 deaths per week. Up to 500,000 people have been displaced as a result of the guerrilla war, and many are living as refugees in insecure camps in southern Mexico.

Constitutional background. The suspended Constitution of 1965 established a 66-member unicameral Congress elected by universal and (for literates) compulsory adult suffrage under a system of proportional representation. Executive power rested with a similarity-elected President, assisted by a Vice-President and a Cabinet. The National Constituent Assembly elected in July 1984 had 88 members, 65 representing districts and 23 from national lists.

Legislation enacted in 1983 obliged all political parties to reapply for official recognition. The (communist) PGT was specifically barred from electoral participation because of its involvement in the guerrilla campaign, and other parties were required to obtain at least 4 per cent of the national vote in order to retain legal status.

Recent election results. The presidential election of March 7, 1982 – annulled by the military regime – attracted a turnout of less than 50 per cent. Gen. Angel Aníbal Guevara, the candidate of the conservative FDP coalition, received 38.9 per cent of the valid votes, less than the overall majority required for outright victory; he was, however, endorsed as President by Congress on March 13. Mario Sandóval of the far-right MLN won 28.2 per cent, Alejandro Maldonado of the centrist UNO coalition 22.7 per cent and Gustavo Anzueto of the right-wing CAN 10.2 per cent. In the simultaneous congressional election, the 66 seats were distributed as follows: FDP 33, MLN 21, CAN 3, UNO 2, others 7. According to initial figures, the National Constituent Assembly election on July 1, 1984, attracted a turnout of 1,855,619 of the 3,500,000 or so eligible voters; the votes (and the 88 seats) were distributed as follows: MLN–CAN coalition 245,514 votes (23 seats), UCN 269,372 (21), PDGG 318,300 (20), PR 142,565 (10), PNR 129,664 (5), PID 102,829 (5), 61,069 (1), FUN 45,191 (1), OCAS 39,795 (1); others 147,244 (1); blank and invalid ballots totalled 354,076.

Alianza Democrática (AD)
Democratic Alliance
Leadership. Leopoldo Urrutia (leader)
Orientation. Centrist
Founded. 1983
History. This movement, whose leader formerly belonged to the PR (see below), contested the 1984 constituent assembly elections without success.

Asociación Nacional Campesina (ANC)
See Frente Popular (below).

Banda de los Buitres
Band of the Vultures
Orientation. Right-wing guerrilla group
History. This group was active in the late 1970s and early '80s.

Banda de los Halcones
Band of the Hawks
Orientation. Right-wing guerrilla group
History. This group was active in the late 1970s and early '80s.

Banda del Rey
The King's Band
Orientation. Right-wing guerrilla group

History. This group was active in the late 1970s.

Central Auténtica Nacionalista (CAN)
Authentic Nationalist Confederation

Leadership. Gen. (retd) Carlos Manuel Araña Osorio (leader)

Orientation. Right-wing

Founded. 1980

History. The CAN was set up as the successor to the Central Arañista Organizado (CAO – Organized Arañist Confederation), and, like the CAO, consisted of supporters of Araña, who served as President in 1970–74 as the leader of the MLN (see below) in the 1978 elections The CAO had joined the PID and the PR (see below) in the successful centre-right alliance.

In March 1982 the CAN's presidential candidate, Gustavo Anzueto Vielman, was accorded 99,047 votes, or 10.2 per cent, and the party won three seats in Congress; it initially supported the March coup, but in September announced its opposition to the proposed Council of State and called for "free and clean" elections. For the July 1984 consituent assembly elections it allied with the MLN, jointly winning 23 seats to form the largest bloc (which the PID – see below – later joined).

Central Nacional de Trabajadores (CNT)
National Confederation of Workers

Leadership. Julio Celso de León (general secretary)

Orientation. Trade union organization

Founded. 1972

History. The CNT was established as a national trade union body to represent urban and rural employees in the public and private sectors. Due to repressive activities by government and ultra-right forces, the CNT was forced to go underground in 1980.

Membership. 24,000

Associated organizations. The CNT is close to the FAR guerrilla group (see below).

Los Centuriones
The Centurions

Orientation. Right-wing guerrilla group

History. This group was active in the late 1970s and early '80s.

Comando Anticomunista del Sur (CADS)
Southern Anti-Communist Commando

Orientation. Right-wing death squad

History. This group was active from May 1980.

Comando de las Fuerzas Populares
Commando of Popular Forces

Orientation. Left-wing guerrilla group

Founded. Dec. 9, 1981

History. This group issued a statement on its formation announcing that it was "ready for armed action against the government". The Comando is not represented in the main guerrilla coalition, the RUOG-URNG (see below).

Comandos Guerrilleros Guatemaltecos en Formación (CGGF)
Guatemalan Guerrilla Commandos in Formation

Orientation. Guerrilla group

Founded. 1984

History. This previously-unknown group claimed responsibility for the kidnapping in October 1984 of a student.

Comité para Derechos Humanos en Guatemala (CDHG)
Guatemala Committee for Human Rights

Address. Based in Mexico City

Leadership. Luis Alberto Padilla (president); Pedro Juárez (administrator)

Orientation. Human rights concerns

History. This organization, which for the safety of its members is obliged to operate from exile, filed most of the 809 habeas corpus suits received by the Guatemalan Supreme Court in January–October 1984 in respect of "disappeared" persons.

International affiliations. The committee is supported and supplemented in its work by several solidarity and human rights groups in Europe and North America.

Comité Guatemalteca de Unidad Patriótica (CGUP)
Guatemalan Committee of Patriotic Unity

Leadership. Luis Cardoza y Aragón (head of co-ordinating committee)

Orientation. Revolutionary broad front

Founded. Feb. 16, 1982

History. The formation of the CGUP, a coalition of opposition groups, was announced by Guatemalan exile leaders of various political affiliations in a statement issued simultaneously in Mexico, Panama and France. The 26 leaders who signed the founding document established an eight-member co-ordinating committee headed by Cardozo, a veteran politician who had been a member of the Arbenz government overthrown in 1954; other members of the committee included Guillermo Toriello Garrido of the CUC (see above), formerly Arbenz's Foreign Minister, and Carlos Gallardo of the PSD (see below).

Policies. The CGUP endorsed the basic programme of the URNG guerrilla coalition (see below), stating that popular revolutionary war was the only road left open, but that it had no direct links with the guerrillas. The CGUP also denounced the March 1982 elections as a "farce", saying that "electoral fraud, corruption, persecution and the assassination of democratic leaders and of hundreds of party members" had been "the permanent practices of the regime". It declared that the revolution was aimed at "constructing a new society responding to the interests and aspirations of the people, confronting the bloodiest dictatorship which Latin America has ever known".

Membership. The founding members of the CGUP were the FDCR and the FP-31 (see below); it also had the support of several members of the FUR (see below).

Comité de Unidad Campesina (CUC)
Peasant Unity Committee

Orientation. Peasant land rights group

History. The CUC is active in support of peasant struggles mainly in the western Departments.

Policies. The group is socialist, *indigenista* and influenced by liberation theology.

Associated organizations. The CUC forms part of the FP-31 (see below) and has links with the EGP (see below) and with Chuch-based radical groups. One of its members was prominent in the foundation of the CGUP (see above).

Coordinadora Democrática Guatemalteca
Guatemalan Democratic Co-ordinating Board

Orientation. Centre-left

Founded. Feb. 21, 1984

History. This alliance of centrist and leftist parties was formed in order to press for the fair and proper conduct of the July 1984 constituent assembly elections. It may now be defunct.

Policies. The CDG demanded that the government and armed forces remain impartial in the election, and sought various electoral reforms designed to reduce the likelihood of fraud. It denounced the "climate of violence" and called for the cessation of paramilitary activities.

Membership. The member parties included the PDCG, the UCN, the PSC, the FCD and eight smaller parties.

Coordinadora Democrática Nacional (CDN)
National Democratic Co-ordinating Board

History. The CDN, which succeeded the Coordinadora Nacional Guevarista (and which was at first known as the Nueva Coordinadora Nacional Democrática), contested the 1984 constituent assembly elections in coalition with the FDP, but failed to win any seats.

Coordinadora Nacional Guevarista

See Coordinadora Democrática Nacional (above).

Cristianos para el Respeto a la Vida
Christians for Respect for Life

History. Members of this group kidnapped a nephew of Gen. Ríos Montt on Oct. 13, 1982, but he was freed by security forces six weeks later.

Ejército Guerrillero de los Pobres (EGP)
Guerrilla Army of the Poor

Leadership. Rolando Morán (commander)

Orientation. Left-wing guerrilla movement

Founded. 1972

History. The EGP greatly extended its activities in 1976, with the result that by the end of the year it controlled certain areas in the northern mountain region. While the movement was active mainly among the country's landless peasants, it has also been involved in incidents in the capital city.

On Nov. 6, 1976, the EGP bombed a hotel in the capital in retaliation for the killing of two of its members by the hotel owner's bodyguard. In early 1977 the group extended its activities in southern Guatemala. On Dec. 31 it kidnapped a former minister, but released him on Jan. 30, 1978, in return for a cash ransom, the publication in the press of a manifesto and safe conduct out of the country for an EGP member who had sought refuge in the Costa Rican embassy. Following the deaths of at least 43 people on May 29, in a confrontation between the army and peasants at Panzós, President Laugerud accused the EGP and both Catholic and Protestant clergy of inciting peasant invasions of private estates. After a march in protest at the killings, an EGP bomb killed 14 military policemen in Guatemala City on June 14.

A group of 27 Indian peasants from the department of Él Quiché, which had been under virtual military occupation since 1975 because of the activities of the EGP and the ORPA (see below), occupied the Spanish embassy in Guatemala City on Jan. 31, 1980. When police stormed the building, against the express wishes of the ambassador, a petrol bomb was thrown and 39 people burnt to death, the only survivors being the ambassador and a peasant, Yuxa Shona, who was later killed by a death squad (see Frente Yuxa Shona, below). Spain immediately broke off diplomatic relations with Guatemala, and did not restore them until Sept. 22, 1984, when Guatemala formally apologized for the forced entry and agreed to accept the "judicial consequences" thereof.

On Sept. 5, 1980, Elias Barahona, press secretary at the Ministry of the Interior, announced that he was a member of the EGP and had infiltrated the government four years earlier; he alleged that the ESA and EM death squads (see below) were controlled directly by the President, the Minister of the Interior and several generals.

The EGP has considerable influence among the Indian population and has repeatedly occupied villages temporarily, partly to carry out recruitment. Large numbers of people have been killed in punitive raids by the army. By June 1981 the EGP claimed to have extended their "people's war" to 19 of Guatemala's 22 departments and to be concentrating on the Verpaz oil region near the Mexican border in the north-west.

In February 1982 the EGP joined the unified guerrilla command, the URNG. In September 1982 four members of the EGP became the first Guatemalans to be executed judicially, as opposed to being killed by death squads, during the present conflict. The group carried out attacks in El Quiché in early 1984. Ten of its members were reported to have accepted an amnesty and given themselves up in El Petén in May. On Sept. 7–8 it was involved in clashes in which it claimed to have killed 23 army troops for the loss of two of its own fighters, in Huehuetenango and El Quiché. At the end of 1984 the group claimed to have carried out 181 operations, inflicting losses on the army of 686 dead and 211 wounded.

Policies. The EGP is socialist, *indigenista* and influenced by liberation theology.

Structure. The two main bodies of the EGP military force in 1985 are known as the Frente Ho Chi Minh, centred on El Quiché, and the Frente Ernesto Che Guevara, in Huehuetenango. It is organizing a third front, the Frente Augusto César Sandino, also in El Quiché.

Membership. The EGP has an armed force of about 4,000, and an additional 12,000 unarmed members.

Publications. *Informador Guerrillero*, official organ

Associated organizations. The EGP is a member of the RUOG-UNRG coalition (see below). It has links with the CUC (see above), with the FP-31 (see below) and with Church-based radical groups.

Ejército Secreto Anticomunista (ESA)
Anti-Communist Secret Army

Orientation. Ultra-right death squad

137

Founded. 1976

History. This organization has been responsible for the killing of numerous politicans, officials, trade unionists, student leaders and others whose names appeared on frequently published "death lists". It is thought to be linked with the right-wing MLN (see below), led by Mario Sandóval Alarcón.

The ESA was thought to be involved in the killing of the president of the university students' association on Oct. 20, 1978, and that of Manuel Colom Argueta, the country's leading opposition figure (and former mayor of the capital, 1970–74) on March 22, 1979. In a statement issued in January 1980, Jesuits said that the ESA had carried out 3,252 murders "with absolute impunity" between January and October 1979; there followed death threats from the ESA against the 52 Jesuit priests working in Guatemala.

International affiliations. A right-wing group of the same name operates in El Salvador.

Escuadrón de la Muerte (EM)
Death Squad

Orientation. Ultra-right death squad

History. The EM and other death squads, notably the ESA (see above), have killed thousands of alleged left-wing activists or sympathizers; in 1980 alone, several hundred such deaths were occurring every month.

Policies. The EM has specialized in the assassination of labour movement and peasant leaders.

Frente Anticomunista del Nororiente (FANO)
Anti-Communist Front of the North-East

Orientation. Right-wing death squad

History. This group was active from May 8, 1980.

Frente Cívico Democrático (FCD)
Civic Democratic Front

Leadership. Danilo Barillas, Jorge González del Valle (leaders)

Orientation. Centrist opposition

History. The FCD was formed as a splinter group of the PDCG, one of its founders – González – having previously been president of the national bank. It obtained legal status in 1984 and contested the July 1984 constituent assembly elections without success; it joined an electoral alliance with the PDCG (see below) in January 1985.

Frente Demócrata Guatemalteco
Guatemalan Democratic Front

Leadership. Clemente Marroquín Rojas (leader)

Orientation. Centrist opposition

History. This body was active in the early 1980s.

Frente Democrático Popular (FDP)
Popular Democratic Front

Orientation. Centrist

History. The FDP coalition (not to be confused with the other FDP – see below) was formed to present a centrist candidate in the March 1982 presidential and congressional elections; it obtained the largest number of votes, but not an absolute majority, for its presidential candidate, and 33 of the 66 seats in Congress. A military coup on March 23 prevented the installation of the President-elect and dissolved the Congress. The member parties subsequently operated independently of the FDP.

Membership. The constituent parties of the Front were the FUN, the PID and the PR (see below).

Frente Democrático contra la Represión (FDCR)
Democratic Front against Repression

Leadership. Rafael García (leader)

Orientation. Human rights concerns

Founded. March 1979

History. The FDCR was formed as an alliance of parties and organizations, initially 72 in number, in order to denounce at national and international level all actions of repression committed in Guatemala against "popular and democratic" sectors, and to provide aid to the widows and orphans of victims of such actions.

Associated organizations. The FDCR is regarded as close to the ORPA (see below); it is a member of the CGUP coalition (see above).

Frente Nacional de Unidad (Frenu)

See PDCG (below).

Frente de Participación Popular

See PDCG (below).

Frente Popular
Popular Front

Leadership. Angel Flores (general secretary)

Orientation. Centre-left

Founded. Sept. 26, 1984

History. This broad front of parties and civic groups was formed as an electoral alliance for the presidential poll scheduled for July 1985.

Membership. The founding members of the front were the Asociación Nacional de Campesinos (ANC – National Peasant Association), the Comité de Mejoramiento Urbano de Guatemala (Guatemalan Urban Improvement Committee), the Frente de Trabajadores (Workers' Front), the FUR (see below), the FN (see below), the M-20-X (see below), the MHID (see below), the Movimiento Maya Guatemalteco (Guatemalan Maya [Indian] Movement), the PSN (see below), and the Unión Popular (see below).

Frente Popular 31 de Enero (FP-31)
Popular Front of January 31

Orientation. Left-wing direct action group

Founded. January 1981

History. The FP-31, named after the date of the 1980 attack on the Spanish embassy (see EGP, below), was formed as a coalition of labour, peasant, student and other groups. A dozen members of the group occupied the Brazilian embassy in Guatemala City on May 12, 1982, in order to draw attention to the killings by the security forces in rural areas; 10 hostages, including the ambassador, were released unharmed in return for safe conduct out of the country for the group.

Membership. The member organizations are the Federación de

Trabajadores de Guatemala (FRG – Guatemalan Workers' Federation), the CUC (see above), the Frente Revolucionario Estudiantil Rubén García (Rubén García Revolutionary Student Front), the Nucleos Obreros Revolucionarios Felipe Antonio García (Felipe Antonio García Revolutionary Workers' Nuclei), and two other groups, one of revolutionary Christians and the other of peasant squatters.

Associated organizations. It is a member of the CGUP coalition (see above).

Frente Tecum Uman
Tecum Uman Front

Orientation. *Indigenista* guerrilla group

Founded. 1982

History. The first major action by this group was the ambushing on Aug. 17, 1982, of government troops in Chimaltenango department, causing 40 casualties.

Frente de Trabajadores

See Frente Popular (above).

Frente de Unidad Nacional (FUN)
National Unity Front

Leadership. Gabriel Girón Ortiz, Col. Enrique Peralta Azurdia (leaders)

Orientation. Right-wing

Founded. 1977

History. Peralta joined the FUN after obtaining second place in the 1978 presidential election as the candidate of the MLN. In March 1982 the FUN was part of the FDP alliance (see above) which obtained the largest share of votes in the presidential and congressional elections.

It contested the July 1984 constituent assembly elections in its own right, winning one seat, but its representative – Santos Hernández – was almost expelled from the assembly after it transpired in August that he was illiterate and therefore technically ineligible for election. After MLN representatives voted in favour of permitting him to remain, he defected to that party in September, but was assassinated on Oct. 26.

Policies. The FUN is seen as representing business interests.

Frente Unido de la Revolución (FUR)
United Revolutionary Front

Leadership. Guillermo Colom Argueta, Andrino Diéguez, Angel Lee Duarte (leaders); César Augusto Toledo Peñate (general secretary)

Orientation. Social democratic

Founded. 1977

History. The FUR succeeded the Unión Revolucionaria Democrática (URD – Revolutionary Democratic Union), formed as a splinter group of the PR (see below) and the Frente Nacional Opositora (see PDCG, below). It was involved in the formation in early 1979 of the FDCR (see above).

The former leader of the URD, Alberto Fuentes Mohr (a former cabinet minister), was assassinated in January 1979 by the ESA (see above), and in March of that year Manuel Colom Argueta, the leader of the FUR (which had just obtained legal recognition) was similarly murdered. The leadership of the FUR suffered many such losses over the next three years, and in 1982 it declined for that reason to take part in the presidential and congressional elections. On the other hand, the FUR was the only opposition party prepared to participate in the Council of State installed by the Ríos Montt regime on Sept. 14, 1982.

In 1984 the party contested the constituent assembly elections, but failed to secure representation.

Associated organizations. Members of the FUR were involved in the formation of the pro-guerrilla CGUP group (see above). The FUR joined the Frente Popular (see above) in September 1984, and allied itself in January 1985 with the Fuerza Nueva, the PSD and the URD (see below).

Frente Voluntario de Defensa (FVD)
Voluntary Defensive Front

Orientation. Left-wing guerrilla group

History. This small group was first active in mid-1980.

Frente Yuxa Shona
Yuxa Shona Front

Orientation. Left-wing guerrilla group

Founded. March 1980

History. This group was named after a survivor of the siege at the Spanish embassy in January 1980 (see EGP, above), who was kidnapped from hospital and killed by a right-wing death squad on Feb. 1.

Associated organizations. The group has been variously reported as in sympathy with the EGP, the FAR and the ORPA (see below).

Fuerza Democrática Popular (FDP)
Popular Democratic Force

History. This group unsuccessfully contested the 1984 constituent assembly elections in alliance with the CDN (see above).

Fuerza Nueva (FN)
New Force

Leadership. Carlos Rafael Soto (leader)

Orientation. Social democratic

Founded. 1984

History. The first president of the FN, Jorge Gálves Loaica, was kidnapped, tortured and killed by a right-wing death squad in February 1984; he had been carrying FN registration lists naming some 1,200 supporters. Fuerza Nueva joined the Frente Popular (see above) in September 1984 and entered into an alliance with three other parties – the FUR (see above), the PSD and the URD (see below) – in January 1985.

Fuerza Popular Organizada
Organized Popular Force

History. This group was reportedly active in 1984.

Fuerzas de Acción Armada (FADA)
Armed Action Forces

Orientation. Guerrilla group

History. This group was responsible for the killing on Jan. 25, 1979, of Alberto Fuentes Mohr, a former Foreign Minister (in 1966–70) and a supporter of the centre-left Frenu alliance.

Fuerzas Armadas Rebeldes (FAR)
Rebel Armed Forces

Leadership. Nicolás Sis (commander); Pablo Monsanto

Orientation. Left-wing guerrilla group

Founded. December 1962

History. The FAR was formed in succession to the Movimiento Revolucionario 13 de Noviembre (MR-13 – November 13 Revolutionary Movement), which had arisen out of a rebellion by a group of officers on Nov. 13, 1960, and was led by Luis Turcios Lima (who died in 1966), Marco Antonio Yon Sosa ("El Chino", who was killed in a clash with troops in May 1970) and Luis Trejo Esquivel. On its formation the FAR was joined by part of the PGT (see below), forming the party's military commission; from 1970 the FAR went into decline but in 1972 it was reorganized with the aim of constituting a mass party, and later it reverted to armed struggle. By 1980 it operated in northern areas and also near Lake Izabál in eastern Guatemala; it is currently strongest in the capital city and in the departments of El Petén and Chimaltenango. The group kidnapped the sister of the then President Ríos Montt in June 1983, and the sister of President Mejía in September, but freed both after the publication of its manifesto in various newspapers in October. In January 1984 the FAR began an offensive in El Petén; on Sept. 13 it destroyed an important bridge in that department.

Associated organizations. The FAR joined the unified guerrilla command, the UNRG (see below), in February 1982. It is close to the clandestine CNC (see above) and to another labour federation, the Comité Nacional de Unidad Sindical Guatemalteca (CONUS – National Committee for Trade Union Unity in Guatemala).

Grupo de Apoyo Mutuo para Familiares de Desaparecidos
Mutual Support Group for the Families of Disappeared Persons

Leadership. Nineth de García (spokesperson)

Orientation. Human rights concerns

Founded. 1984

History. This grouping represents the relatives of persons abducted by gunmen or otherwise "disappeared" as a result of the security situation. It denounces individual cases of abduction, pursues such legal remedies as are available, and seeks all possible publicity for the issue. In mid-1985 it was regarded as the country's leading human rights organization. Two of its leaders, Héctor Rolando Gómez and Maria Goydo de Cuevas, were assassinated by a death squad in April 1985 (the latter together with her brother and infant son) after President Mejía denounced it as a "subversive organization". Another member of the group was similarly killed in August.

Membership. About 620 families (early 1985)

Juventud Organizada del Pueblo en Armas (JOPA)
Organized Youth of the People at Arms

Orientation. Right-wing death squad

History. This group, the name of which parodies that of the left-wing ORPA (see below), was established in March 1980.

Libertad 15 de Septiembre
September 15 Freedom

Orientation. Right-wing guerrilla group

History. This group was active in the early 1980s.

La Mano Blanca
The White Hand

Orientation. Right-wing death squad

Founded. 1970

History. This group has been active since 1970, when its headquarters were said to be in the police headquarters in Guatemala City. On April 4, 1970, it killed César Montenegro Paniagua, a communist leader whom it suspected of involvement in the abduction and killing by the FAR guerrilla group (see above) of the West German ambassador a week earlier. The group was one of two suspected of the murder of the opposition leader Manuel Colom Argueta on March 22, 1979, the other being the ESA (see above).

The group was reportedly linked to Gen. Carlos Manuel Araña Osorio, President in 1970–74 and a leading member of the MLN (see below).

Milicias Obreras Guatemaltecas (MOG)
Guatemalan Workers' Militias

Orientation. Right-wing guerrilla group

Founded. March 1978

History. This group was active in the early 1980s.

Movimiento Anticomunista Organizado (MANO)
Organized Anti-Communist Movement

Orientation. Right-wing guerrilla group

History. This group was active in the early 1980s.

Movimiento Emergente de Concordia (MEC)
Emerging Movement for Harmony

Leadership. Col. (retd) Francisco Luis Gordillo Martínez (leader); Darío Chávez, Arturo Ramírez

Orientation. Centre-right

Founded. 1983

History. The MEC leader had been a member of the junta formed in March 1982; his party contested the constituent assembly elections of July 1984, but failed to win representation.

Movimiento Humanista de Integración Demócrata (MHID)
Humanist Movement for Democratic Integration

Orientation. Centrist

History. This movement joined the Frente Popular (see above) in September 1984.

Movimiento de Liberación Nacional (MLN)
National Liberation Movement

Address. 5a Calle 1-20, Zona 1, Guatemala City

Leadership. Mario Sandóval Alarcón (leader)

Orientation. Far right-wing

Founded. 1960

History. The MLN had its origins in the US-backed Movimiento de Liberación which overthrew the country's left-wing government in 1954. In

1963, under the leadership of Col. Peralta (see FUN, above), it mounted a military coup against the elected government, but its presidential candidate came third in the election of March 1966. In 1970 its leader, Col. Carlos Araña Osorio (see CAN, above), was elected President and was confirmed in office by a majority in Congress. For the 1974 elections the MLN concluded an alliance with the PID (see below), the MLN's Gen. Kjell Lagerud, being elected and pursuing less right-wing policies than his party usually advocated; Sandóval was his Vice-President.

In 1978 and 1982 the MLN came second in the presidential elections, in 1982 winning 275,487 votes (28.2 per cent) for Sandóval and simultaneously obtaining 21 of the 66 Congress seats. Although the MLN strongly supported the subsequent military coup, a faction within it was suspected in August 1982 of plotting a coup against the Ríos Montt regime. A leading member of the party, Leonel Sisniega, went into exile and in 1983 formed the PUA (see below), which recruited some members of the MLN.

On Sept. 4, 1982, the MLN joined three other parties in denouncing the proposed Council of State and calling for elections. Early in 1983 the party threatened "holy war" against any attempt by Ríos Montt to form a Protestant political party to contest the promised elections, and in August it supported the Mejía coup against Ríos Montt.

For the July 1984 constituent assembly elections the MLN formed an alliance with the CAN (see above), together winning 23 of the 88 seats; the PID (see below) subsequently added its five seats to the MLN-CAN bloc.

Policies. The MLN is Catholic, extremely right-wing and anti-communist.

Structure. Apart from the party organization, the MLN has a paramilitary force the strength of which was estimated in 1983 at 5,000 men.

Membership. 95,000

Movimiento Revolucionario del Pueblo – Ixim (MRP)
People's Revolutionary Movement – Food [Mayan word]

Orientation. Left-wing *indigenista* guerrilla group

Founded. 1982

History. This movement announced its formation with the setting off of low-powered "propaganda bombs" to distribute leaflets in the capital city in August 1982. Members of the MRP kidnapped the daughter of President Roberto Suazo of Honduras on Dec. 14, 1982, but later released her in return for the publication of a manifesto in Guatemalan, Mexican and Central American newspapers.

Movimiento 20 de Octubre (M-20-X)
October 20 Movement

History. This group was a founding member of the Frente Popular (see above) in late 1984.

Nueva Coordinadora Nacional Democrática

See CDN (above).

Nueva Derecha
New Right

Orientation. Far right-wing

History. This group, active in 1984–85, represents right-wing business interests and is very close to the MLN; it has endorsed the MLN leader, Mario Sandóval, in the 1985 presidential election.

Nueva Organización Antiterrorista (NOA)
New Anti-Terrorist Organization
Orientation. Right-wing guerrilla group

History. This group was active from 1982.

Ojo por Ojo
An Eye for an Eye
Orientation. Right-wing death squad

History. This is one of the older right-wing guerrilla groups, having been active in the early 1970s.

Orden de la Muerte
Order of Death
Orientation. Right-wing death squad

History. This organization was active in the early 1980s.

Organización Campesina de Acción Social (OCAS)
Peasant Organization for Social Action
Orientation. *Indigenista*

History. This almost exclusively Indian party won a single seat in the July 1984 constituent assembly elections.

Organización Cero
Zero Organization
Orientation. Right-wing death squad

History. This organization was active in the early 1980s.

Organización Revolucionaria del Pueblo en Armas (ORPA)
Revolutionary Organization of the People at Arms
Leadership. Rodrigo Ilom (known as Gaspar Ilom; commander); Lucrecia Matzar

Orientation. Left-wing guerrilla group

Founded. September 1979

History. The ORPA (the name is sometimes rendered as Organización del Pueblo en Armas) was formed after a split in the FAR, as a political and military movement to be built up secretly, at first in rural areas, mainly among the indigenous communities, and later among all sections of the people. In 1980 it was active mainly in western and central departments but also in the capital and in some southern areas. In September 1980 it moved into tourist-frequented areas on the shores of Lake Atitlán, west of the capital, leading to an army counterinsurgency campaign in that region. In July 1981 security forces attacked ORPA bases in the capital.

By mid-1984 the ORPA was reckoned the most effective of the four main guerrilla groups, and was particularly active in Quetzaltenango and San Marcos. It claimed to have inflicted 122 casualties on the army after 10 days of fighting in San Marcos in August.

Policies. The ORPA is anti-racist and stands for the development of the indigenous people's cultures.

Associated organizations. The ORPA has co-operated closely with the guerrilla forces of the PGT (see below); it is linked to the FDCR (see above) and in February 1982 it joined the main guerrilla coalition, the RUOG-URNG (see below).

Pantinamit

Leadership. Fernando Tezahuic Tohín (leader)

Orientation. *Indigenista* (i.e. represents the interests of the Indian peasantry)

Founded. 1977

History. This organization was active in the early 1980s.

Partido de Cooperación Democrática Nacional (PCDN)

National Democratic Co-operation Party

Leadership. Acisclo Valladares Molina (leader)

Orientation. Right-wing

History. The leader of the PCDN was a prominent member of the MLN (see above) until the coup which ousted Gen. Ríos Montt. The party contested the 1984 constituent assembly elections without success. Its candidate in the 1985 presidential election was announced as Jorge Serrano Elías, the first president of the Council of State created in 1982.

Policies. The PCDN is very much identified with the Protestant fundamentalism of the Ríos Montt regime.

Partido Democracia Cristiana Guatemalteca (PDCG)

Christian Democratic Party of Guatemala

Address. The PDCG was forced to close its head office (8 Avenida 14–53, Zona 1, Guatemala City) in 1980.

Leadership. Mario Vinicio Cerezo Arévalo (general secretary)

Orientation. Christian democratic

Founded. July 1968

History. In the presidential election of 1970 the PDCG candidate came third; in 1974 it took part in the Frente Nacional Opositora (National Opposition Front), whose candidate came second; in 1978 it joined the Partido Revolucionario Auténtico (Authentic Revolutionary Party) and the Frente de Participación Popular (Popular Participation Front) in the Frente Nacional de Unidad (Frenu – National Unity Front), whose candidate came third. In 1980 the party suffered attacks by right-wing paramilitaries, and after the killing in June of two PDCG activists all party offices were closed. In the 1982 elections it was part of the UNO alliance (see below), whose candidate came third. At the same time the UNO gained three seats in Congress.

Later the PDCG broadly supported the Ríos Montt regime, while expressing concern that its measures "might lead to polarization and the creation of a climate of fear". It was one of four parties which on Sept. 4, 1982, condemned the new Council of State as "a mask" for the regime, and called for "free and clean" elections.

Prior to the July 1984 constituent assembly elections the PDCG formed a Democratic Co-ordinating Board with 11 other centre-left parties in order to press for reform of the electoral law and impartiality on the part of the media. The party secured 20 of the 88 seats in the elections.

There is a right-wing faction of the party led by a lawyer, Dr Francisco Villagrán Kramer, who was Vice-President of Guatemala in 1979–80.

Policies. The PDCG is liberal and reformist, left-of-centre in Christian democratic terms.

Membership. 89,000

International affiliations. The party is a member of the Christian

Democratic International and of the Christian Democratic Organization of America.

Partido Guatemalteco del Trabajo (PGT)
Guatemalan Party of Labour

Leadership.   Carlos González (general secretary); Mario Sánchez

Orientation.   Communist guerrilla group

Founded.   September 1949, as Partido Comunista de Guatemala (PCG – Communist Party of Guatemala)

History.   The party was founded at a clandestine congress involving members of a left-wing coalition, the Vanguardia Democrática (Democratic Vanguard). It was one of the first and best-organized communist parties in Central America. In 1954 the party was outlawed; from then on it worked underground, and from 1961 it conducted armed struggle. At its second congress, in December 1962, it adopted its present name.

In 1969 the party adopted a new programme aimed at agrarian, anti-imperialist and socialist revolution. In 1972–74, the entire central committee of the PGT was killed, either judicially or by ultra-right death squads. The party elected a new leadership which adopted a non-military strategy, leading to a split in the membership; most of the pacifist tendency went into exile or were killed, while a majority of members reverted to the armed struggle and became involved in the FAR (see above).

By 1980 PGT guerrillas were active in Guatemala City and areas to the south and west of it. The party is currently divided into three factions: the PGT – Camarilla, the PGT – Comisión Nuclear (PGT-CN – Commission of the Nucleus) and the PGT – Núcleo de Conducción y Dirección (PGT-NCD – Nucleus of Direction and Leadership). The Camarilla faction became active in the guerrilla struggle in 1981.

In October 1983 the PGT secured the publication of a manifesto in various North and Central American countries in return for the release of a conservative newspaper executive whom it had kidnapped earlier in the month.

Associated organizations.   The guerrilla forces of the PGT are represented in the main guerrilla coalition, the RUOG-URNG (see below).

International affiliations.   The PGT is recognized by the Soviet Communist Party and its allied parties.

Partido Institucional Democrático (PID)
Institutional Democratic Party

Address.   2a Calle 10-73, Zona 1, Guatemala City

Leadership.   Oscar Humberto Rivas García (leader); Jorge Lamport Rodil, Donaldo Alvarez Ruiz

Orientation.   Centre-right

Founded.   1965

History.   In the presidential election of 1966 the PID candidate came second. In the 1970 and 1974 elections it was in alliance with the MLN (see above) but in those of 1978 it co-operated with the PR (see below). In 1982 it was part of the victorious FDP alliance (see above).

The PID contested the 1984 constituent assembly elections, winning five seats and forming an alliance with the right-wing MLN-CAN coalition. In late September 1984 the PID's vice-president, Ramiro Quijada Fernández, was assassinated.

Policies. The PID has opposed the making of any concessions to the left-wing guerrilla movements.

Membership. 60,000

Partido Nacionalista Renovador (PNR)
Nationalist Renewal Party

Leadership. Alejandro Maldonado Aguirre (leader); Mario Castrejón (general secretary)

Orientation. Centre-right

History. The PNR gained official recognition as a political party in August 1979. Its leader, a former MLN member, contested the 1982 presidential election as the candidate of the UNO coalition (see below), coming third. The party joined three other parties on Sept. 4, 1982, in condemning the Ríos Montt regime's proposal for a Council of State, and in calling for "free and clean" elections.

In July 1984 the PNR contested the constituent assembly elections, winning five of the 88 seats; its contingent decided in July to sit with the 10 representatives of the PR (see below).

Membership. 72,000

Partido Petenero
El Petén Party

Orientation. Regionalist

Founded. 1983

Policies. The party operates in and represents the interests of El Petén, which with 113,000 inhabitants is the second-smallest of the 22 departments.

Partido Populista
Populist Party

History. This party was active in the early 1980s.

Partido Revolucionario (PR)
Revolutionary Party

Address. 14a Avenida 1-42, Zona 6, Guatemala City

Leadership. Jorge García Granados (leader)

Orientation. Democratic

Founded. 1957

History. The PR came to power in March 1966, winning 30 of the 55 seats in congress. In 1970, however, it came second to the MLN (see above). After a left-wing breakaway group formed the URD (see FUR, above), the mainstream PR contested the 1974 elections in alliance with the centrist FDG (see above), but the joint candidate came third. In 1978 most of the PR allied with the CAO and the PID (see above) to present a joint, successful, presidential candidate, but a radical faction – the Partido Revolucionario Auténtico (Authentic Revolutionary Party) – supported the Frenu candidate (see PDCG, above).

In 1982 the PR joined the FDP alliance (see above), which was accorded the largest number of votes in the March presidential and congressional elections but was prevented by a coup from forming a government. The PR contested the 1984 elections in its own right, winning 10 seats in the constituent assembly and from July forming an alliance with the PNR.

148

Policies. The PR advocates land reform, administrative reform and accelerated national development.

Membership. 100,000

Partido Revolucionario Auténtico

See PDCG and PR (above).

Partido Revolucionario de los Trabajadores Centroamericanos (PRTC)
Central American Revolutionary Workers' Party

Orientation. Trotskyist

History. This group was active in 1984.

International affiliations. The PRTC is linked with similarly-named parties operating in El Salvador and Honduras.

Partido Social Cristiano (PSC)
Social Christian Party

History. This group sought legal recognition for the first time in 1984.

Partido Social Nacionalista (PSN)
Nationalist Social Party

Orientation. Centre-left

History. The PSN was a founding member of the Frente Popular (see above) in September 1984.

Partido Socialista
Socialist Party

Orientation. Socialist

Founded. 1980

History. This party was active in 1984.

Partido Socialista Democrático de Guatemala (PSD)
Democratic Socialist Party of Guatemala

Address. 12 Calle 10-37, Zona 1, Guatemala City; the party has until recently been based in exile in San José, Costa Rica

Leadership. Carlos Gallardo Flores (leader); Mario Solorzano (general secretary); Enrique de León (international secretary); Arnoldo Rodas

Orientation. Social democratic

History. The PSD lost many of its leading members to right-wing death squads in the late 1970s and early 1980s, especially in 1979, it subsequently went underground. Its leader became in February 1982 one of eight members of the co-ordinating committee of the CGUP (see above). The party did not take part in the 1984 elections and entered into an alliance with three other parties in January 1985. Its leaders returned from exile in January and February.

Associated organizations. The parties with which the PSD has allied itself are the FUR and Fuerza Nueva (see above) and the URD (see below). The party supports the guerrilla campaign through the RUOG-UNRG (see below) and the CGUP (see above).

International affiliations. The PSD is a full member of the Socialist International.

Partido de Unificación Anticomunista (PUA)
Anti-Communist Unity Party

Leadership.   Leonel Sisniega Otero (leader)

Orientation.   Far right-wing

Founded.   1983

History.   The founder and leader of the party was previously a prominent member of the MLN (see above), but went into temporary exile and left the party after allegations in August 1982 that a coup was being planned against the Ríos Montt regime. He went on to found the PUA, which attracted the support of some former MLN members.

The PUA contested the 1984 constituent assembly elections, winning one seat.

El Rayo
The Thunderbolt

Orientation.   Right-wing death squad

History.   This organization was active in the early 1980s.

Representación Unitaria de la Oposición Guatemalteca

See URNG (below).

La Sombra
The Shadow

Orientation.   Right-wing death squad

History.   This organization was active in the early 1980s.

Unidad Revolucionaria Nacional Guatemalteca (URNG)
Guatemalan National Revolutionary Unity

Leadership.   Raúl Molina Mejía (leader of RUOG)

Orientation.   Left-wing political-military front

Founded.   Feb. 8, 1982

History.   The URNG (also known as the Representación Unitaria de la Oposición Guatemalteca – RUOG – United Representation of the Guatemalan Opposition) is a common front of guerrilla organizations opposed to the government. The formation of the URNG united the four main guerrilla organizations which had on several earlier occasions (November 1979, May 1980 and January 1981) announced their intention of forming an alliance.

Policies.   The URNG announced in a statement widely distributed in Guatemala City in 1982 that it intended to pursue a "popular revolutionary war" as the sole means left to the people "to free themselves from oppression, exploitation, discrimination and dependence on foreign countries". The statement also denounced "the most odious genocide perpetrated in the whole of the western hemisphere", claiming that the regime and its supporters in the death squads were killing an average of 36 persons per day. After temporarily occupying a number of radio stations, the URNG broadcast a statement outlining its objectives as (i) an end to repression and a guarantee of life, peace and fundamental human rights for all citizens; (ii) provision for the basic needs of the majority of the people; (iii) equality between the indigenous and ladino communities; (iv) the creation of a new society in which all sectors of the population would be represented in government, and (v) non-alignment and international co-operation. The group condemned the 1984 constituent assembly elections as an effort "to cover up an eroded repressive military apparatus, following the failure of several years of counterinsurgency campaigns resulting in death and destruction".

Membership.   Guerrilla groups represented in the URNG command are the EGP, the FAR, the ORPA and the PGT (see above).

Associated organizations.   The RUOG-URNG is close to the PSD (see above) and its allies. It is also supported by the CGUP (see above).

Unión del Centro Nacional (UCN)
National Centre Union

Leadership.   Jorge Carpio Nicolle (leader); Ramiro de León Carpio (general secretary)

Orientation.   Centrist

Founded.   July 1983

History.   This party was formed by Jorge Carpio, a well-known newspaper publisher. It was extremely successful in its first electoral contest, winning 269,000 votes and 21 seats in the July 1984 constituent assembly elections.

Publications.   The policies of the party are likely to be reflected in Carpio's morning and evening papers, *El Gráfico* (circulation 60,000) and *La Razón* (circulation 20,000).

Unión Nacional Opositora (UNO)
National Opposition Union

Orientation.   Centrist

History.   The UNO coalition presented Alejandro Maldonado Aguirre as its candidate in the March 1982 presidential election, winning – according to the official count – 221,810 votes (22.7 per cent) and third place. It won two seats in the simultaneous congressional elections. The member parties have subsequently operated independently.

Membership.   The UNO was formed by the PDCG and the PNR (see above).

Unión Popular
Popular Union

History.   This small group was a founding member of the Frente Popular (see above) in 1984.

Unión Revolucionaria Democrática (URD)

See FUR (above).

Haiti

Capital: Port-au-Prince   **Population: 5,300,000**

Haiti won independence from France in 1804, but was invaded by the United States in 1915. Its sovereignty was not restored until 1934. A military coup in 1950 gave power to Gen. Paul Magloire, who was ousted in 1956; Dr Francois (Papadoc) Duvalier was elected as President in 1957 and rapidly established a dynastic dictatorship with the support of a private army now officially known as the Volontaires pour la Sécurité Nationale but more widely known as the Tontons Macoutes. Duvalier became President-for-Life in 1964 and on his death in 1971 he was succeeded by his son Jean-Claude, a succession which in a referendum in February 1971 was allegedly approved by 2,391,916 votes to nil. The regime of the Duvalier family has been repeatedly condemned by the international community for corruption and systematic violation of civil and human rights. Numerous arrests and executions of alleged plotters against the regime were carried out between 1967 and 1970, and several attempts by exiles in Florida to land guerrilla forces in Haiti were foiled by Haitian and US authorities in 1966–67 and in the early 1980s. By 1970 there were about 400,000 Haitians living in exile, and political groups formed by them ranged over the whole political spectrum from right-wing conservative to communist. Massive emigration continued in the 1970s, and tens of thousands made the sea crossing to Florida in the early 1980s, most being refused political asylum and either imprisoned or returned to Haiti.

In 1979 Christian democratic opposition groups were formed illegally inside Haiti; repression continued as before and in May 1984 a decree outlawed all political activities other than those of the Duvalier family's Parti de l'Unité Nationale. Elements of the Catholic Church have been to the fore in non-party anti-government protest in recent years.

Riots occurred in the capital and in the northern town of Gonaïves during 1984, and an anti-government plot was allegedly discovered in November, leading to a new wave of arrests. Various constitutional reforms have been enacted, most recently in 1983 and April 1985; the latter revision was the subject of a referendum on July 22, the official result of which was given as 2,375,011 votes in favour (99.98 per cent) and 440 votes against (0.02 per cent).

Constitutional background.   Under the latest (April 1985) revision of the Constitution of 1950, Haiti is defined as a republic with a President appointed for life and having the power to nominate his successor. The President appoints a Prime Minister and a

Cabinet, some of whose members – the Ministers of State – form an Inner Cabinet. There is a unicameral National Assembly whose 59 members are, according to the Constitution, elected by universal adult suffrage for six-year terms. The President is able to dissolve the Assembly and rule by decree, and in effect has absolute power. The latest version of the Constitution provides for the establishment of political parties, subject to the approval of the interior ministry; such parties would have to support the life presidency, have no foreign affiliations, have at least 15,000 members and reject "totalitarian, fascist, communist or nazi" ideologies.

Recent election results. In a process which took place on Feb. 12, 1984, the sole legal party – the PUN – was declared to have won all 59 seats in the Assembly, no opposition candidates being permitted to stand. Elections under the revised Constitution are scheduled for 1987.

Action démocratique
Democratic Action

Leadership. Alexandre Lerouge (leader)

Orientation. Centrist

History. This group attempted to hold a joint meeting with the PDCH (see below) on Sept. 12, 1985, but its leader was arrested together with Sylvio Claude; both were released some hours later.

Brigade Hector Riobé
Hector Riobé Brigade

Orientation. Anti-Duvalier guerrilla group

History. This group carried out several air attacks on targets in Haiti in mid-1982, among them one on vehicles near the main presidential palace and another on the President's ranch north of Port-au-Prince. It was also responsible for scattering anti-government leaflets from a light aircraft, and for bombings in Port-au-Prince in December 1982 and in 1983; five people were killed in the three 1983 blasts. Five alleged members of the Brigade were sentenced to life imprisonment on Sept. 21, 1984, for carrying out the 1983 attacks, but they were released in April 1985, with 31 other prisoners, after the intervention of a visiting US congressman.

Conseil pour la libération nationale d'Haïti
Council for the National Liberation of Haiti

Leadership. Roland Magloire (leader)

Orientation. Anti-Duvalier guerrilla group

History. This organization of Haitian exiles, led by the nephew of former President Paul Magloire (in office 1950–56), was involved in an attempt to invade Haiti from Florida on March 16, 1982, but the 16 mercenaries setting out in two cabin cruisers were arrested by US coast guards.

Jeunesse d'Haïti
Youth of Haiti

Orientation. Democratic

History. This organization staged an anti-government rally in Port-au-Prince on June 22, 1985.

Ligue haïtienne des droits humains
Haitian League for Human Rights

Leadership. Gérard Gourgue (president); Lafontant Joseph (general secretary)

Orientation. Opposition

History. Joseph Maxi, a lawyer and a founder-member of this movement, was reported to have been arrested after the parliamentary elections of February 1979, together with 12 others, in connection with an alleged anti-government plot. A meeting of the League in Port-au-Prince in early November 1979 was attacked by police who beat up a number of those present, including personnel of the Canadian, French, West German and US embassies. One of those beaten died of his wounds. Among 400 people briefly detained later in November, when it was officially claimed that a plot against the government had been discovered, was the League's general secretary.

Mouvement ouvriers-paysans (MOP)
Workers' and Peasants' Movement

Orientation. Anti-Duvalier group

History. Representatives of the MOP attended the Continental Conference of Solidarity with the People of Haiti in September 1981 in Panama (see PDCH, below).

Parti démocratique chrétien d'Haïti (PDCH)
Christian Democratic Party of Haiti

Leadership. Dr Sylvio Claude (president); Abel Cangé (general secretary)

Orientation. Christian democrat; opposes Duvalier regime

Founded. July 5, 1979

History. Claude stood unsuccessfully in the 1979 National Assembly elections and was then briefly deported from Haiti before returning to form the PDCH. An open-air political meeting organized by him in Port-au-Prince for Aug. 28, 1979, was attacked by some 2,000 people, and on the following day the party's offices were ransacked by the police. After broadcasting a report of the events Claude was arrested on Aug. 30 with some 200 others, including Prof. Grégoire Eugène (see PDCH-27 juin, below); Claude was, however, released on May 2, 1980, after a hunger strike.

On Oct. 13 Claude was rearrested after asking in his newspaper, *La Conviction*, how long Duvalier would remain dictator, and on Aug. 26, 1981, he was with 21 others including his son and daughter, sentenced to 15 years in prison for "incitement to revolt and attempting to create a climate of disorder and to start fires". However, in February 1982 Duvalier annulled the sentences, and a retrial on Aug. 27–28, ordered by the Appeals Court, reduced the sentences to six years each; at the end of September all the accused were released to house arrest. Claude escaped from house arrest and went into hiding.

The party currently operates clandestinely in Haiti.

Policies. Representatives of the party were present at the Continental Conference of Solidarity with the People of Haiti, held in Panama in

September 1981 and attended by about 40 Haitian exiles from nine countries. The conference called for the restoration of democratic freedoms, for an amnesty for 90 named political prisoners (the official total of such prisoners was then 55, compared with unofficial estimates of over 300), and for the unconditional return of exiles.

Publications. *La Conviction*, weekly, often suppressed

Parti démocratique chrétien d'Haïti de 27 juin (PDCH – 27 juin)
June 27 Christian Democratic Party of Haiti

Leadership. Grégoire Eugène (leader)

Orientation. Christian democrat; opposes Duvalier regime

Founded. July 1979

History. The PDCH – 27 juin, also known as the Parti social chrétien (Social Christian Party), operates illegally and clandestinely in Haiti. Its leader was an unsuccessful candidate in the 1979 parliamentary elections. In his fortnightly journal, *Fraternité*, he had criticized the Duvalier regime, and on June 17, 1979, he had published a book in which he maintained that the Constitution of Haiti permitted the formation of political parties. He was temporarily detained after the rally held on Aug. 28, 1979 by the PDCH (see above), and was again arrested, with some 400 other opposition figures, human rights activists and journalists late in November 1980. He was one of a number of people exiled to the United States on Dec. 2, 1980, but was permitted to return to Haiti in February 1984. He was arrested in June of that year but freed in September.

Publications. Eugène is the publisher of a weekly political magazine, *Fraternité*.

Parti national chrétien d'Haïti
Haitian National Christian Party

Leadership. Rev. René des Rameaux (leader)

Orientation. Anti-Duvalier group

Founded. Aug. 29, 1979

History. This illegal party was formed in St Louis du Nord.

Parti national populaire d'Haïti
Haitian National Popular Party

Leadership. Bernard Sansaricq (leader)

Orientation. Anti-Duvalier group

Founded. 1981

History. The formation of this party was announced in leaflets signed by Sansaricq, a right-wing exile leader, and dropped from a light aircraft over Port-au-Prince late in October 1981. The leaflets called for a rising against the Duvalier regime. Shortly afterwards the presidential yacht was said to have been hijacked, and there followed numerous arrests of political and trade union figures.

An invasion attempt led by Sansaricq – who was reportedly involved in similar attempts in 1964 and 1968 – was launched from the British colony of the Turks and Caicos Islands on Jan. 9, 1982. The Haitian Ministry of the Interior and of National Security stated on Jan. 22 that, of 44 "terrorists" involved, 26, including Sansaricq, had been arrested by the US authorities; eight had been killed by Haitian government forces and 10 had fled. Four Haitian soldiers were reported to have been killed.

Parti national progressiste
National Progressive Party

Orientation. *Jean-claudiste*

Founded. Aug. 23, 1985

History. This organization announced its formation in a letter published in a pro-government newspaper.

Policies. The party defined its policies as seeking, "like *duvalierisme*, the greatest good for the greatest number"; moreover, it supported "economic revolution, the acceleration of democratization and the opening [of Haiti] to the outside world".

Membership. Its initial membership was 118.

Parti social chrétien

See PDCH – 27 juin (above).

Parti unifié des communistes haïtiens (PUCH)
Unified Party of Haitian Communists

Leadership. Jacques Dosilien (general secretary)

Orientation. Communist

Founded. November 1968

History. The PUCH was formed by the merger of the Parti populaire de libération nationale (People's National Liberation Party), formed in 1954, with the Parti de l'unité populaire d'Haïti (Haiti People's Unity Party), formed in 1959. It held a congress in exile in November 1978, and was represented at the Panama conference of 1981 (see PDCH, above).

Policies. At its 1978 congress the PUCH adopted a programme demanding that "imperialist pillage" of Haiti's national wealth be ended; that the anti-communist law be abolished; that the life presidency be abolished; that political prisoners be released, political exiles allowed to return unconditionally, and a general amnesty be proclaimed. The congress affirmed the party's adherence to Marxism–Leninism and proletarian internationalism, and condemned the Chinese Communist leadership.

International Affiliations. The PUCH is recognized by the Communist Party of the Soviet Union and its allied parties.

Parti de l'unité nationale (PUN)
National Unity Party

Address. Assemblée Nationale, Port-au-Prince

Leadership. Jean-Claude Duvalier (leader)

Orientation. *Jean-claudiste*; supports the policies of President-for-Life Duvalier.

Founded. 1963, as Parti unique de l'action révolutionnaire et gouvernmentale (PUARG – Sole Party of Revolutionary Government Action)

History. The party was founded by President François ("Papadoc") Duvalier, who was succeeded by his son in 1971. It is the sole authorized political party, its central object being to support the policies of the country's President. In May 1984 all non-PUN political activity was outlawed.

Publications. The main daily newspapers – Le Nouveau Monde and Le Matin – adopt pro-government positions.

Le Petit Samedi Soir

History. This independent weekly magazine, edited by Dieudonné Fardin and with a circulation of 10,000, has provided a forum for the expression of opposition opinion, as a result of which it has frequently come into conflict with the authorities.

Rassemblement démocratique nationaliste et progressiste (RNDP)
Progressive Nationalist and Democratic Assembly

Leadership. Leslie Manigat (leader)

Orientation. Anti-Duvalier group

Founded. March 1981

History. The RNDP was founded in Caracas, Venezuela, and exists only in exile.

Tontons Macoutes

See Volontaires de la Sécurité Nationale (below).

Union des forces patriotiques et démocratiques haïtiennes (IFOPEDA)
Union of Democratic and Patriotic Forces of Haiti

Orientation. Anti-Duvalier group

History. Representatives of this organization attended the Continental Conference of Solidarity with the People of Haiti in September 1981 in Panama (see PDCH, above). In 1985 the group staged a rally in Paris to denounce the constitutional referendum (see introduction).

Volontaires de la Sécurité Nationale (VSN)
National Security Volunteers

Orientation. Right-wing paramilitary group

History. This organization, better known as the Tontons Macoutes (Creole for "bogeymen"), was formed as a private army of the Duvalier dictatorship. Its ruthless response to any manifestation of dissent has ensured the survival of the regime for almost 30 years.

Honduras

Capital: Tegucigalpa   **Population: 3,800,000**

Honduras gained separate independence in 1836. Power has alternated in the present century between civilian, military and coalition civilian–military governments, mostly involving the Partido Liberal de Honduras (PLH) or the conservative Partido Nacional (PN). Liberal regimes elected in 1954 and 1957 were overthrown by the military, traditionally an ally of the PN; the country was under almost uninterrupted military rule from 1963 to 1981, but in 1981 a liberal government was elected under Dr Roberto Suazo. From its inauguration in January 1982 the Suazo regime was subject to close supervision by the armed forces; there were waves of repression in 1982–83 and guerrilla activity of both right and left, although the army inflicted a major defeat on leftist guerrillas at Olancho in October 1983, killing 100 rebels. In 1984–85 political life was dominated by the crises arising from splits within the major parties, partly over the question of the presidential succession, and by a conflict between the executive and the legislature concerning judicial appointments.

Many thousands of refugees from the civil war in El Salvador were by 1982 accommodated in camps just inside Honduras, while various right-wing Nicaraguan guerrilla forces have set up training and operational bases on the border. The Honduran armed forces have been directly engaged in counterinsurgency operations in El Salvador and have tolerated and, according to some reports, assisted the Nicaraguan *contras*. During 1984 a revolt by junior officers forced the replacement of a right-wing commander-in-chief of the armed forces with Gen. Walter Reyes, who is generally perceived as less willing to involve Honduras in regional conflicts.

Constitutional background. The Republic has an executive President, who is appointed by the party winning the largest number of votes in legislative elections, and who presides over a Cabinet; there is a unicameral National Assembly of 82 members, chosen with a system of proportional representation. Members of the Assembly are elected by universal and compulsory adult suffrage for four-year terms. The current Constitution came into effect in 1982.

Recent election results. Elections due to take place on Nov. 24, 1985, were too late for inclusion in this book. Unlike previous presidential elections, those of 1985 were to be contested by the candidates of party factions, rather than by single official candidates from each party. At the previous elections on Nov. 29, 1981, the PLH candidate, Dr Roberto Suazo Córdova, was elected President, taking office on Jan. 27, 1982. Simultaneous elections to the National Assembly gave the PLH 44 seats, the PN 34, the PINU 3 and the PDC 1; the turnout of registered electors was about 80 per cent.

Alianza Campesina de Organizaciones Nacionales de Honduras (ALCONH)
Peasant Alliance of National Organizations of Honduras

Leadership.   Reyes Rodríguez Arévalo (leader)

Orientation.   Peasant land rights movement

Founded.   Oct. 10, 1980

History.   The ALCONH was established as a "revolutionary and belligerent" peasant group under the leadership of Rodríguez, the president of the main peasant union, the ANACH (see PINU, below).

Alianza Liberal del Pueblo (Alipo)
People's Liberal Alliance

Orientation.   Radical liberal tendency

Founded.   1978

History.   The Alipo was formed as a radical tendency within the PLH, merging the Movimiento Villeda Morales (MVM – Villeda Morales Movement, named after a former President) of San Pedro Sula with the Izquierda Democrática (Democratic Left) of Tegucigalpa. The Alipo remained in a minority within the PLH at the party convention of 1981. The founders of Izquierda Democrática, the brothers Carlos Roberto and Jorge Arturo Reina, announced in February 1984 the formation of a separate liberal tendency, the MLDR (see below).

Asociación Nacional de Campesinos de Honduras (ANACH)

See ALCONH (above) and FUNACAMH (below).

Asociación para el Progreso de Honduras (APROH)
Association for the Progress of Honduras

Leadership.   Gen. (retd) Gustavo Alvarez Martínez (leader); Miguel Facussé (vice-president); Oswaldo Ramos Soto (secretary)

Orientation.   Right-wing

Founded.   January 1983

History.   The APROH is an anti-communist and right-wing organization of army officers and businesspeople. It was declared illegal by the Suazo government on Nov. 3, 1984, after the arrest in the USA of several associates of Alvarez – a former commander-in-chief of the Honduran armed forces – on charges of conspiracy to assassinate Suazo and of smuggling cocaine to finance the plot.

Policies.   Although originally described as a civic group aimed at promoting foreign investment in Honduras, the APROH has been widely regarded as a front for right-wing political activities.

Associated organizations.   The APROH received in January 1983 a gift of US$5,000,000 from the strongly anti-communist Unification Church, which had established a significant presence in Honduras in early 1983 but declined after being denounced by the Catholic hierarchy and the media (see also Uruguayan section).

Comando Guerrillero Popular
People's Guerrilla Command

Leadership. José Alberto Munguia Vélez, José Antonio Montalván Munguia (leaders)

Orientation. Left-wing guerrilla group

Founded. April 1980

History. On July 3, 1981, it was announced that a bomb factory of this group had been discovered in the Miraflores district of the capital.

Comité de Defensa de Derechos Humanos en Honduras (CODEH)
Committee for the Defence of Human Rights in Honduras

Leadership. Ramón Custodio López (director)

Orientation. Human rights concerns

History. The CODEH, as one of the main pressure groups on human rights issues, was involved in the campaign which led to the establishment in June 1984 of a special military commission of inquiry into the disappearance in 1981–84 of 112 people. It also opposes and publicises arbitrary and illegal arrests, torture and other abuses of human rights, and in May 1985 denounced the activities of the US Central Intelligence Agency in Honduras.

Comité de Familiares de los Desaparecidos de Honduras (COFADEH)
Honduran Committee of the Families of Disappeared Persons

Orientation. Human rights concerns

History. This pressure group has been active in the early 1980s as the representative of families of political activists and others who "disappeared" as a consequence of the political situation, most of whom are thought to have been killed by the security forces or by right-wing death squads.

Coordinadora Democrática Constitucional Opositora (CODECO)
Democratic and Constitutional Opposition Co-ordinating Body

Orientation. Centrist opposition

Founded. February 1985

History. This parliamentary alliance was formed by members of the PN, the PDC and left-wing liberals.

Policies. The CODECO regards the Suazo regime as US-dominated, undemocratic and corrupt, and accuses it of violations of human rights, disregard for the Constitution and interference in the internal affairs of political parties, businesses, trade unions, professional bodies and student organizations.

Directorio Nacional Unido (DNU)
United National Directorate

Orientation. Left-wing guerrilla front

Founded. April 1983

History. The DNU was formed at a meeting in Nicaragua as a strategic and political co-ordinating body for the various left-wing guerrilla groups operating in Honduras.

Membership. The members are the FMLH, Froylan Turcios, the FPR, the MPLC, the MUR and the PRTCH (see below).

Associated organizations. The DNU is politically close to the PCH (see below).

Federación de Cooperativas Agropecuarias de la Reforma Agraria Hondureña (FECORAH)

See FUNACAMH (below).

Frente Morazanista para la Liberación de Honduras (FMLH)
Morazanist Front for the Liberation of Honduras

Orientation. Left-wing guerrilla group

Founded. September 1979

History. The FMLH (which is also referred to as the Frente Morazanista de Liberación Nacional, FMLN) has joined the guerrilla co-ordinating body, the DNU (see above). It is named after a 19th-century military leader, Francisco Morazán.

Policies. On Aug. 2, 1980, a statement from the Front defined its objective as the establishment of a people's government to give land to the peasants and eliminate the social and economic problems afflicting the masses.

Frente Nacional de Campesinos Independientes de Honduras

See FUNACAMH (below).

Frente Patriótico Hondureño (FPH)
Honduran Patriotic Front

Leadership. Mario Orlando Iriarte (president)

Orientation. Left-wing

Founded. October 1979

History. This alliance of socialist and communist parties and organizations had some 50 member groups in 1980, including the PCH, the PCML and the Paso (see below). It campaigned for abstention in the April 1980 elections to a constituent assembly.

Associated organizations. The FPH is close to one of the smaller trade union federations, the Federación Unitaria de Trabajadores de Honduras (FUTH – United Federation of Honduran Workers), which has 50,000 members, is led by Napoleón Acevedo Granados and forms part of the FPR (see below).

Frente Popular contra la Represión (FPR)
Popular Front against Repression

Orientation. Left-wing human rights group

Founded. Late May, 1981

History. The FPR was founded by a group of labour, peasant and education unions to expose and protest against abuses of human rights.

Policies. The Front has alleged that government repression is being used to "delay the Honduran revolutionary process by the physical elimination of leading members of popular organizations" on the Guatemalan model.

Membership. The founding members of the FPR were the trade union federation FUTH (see FPH, above), the peasant coalition FUNACAMH (see below), the teaching union Frente Unido Magistral (FUM – United Educator's Front), the Frente Estudiantil Universitario de Honduras (FEUH – Honduras University Students' Front) and the Frente Estudiantil Secundario (Fese – Secondary Students' Front).

Frente de Unidad Liberal (FUL)
Liberal Unity Front

Orientation. Liberal

Founded. 1980

History. This faction of the PLH (see below) refused to attend the party's 1981 convention after being denied registration by the PLH executive as a tendency within the party.

Frente de Unidad Nacional Campesino de Honduras (FUNACAMH)
Honduran Peasant's National Unity Front

Orientation. Left-wing peasant federation

Founded. October 1975

History. This federation of peasant co-operatives and unions has co-ordinated a campaign, involving the occupation of lands and strikes by peasant producers, to accelerate the government's land reform programme and end abuses.

Membership. The six main organizations to join the FUNACAMH were the ANACAMH (see PINU, below), the Federación de Cooperativas Agropecuarias de la Reforma Agraria Hondureña (FECORAH – Honduran Land Reform Agricultural Co-operatives Federation), the Unión Nacional de Cooperativas Populares de Honduras (UNACOOPH – Honduran National Union of Popular Co-operatives), the UNCAH (see URP, below), the Frente Nacional de Campesinos Independiente de Honduras (National Front of Independent Peasants of Honduras) and the Unión Nacional de Campesinos (UNC – National Peasants' Union).

Frente Unitaria de Trabajadores de Honduras (FUTH)

See FPH (above).

Froylan Turcios

Orientation. Left-wing guerrilla group

History. The Foylan Turcios group, named after an early 20th-century left-wing writer, claimed responsibility for bomb attacks on power stations in July 1982, causing substantial material damage and the deaths of five people. The military authorities alleged that the bombings were the work of the Salvadorean FMLN (see entry under El Salvador), but the leader of the PCH (see below), Rigoberto Padilla, was among those arrested in connection with the incidents; he was later released. The group has joined the guerrilla co-ordinating body, the DRU (see above).

Fuerzas Armadas Populares (FAP)
Popular Armed Forces

Orientation. Left-wing guerrilla group

Founded. 1984

History. In January 1984 "propaganda bombs" – low-powered explosive devices designed to scatter leaflets – were used in Tegucigalpa to issue leaflets in the name of the FAP threatening to "exterminate" US military advisers and Salvadorean troops using training bases in Honduras.

Fuerzas Revolucionarios Populares Lorenzo Zelaya (FRP)
Lorenzo Zelaya Popular Revolutionary Forces

Orientation. Left-wing guerrilla group

History. The FRP was derived from a Maoist faction which broke away from the PCH (see above) in 1975. It was responsible for bomb attacks on the Argentinian and Chilean embassies in Tegucigalpa in mid-April, 1982, and for the hijacking on April 28 of an aircraft on a domestic flight. The hijackers failed to win the release of 52 alleged political prisoners and the payment of a ransom, but secured safe passage to Cuba after a three-day confrontation. In later actions the group bombed US and Salvadorean commercial offices in Tegucigalpa on Aug. 4, leading to a wave of arrests and reprisals by security forces and right-wing paramilitaries. The group has joined the guerrilla co-ordinating body, the DNU (see above).

Izquierda Democrática

See Alipo (above) and MLDR (below).

La Mano Blanca
The White Hand

Orientation. Ultra-right death squad

History. This group was reported to have issued death threats to alleged members of left-wing groups in the late 1970s and early 1980s, and to have carried out some of those threats; it was said to have links with similar groups elsewhere in Central America.

Movimiento Democratizador Nacionalista (Modena)
Nationalist Democratization Movement

Orientation. Right-wing

History. This dissident faction within the PN (see below) was active in 1984.

Movimiento Liberal Democrático Revolucionario (MLDR)
Revolutionary Democratic Liberal Movement

Leadership. Jorge Arturo Reina (president); Armando Aguilar Cruz (general secretary)

Orientation. Radical liberal

Founded. Feb. 14, 1984

History. This radical faction of the PLH (see below) was formed by Reina, who had previously been a leader of the Izquierda Democrática faction (which had since 1978 been part of the Alipo – see above).

Movimiento Popular de Liberación Cinchonero (MPLC)
Cinchonero People's Liberation Movement

Orientation. Left-wing guerrilla group

History. The Cinchoneros, originally a faction of the PCH, later became the armed wing of the URP (see below). The MPLC stormed the Chamber of Commerce building in San Pedro Sula on Sept. 17, 1982, and took 107 hostages including two government ministers and the governor of the central bank; the guerrillas involved secured safe passage to Cuba but none of their other demands were met, among them the expulsion of the foreign military advisers, the repeal of the April 1982 security legislation, the expulsion of Nicaraguan *contras* and an end to "the repression of the Honduran people". The organization claimed responsibility in August 1983 for bombings in San Pedro Sula, La Ceiba and La Lima, which it said had been carried out "to express the Honduran people's repudiation of US intervention in Central America". The group has joined the guerrilla co-ordinating body, the DNU (see above).

International affiliations. The MPLC has been reported as having links with the Salvadorean guerrilla front, the FMLN (see separate section).

Movimiento Rodista

See PLH (below).

Movimiento de Unidad y Cambio (MUC)
Unity and Change Movement

Orientation. Right-wing

History. The MUC operated in 1985 as a dissident faction within the PN (see below).

Movimiento de Unidad Revolucionaria (MUR)
Revolutionary Unity Movement

Orientation. Left-wing guerrilla group

History. The MUR is a member of the guerrilla co-ordinating body, the DRU (see above).

Movimiento Villeda Morales (MVM)

See Alipo (above).

Partido Comunista de Honduras (PCH)
Communist Party of Honduras

Leadership. Rigoberto Padilla Rush (former general secretary; in exile)

Orientation. Orthodox communist

Founded. 1927; reorganized 1954

History. The PCH was illegal between 1932 and 1944; it operated in 1944–46 and 1948–53 as the Partido Revolucionario Democrático de Honduras (Democratic Revolutionary Party of Honduras). Anti-Soviet factions of the PCH broke away in 1960 and in 1965–67; another split in 1980 resulted in the formation of the URP (see below). The PCH was accorded official recognition in 1981. It has joined the PCML and the Paso (see below) in the FPH alliance (see above). In 1983 it committed itself to the armed struggle in association with the guerrilla organizations of the DNU (see above).

Policies. The party is regarded as pro-Soviet. At a congress in 1972 it adopted a policy programme reaffirming its commitment to Marxism–Leninism and proletarian internationalism, and calling for "struggle against the domination of US imperialism and the reactionary bourgeoisie and landowners", and for "an anti-imperialist, agrarian, popular and democratic revolution".

Associated organizations. See FPH (above). The PCH is politically close to the guerrilla co-ordinating body, the DNU (see above).

International affiliations. The PCH is recognized by the Communist Party of the Soviet Union and its allied parties.

Partido Comunista Marxista–Leninista (PCML)
Communist Party (Marxist–Leninist)

Orientation. Revolutionary communist

History. The PCML has joined the PCH (see above) and the Paso (see below) in the FPH alliance (see above).

Partido Demócrata Cristiana (PDC)
Christian Democratic Party
Leadership.　Dr Hernán Corrales Padilla (leader); Efraín Díaz Arrivillaga (president)

Orientation.　Christian democratic

History.　The PDC gained legal status on July 15, 1980, and in the 1981 elections gained one seat in the Assembly.

Policies.　The party opposes the PLH government, which it accused in September 1982 of planning a systematic extermination of opposition members.

Associated organizations.　The party has a trade union affiliate, the Central General de Trabajadores (CGT – General Confederation of Workers).

International affiliations.　The party belongs to the Christian Democratic International and to the Christian Democratic Organization of America.

Partido de Innovación y Unidad (PINU)
Innovation and Unity Party
Address.　Apartado 105, Tegucigalpa, DC

Leadership.　Dr Miguel Andoníe Fernández (leader)

Orientation.　Leftist

Founded.　1970

History.　The PINU gained legal status in 1978 and won three seats both in the constituent assembly elected in April 1981 and in the legislature elected in November of that year.

Associated organizations.　The 80,000-member Asociación Nacional de Campesinos de Honduras (ANACAMH – National Association of Honduran Peasants) has as its general secretary a PINU member of the National Assembly, Antonio Julián Méndez; it forms part of the FUNACAMH (see above).

Partido Liberal de Honduras (PLH)
Liberal Party of Honduras
Leadership.　Dr Roberto Suazo Córdova (leader); Romualdo Bueso Peñalba (president); Pompilio Romero Martínez (general secretary)

Orientation.　Liberal

Founded.　1890

History.　The PLH first came to power in 1957, when it gained 37 of the 58 seats in a constituent assembly. Its candidate was elected President, but was overthrown in 1963. The party contested elections for a constituent assembly in 1965, but its successful candidates boycotted the proceedings until the conversion of the assembly into a legislature. It contested the 1971 elections in a "pact of national union" with the PN (see below), each of the parties securing 32 seats in congress and the presidency going to the PN as the party with the larger share of the vote. The pact broke down in 1973 with the withdrawal of the PN after a dispute over government appointments.

In the next elections, in 1980, the PLH gained 35 of the 71 seats and joined a civilian–military coalition government with the PN. The PLH won the 1981 election with an absolute majority for Suazo as its presidential candidate and 44 of the 82 seats; it then formed a government on its own. By then, however, the party was comprised of a number of contending factions including Suazo's conservative Rodista tendency (also known as the

Movimiento Rodista, and named after the late PLH leader, Modesto Rodas Alvarado, who died in 1979) and the radical Alipo and FUL factions (see above). In November 1982 six PLH members of congress joined the opposition, creating a crisis for the government resolved by the reaffiliation of three of them and the dismissal of a fourth. The appointments of Bueso and Romero to their leadership positions followed the resignation in 1983 of the previous party president, José Azcona del Hoyo, who alleged "irregularities" in the party's internal election processes. In February 1984 the MLDR faction (see above) split from the mainstream PLH.

Policies. The PLH promotes democratic principles, social reform and Central American integration.

Partido Nacional (PN)
National Party

Leadership. Ricardo Zúñiga Augustinus (leader)

Orientation. Right-wing

Founded. 1923

History. The PN was in power from 1932 to 1957, including a period of dictatorship by the then party leader, Gen. Tiburcio Carías Andino, in 1939–49. In 1957 it was defeated by the PLH (see above) in elections to a 58-member consituent assembly, in which it won only 18 seats. It held a majority in the 1965 constituent assembly and supported for the presidency the military candidate, who had overthrown the liberal government in 1963. In 1971–73 it formed part of a military–civilian coalition government as part of a "pact of national unity" (see PLH).

In elections on April 20, 1981, to a constituent assembly, the PN obtained 33 of the 71 seats; it joined another military–civilian government together with the PLH. In November its presidential candidate, Zúñiga, came second with 40.9 per cent of the vote, while the party obtained 34 of the 82 seats in the National Assembly. The PN has developed a number of internal factions, including the Modena and the MUC (see above) and the TNT (see below).

Policies. As a party of the right, the PN favours modest domestic reforms, economic and social development and Central American integration.

Partido Revolucionario Hondureño (PRH)
Honduran Revolutionary Party

Address. Apartado 1319, San Pedro Sula

Leadership. Francisco Rodolfo Jiménez Caballero (general secretary)

Orientation. Social democratic

Founded. Aug. 28, 1977

History. Preparations for the foundation of the PRH began in December 1974 at the initiative of a group of labour and peasant leaders allied with professional elements. Since its formal constitution in 1977 the PRH has not been officially recognized as a political party and has not won representation in the Assembly.

Structure. The party has a national assembly and other assemblies at departmental and local levels. The assemblies elect executive committees at each level.

Membership. 8,300

Publications. *Mensaje Revolucionario*, weekly

Partido Revolucionario de los Trabajadores Centroamericanos de Honduras (PRTCH)

Central American Revolutionary Workers' Party of Honduras

Leadership. "Comandante Manuel Federico" (general secretary)

Orientation. Left-wing guerrilla group

History. The PRTCH, founded in 1975 is a member of the guerrilla co-ordinating body, the DNU (see above). Its leader, José María Reyes Matos, was killed in action in 1983.

International affiliations. The PRTCH is linked with similarly-named parties in El Salvador and Guatemala.

Partido Socialista (Paso)

Socialist party

Leadership. Mario Virgilio Caras, Rogelio Martínez Reina (leaders)

Orientation. Socialist

History. The Paso joined the PCH and the PCML in the FPH alliance (see above), but did not present any candidates for the elections of November 1981. During 1981 both Caras and Martínez were detained, apparently by security forces; they stated on their release that they had been tortured and interrogated about alleged arms traffic to Salvadorean guerrillas.

Tendencia Nacionalista de Trabajo (TNT)

Nationalist Labour Tendency

Orientation. Right-wing, labour movement oriented

History. The TNT operated in 1984 as a dissident faction of the PN (see above).

Unión Nacional de Campesinos (UNC)

See FUNACAMH (above).

Unión Nacional de Campesinos Auténticos de Honduras (UNCAH)

See FUNACAMH (above) and URP (below).

Unión Nacional de Cooperativas Populares de Honduras (UNACOOPH)

See FUNACAMH (above).

Unión Revolucionaria del Pueblo (URP)

People's Revolutionary Union

Leadership. Tomás Nativi, Fidel Martínez (leaders)

Orientation. Peasant-based Marxist group

Founded. 1980

History. The URP was formed as a result of a split within the PCH (see above). Its leaders, Nativi and Martínez, were reported in 1981 to have been killed in clashes with the army, but the URP claims that both are being held in prison.

Membership. 8,300

Associated organizations. The URP is linked with the MPLC guerrilla group (see above), and has a peasant union affiliate, the Unión Nacional de Campesinos Auténticos de Honduras (UNCAH), which claims 20–30,000 members and belongs to the FUNACAMH federation (see above).

Mexico

Capital: México   **Population: 78,000,000**

Mexico, which achieved independence from Spain in 1821, was involved in various domestic and foreign conflicts until the installation of the dictatorship of Porfirio Díaz (the *"Porfiriato"*), which lasted from 1876 until 1910. The revolutionary period of 1910–17 was followed by another period of authoritarian rule, by Plutarco Elías Calles, who established a government party which, under various names and with a shifting ideological orientation, has dominated Mexican political life up to the present. The party – known since 1946 as the Partido Revolucionario Institucional (PRI), a name which embodies its philosophy that popular demands can and should be expressed and dealt with by the state apparatus – has, through populist policies, electoral manipulations, occasional reforms and the exercise of nationwide patronage and selective repression, prevented the emergence of an effective opposition.

The most radical of the PRI presidencies (known, from their duration, as *sexenios*) was that of Lázaro Cárdenas (1934–40), who carried out land reforms and nationalized the oil industry. It was during one of the more right-wing *sexenios* (Gustavo Díaz Ordaz, 1964–70) that, after 50 years of relative calm, serious disturbances broke out in Mexico City in 1968. A student strike developed into a full-scale revolt against the ruling PRI by left-wing, but mainly middle-class, students, which was suppressed by the armed forces with substantial loss of life and hundreds of arrests.

Various left-wing guerrilla groups were active during the 1970s, in particular in Guerrero, the poorest of the 31 states: trials of captured guerrillas have taken place from time to time. The groups included the Fuerzas Armadas Revolucionarias Populares, the Liga Comunista 23 de Septiembre, the Movimiento de Acción Revolucionaria, the Partido de los Pobres and the Unión del Pueblo. During the 1970s right-wing militias, such as the Brigada Blanca, the Halcones, the Tecos and various university gangs known as *porros*, were alleged to have carried out intimidation, kidnappings, torture and killings with the tacit support of the authorities. Measures taken by the security forces against the left, and more recently the treatment of the indigenous communities and of refugees from Central America, gave rise to campaigns by human rights groups in the late 1970s and early '80s. Guerrilla activities of left and right declined considerably in the 1980s, although in 1984 right-wing death squads were suspected of having assassinated an investigative reporter and an (amnestied) former leader of the Partido de los Pobres, which resumed its activities in 1985.

The most recent *sexenios* have been those of Luis Echeverría Alvarez (1970–76), José López Portillo (1976–82) and Miguel de la Madrid Hurtado (from 1982). López Portillo initiated a process of political liberalization which permitted a number of parties of the left, and a smaller number on the right, to expand their activities, acquire legal status and participate in elections. He also pursued economic policies which led to a massive increase in the public debt and severe difficulties with foreign and multilateral creditors. The current regime has introduced deflationary policies and other measures, such as the nationalization of the banking sector, designed to increase the government's control over the economy.

Constitutional background. Under the 1917 Constitution, as revised, the United Mexican States are a federal republic consisting of 31 states and a federal capital district, with an executive President heading a Cabinet. The bicameral National Congress consists of a 400-member Federal Chamber of Deputies – 300 elected by majority vote in single-member constituencies, and 100 by proportional representation – and a 64-member Senate with two seats for each state and for the federal district. Each state elects a governor and a Chamber of Deputies. Elections are by universal adult suffrage, with a six-year term for the President and governors and a three-year term for senators and for federal and state deputies.

To qualify to take part in elections a party must have at least 65,000 members, including 300 in each of any 150 constituencies of the chamber or 3,000 in each of any 16 states: other parties which have been active for four years may gain provisional recognition but must win at least 1.5 per cent of the total national vote to retain their recognition. No candidate may stand for election unless affiliated to a recognized party. Parties receive some official assistance for congressional elections, including free postal services and television and radio time.

Recent election results. A presidential election on July 4, 1982, was won by Miguel de la Madrid Hurtado of the PRI, whose share of the vote was officially stated to be 74.4 per cent. His candidature was also supported by the PARM and the PPS, but other candidates stood for the PAN, the PSUM, the PDM, the PST and the PSD (for explanation of acronyms, see below). According to provisional results of elections to the Federal Chamber of Deputies on July 7, 1985, the PRI gained 292 of the 300 seats filled by majority vote; 6 went to the PAN and 2 to the PARM. Of the 100 seats filled by proportional representation, the PAN gained 32, the PSUM 12, the PDM 12, the PST 12, the PPS 11, the PARM 7, the PMT 6 and the PRT 6.

Acción Comunitaria (ACOMAC)
Community Action

Orientation. Centrist

History. ACOMAC registered as a "civic association with political ends" in December 1978.

Policies. The group has stated that its aim is "to promote progressive social change" to allow "the better application of social justice".

Acción Democrática de Rescate Electoral (ADRE)
Democratic Action for Electoral Salvation

Orientation. Conservative

Founded. January 1983

History. The ADRE was formed as an electoral alliance of two conservative parties, the PAN and the PDM (see below).

Asamblea Nacional Popular Obrero y Campesino
National Workers' and Peasants' Popular Assembly

Orientation. Left-wing

History. This coalition of more than 100 small groups called a national strike on June 5, 1984, to protest against the government's economic austerity programme; the strike received very limited support.

Coalición Obrera, Campesina y Estudiantil del Istmo (COCEI)
Coalition of Workers, Peasants and Students of the Isthmus

Orientation. Left-wing

History. This leftist grouping was organized in the Tehuantepec isthmus in the late 1970s. It won the municipal elections in Juchitán, Oaxaca, in March 1981, but the council was suspended by the PRI-controlled state legislature in August 1983. The COCEI occupied the town hall until in December a police and military operation resulted in the arrest of the group's leaders and the installation of a PRI-dominated council which was stated to have been elected in November.

Coordinadora Nacional Plan de Ayala
Ayala Plan National Co-ordinating Body

Orientation. Peasants rights concerns

History. This coalition of independent (i.e. non-PRI) peasant federations was active in 1985.

Coordinadora Nacional de Pueblos Indígenas
National Co-ordinating Body for Indigenous Peoples

Orientation. *Indigenista*

History. This coalition of indigenous minority groups issued a statement in 1985 accusing the US Central Intelligence Agency of operating in Mexico through the Seventh Day Adventist sect.

Ejército de los Pobres

See Partido de los Pobres (below).

Movimiento de Acción Popular (MAP)

See PSUM (below).

Movimiento de Acción y Unidad Socialista (MAUS)

See PSUM (below).

Movimiento Comunista Libertario
Libertarian Communist Movement

Leadership. Evaristo Pérez Arreola

170

History. This group was formed by PCM members who refused in 1981 to join the PSUM (see below).

Partido Acción Nacional (PAN)
National Action Party

Address. Angel Urraza 812, Colonia del Valle, 03109 México, DF

Telephone. 5590777

Telex. 1764164

Leadership. Pablo Emilio Madero (president); Bernando Rátiz Vázquez (general secretary)

Orientation. Conservative

Founded. September 1939

History. The PAN was founded as "the sole independent opposition party in Mexico", and has stood against the PRI in congressional elections since 1943, local government elections since 1946 and most presidential elections since 1952. It was, however, widely regarded until recently, together with the PARM (see below), as a "tame" opposition permitted to win a limited number of seats in order to give pluralist credibility to a fairly monolithic system. However, in the past few years, and particularly since the opening up of the political system under President López Portillo, the PAN has increasingly been seen as representing a genuine conservative alternative to the populist policies of the PRI.

As the leading opposition party in the 1982 presidential election it gained 16.4 per cent of the vote for its candidate, the party president. It also won 55 of the 400 seats in the Chamber. In 1983 it entered into an electoral alliance, known as ADRE (see above) with a smaller right-wing party, the PDM (see below). The PAN made major gains in municipal elections in July 1983, bringing the total of state capitals under its control to five (of 31), but municipal elections later in the year and in 1984–85 were declared, despite evidence to the contrary, to have been won by the PRI.

Policies. The PAN is a social Christian party, advocating human rights, common welfare and the establishment of "a democratic government of national solidarity". It is regarded as a Catholic party.

Structure. The supreme organ of the party is the national convention, and between conventions the national assembly. The convention elects a national council, which appoints a national committee. There are also committees at state and district level, most of the membership and electoral support being in the north of the country.

Membership. 500,000

Publications. *La Nación*, circulation 100,000

Partido Auténtico de la Revolución Mexicana (PARM)
Authentic Party of the Mexican Revolution

Address. Río Nazas 168, México DF

Leadership. Jesús Guzmán Rubio (president); Rubén Rodríguez Lozano (general secretary)

Orientation. Centre-right

Founded. March 1954

History. The PARM was formed by a dissident faction of the PRI and was, together with the PAN and the PPS, tolerated by the PRI as a token opposition party from the 1950s to the 1970s. After elections held in 1958 it was given one of 156 seats in the Federal Chamber of Deputies; in 1964 it was

171

given five of the 210 seats contested, and by 1979 it held 10 seats. Following the emergence of more vociferous opposition forces in the political liberalization of the late 1970s, it failed to maintain its electoral base and in 1982 it did not contest the presidential election in its own right, but contributed its 1.1 per cent of the vote to the PRI candidate; it lost all its seats in the Chamber.

Policies. The ideology of the PARM has traditionally been somewhat vague; the main thrust of its argument has been that the ruling PRI has deviated from the ideals of the 1917 Revolutionary Constitution. However, it has been widely regarded as a conservative organization. It has defined itself as against "exploitation and injustice, for civil rights and liberties, for economic development and social justice, against misery and ignorance, for the sovereignty and self-determination of all nations and against all forms of dictatorship".

Structure. The PARM has an eight-member supreme presidium, a 21-member national executive committee, and committees at state, district and municipal levels.

Membership. 191,500

Publications. El Auténtico

Partido Comunista Mexicano (PCM)

See PSUM (below).

Partido Demócrata Mexicano (PDM)
Mexican Democratic Party

Address. Edison 89, Colonia Tabacalera, México 1, DF

Leadership. Gumersindo Magaña Negrete (president); Roberto Picón Robledo (organizing secretary)

Orientation. Right-wing

Founded. May 1971

History. The PDM evolved from the Unión Nacional Sinarquista (UNS – National Synarchist Union), the successor to a quasi-fascist movement which was popular in Mexico for a period in the late 1930s. Since reorganizing in the early 1970s, with a toned-down conservative ideology, the movement has gained considerably in strength and has spread beyond the traditional UNS strongholds in the north. Between May 1971 and May 1975 it organized in 22 states, and by 1978 it had committees in all of the then 28 states. In May 1978 it was allowed to register as a political party, and maintained its registration by exceeding 1.5 per cent in the 1979 congressional elections (in which it won 10 of the 100 proportional representation seats in the Federal Chamber of Deputies). In July 1982 the PDM obtained 1.9 per cent of the presidential vote, its candidate being Ignacio González Gollaz, and held eight seats in the Chamber.

Policies. The PDM is strongly anti-communist and is identified with Catholic moral precepts. It advocates an "integral and humanist democracy", a pluralist government, industrial co-ownership and the protection of the family.

Structure. The party has a national congress, a 20-member national consultative body, a national executive committee and state, district and local committees.

Membership. 450,000

Publications. El Demócrata, circulation 30,000

Associated organizations. In 1983 the PDM entered into an electoral alliance, known as ADRE (see above) with the country's main right-wing party, the PAN (see above).

Partido Mexicano de los Trabajadores (PMT)
Mexican Workers' Party

Address. Bucareli 20, 6° y 8°, México 1, DF

Leadership. Herberto Castillo (president); José Alvarez Icaza (secretary)

Orientation. Socialist

Founded. September 1974; reorganized 1977

History. The PMT was founded by Castillo and drew much of its membership from left-wing Catholic activists and former supporters of the student protest movements of the late 1960s and early 1970s. Having gained electoral registration, after some difficulties, in July 1984, it entered into an electoral alliance in February 1985 with other socialist, liberal and communist parties including the PPS, the PRT, the PST, the PSUM and the UPAC (see below).

Policies. The PMT has been involved in the campaign for electoral reforms and against the monopolization of power by the PRI. It has called for "the defence of the nation's human and material resources, especially of energy", and for the elimination of discrimination, inequality and injustice.

Structure. The highest organ of the party is the national assembly, ordinarily held every three years and consisting of delegates from all state, municipal and local committees. There is a national plenum consisting of a nine-member national committee and the presidents of state committees.

Membership. Estimates vary from 20,000 to 100,000

Publications. *Insurgencia Popular*, monthly, circulation 10,000

Partido de los Pobres
Party of the Poor

Orientation. Left-wing guerrilla group

History. This group (also known as the Ejército de los Pobres – Army of the Poor), founded in the late 1960s and led by Lucio Cabañas, was responsible for killing 10 soldiers near Acapulco on June 25, 1972, and for kidnapping a PRI senator and four aides on May 30, 1974 (all five being freed by army action on Sept. 7). Cabañas was reprotedly killed on Dec. 2, after a five-month counterinsurgency operation in Guerrero state in which at least 800 peasants were reported to have been killed; rumours of this survival continued for some years thereafter, although the movement itself appeared to be dormant.

The then deputy leader of the movement, Francisco Fierro Loza, accepted a government amnesty and emerged from hiding in 1984. On July 7 he was assassinated by unidentified gunmen. The movement resumed its guerrilla activities with the kidnapping in May 1985 of the leader of the communist PSUM (see below), who was released after the payment of a substantial ransom by the PSUM leadership.

Partido Popular Socialista (PPS)
Popular Socialist Party

Address. Avenida Alvaro Obregón 185, Colonia Roma, 06977 México, DF

Telephone. 5330816

Leadership. Jorge Cruikshank García (general secretary)

Orientation. Marxist

Founded. June 1948

History. A call for the formation of a Popular Party was made at an anti-Franco meeting in Mexico on July 18, 1946, by Vicente Lombardo Toledano, then vice-president of the World Federation of Trade Unions and president of its regional affiliate, the Confederación Latinoamericana de Trabajadores. The constituent assembly of the party took place on June 20, 1948, and it adopted its present name in October 1960, when it defined itself as a party of the proletariat. In 1964 it obtained 10 seats in the Federal Chamber of Deputies. In 1964, 1976 and 1982 it supported the PRI candidate in the presidential elections, but contested congressional elections in its own right; the official count in 1976 gave it about 1,000,000 votes and 11 seats in the Chamber, and Cruikshank became the first opposition candidate to obtain a seat in the Senate since 1929. In 1979 11 PPS candidates were elected to the Chamber, and in 1982 Cruikshank, having completed his Senate term, was one of 11 new PPS deputies elected. The PPS contribution to the vote for the PRI presidential candidate in 1982 was 1.6 per cent.

Policies. The PPS describes itself as "a working-class party based on Marxism–Leninism" and aiming to "build socialism in Mexico, developing the Mexican revolution through the unity of patriotic and democratic forces to confront North American imperialism and the country's oligarchic bourgeoisie". Despite the tenor of its public pronouncements, the PPS was regarded for most of the three decades after its foundation as a "tame" opposition party fulfilling the same function for the PRI as did the PAN and the PARM on the right, and its policies were very close to those of the left wing of the government party. However, it has increasingly functioned as a genuine anti-PRI party and has allied with new opposition parties. Its foreign policies are regarded as pro-Soviet.

Structure. Since 1960 the organizing principle of the PPS has been democratic centralism; the highest organ of the party is the national assembly which meets every three years and elects a central committee. That body meets twice a year and appoints a general secretary and a national leadership. The PPS youth wing is the Juventud Popular Socialista.

Publications. *Nueva Democracia*, theoretical quarterly, circulation 5,000; *El Combatiente*, weekly, 25,000

Associated organizations. In February 1985 the PPS entered into an electoral alliance with other socialist, liberal and communist parties including the PMT (see above) and the PRT, the PST, the PSUM and the UPAC (see below). The PPS controls the Unión General de Obreros y Campesinos de México (UGOCM – General Union of Workers and Peasants of Mexico).

Partido del Pueblo Mexicano (PPM)

See PSUM (below).

Partido Revolucionario Institucional (PRI)
Institutional Revolutionary Party

Address. Insurgentes Norte 61, 06350 México, DF

Leadership. Miguel de la Madrid Hurtado (President of Mexico, effective leader); Adolfo Lugo Verduzco (president); Irma Cue de Duarte (general secretary)

Orientation.   Approximately social democratic

Founded.   March 4, 1929, as Partido Nacional Revolucionario (PNR – National Revolutionary Party)

History.   The party was founded in 1929 as a coalition of local and state groups supporting the regime which had developed from the revolutionary period of 1910–17. It became the Partido de la Revolución Mexicana (PRM – Party of the Mexican Revolution) in 1938, and assumed its present name in 1946.

The party, together with its allied organizations in the labour, agrarian and "popular" sectors, has dominated Mexican political life since its foundation. It consistently wins overwhelming majorities in congressional elections, and receipt of the PRI nomination for the presidency – a decision arrived at by private consultations among the party leadership – guarantees election. Many PRI governments have been accused – particularly by their successors – of corruption and nepotism, and the start of each presidency is marked by the replacement of thousands of officials at every level. The party has often been accused of ballot-rigging on a large scale, but such charges appear to have become less frequent since the liberalization initiated in the late 1970s (although they recurred in 1983–85 – see PAN, above).

The PRI won 299 of the 400 seats in the Chamber of Deputies in the elections of July 1982, and secured 74.4 per cent of the vote for its presidential candidate, de la Madrid.

Policies.   The ideological orientation of the PRI depends largely on that of the faction represented by the incumbent President, and has veered from the socialist nationalism of the Cárdenas era (1934–40) to the conservatism of the Echeverría government (1970–76). In recent years the party has, as a rule, been more conservative on domestic than on foreign issues, and has played a leading role in the Third World and in the non-aligned movement. The current regime has led a "moral renewal" campaign aimed at eliminating corruption.

Structure.   The party has a complicated structure based on labour, peasant and civic associations, which meet in annual congress. There is a national executive committee. In 1984 the party decided to establish a national council to increase women's participation in the party and in national political life. The actual operation of the party has tended to be hierarchical, with candidates for electoral office imposed on lower levels of the party by the national and state leaderships – a system known as *dedazo* ("fingering") – but it was announced in 1984 that reforms were to be introduced to give a greater say to the individual members.

Publications.   *La República*; *La Línea*

Associated organizations.   The PRI has its own trade union movement, the central organs of which are the Congreso del Trabajo (Labour Congress) and the Confederación de Trabajadores de México (CTM – Mexican Confederation of Workers). In the rural sector it is represented by various peasant organizations.

Partido Revolucionario Socialista
Revolutionary Socialist Party

History.   This group gained registration as a political party on March 8, 1985. It has a collective presidency and describes its objective as "the unification of the Mexican left".

Partido Revolucionario de los Trabajadores (PRT)
Revolutionary Workers' Party

Leadership. Rosario Ibarra de la Piedra (leader); José Manuel Aguilar Mora (general secretary)

Orientation. Trotskyist

History. In 1982 the PRT unsuccessfully contested the congressional elections and its presidential candidate, Ibarra de la Piedra, gained 1.9 per cent of the vote. In February 1985 the PRT entered into an electoral alliance with other socialist, liberal and communist parties including the PMT and the PPS (see above) and the PST, the PSUM and the UPAC (see below).

International affiliations. Fourth International United Secretariat

Partido Social Demócrata (PSD)
Social Democratic Party

Leadership. Manuel Moreno Sánchez (leader)

Orientation. Social democratic

History. In 1982 the PSD contested the presidential election, its candidate – Moreno – gaining only 0.2 per cent of the vote. It also fought the congressional elections without success and subsequently lost its legal status as a political party.

Partido Socialista Revolucionario (PSR)

See PSUM (below).

Partido Socialista de los Trabajadores (PST)
Socialist Workers' Party

Address. Avenida México 199, Colonia Hipódromo Condesa, 06170 México, DF

Leadership. Rafael Aguilar Talamantes (president); Graco Ramírez Abreu (general secretary)

Orientation. Marxist–Leninist

Founded. July 1973

History. The PST was founded by individuals associated with the student protest and guerrilla movements of the late 1960s and early '70s. In June 1977 it formed an alliance with other groups including the Movimiento de Acción y Unidad Socialista (MAUS – Socialist Action and Unity Movement) with the aim of obtaining legal recognition as a political party. The PST was granted temporary registration in May 1978, confirmed after it gained 10 of the 100 proportional representation seats in the Chamber in the 1979 elections. In 1982 it won 11 seats and its presidential candidate, Candido Díaz Cerecedo, won 1.5 per cent of the vote. Despite its espousal of Marxist ideology, the PST has in the past declined to work against the ruling PRI (see above), maintaining that the best hope for the socialist transformation of Mexico lay in the radicalization of the PRI and its labour movement allies. However, in February 1985 the PST entered into an electoral alliance with other socialist, liberal and communist parties including the PMT, the PPS and the PRT (see above) and the PSUM and the UPAC (see below).

Policies. As a Marxist–Leninist party, the PST stands for "the union of scientific socialism with the workers' movement and the people themselves"; free trade unions; the nationalization of foreign companies and banks; government control of basic industries and natural resources, and a

176

state monopoly in foreign trade; collectivization of land, democratization of education and a general amnesty for political prisoners.

Structure. The PST has a national assembly which elects a central committee; from the central committee are drawn the political commission, the executive commission and the national leadership council.

Membership. 132,000

Publications. *El Insurgente Socialista*, organ of central committee; *El Eslabón*, internal bulletin

Associated organizations. The PST has links with two independent trade union federations, the Confederación Nacional de Campesinos (CNC – National Confederation of Peasants) and the Unión Nacional de Trabajadores Agrícolas (UNTA – National Union of Agricultural Workers).

Partido Socialista Unificado de México (PSUM)
Unified Socialist Party of Mexico

Address. Monterrey 159, Colonia Roma, 06700 México, DF

Telephone. 5841972

Telex. 1772925

Leadership. Arnaldo Martínez Verdugo (general secretary)

Orientation. Marxist

Founded. November 1981

History. The PSUM was formed by the merger of five left-wing parties – the PCM, the MAP, the MAUS, the PPM and the PSR – but excluding the PMT (see above), to which the PSUM is ideologically close, and certain other leftist parties.

The Partido Comunista Mexicano (PCM – Mexican Communist Party) had been founded in November 1919 and was recognized by Soviet-bloc communist parties. It was banned after an abortive revolt in 1929, was legalized in 1935 but was not registered for electoral purposes until 1978. In the 1970s it adopted a "Eurocommunist" position.

The Movimiento de Acción Popular (MAP – Popular Action Movement) was founded in January 1981 by Marxist trade unionists and intellectuals.

The Movimiento de Acción y Unidad Socialista (MAUS – Socialist Action and Unity Movement) was founded in 1969 and was led at the time of its merger in the PSUM by Miguel Angel Velasco. It had supported the efforts in 1977–78 which led to the registration of the PST (see below) as a political party.

The Partido del Pueblo Mexicano (PPM – Mexican People's Party), led in 1981 by Alejandro Gascón Mercado, was founded in 1976 after left-wing elements broke away from the pro-government PPS (see above).

The Partido Socialista Revolucionario (PSR – Revolutionary Socialist Party), led in 1981 by Roberto Jaramillo Flores, was founded in 1974 as the Movimiento de Organización Socialista (Movement for Socialist Organization).

The PSUM partners (excluding the MAP) had obtained 703,000 votes and 18 seats in the Chamber of Deputies in the 1979 elections; in 1982, the unified party was allied with the PST and the Corriente Socialista, obtaining 17 seats in the Chamber and 3.7 per cent of the vote for its presidential candidate, Martínez Verdugo. In February 1985 the PSUM entered into an electoral alliance with other Marxist, socialist and liberal parties including the PMT, the PPS, the PRT and the PST (see above) and the UPAC (see below). A week before the elections of July 1985, Martínez Verdugo was kidnapped by the Partido de los Pobres (see above), but he was released on July 18 in return for a US$300,000 ransom.

Policies. The PSUM seeks to link the Mexican revolutionary tradition with the theory of scientific socialism to foment "a new political, economic and cultural revolution" which would bring the working class and its allies to power in "a new society based on the labour of its partners and in which wealth would be the property of society". The party's programme calls for the nationalization of basic industries, banks, land, the media, transport and the public services essential to the country's economic development. It describes itself as both patriotic and internationalist, its foreign policy being broadly in line with that of the Soviet Communist Party.

Structure. The PSUM is a democratic centralist party, with as its highest authority a national congress (held every three years), which elects a central committee with a 17-member political commission and a seven-member secretariat.

Membership. 600,000

Publications. *Así Es*, weekly; *Memoria*, bimonthly

International affiliations. The party regards itself as part of the international communist movement; it maintains relations with communist and workers' parties and democratic and revolutionary movements around the world, including both the Chinese and Soviet parties.

Unidad de la Izquierda Comunista (UIC)
Unity of the Communist Left

Orientation. Communist

Founded. 1973

History. The UIC was formed after a split in the PCM between a majority faction favouring a broad front strategy and this group which has pursued an ideologically narrower line. It was officially recognized as a national political association in December 1978.

Policies. The foreign policies and theoretical orientation of the UIC are very closely in line with those of the Soviet Communist Party. The group supports "the fight of the workers and people of Mexico for political power and for the participation of the working classes and democratic forces in government at all levels".

Unificación y Progreso (UPAC)
Unification and Progress

Orientation. Liberal

History. The UPAC registered as a national political association in December 1978. In February 1985 it joined socialist and communist parties in an electoral alliance.

Policies. The aim of the UPAC is "to recover the true ideals of Mexican social liberalism".

Associated organizations. See PMT, PPS, PRT, PST and PSUM (above).

Nicaragua

Capital: Managua   **Population: 3,100,000**

Nicaragua gained separate independence in 1838. It was subjected to US military intervention in 1912–25 and 1927–33, after which the country was left in the control of the Somoza family, which ruled directly or indirectly, and controlled a vast proportion of the national economy, until the overthrow of the right-wing regime headed by Gen. Anastasio Somoza Debayle by a popular revolutionary movement, the Frente Sandinista de Liberación Nacional (FSLN), in a long and bloody war ending in 1979.

The FSLN, which is named after an anti-US guerrilla leader, Augusto César Sandino (killed by the Somozas' National Guard in 1934), adopted left-wing policies and has met with vigorous opposition from the United States and from internally- and externally-based counter-revolutionary movements (the *contras*), some of which have been funded by the US government; these groups include former supporters of the Somoza regime (*somocistas*) and others including defectors from the Sandinistas. The FSLN has also been opposed by liberal, conservative and Christian democratic parties, which have alleged that the FSLN was attempting to establish a Marxist dictatorship.

Immediately after the revolution the FSLN held power through its majority support in a provisional government junta and, from 1980, on a Council of State incorporating 31 other organizations; in November 1984, however, presidential and legislative (and constituent) elections resulted in a substantial victory for the FSLN, which formed a new government on Jan. 10, 1985.

Constitutional background. The Republic of Nicaragua is governed under interim constitutional statutes by an executive President serving a six-year term and a 96-member National Constituent Assembly, replacing the earlier Council of State and acting as a legislature; the President and Assembly were elected by universal adult suffrage. The Assembly is currently preparing a new Constitution to replace that of 1974, and is expected to have completed its work by 1987.

Recent election results. In an election held on Nov. 4, 1984, Daniel Ortega Saavedra of the FSLN won the presidency with 66.9 per cent of the votes, the candidate of the PCD winning 14 per cent, that of the PLI 9.6 per cent and that of the PPSC 5.6 per cent. Simultaneous elections to the National Constituent Assembly gave the FSLN 61 of the 96 seats, with 14 for the PCD, 9 for the PLI, 6 for the PPSC and two each for the MAP–ML, the PSN and the PCN.

Alianza Revolucionaria Democrática (ARDE)
Democratic Revolutionary Alliance

Leadership. Alfonso Robelo Callejas (political leader); Fernando Chamorro Rapaccioli (known as El Negro; military commander); Adolfo ("Popo") Chamorro

Orientation. Alliance of *contra* groupings

Founded. September 1982

History. The ARDE was formed in San José, Costa Rica, as a political–military coalition of non-*somocista* anti-FSLN groups, some of which did not regard themselves as either anti-Sandinista or counter-revolutionary; its first military commander, Edén Pastora, was a defector from the FSLN (see FRS, below). In a statement issued in December 1982 the ARDE called on the Nicaraguan government to hold elections before June 1983 to end the violence in the country. On April 15, 1983, it issued an ultimatum demanding the withdrawal from Nicaragua of Cuban military personnel, and in May it commenced guerrilla operations against Nicaragua from bases in Costa Rica. Most of its activities have to date been in the southern border area.

During 1983 and early 1984 ARDE attacks consisted mainly of hit-and-run raids across the border. In September 1983, however, it launched a series of more ambitious actions coinciding with an offensive of the FDN (see below); on Sept. 8 the ARDE claimed responsibility for a rocket attack on Managua airport by two planes, one of which was shot down, and Pastora claimed that the attack was launched from an allegedly ARDE-controlled area of 4,200 sq km around San Juan del Sur. A main border post and power lines were destroyed by the ARDE at Peñas Blancas on Sept. 28. From Dec. 27 a new ARDE offensive, again coinciding with an FDN offensive, involved about 3,000 of its guerrillas, but by late January 1984 the Sandinistas had repelled the *contra* forces after heavy fighting.

The ARDE claimed responsibility for the mining of the Atlantic port of El Bluff on Feb. 24, 1984, leading to the sinking of a trawler with nine deaths on Feb. 25. Along with other minings claimed by *contra* forces, this incident was later found to be the work of employees of the US Central Intelligence Agency. The capture by ARDE forces of the Nicaraguan town of San Juan del Norte for four days in April led the Sandinista government to protest to the Costa Rican authorities, who then raided the ARDE offices in San José, closed down its radio communications centre and arrested 12 of its officials. The presence of ARDE guerrillas on Costa Rican territory, and occasional incursions from either side of the border, continued to cause difficulties in relations between Costa Rica and Nicaragua later in 1984 and in 1985.

The ARDE and the FDN, which after some months of negotiation announced their alliance in July 1984, offered to call a ceasefire in 1984 conditional on the acceptance by the government of demands put by the prospective presidential candidate of the CDN (see below), including an amnesty, the lifting of the state of emergency and a "national dialogue" including the *contra* forces. Discussions on the demands broke down in October. In September the ARDE and the FDN combined with Misura (see below) to form the UNIR (see below).

The presence of *somocista* ex-Guardsmen in the FDN caused a division within the ARDE, Pastora's resignation as military commander on Oct. 25 and subsequently his departure from the group; his successor, Chamorro, was the leader of the UDN–FARN (see below). At a press conference held by Pastora shortly after the decision in May (by 24 votes to three) of the ARDE directorate to unite with the FDN, a bomb exploded, killing nine people and injuring 25, including Pastora. Although Pastora had in October 1983 accused Robelo of plotting against his life, Pastora confirmed on Sept. 6, 1984, that there would be continued co-ordination of the military activities of his FRS with those of the ARDE.

In March 1985 the ARDE was one of the *contra* organizations to support proposals for a "national dialogue" put forward by leaders of the CDN opposition coalition (see CDN, below). In June it joined the CDN and the FDN in the UNO opposition alliance, but elements of the ARDE were among the groups which subsequently formed the (seemingly rival) BOS alliance (see below).

After the ARDE launched a seaborne attack on Bluefields on May 16, a Sandinista army counteroffensive – *Operación Soberanía* – opened on May 23 with the aim of pushing ARDE forces back into Costa Rica. By early July the army had taken all eight FDN camps known to be based in Nicaraguan territory, and the organization's leaders were complaining of a shortage of funds and materiel.

Policies. The ARDE has described itself as comprised of "democratic revolutionaries" who "want to make deep social, political and economic changes in Nicaragua" but without the "totalitarianism" of the FSLN. It has stated its willingness to enter into talks with the FSLN but, if no dialogue were offered, to continue its military campaign.

Membership. The founding members of the coalition were the FRS, the MDN, the Misurasata group led by Brooklyn Rivera and the UDN–FARN; the current members are the FTN, the FSDC (which joined on Sept. 1, 1983), the non-Rivera faction of the Misurasata–SICC, the MDN, the STC and the UDN–FARN (see below).

Publications. The main platform for the dissemination of ARDE propaganda is the *contra* radio station, *Voz de Sandino*.

Asamblea Nicaragüense de Unidad Democrática (Anude)
Nicaraguan Assembly of Democratic Unity

Leadership. José Dávila Membereno (one of founders)

Orientation. *Contra* political group

Founded. September 1982

History. The Anude was formed by right-wing emigré politicians including Dávila, a leader of the exiled FSDC section of the PSCN (see below). It was founded in Costa Rica and Dávila was in August 1985 a founder of the Costa Rica-based BOS *contra* alliance (see below).

Policies. Dávila has stated that Anude supports the formation of a united opposition front, and that in his view only violence would remove the Sandinistas.

Associated organizations. Although claiming to represent right-wing elements which had opposed the Somoza regime, Anude appeared to maintain links with *somocista* groups.

International affiliations. Dávila was quoted in 1983 as saying that the group had offices in Costa Rica, Venezuela and Europe, and maintained links with the military forces of Honduras.

Bloque Opositora del Sur (BOS)
Southern Opposition Bloc

Leadership. Edén Pastora Gómez, José Dávila Membereno, Alfredo César Aguirre (leaders)

Orientation. *Contra* alliance

Founded. Aug. 2, 1985

History. The formation of this alliance of Costa Rica-based *contras* followed the creation of the UNO alliance (see below) grouping ARDE (see above), with which the BOS founders had previously been associated, with the CDN and FDN opposition movements (see below).

Policies. The BOS claimed that its members had been discriminated against by the US backers of the *contra* forces, presumably on the grounds that they were not keen to associate with *somocista* elements in the FDN and similar groups; it set out conditions for the unification of all *contra* activities, in the UNO or any other umbrella organization, which included a common political project, equal status for member parties and "a change of attitude" by those who had discriminated against BOS members.

Members. The advertisement in a Costa Rican newspaper which announced the formation of the BOS carried the names of a number of organizations, including Rescate y Conciliación Nacional, various exile trade union groups and the ARDE, but not the FRS, the FSDC, the Anude or other likely sympathizers.

Central de Trabajadores Nicaragüenses (CTN)
Nicaraguan Workers' Federation

Address. Iglesia Santa Ana, 1½ cuadras al occidente, Managua, JR

Telephone. 25981

Leadership. Carlos Huendes (leader); Agustín Jarquín Anaya (general secretary)

Orientation. Social Christian trade union body

Founded. 1943; banned 1949; reorganized as Movimiento Sindical Autónomo Nicaragüense (Mosan – Nicaraguan Autonomous Trade Union Movement) in 1962; reorganized as CTN 1972

Associated organizations. Although nominally independent of party politics, the CTN has long been identified with the PSCN in the Christian democratic movement. The organization is affiliated to the CDN (see below).

International affiliations. World Confederation of Labour; Confederación Latinoamericana del Trabajo

Confederación de Unificación Sindical (CUS)
Confederation for Trade Union Unification

Address. Apartado 4845, Managua, JR

Telephone. 42039

Leadership. Mariano Mendoza (leader); Alvin Guthrie (general secretary)

Orientation. Opposition trade union body

Founded. 1972

History. The CUS was formed by members of the Confederación Sindical Nicaragüense, which was itself formed in 1964. It has joined the CDN opposition coalition.

Policies. The CUS professes to be a social democratic organization but is in practice anti-Sandinista and identified with the right.

Membership. 1,670 (in a labour force of about 864,000)

Publications. Monthly bulletin

Associated organizations.   A total of 17 trade unions are affiliated to the CUS.

International affiliations.   The CUS receives money and services from the American Institute for Free Labor Development (AIFLD), and is closely connected with the main sponsor of the AIFLD, the US AFL–CIO trade union confederation. It is also affiliated to the International Confederation of Free Trade Unions and to the Organización Regional Interamericana de Trabajadores.

Consejo de Acción y Unidad Sindical (CAUS)
Trade Union Council for Action and Unity

Orientation.   Pro-Chinese communist

Founded.   1963

History.   The CAUS has since 1967 been the trade union arm of the PCN (see below).

Consejo Superior de la Empresa Privada (Cosep)
Higher Council of Private Enterprise

Address.   Apartado 5430, Managua, JR

Telephone.   27130

Leadership.   Enrique Bolaños Geyer (president)

Orientation.   Anti-government business association

History.   The Cosep joined the CDN opposition alliance in July 1981. Three individual members of the Council were in October 1981 sentenced to imprisonment for economic offences, but were released on bail in February 1982 in an apparent gesture of goodwill towards the private sector.

In February 1985 Bolaños was quoted as saying that contacts between CDN leaders and *contra* forces made the CDN "inoperative". Bolaños was one of nine people held briefly in March on suspicion of conspiracy to destabilize the government, and in June he lost two-thirds of his substantial landholdings in Masaya as part of the agrarian reform programme.

Membership.   The members of the Cosep are national federations and chambers of commerce and industry and the 650-member Instituto Nicaragüense de Desarrollo (INDE), also led by Bolaños and consisting of private businessmen.

Coordinadora Democrática Nicaragüense Ramiro Sacasa (CDN)
Ramiro Sacasa Democratic Co-ordinating Body of Nicaragua

Leadership.   Dr Eduardo Rivas Gasteazoro (president); Dr Arturo José Cruz, Adán Fletes, Pedro Joaquín Chamorro

Orientation.   Anti-government

Founded.   July 1981

History.   This group (usually known as the Coordinadora Democrática or as the CDN) was set up as an alliance of the main internal opposition parties and other groupings. It frequently accused the Sandinista government of breaches of human rights, withdrew from the Council of State in March 1984 and boycotted the elections of November 1984 after its prospective presidential candidate, Cruz (a member of the revolutionary junta in 1980–81), had failed to secure concessions from the government including the opening of a "national dialogue" with the representation of *contra* forces; the ending of the state of emergency; an amnesty for political offenders; an end to government control of the media; an independent judiciary and the separation of the FSLN from the government apparatus. Discussions on the CDN demands, and a possible postponement of the elections to permit their participation in the campaign, continued until one month before the November polling day.

In February and March 1985 the CDN leaders Cruz and Chamorro held discussions with *contra* leaders of the ARDE (see above), the FDN, the FPS and Misura (see below), resulting in serious disagreements within and between the member parties of the CDN and in the issue in March of joint documents in which the CDN and *contra* leaders reiterated the demands concerning the "national dialogue" and added others concerning fresh elections and a ceasefire. In June 1985 the CDN joined the main *contra* groups in the UNO opposition alliance (see below).

Membership. The original members of the group were the PSCN, the PCDN, the PLC, the PSD, the Cosep, the CUS and the CTN; members in 1985 are the PLC, the PSD, the PSCN and a minority faction of the PCD (see below).

Coordinadora de la Oposición Nicaragüense (CON)
Nicaraguan Opposition Co-ordinating Board

Orientation. Political opposition group

Founded. March 1985

History. The formation of the alliance of opposition political groupings was announced in San José, Costa Rica.

Policies. The CON reportedly called for the solution of the "extremely serious crisis" in Nicaragua by means of dialogue.

Membership. According to media reports the CON members were the PLI, the PSCN, the MDN, the Partido Conservador Nicaragüense and the Movimiento Social Democrático.

Ejército de Liberación Nacional (ELN)
National Liberation Army

Leadership. Pedro Ortega (known as Juan Carlos; leader)

Orientation. Very right-wing *contra* group

Founded. 1979

History. The ELN was formed and is led by former members of Somoza's National Guard. It is based in Honduras. Late in 1980 the group claimed to have 4,000–6,000 armed men inside Nicaragua and several hundred elsewhere; it also claimed to have influence with the east coast Misurasata group (see below). It operates independently of the UND–FARN.

Policies. The group claims to favour free elections, free enterprise and respect for human rights.

Federación de Trabajadores Nicaragüenses (FTN)
Nicaraguan Workers' Federation

Leadership. Zacarías Hernández (leader)

Orientation. *Contra* labour federation

History. The FTN, which is based in Costa Rica, is a member of the ARDE coalition (see above). It does not appear to have a significant following inside Nicaragua.

Frente Obrero (FO)
Workers' Front

Orientation.   Pro-Chinese communist

Founded.   1974

History.   The armed members of the FO had up to 1979 formed the Milicias Populares Antisomocistas (Milpas – Anti-Somocista People's Militia). The FSLN government, stating that the FO and the Milpas were threatening production by provoking urban and rural labour unrest in some areas, arrested about 70 FO members up to October 1979; on Jan. 25, 1980, it closed down the FO daily, *El Pueblo*; and on April 10, 1980, a member of the junta said that the FO and the PCN were to be excluded from the Council of State.

Associated organizations.   The FO is an affiliate of the PCN (see below).

Frente Patriótico para la Revolución (FPR)
Patriotic Front for the Revolution

Leadership.   Gustavo Tablado (co-ordinator)

Orientation.   Pro-government

Founded.   July 23, 1980

History.   The FPR was formed to group together those parties supporting the Sandinista revolution.

Membership.   Its founding members were the FSLN, the PLI, the PPSC and the PSN (see below); the PLI withdrew in February 1984 in order to contest the November elections in opposition to the FSLN.

Frente Revolucionaria Sandinista (FRS)
Sandinista Revolutionary Front

Leadership.   Edén Pastora Gómez (leader)

Orientation.   *Contra* guerrilla group

History.   Pastora played a significant role in the guerrilla struggle of the FSLN against the Somoza dictatorship, during which, using the nom de guerre "Comandante Cero", he became something of a popular hero. On July 7, 1981, he resigned as Deputy Minister of Defence in the revolutionary government and as head of the Sandinista people's militia; he went into exile and founded the FRS as an anti-FSLN guerrilla group professing a democratic and left-wing, but strongly anti-communist, philosophy. The group, which is based in Costa Rica, was a founding member of the ARDE coalition (see above), but withdrew from it after the ARDE leadership voted in May 1984 to form an alliance with the FDN (see below), a *contra* group dominated by *somocista* elements. Nine people were killed in an apparent attempt to assassinate Pastora later in May. The FPS nevertheless agreed to co-operate with the ARDE, and in March 1985 it joined the ARDE, the FDN and Misura in reaching agreement on peace proposals advanced by the CDN opposition leadership (see CDN, above).

Frente Sandinista de Liberación Nacional (FSLN)
Sandinist National Liberation Front

Leadership.   Daniel Ortega Saavedra (President of the Republic, head of FSLN executive commission); Bayardo Arce Castaño (deputy head of e.c.); Tomás Borge Martínez, Cdr Humberto Ortega Saavedra, Cdr Jaime Wheelock Román (other members of e.c.)

Orientation.   Socialist

Founded. 1962

History. The FSLN, which is named after Gen. Augusto César Sandino – a revolutionary leader killed by the National Guard in 1934 – was set up to conduct a guerrilla war against the Somoza regime. It gained substantial support among workers, business and professional people and the clergy, and was by far the most important of the guerrilla groups taking part in the revolution which overthrew Anastasio Somoza in 1979.

On March 8, 1979, the three factions which had developed within the FSLN – the Guerra Popular Prolongada (GPP – Prolonged Popular War), the Tendencia Proletaria (Proletarian Tendency) and the Tercerista (Third Line or Insurrectionist) groups – agreed on a joint programme and strategy, and on June 16 formed (in Costa Rica) a "provisional government junta of national reconstruction" including representatives of other anti-Somoza groupings. On July 19 this provisional government took control in Managua.

The FSLN has since been the main party of government. In September 1979 the junta prohibited the use of the description "Sandinista" by any party other than the FSLN, which was described as "the legal vanguard of the Nicaraguan revolutionary process" and the sole "defender and loyal interpreter of the principles and objectives of Sandinista ideology". The Front has since 1980 been the leading member of the FPR coalition of pro-government parties (see above).

The radical policies pursued by the FSLN led to the defection in 1981 of a deputy minister, Edén Pastora, who went on to form the FRS (see above). That group, and others mainly in the FDN and ARDE alliances, conducted a counter-revolutionary guerrilla war against the FSLN government from bases in neighbouring countries.

The FSLN presidential and vice-presidential candidates, Daniel Ortega and Dr Sergio Ramírez Mercado, won the November 1984 elections, in which the movement also gained 61 of the 96 seats in the Constituent Assembly.

Policies. The FSLN programme issued in 1979 called for national reconstruction (partly using the expropriated assets of the Somoza family), a non-aligned foreign policy, improved standards of living, increased participation of the masses in decision-making and state participation in the economy.

Structure. The FSLN is controlled by five-member executive commission which in August 1985 replaced the earlier directorate of nine members. It is supported at local level by Comités de Defensa Sandinista (CDS – Sandinista Defence Committees) which, in conjunction with the army (the Ejército Popular Sandinista – Sandinista People's Army), runs a civil defence programme, and assists the government in public health and education programmes.

Membership. 60,000

Publications. Barricada, daily in Spanish, weekly in English; daily circulation 95,000. The FSLN is also supported by the daily *Nuevo Diario*, circulation 45,000, and the weekly *Poder Sandinista*; it has its own radio station, *Radio Sandino*.

Associated organizations. See FPR (above). The pro-Sandinista trade unions are represented by the Central Sandinista de Trabajadores (CST – Sandinista Workers' Congress).

International affiliations. Although not a part of the world communist movement, the FSLN enjoys friendly relations with the communist and workers' parties of most countries and also with many social democratic and other left and centre-left parties. It is supported in many European and North American countries by solidarity committees.

Frente de Solidaridad Demócrata Cristiana (FSDC)
Christian Democratic Solidarity Front

Leadership.   José Dávila Membereno (leader)

Orientation.   Christian democrat *contra* group

History.   The FSDC, a right-wing exiled faction of the PSCN, joined the ARDE coalition (see above) with effect from Sept. 1, 1983. In August 1985 its leader was reported to have joined the Bloque Opositor del Sur (see above).

Fuerzas Armadas Anticomunistas (FARAC)
Anti-Communist Armed Forces

Orientation.   *Somicista*

History.   Seven members of the FARAC were on Aug. 20, 1980, sentenced to imprisonment for counter-revolutionary activities. The organization has not recently been reported as active.

Fuerzas Armadas Democráticas (FAD)
Democratic Armed Forces

Leadership.   Bernardino Larios (last identified leader)

Orientation.   *Somocista*

History.   The then leader of the FAD, Carlos García Solorzano, who was head of the National Security Office under Somoza, was arrested with other FAD members on May 9, 1980, and on Aug. 25 he was sentenced to 14 years' imprisonment. Larios, a former Lieutenant-Colonel in Somoza's National Guard who had served as Minister of Defence in the first post-revolutionary government, was arrested on Sept. 19 and charged with conspiring to assassinate members of the FSLN directorate; on Oct. 31 he was sentenced to seven years in prison (although he was freed by the Supreme Court in March 1984 on technical grounds). On Oct. 10 a Spanish diplomat allegedly in contact with the FAD was expelled from Nicaragua, and on Nov. 30 Jorge Salazar Argüello, the head of a landowners' organization and allegedly a financial backer of the FAD, was shot dead in a confrontation with police.

Fuerzas Armadas Revolucionarias Nicaragüenses (FARN)

See UDN–FARN (below).

Fuerzas Democráticas Nicaragüenses (FDN)
Nicaraguan Democratic Forces

Leadership.   Adolfo Calero Portocarrero (commander-in-chief); Enrique Bermúdez (military commander); Indalecio Rodríguez (head of civil services); with a head of communications, this group comprises the FDN civilian–military command

Orientation.   Right-wing *contra* group

Founded.   November 1981

History.   The formation of the FDN (the name is sometimes rendered in the singular, Fuerza Democrática Nicaragüense) was announced on Nov. 27, 1981, by a radio station claiming to be based in Nicaragua. The movement was, and is, based in Honduras, on Nicaragua's northern border, leading to considerable friction between the Nicaraguan and Honduran governments. Of its founders, three – Edgar Chamorro Coronel, Alfonso Callejas and Mario Zeledón – were businessmen; Bermúdez was a colonel in Somoza's forces, and Lucia Cardenal was the widow of Jorge Salazar (see FAD, above). Calero, who joined on Feb. 9, 1983, was then the leader of the PCD (see below); on Oct. 8 he was named by the FDN as "president in exile" of Nicaragua.

On Dec. 14, 1982, the Sandinista government announced that its forces had repelled an FDN invasion aimed at establishing bases inside Nicaraguan territory. In January 1983 the FDN announced that it was prepared to suspend armed operations if the government agreed to hold elections by September under the supervision of the Organization of American States; however, further clashes in February resulted in the deaths of 55 *contra* and five government troops. It launched a major offensive in August, and on Aug. 10 killed 11 civilians and one soldier travelling on a bus near Jinotega. On Aug. 11–12 it destroyed bridges near Jinotega; on Aug. 15 it attacked San Rafael del Norte, reportedly losing 20 dead; and other fighting around northern towns reportedly resulted in 200 *contra* and 31 Sandinista deaths by Aug. 26. On Sept. 9 the FDN claimed responsibility for a rocket attack by US-made T-38 jets on the oil port of Corinto; on Oct. 7 it claimed responsibility for the mining of Corinto harbour (although later reports attributed responsibility to the US Central Intelligence Agency), and on Oct. 10 it claimed responsibility for further sabotage at Corinto. Early in December it announced its intention to establish a provisional government on Nicaraguan territory, of which it claimed to control 8,000 sq km; it launched an offensive, reportedly involving 9,000 guerrillas, on Dec. 13, but after clashes in various parts of the country the Sandinista forces had a clear advantage by late January 1984. On Dec. 28 the FDN created a civilian–military command, reducing the former nine-member directorate to four members.

Air raids and minings of ports resumed in February and March, 1984. By mid-June the FDN, which claimed to have 10,000 guerrillas on three fronts (in northern, central and southern departments), had clashed with Sandinista army and militia units on 156 occasions in the course of an offensive launched late in March; the deployment of about 5,000 FDN fighters, with 3,000 in reserve in Honduras, led the Nicaraguan army to describe this as the largest offensive to date, and it claimed that the FDN had the use of CIA transport aircraft and of CIA-operated supply bases at Las Vagas, Banco Grande and El Aguacate in southern Honduras. Incidents up to mid-June included an attack on San Juan del Río Coco in Nueva Segovia department (May 19–22, 60 FDN and 15 Sandinista casualties reported); an attack by FDN planes on Somoto, Madríz department (June 1); an attack by 600 FDN men on Ocotal, Nueva Segovia (June 2, 45 Sandinistas killed); and later in the offensive, clashes in Jinotega and Zelaya Norte (June 20, 100 FDN and 32 Sandinista dead); the destruction of a major FDN base at Turuwas, Jinotega (June 27, 278 FDN dead); incidents in Matagalpa (Aug. 16–18, 52 FDN and five Sandinista casualties); the bringing down of an FDN supply aircraft in Jinotega (Aug. 27, eight FDN dead) and of a Sandinista helicopter in Matagalpa (Aug. 28). Casualty figures and other details were invariably disputed between the two sides.

By 1984 the FDN was one of the two largest *contra* groupings, the other being the ARDE (see above), and was coming under heavy pressure from the United States – which funded both organizations – to form an alliance. Both groups supported the prospective candidate of the CDN (see above) in the period leading up to the 1984 presidential elections (in which, however, he did not take part), and on July 24 the formation of an FDN–ARDE alliance was announced; on Sept. 5 this was expanded to become the UNIR (see below). The presence in the FDN of many *somocista* ex-members of the National Guard caused a split in the ARDE.

In June 1984 a Catholic priest, Fr Luis Amado Peña, was arrested on charges of conspiring to open an FDN guerrilla front inside Nicaragua; he was found guilty by a commission of the Council of State, and 10 foreign priests were subsequently expelled from Nicaragua, but Fr Amado was pardoned after protests by the Catholic hierarchy in what was interpreted as a move to ease tensions between Church and state. In November Edgar Chamorro Coronel, head of communications in the FDN command, was expelled from the group for communicating details of its CIA support to the press.

In early 1985 there were a number of reports of human rights violations, including the execution of prisoners, by the FDN; after adverse reactions in the US Congress and elsewhere the organization announced the introduction of a "code of conduct" in August. In March 1985 the FDN and other *contra* groups agreed on peace proposals put forward by leaders of the CDN opposition coalition (see above), and on June 12 it announced the formation (with the CDN and the ARDE) of the UNO opposition alliance; this, like the formation of the UNIR, caused dissension in the ranks of the ARDE. In July the FDN launched a major offensive from its Jinotega bases, but by October it had failed to take any major towns and was encountering severe resistance.

Policies. The FDN stated on its formation that its aim was "to liberate our people from Marxist totalitarianism".

Structure. The FDN was originally an alliance of the Misurasata, the UDN and the Legión 15 de Septiembre (see below), but now operates in effect as a single organization. In 1981 it appointed a nine-member directorate, reduced in 1983 (see above) to four members.

Membership. Estimates of the strength of the FDN vary greatly; most are around the 10,000 mark. In June 1985 Calero claimed that the group had 17,000 members and would increase this to 30,000 by the end of 1985.

International affiliations. The FDN receives very substantial support from the US Central Intelligence Agency and from private sources in the USA; it is also thought to have received aid from official sources in other countries, reportedly including Argentina, Guatemala, Israel, Taiwan and Venezuela.

Jeane Kirkpatrick Task Force

Orientation. *Contra* guerrilla group

Founded. Late 1984

History. The formation of this group, named after the then US ambassador to the United Nations, was reported in October 1984.

Kisán

Leadership. Diego Wykliffe (leader)

Orientation. Indian *contra* group

Founded. September 1985

History. This Indian guerrilla organization was founded at a meeting in southern Honduras on Aug. 31–Sept. 3, 1985, attended by 895 people. It was decided that the organization should seek membership of the UNO alliance (see below) and should ask for $300,000 in US government funding.

Structure. The group is led by a seven-member committee.

Legión 15 de Septiembre
September 15 Legion

Orientation. Somocista

Founded. 1979

History. This military organization of former soldiers in Somoza's National Guard was a co-founder of the FDN (see above) in 1981, and has not subsequently conducted independent operations.

Misatán

Orientation. Indigenista

Founded. July 24, 1984

History. This organization was formed at a meeting in Puerto Cabezas with the intention of replacing Misurasata (see below) as the official channel of communication between the government and the Indian population.

Policies. Misatán is committed to the reunification of Indian communities divided by the *contra* war, and seeks the recognition of Miskito as the second official language of Nicaragua.

Membership. The founding meeting was attended by delegates of 63 indigenous communities, representing about 200,000 people.

Misura

Orientation. Indian *contra* group

Founded. July 1982, as Guerrilla Miskito

History. The Guerrilla Miskito, formed by members of the east coast Miskito population of Sumo and Rama Indians, broke away from Misurasata (see below) and took up arms against the Sandinistas in 1982. Its leader, Steadman Fagoth Müller, had been Misurasata's representative on the Council of State when in February 1981 he was arrested and accused of having been a security agent of the Somoza regime. He was released on bail and fled to Honduras in May 1981, where he continued to play an important role in Misurasata until the formation of his own group.

In December 1983 the Guerrilla Miskito rejected a suggestion that it merge with other contra groups including the ARDE (see above), on the grounds that Edén Pastora, then commander of the ARDE, had "close and direct links with Sandinismo". As the Misura it joined the leading *contra* groups in the UNIR (see below) in late August 1984, after Pastora and his FRS (see above) had left the ARDE. The organization joined with other *contra* groupings in March 1984, including the FRS, in supporting proposals for a "national dialogue" advanced by leaders of the CDN opposition coalition (see above).

In January 1985 Fagoth was deported from Honduras after the Nicaraguan authorities had unsuccessfully requested his extradition in connection with the capture and attempted ransoming of 23 Sandinista troops. In mid-August 1985 Misura expelled and arrested Fagoth, charging that he had kidnapped 12 members of the group and that he had betrayed it.

Membership. The fighting strength of the group is estimated at 3,000 members.

Misurasata (pro-ARDE faction)

Leadership. Joaquín Suazo Jessy, Guillermo Espinoza, Rafael Zelaya (leaders)

Orientation. Sumo and Rama Indian *contra* group

Founded. Late 1984

History. Misurasata was a founding member of the ARDE political–military coalition (see above). It is at present divided into this minority hard-line anti-Sandinista faction, which emerged in December 1984 and is still affiliated to the ARDE, and a faction led by the movement's founder, Brooklyn Rivera (see below), which has entered a dialogue with the FSLN.

Misurasata (Rivera faction)

Leadership. Brooklyn Rivera (leader)

Orientation. Sumo and Rama Indian and Creole opposition group

Founded. 1982

History. Misurasata, also known as Misurasata-SICC (for Southern Indigenous Creole Council), was founded and led by Rivera and in 1982, after instances of inhumane or arbitrary treatment of Atlantic coast indigenous communities by the Nicaraguan authorities, it became a member of the ARDE coalition. A faction led by Steadman Fagoth (see Misura, above) broke away from Rivera's Misurasata, the military wing of which was then known as Los Astros, in mid-1982.

After waging an unsuccessful guerrilla campaign in 1982–84, and leading a massive migration of Miskito Indians to Honduras, Rivera held talks with the government in October 1984, in which he presented four conditions for a ceasefire: the recognition of Misurasata as representing the Atlantic coast area; the release of Miskito prisoners; regional autonomy discussions; and a guarantee of freedom of expression. Misurasata subsequently divided between this faction, which has left the ARDE and is willing to hold a dialogue with the FSLN government, and a hard-line anti-Sandinista faction (see above), headed by Suazo Jessy and still belonging to the ARDE.

The negotiations with the government continued in December 1984, but were broken off in January 1985 after failure to agree on whether the granting of autonomy should precede or follow the cessation of hostilities. Talks were resumed in April and broke down in May, but the Sandinista government unilaterally introduced a ceasefire and from July secured the voluntary return of many of the Miskito refugees from Honduras.

Movimiento Acción Popular Marxista–Leninista (MAP–ML)
Popular Action Movement – Marxist–Leninist

Leadership. Isidro Téllez (leader)

Orientation. Ultra-left

History. This small group contested the November 1984 elections, winning two seats in the Constituent Assembly; its presidential and vice-presidential candidates, Téllez and Juan Alberto Enríquez, polled less than 2 per cent of the valid votes.

Movimiento Anticomunista Nicaragüense
Nicaraguan Anti-Communist Movement

Orientation. *Contra* guerrilla group

Founded. Mid-1985

History. The first recorded action of this organization was the kidnapping and subsequent release of a group of US Christian activists and

191

journalists travelling on the Río Coco (on the Costa Rican border) in early August 1985.

Movimiento Democrático Nicaragüense (MDN)
Nicaraguan Democratic Movement

Leadership. Alfonso Robelo Callejas (leader); Fabio Gadea Mantilla

Orientation. Businessmen's *contra* group

Founded. April 1978

History. The MDN was founded by businessmen opposed to the Somoza regime. It became a component of the Frente Amplio Opositor (Opposition Broad Front) formed in July 1978, and participated in the first post-revolutionary government, but came into conflict with the Sandinistas and withdrew from the Council of State after the banning of an MDN-led rally on Nov. 9, 1980.

In November 1981 the MDN declined to co-operate with the PSCN and the PSD (see below) in seeking a dialogue with the government, and in June 1982 Robelo left Nicaragua after the forfeiture of his property for subversive activities. In August the MDN was involved in clashes between Catholic students and young Sandinistas, in which two people were killed, 20 injured and 80 arrested. In December it became a founding member of the ARDE coalition (see above); it called for elections to be held before June 1983, but stated that it would not abandon its "military option".

Movimiento Tercera Vía (M-3V)
Third Way Movement

Leadership. Abelardo Taboada, Luis Riva, Eduardo Sánchez, Sebastián González (leaders)

Orientation. *Contra* group

Founded. October 1983

History. This group was founded in San José, Costa Rica, to "provide an option which would fill the void between the northern [FDN] forces and the [southern] ARDE". It worked closely with both groups from late 1983.

Membership. Its fighting strength in late 1984 was estimated at 300.

Partido Comunista de Nicaragua (PCN)
Communist Party of Nicaragua

Leadership. Elí Altamirano (general secretary)

Orientation. Pro-Chinese communist

Founded. 1967

History. The PCN broke away from the mainstream Nicaraguan communist party (see PSN, below). It was illegal under the Somoza regime but was legalized after the Sandinista revolution; it was not allowed to participate in the Council of State and on Oct. 6, 1981, issued a document on the "serious economic crisis and the deviation of the Sandinista revolution". The authorities, having accused the PCN of "organized and systematic sabotage against the national economy", arrested Altamirano and three other party members on Oct. 29, and on Oct. 29 they were sentenced to seven months in prison.

In November 1984 the PCN won two seats in the elections to a Constituent Assembly; its candidates for the presidency and vice-presidency, Alán Zambrana and Manuel Pérez Estrada, won less than two per cent of the valid votes.

Publications. *Avance*, founded in 1984

Associated organizations. The PCN has a trade union wing, the CAUS (see above), and is linked with the FO (see above).

Partido Conservador (PC)
Conservative Party

Leadership. Mario Rappaccioli, Miriam Argüello (leaders)

Orientation. Conservative

History. This grouping is the hard-line anti-Sandinista faction of the Partido Conservador Demócrata (see below), and joined other opposition parties in the CDN (see above) in boycotting the November 1984 elections.

Partido Conservador Demócrata de Nicaragua (PCDN)
Democratic Conservative Party of Nicaragua

Leadership. Rafael Córdova Rivas, Dr Clemente Guido, Enrique Sotelo (leaders)

Orientation. Conservative

Founded. 1979

History. The PCDN (also known as the PCD) was the largest legal opposition party in the latter years of the Somoza regime. The party, then led by Adolfo Calero Portocarrero, left the Council of State in November 1980 and in July 1981 joined the CDN opposition coalition. Calero went into exile and joined the FDN (see above) in 1983; the party remained active, with a substantial following, inside Nicaragua, and opposed such FSLN policies as the introduction of compulsory military service.

The party subsequently split into CDN and non-CDN factions, and while the former (see Partido Conservador, above) joined in the CDN boycott, the latter presented a candidate in the 1984 presidential election, Guido, who won 14 per cent of the vote, with as his running mate Mercedes Rodríguez de Chamorro; this faction of the PCD also secured 14 of the 96 seats to become the largest opposition grouping in the National Constituent Assembly.

Partido Liberal Constitucionalista (PLC)
Constitutionalist Liberal Party

Leadership. Alfredo Reyes Duque Estrada (general secretary)

Orientation. Conservative, anti-government

History. Derived from the centrist wing of the pre-revolutionary Partido Liberal Nacional (National Liberal Party), the PLC united with other parties in 1981 to form the CDN coalition (see above). It was one of 32 organizations represented on the Council of State, although it opposed the Sandinista government. In February 1984 the decision of the party executive to join in the CDN boycott of the November elections led to the resignation of the party president, Dr Julio Centeno.

Partido Liberal Independiente (PLI)
Independent Liberal Party

Address. Ciudad Jardín, F29 frente a Optica Selecta, Managua, JR

Telephone. 40743

Leadership. Dr Virgilio Godoy Reyes (president)

Orientation. Liberal

Founded. 1946

History. The PLI was formed by liberals opposed to the Somoza-controlled Partido Liberal Nacional. Like other opposition parties it boycotted elections held under the Somoza regime. It was one of the founding members of the pro-government FPR (see above) in 1980; Godoy became Minister of Labour in the Sandinista government, but resigned in February 1984, and took the party out of the FPR to contest the November elections independently.

Godoy won 9.6 per cent of the vote for the presidency, with Constantino Pereira as vice-presidential candidate, and the party secured nine seats in the Constituent Assembly.

Publications. *Alternativa Liberal,* founded in 1984

International affiliations. Liberal International

Partido Popular Social Cristiano (PPSC)
Popular Social Christian Party

Leadership. César Delgadillo Machado (leader)

Orientation. Left-wing social Christian

Founded. 1976

History. The PPSC has joined the pro-Sandinista FPR coalition (see above). In November 1984 its presidential and vice-presidential candidates, Mauricio Díaz and Guillermo Mejía, won 5.6 per cent of the vote; the party also won six seats in the Assembly.

Partido Popular Social Cristiano Auténtico (PPSCA)
Authentic Popular Social Christian Party

Orientation. Social Christian

History. The PPSCA was formed after a split in the PPSC (see above).

Partido Social Demócrata (PSD)
Social Democratic Party

Leadership. Wilfredo Montalván (general secretary); Pedro Joaquín Chamorro Barrios, Guillermo Potoy

Orientation. Right-wing social democratic

Founded. September 1979

History. The PSD was formed by dissident members of the PSCN (see below). It united with other parties in July 1981 to form the CDN coalition (see above), but Montalván and another party member took up seats on the Council of State on Nov. 28. The party boycotted the November 1984 elections and on Dec. 9 Chamorro, the publisher of the opposition daily *La Prensa* (circulation 75,000), announced his decision to remain in exile because of press censorship. In February 1985 he entered into contact with leaders of the FDN and ARDE *contra* forces (see above), together with Arturo Cruz of the CDN, and the ensuing controversy resulted in severe disagreements among the CDN parties and in the conclusion of various agreements with the *contras* (see CDN, above).

Partido Socialcristiano Nicaragüense (PSCN)
Nicaraguan Social Christian Party

Address. Iglesia Larreynaga, 1½ c. al Lago, Apartado 4774, Managua, JR

Telephone. 41259

Leadership. Agustín Jarquín Anaya (president); Dr Luis Vega Miranda (general secretary)

Orientation. Right-wing social Christian

Founded. 1957

History. The PSCN (the name of which is sometimes rendered as Partido Social Cristiano) supported the Unión Nacional de la Oposición (UNO – National Opposition Union) in the 1967 elections. It suffered a split in 1979, leading to the formation of the PSD (see above). It was represented in the Council of State established after the 1979 revolution, but resigned its seat in November 1980; the party, then led by Adán Fletes Valle, united with groups including the PSD and the PLC in July 1981 to form the CDN coalition (see above). In November it called for a "dialogue of national reflection" and for all-party talks.

In July 1983 the PSCN demanded the release of five party members arrested on security charges between May 1982 and April 1983, and alleged that the Sandinista government was persecuting the Catholic Church. The party president nevertheless criticized the April 1984 pastoral letter in which the Nicaraguan bishops asked for the inclusion of the *contras* in a "national dialogue".

Structure. The PSCN has a seven-member national executive (which includes the president and general secretary) elected at party conferences, the 10th of which was held in September 1983.

Membership. 42,000

Publications. El Socialcristiano

Associated organizations. See CDN (above). Some exiled members of the PSCN belong to the FSDC and Anude groups (see above). The party's trade union affiliates include the Frente de Trabajadores Socialcristiano (FRETRA SC – Social Christian Workers' Front), formed in 1980, and the Unión Nacional Campesina (UNC – National Peasant Union), formed in 1983; it is also very influential in the CTN (see above).

International affiliations. Christian Democratic International

Partido Socialista Nicaragüense (PSN)
Nicaraguan Socialist Party

Address. 1er Callejón, Colonia Mántica, Frente a Barricada, Managua, JR

Leadership. Luis Sánchez Sancho (general secretary)

Orientation. Orthodox communist

Founded. 1939

History. The PSN was illegal until the 1979 revolution, but was actively involved in the struggle against the Somoza regime, particularly on the trade union front. The party joined the pro-Sandinista FPR coalition (see above) in 1980, and its representative on the Council of State was appointed vice-president of that body. In 1984 it won two seats in the Assembly which replaced the Council, but its candidate in the presidential election, Domingo Sánchez Salgado (running with Adolfo Evertz Vélez), won less than 2 per cent of the vote.

Policies. Pursuing democratic, pluralist and non-aligned policies, the PSN works for the conversion of the Sandinista revolution into a socialist one.

International affiliations. The PSN is recognized by the communist parties of the Soviet Union and its allies.

Rescate y Conciliación Nacional de Nicaragua
Nicaraguan Rescue and Conciliation

Leadership. Alfredo César Aguirre (leader)

Orientation. Opposition

Founded. October 1983, as Recovery of the Original Nicaraguan Revolution

History. This organization was founded by Aguirre, a former president of the central bank living in exile since mid-1982, and Lionel Poveda. In August 1985 it joined other exile groupings in the Costa Rica-based BOS alliance (see above).

Policies. The group opposes the FSLN government, which it regards as a dictatorship.

Salvación Internacional de Nicaragua del Comunismo (SINC)
Nicaraguan International Rescue from Communism

Orientation. Right-wing guerrilla group

History. Seven members of this organization were imprisoned in Costa Rica in December 1980 for attacks on a left-wing radio station, *Radio Noticias del Continente* (which was closed down by the Costa Rican government on Feb. 20, 1981). Five other members hijacked an aircraft with 22 people on board at San José on Oct. 29, 1981, and secured the release of six of the prisoners, who were flown with the hijackers to El Salvador; they were arrested there and in November it was announced that they were all to be extradited to Costa Rica.

Solidaridad de Trabajadores Cristianos (STC)
Christian Workers' Solidarity

Leadership. Donald Castillo (leader)

Orientation. Christian workers' *contra* group

History. The STC is a member of the ARDE coalition (see above).

Unidad Nicaragüense para la Reconciliación (UNIR)
Nicaraguan Unity for Reconciliation

Leadership. Alfonso Robelo Callejas, Adolfo Calero Portocarrero, Steadman Fagoth Müller (leaders)

Orientation. *Contra* alliance

Founded. Late August 1984

History. The formation of this political–military alliance of three large *contra* groupings was announced on Sept. 5, 1984, and represented the culmination of months of heavy pressure from the US sponsors of the counter-revolutionary war for the unification of the guerrilla command.

Membership. The founding members of the UNIR were the ARDE and the FDN, which had allied with each other in July 1984, and Misura (see above).

Unión Democrática Nicaragüense – Fuerzas Armadas Revolucionarias Nicaragüenses (UDN–FARN)
Nicaraguan Democratic Union – Nicaraguan Revolutionary Armed Forces

Leadership. Fernando Chamorro Rapaccioli (leader)

Orientation. *Contra* guerrilla group

History. The UDN was formed by conservative businessmen, some of whom had opposed the Somoza regime but all of whom opposed the Sandinista revolution. It formed a military wing, the FARN, which carried out several attacks in 1980 and claimed 2,000 members at the end of the year. It stated late in 1980 that it would not enlist former National Guardsmen who sought a return to right-wing dictatorship. In March 1981 the FARN claimed to have a 600-man "freedom force" in Honduras which, with "thousands of supporters" from Guatemala and Miami, would launch an invasion to "liberate" Nicaragua. Nicaraguan protests at guerrilla incursions from Honduras led to talks between Daniel Ortega, then co-ordinator of the government junta, and President Paz García of Honduras in May 1981. A group of 25 UDN and other *contra* leaders, half of whom were tried in absentia, were sentenced on Aug. 25, 1981, to prison terms and fines for subversive activities.

After leading the FDN (see above) in 1982, the UDN-FARN became in December 1982 a founder member of the ARDE coalition (see above); Chamorro subsequently succeeded Edén Pastora as military commander of the ARDE following the formation of an alliance with the FDN.

Unión Nicaragüense de la Oposición (UNO)
Nicaraguan Opposition Union

Orientation.   Opposition coalition

Founded.   June 12, 1985

History.   This alliance was founded by Arturo Cruz of the CDN, Adolfo Calero of the FDN and Alfonso Robelo of the FDN at a meeting in San Salvador, El Salvador. Its purpose was to provide an umbrella organization for political and guerrilla opposition groupings. As with the earlier formation of the UNIR (see above), this initiative led to dissension in the ranks of some of the organizations involved, and particularly the ARDE.

Panama

Capital: Panamá **Population: 2,175,000**

The Republic of Panama seceded from Colombia in 1903, helped and encouraged by the United States, which proceeded to build and run the Panama Canal. The country experienced considerable political instability in its early decades, with frequent and often forcible changes of government. In October 1968 a coup was carried out by the National Guard under the command of Col. Omar Torrijos Herrera; the National Assembly was dissolved and the activities of all political parties were suspended. Torrijos instituted a period of populist and reformist government, his policies including agrarian reform and attempting to regain Panamanian sovereignty over the US-controlled Canal Zone. A National Assembly of Community Representatives (ANRC) was elected in August 1972 and authorized the then Gen. Torrijos to govern by decree for six years.

A new ANRC was elected in August 1978, and installed Dr Arístides Royo as President, although effective power remained with Torrijos. Political parties were legalized in October 1978; in 1979 supporters of the government formed the Partido Revolucionario Democrático (PRD), which gained the support of 398 of the 505 members of the ANRC. A National Legislative Council, to act as an upper chamber, was formed in 1980 of 19 elected members and 37 appointed from the membership of the ANRC.

Torrijos died in an air crash in July 1981, and was succeeded as head of the National Guard by Col. Florencio Flores and from March 1982 by Col. Rubén Darío Paredes, who followed pro-Western and anti-communist policies. Paredes replaced President Royo in July with the former Vice-President, Ricardo de la Espriella. Paredes resigned in August 1983 with the intention of contesting elections due to take place in 1984. The National Guard, then under the command of Gen. Manuel Antonio Noriega Morena, replaced the President with his own Vice-President, Dr Jorge Illueca, in February 1984.

Presidential and legislative elections took place in May and the declared winner was Dr Ardito Barletta of the PRD, the candidate of the Unade coalition, who took office in October and pursued the conservative policies favoured by Noriega. Barletta was obliged to resign in September 1985, and was replaced by Eric Arturo del Valle, leader of the small Partido Republicano, after a political crisis resulting partly from the murder (allegedly by Panamanian security agents) of a former deputy minister of health.

Internal disturbances in recent years have been confined mainly to industrial unrest and student demonstrations, the latter often directed against US policies in Latin America. There were reports of unsuccessful coup plots in October 1979 and September 1983.

Constitutional background. As a result of constitutional reforms adopted by referendum in April 1983, the ANRC was replaced in 1984 by the unicameral Legislative Assembly, consisting of 67 members elected for five-year terms by universal and compulsory adult suffrage. One representative and one alternate are elected in each of 67 polling districts. The presidential election is decided by a simple majority of the popular vote, failing which the Assembly appoints the President by a simple majority. The President, who holds executive power and appoints the Cabinet, is assisted by two elected Vice-Presidents.

Recent election results. The May 6, 1984, elections were followed by a 10-day period in which the government closely supervised the counting of ballots before declaring that the pro-government Unade had won the presidential election by a margin of 1,713 votes, with 300,748 votes for Barletta, 299,035 for Dr Arnulfo Arias Madrid of the Partido Panameñista Auténtico (PPA) and 15,976 for Paredes who, failing to secure the PRD nomination, had stood as the candidate of the Partido Nacionalista Popular. There were four minor candidates. The count in the legislative election gave 40 of the 67 seats to the Unade and 27 to the opposition Alianza Democrática Opositora, which included the PPA.

Alianza Democrática Opositora (ADO)
Democratic Opposition Alliance

Orientation. Right-wing

History. The ADO was formed as an electoral alliance of three conservative opposition parties. It won 27 of the 67 seats in the May 1984 election to the Legislative Assembly, which it claimed were fraudulent; its presidential candidate, the leader of the PPA, was deprived of victory by a very narrow margin.

Membership. The founding parties were the Molirena, the PDC and the PPA (see below).

Frente Amplio Popular (Frampo)
Popular Broad Front

Leadership. Renato Pereira (leader)

Orientation. Populist, centre-left

Founded. 1979

History. The Frampo was founded by supporters of Gen. Torrijos with the object of providing a broader political base for the military regime than its Partido Revolucionario Democrático (see below). It was supported by left-wing groups including an Independent Lawyers' Movement. It was part of the Unade coalition (see below) which won the 1984 legislative elections, but was deprived of its legal status and declared defunct in November 1984.

Membership. 36,000

Associated organizations. See Unade (below).

Frente Nacional Opositora (Freno)
National Opposition Front

Orientation. Alliance of populist and left-wing groups

Founded. 1979

History. The Freno was formed as an alliance of unregistered political parties of various ideological persuasions ranging from right-wing to Trotskyist.

Membership. Its members include the MID, the PDS, the PLA, the PSDP and the PST (see below).

Frente Nacional de Panamá (FNP)
Panamanian National Front

Leadership. Abraham Crocamo (leader)

Orientation. Right-wing

Founded. 1979

History. It was announced on Oct. 24, 1979, that the government had uncovered a coup plot led by Crocamo, a former National Guard officer later identified as leader of the FNP, and supported by members of the Partido Panameñista (see below) and by foreign mercenaries. Several arrests followed the announcement but Crocamo escaped to Costa Rica in January 1980 and to Venezuela in February.

Frente Popular Unido (Frepu)
United Popular Front

Leadership. José Renán Esquivel (1984 presidential candidate)

History. This organization unsuccessfully contested the 1984 presidential election. It lost its legal status in November 1984.

Movimiento Independiente Democrático (MID)
Independent Democratic Movement

History. The MID has been denied official recognition as a political party and has joined the Freno alliance (see above) of unregistered parties.

Movimiento Liberal Republicano Nacionalista (Molirena)
Nationalist Republican Liberal Movement

Leadership. César Arrocha Graell (leader)

Orientation. Conservative

Founded. 1981

History. The Molirena was officially registered on Oct. 21, 1981, and was authorized to recruit members from January 1982.

Membership. 51,000

Associated organizations. The party contested the 1984 legislative elections as part of the ADO opposition coalition (see above), which won 27 of the 67 seats in the Assembly.

Movimiento Revolucionario No Alineado
Revolutionary Non-Aligned Movement

History. The Movement was active in the early 1980s but has not obtained official recognition as a political party.

Partido Acción Nacional (PAN)
National Action Party

History. The PAN was reported active in 1984 but has not been accorded legal status as a political party.

Partido Acción Popular (PAPO)
Popular Action Party

Leadership. Carlos Iván Zúñiga (leader)

Orientation. Centre-left social democratic

History. The PAPO was the only party to oppose the constitutional reform approved in the referendum of April 24, 1983. Its leader unsuccessfully contested the 1984 presidential election. It was deprived of its legal status and declared defunct in November 1984; the party leader was abducted and beaten up by armed men in August 1985.

Membership. 33,000

Partido Demócrata Cristiano (PDC)
Christian Democratic Party

Address. Apartado 6322, Panamá 5

Leadership. Ricardo Arias Calderón (president); Raúl E. Figueroa (general secretary)

Orientation. Conservative, Christian democratic

Founded. 1960

History. The PDC came third in the presidential election of 1968. It won two seats and 20.6 per cent of the votes in the legislative elections of 1980. It is now a leading member of the ADO opposition (see above), which won 27 of the 67 seats in the 1984 legislative elections.

Membership. 36,000

International affiliations. The PDC is a member of the Christian Democratic International.

Partido Demócrata Socialista (PSD)
Democratic Socialist Party

Orientation. Centre-left

History. The PSD is a member of the Freno alliance (see above); it has been denied official recognition as a political party.

Partido Federalista Nacionalista Popular (PFNP)
Federalist Nationalist Popular Party

History. The PFNP has not been accorded legal status as a political party.

Partido Independiente de la Clase Obrera (PICO)
Independent Working Class Party

History. The PICO has not obtained legal status as a political party.

Partido Laborista (PALA)
Labour Party

Leadership. Carlos Eleta Almarán (director); Azael Vargas

Orientation. Right-wing

Founded. Sept. 8, 1982

History. This party initially supported the candidature of Gen. Rubén Darío Paredes in the 1984 presidential elections, but on the latter's withdrawal from the PRD (see PNP, below) the PALA transferred its support to Nicolás Ardito Barletta, also of the PRD (see below). It was given three seats in the Barletta Cabinet formed in October 1984.

Associated organizations. The PALA contested the 1984 legislative elections as part of the winning Unade coalition (see below).

Partido Laborista Agrario (PLA)
Agrarian Labour Party

Orientation. Conservative and populist

Founded. 1940

History. The PLA is a member of the Freno alliance (see above), and has been denied official recognition as a political party.

Partido Liberal Nacional (PLN)
National Liberal Party

Address. Apartado 8420, Panamá 7

Leadership. Roderick Esquivel (leader)

Orientation. Liberal

History. The PLN, founded as the Partido Liberal (PL), was defeated in the presidential elections of 1968. It was the only opposition party whose leader participated in the sessions of a commission convened in 1978 to consider the legalization of parties, the implementation of an electoral law and constitutional changes. In August 1982 the PL gained representation in the Cabinet led by the PRD (see below). After the 1984 elections it was given three seats in the Barletta Cabinet formed in October.

Membership. 47,000

Associated organizations. The PLN contested the 1984 legislative elections as part of the victorious Unade coalition (see below).

International affiliations. The party is affiliated to the Liberal International.

Partido Nacionalista Popular (PNP)
Popular Nationalist Party

Leadership. Olimpio Sáenz (leader)

Orientation. Conservative

Founded. 1983

History. The PNP was founded to promote the policies of Gen. Rubén Darío Paredes, the former commander of the National Guard, after he failed to win the PRD candidature for the 1984 presidential election. He stood as the PNP candidate but secured less than 16,000 votes. The party was deprived of its legal status and declared defunct in November 1984.

Membership. 31,000

Partido Panameñista (PP)
Pro-Panamanian Party

Leadership. Luis Suárez, Alonso Pinzón (leaders)

Orientation. Right-wing

History. This party was formed as a result of a split in the original Partido Panameñista, most of whose members remained in the "authentic" party (see PPA, below). It lost its legal status and was declared defunct in November 1984.

Associated organizations. The party contested the 1984 legislative elections as part of the victorious Unade coalition (see below).

Partido Panameñista Auténtico (PPA)
Authentic Pro-Panamanian Party

Leadership. Dr Arnulfo Arias Madrid (leader)

Orientation. Right-wing

Founded. 1938, as Partido Panameñista (PP)

History. Arias Madrid was deposed three times after election as President of Panama, holding office in 1940–41, in 1949–51 and again, after his election as the candidate of a five-party alliance, the Unión Nacional (National Union), for the 11 days immediately before the 1968 military coup which had brought Torrijos to power. The party has traditionally opposed the political power of the National Guard. Supporters of this movement were allegedly involved in the 1979 coup plot attributed to the FNP (see above).

The party leader was the main opposition candidate in the May 1984 presidential election, and his supporters claimed that the narrow government victory was the result of fraud.

Policies. The PPA describes its stance as nationalist and anti-communist.

Membership. 70,000

Associated organizations. The PPA became the leading member of the ADO congressional opposition group (see above).

Partido del Pueblo de Panamá (PPP)
Panama People's Party

Leadership. Rubén Darío Sousa (general secretary)

Orientation. Communist

Founded. 1943

History. The PPP succeeded the Partido Comunista de Panamá (PCP – Communist Party of Panama), founded in April 1930 and dissolved in 1943. After some years as a moderate socialist party, the PPP adopted Marxism–Leninism as its ideology in 1951. In September 1968 the party decided to transform itself into "a mass party of the proletariat and other working people" and to support "the progressive socio-economic reforms" of the government, and its campaign for the restoration of national sovereignty over the Panama Canal Zone. Its unsuccessful candidate in the 1984 presidential election was Carlos del Cid. The PPP was deprived of its legal status and was declared defunct in November 1984.

Policies. On foreign issues, the PPP is sympathetic to the line of the Soviet Communist Party; on domestic issues, it has supported Gen. Torrijos and the left of the PRD (see below).

Structure. The PPP has branches in workplaces and in residential districts and has local, zonal and regional committees. Its supreme organ is a national congress, meeting every four years, which elects a central committee. The central committee appoints a political bureau, a national executive committee and a general secretary.

Membership. 36,000

Publications. *Unidad*, monthly

International affiliations. The PPP is recognized by the Soviet Communist Party and its allies.

Partido Republicano (PR)
Republican Party

Leadership. Eric Arturo del Valle (President of Panama, leader)

Orientation. Moderate conservative

History. The party contested the 1984 legislative elections as part of the victorious Unade coalition (see below), winning only two of the bloc's 40 seats. It was given one seat in the Barletta Cabinet formed in October 1984, and the party leader was, as President Barletta's First Vice-President, installed as President when Barletta was obliged to resign in September 1985.

Membership. 40,000

Partido Revolucionario Democrático (PRD)
Democratic Revolutionary Party

Address. Apartado 2650, Panamá 9A

Leadership. Berta Torrijos de Arosemana (president); Dr Jorge Medrano (vice-president)

Orientation. Populist, currently centre-right

Founded. Sept. 22, 1979

History. The PRD was founded by supporters of Gen. Torrijos and, reflecting the ideological diversity of his following, included Marxists, Christian democrats and liberals among its members. Torrijos was the effective leader of the party until his death in an air crash on July 29, 1981. The PRD, as the party favoured by the National Guard, is the country's leading political formation. Its candidate, Nicolás Ardito Barletta, was accorded a narrow victory in the May 1984 presidential elections in which he was opposed by a coalition headed by Arnulfo Arias Madrid, while a coalition led by the party won 40 of the 67 seats in the Legislative Assembly. The PRD was given five posts in the Cabinet formed by Barletta in October. Barletta was, however, ousted in September 1985 and succeeded by the First Vice-President, Eric del Valle of the PR.

Policies. Under the supervision of the current head of the Guard, Gen. Noriega, it has moved from the centre-left line of Torrijos to a more conservative position, particularly on economic issues.

Structure. The PRD has "basic units" each of 25–100 members who elect municipal and provincial leaders and delegates to the national congress. The congress, held every three years, is the party's supreme authority, determining policy and electing a 300-member directorate and a five-member executive committee. The directorate meets every three months to deal with current policy issues, and appoints a 30-member political commission and a secretariat.

Membership. 206,000

Associated organisations. See Unade (below).

Partido Socialdemocrático Panameño (PSDP)
Panamanian Social Democratic Party

Leadership. Winston Robles (leader)

Orientation. Social democratic

History. The PSDP is part of the Freno (see above), and has been denied official recognition as a political party.

Associated organizations. See Freno (above).

Partido Socialista de los Trabajadores (PST)
Socialist Workers' Party

Leadership. Ricardo Barria (1984 presidential candidate)

Orientation. Trotskyist

History. The PST joined the Freno (see above) soon after the latter's establishment in 1979. It contested the 1984 presidential election but polled negligibly. It was deprived of its official recognition and declared defunct in November 1984.

Membership. 30,000

Associated organizations. See Freno (above).

Unión Nacional Democrática (Unade)
National Democratic Union

Orientation. Centre-right

History. The Unade was formed as an electoral coalition of centrist and right-wing parties which collectively gained 40 of the 67 seats in the Legislative Assembly in May 1984.

Membership. The original members of the Unade were the PRD, the Frampo, the PALA, the PLN, the PP and the PR (see above); the PP and the Frampo lost their legal status in November 1984.

Paraguay

Capital: Asunción   **Population: 3,650,000**

From independence in 1811 until the War of the Triple Alliance, in which Paraguay took on the combined forces of Argentina, Brazil and Uruguay, the country was ruled by three successive dictators. After the war (of 1865–70), in which half the population was killed, two major political parties – the Partido Colorado and the Partido Liberal – were formed, and they have dominated the political life of the country ever since (apart from a period of military rule after the 1933–35 Second Chaco War with Bolivia).

Since taking power in a military coup in 1954, Gen. Alfredo Stroessner has on seven consecutive occasions been declared the winner of presidential elections as the candidate of the Partido Colorado. His authoritarian and right-wing government has maintained the country under a "state of siege", renewed almost without interruption at 90-day intervals since 1954 and suspending constitutional rights and civil liberties. Political prisoners have been held in prison for 20 years or more without trial; a very large proportion of the population is living in exile, for political or economic reasons, and there have been frequent and documented instances of torture and arbitrary arrest. The Partido Liberal is currently divided into a number of contending factions the largest of which – the Partido Liberal Radical Auténtico – is among the

205

opposition movements denied legal status as a party. The regime is also opposed by a growing independent trade union movement and by substantial elements of the Catholic hierarchy, while externally its violation of human rights has been censured by bodies such as the Inter-American Human Rights Commission.

Constitutional background. The Constitution of 1967 defines the Republic of Paraguay as "a representative democracy" with an executive President. Legislative power is vested in a Congress consisting of a Senate of at least 30 members and a Chamber of Deputies of at least 60 members, both chambers, and the President, being elected (and re-eligible) for five-year terms by universal adult suffrage. The party which gains a majority in congressional elections is allocated two-thirds of the seats in both chambers, the remainder being divided among the minority parties in proportion to their electoral strength. The President has powers to dissolve Congress.

Under legislation introduced in 1981, parties were prohibited from urging voters to abstain or return blank or spoiled ballot papers as a form of protest; in order to be registered, a party was required to have 10,000 members distributed among at least one-third of the country's electoral districts; communist parties and those with "similar aims" remained banned, and a ban was imposed on parties with international links or which preached "racial, religious or class struggle" or "hatred among Paraguayans".

Recent election results. In a presidential election held on Feb. 6, 1983, exactly 90 per cent of the votes were, according to official results, cast for the Colorado candidate, Stroessner, in a 90 per cent poll, with 8.9 per cent for two small liberal factions, all other parties having called for abstention. In simultaneous congressional elections, the official count gave a majority to the Colorados, giving them, in accordance with the Constitution, 40 seats in the Chamber and 20 in the Senate; the Partido Liberal Radical was given 13 and 6, and the Partido Liberal 7 and 4.

Acuerdo Nacional (AN)
National Accord

Leadership. Collective leadership consisting of leaderships of constituent parties

Orientation. Centre-left

Founded. 1978

History. The Acuerdo Nacional is an opposition coalition not recognized as a political party and consisting of the PRF and several parties which are themselves not recognized. It has been represented at the very few political rallies to have been permitted in recent years, including one on May 14, 1985, attended by 5,000 people.

Policies. The AN has called for a boycott of elections held by the Stroessner regime. In a programme launched in August 1984 it called for the lifting of the state of siege, the release of all political prisoners, the defence of human rights, the abolition of repressive laws, the establishment of a new electoral law and a law on political parties, freedom of expression and the ending of government control over the media, the defence of national sovereignty, an independent judiciary and a fairer distribution of wealth.

Membership. Member parties are the MOPOCO, the PDC, the PLRA and the PRF (see below).

International affiliations. The AN is informally supported by an international alliance of political exiles, the APE (see below).

Acuerdo Paraguayo en el Exilio (APE)
Paraguayan Accord in Exile

Leadership. Arturo Acosta Mena (general secretary)

Orientation. Anti-*Stronista* (i.e. anti-Stroessner)

Founded. 1978

History. The APE was formed at a meeting in Amsterdam as a coalition of exiled members of Paraguayan opposition groupings in Latin America, North America and Europe. Its broad front strategy and its policies are in agreement with the line pursued inside Paraguay by the Acuerdo Nacional (see above), although there is no formal organizational link.

Asociación Nacional Republicana – Partido Colorado (ANR-PC)
National Republican Association – Colorado Party

Leadership. Gen. Alfredo Stroessner Mattiauda (President of Paraguay, effective leader); Dr Juan Ramón Chávez (president); Dr Sabino Augusto Montanaro (first vice-president); Mario Abdo Benítez (secretary)

Orientation. Authoritarian, conservative and *Stronista* (pro-Stroessner)

Founded. Sept. 11, 1887

History. The ANR was founded under the presidency of Triple Alliance War veteran Gen. Bernardino Caballero. The group took the red flag as its emblem, giving rise to its more popular name, the Colorado [Red] Party. In the violent sequence of coups and counter-coups at the end of the last century (there were three Presidents in one day in 1880), the Colorados were the dominant political force, with Caballero holding the presidency for nine years (1882–91).

Following the liberal revolution of 1904 the Colorados were removed from power, but returned in the 1940s. When the liberal leader Marshal Estigarribia was killed in 1940, Gen. Higinio Morínigo assumed the presidency and banned all political parties. His support for the Axis powers in the Second World War made him unpopular following the Allied victory and in 1946, under US pressure, he accepted the installation of a Colorado–Febrerista coalition government. When the Febreristas were expelled from the government in 1947 the Colorados remained in power, although divided between a moderate conservative wing and the very right-wing Guión Rojo faction; armed bands of *guionistas* roamed the streets and filled the prisons with opponents of the Colorados. Morínigo's forces defeated the Liberals and the Febreristas in the civil war of 1947, but in 1948 a palace coup brought Natalicio González to power with the support of the Guión. Subsequent coups led to two short presidencies followed by the democratic regime of Federico Chávez, installed in August 1950.

On May 5, 1954, the commander-in-chief of the armed forces, Gen. Stroessner, staged a coup against Chávez and formed a government based on the right wing of the Colorados. Stroessner and the Colorados were declared the winners in presidential and legislative elections held in 1954, 1958, 1963, 1968, 1973, 1978 and 1983, their share of the vote in 1983 being stated at 90 per cent. Until 1968 the Colorados were the only party represented in the Chamber of Deputies, but there has subsequently been a token liberal presence; the Colorados have since 1968 held 40 of the 60 seats in the Chamber of Deputies, and 20 of the 30 in the Senate.

The party operates with the support of the armed forces and most of the commercial and industrial sector. Branches have been established even in the smallest villages, a personality cult has been developed around Stroessner, and political opponents have been neutralized by imprisonment, exile or other means. The party has from time to time suffered purges and factional splits, including that in 1959 leading to the formation of the Mopoco (see below). The question of the presidential succession has in recent years led to the development of various personalist tendencies, of indeterminate strength, within the party, and there are also identifiable pro-military and pro-civilian factions; these differences were demonstrated in the national convention of September 1984, when neither the "military" candidate, Mario Abdo Benítez, nor the "civilian" candidate, Juan Manuel Frutos, secured election to the crucial position of first vice-president.

Policies.   The party is conservative and emphasizes the need for stability and vigilance against left-wing extremism.

Structure.   The party is highly centralized and is directed by a national executive committee, although annual conventions are held with delegates appointed to represent about 200 local branches.

Membership.   1,300,000; membership is compulsory for members of the armed forces, civil servants, teachers, doctors and other state employees.

Publications.   *La Patria*, daily, circulation 8,000; *La Voz del Coloradismo*, daily half-hour broadcast on 30 radio stations; *El Diario*, new daily newspaper strongly supporting the party

Associated organizations.   The Party has a close relationship with the sole legal trade union federation, the Confederación Paraguaya de Trabajadores (CPT – Paraguayan Confederation of Workers).

International affiliations.   The Colorado Party has no international affiliations other than its association with the World Anti-Communist League, the 12th congress of which it hosted in 1979. It regards affiliation to international party organizations as unpatriotic.

Asociación Nacional Republicana – Partido Colorado en el Exilio (ANR-PC en el Exilio)
National Republican Association – Colorado Party in Exile

Orientation.   Centre-right

Founded.   1973

History.   This movement was formed in exile by a minority faction of the Mopoco (see below), but claims to have a following in Paraguay among the membership of the mainstream Partido Colorado.

Confederación Paraguaya de Trabajadores en el Exilio (CPTE)
Paraguayan Confederation of Workers in Exile

Leadership.   Miguel Angel Aquino (general secretary)

Orientation.   Democratic trade union movement

History.   This organization represents exiled trade unionists and supports the development of the independent unions within Paraguay; it is in sympathy with the policies of the Acuerdo Nacional.

14 de Mayo

See Partido Liberal (below).

Frente Amplio Democrático y Popular (Fadepo)
Popular and Democratic Broad Front

Orientation. Anti-*Stronista*

History. This co-ordinating committee was created in the early 1980s to bring together representatives of the various exiled democratic groups to work out a common strategy for opposing the Stroessner regime.

Ligas Agrarias Campesinas
Peasant Agrarian Leagues

Leadership. Victoriano Centurión (leader)

Orientation. Land rights movement

Founded. Early 1960s

History. This movement attracted considerable support among landless peasants, and organized production and distribution co-operatives serving about 20,000 peasants by 1969. Claiming that the Leagues were communist-inspired, the regime launched a wave of repression in rural areas in the mid-1970s; leaders of the movement were killed, arrested or forced into exile. After some years of clandestine activity, the Leagues re-emerged in 1980 as a result of increasing land conflicts in the eastern region between, on the one hand, Paraguayan peasants, and on the other, Brazilian settlers and others with legal title to farmlands.

After coming into conflict with a group of army officers attempting to develop a sand quarry in the department of Caaguazú, some 30 peasants hijacked a bus on March 8, 1980, and drove it towards the capital with the intention of bringing their grievances to the attention of the President. The bus was halted by an army patrol; the hijackers escaped but there followed an intensive military operation in which about 300 peasants were arrested and several – including Blas Rodas Rojas, a leader of the Leagues – were killed. Among those who escaped was Centurión, a founder – member of the Leagues who had been imprisoned without trial for three years in the 1970s; he obtained asylum in the Panamanian embassy and later left the country.

Of 13 peasants brought to trial in connection with the incident three were released in 1983, four in 1984 and the other six in 1985 (after a hunger strike, and having served two months more than their 4½ year sentences).

Policies. The Leagues are a Christian-oriented movement committed to improving conditions in the countryside by establishing communities based on mutual assistance.

Movimiento de Autenticidad Colorado (MAC)
Colorado Authenticity Movement

Leadership. Alcibiades Melgarejo, Rubén Darió Verón (leaders)

Orientation. Non-*Stronista* conservative

History. The MAC was founded by two dissident lawyers, members of the Colorado Party. Three of its members were arrested without charge in June 1984.

Movimiento de Integración Liberal Radical (MILR)
Radical Liberal Integration Movement

Orientation. Centrist

Founded. 1984

History. This movement originated as a tendency within the Partido Liberal Radical (see below). Its supporters among the delegates walked out of the PLR's January 1985 convention.

Movimiento Popular Colorado (Mopoco)
Popular Colorado Movement

Leadership. Epifanio Méndez Fleitas (leader); Miguel Angel González Casabianca (president); Enrique Riera (first vice-president); César Stumps (second vice-president)

Orientation. Centrist, anti-*Stronista*

Founded. 1959

History. The Mopoco was formed as a result of a split in the Partido Colorado between pro-military supporters and civilian opponents of Stroessner. Méndez had been exiled in 1956 for criticisms of Stroessner's economic policies. The lifting of the state of siege for one month in 1959 led to a number of demonstrations by anti-*Stronista* Colorados, resulting in clashes with the police; the army was called out and, when the lower chamber condemned the treatment of protestors, Stroessner closed down Congress. Hundreds of opposition Colorados were imprisoned and others went into exile and formed the Mopoco under the leadership of Méndez. Although most of the leadership of the movement has remained in exile, it claims to have developed a significant following within Paraguay.

In 1973 a division emerged in the movement, the majority of members favouring co-ordinated action with other opposition forces while a minority, seeking to emphasize the link with mainstream coloradismo, renamed itself the ANR en el Exilio (see above). The majority faction went on to join the Acuerdo Nacional (see above) in 1978. In November 1974, after the arrest and interrogation of several students in Asunción, the Mopoco was alleged to have been involved with the Argentinian ERP guerrilla movement in a plot to kill Stroessner and capture other government figures; about 1,000 people were arrested and many Mopoco supporters fled the country. One of the alleged instigators of the plot was a leader of the Mopoco, Dr Agustín Goiburú, who was seized by Argentinian security forces in Paran and reportedly handed over to the Paraguayan authorities in February 1977, since when he has disappeared. Other members of the movement were kidnapped while in Brazil.

In December 1983 20 prominent members of the Mopoco, including González Casabianca, were permitted to return to Paraguay after more than 20 years in exile; however, they have since been subjected to continual surveillance. In March 1984 the leading daily newspaper, *ABC Color*, published an interview with González Casabianca, leading to the arrest of its editor and publisher and the closure of the paper as a "focus for subversion". In July the Mopoco was prevented from holding a conference, and in January 1985 four Mopoco leaders were reported to have begun a hunger strike after their detention by the police. The party has never been accorded legal status. Both vice-presidents were sent into internal exile in September 1985, the third such sentence against Riera in that year.

Policies. Mopoco is a democratic nationalist party opposed to military intervention in politics and broadly in favour of state involvement in the economy.

Associated organizations. See Acuerdo Nacional (above).

Movimiento Renovación
See Partido Liberal (below).

Organización Político-Militar (OPM)
Political–Military Organization

Orientation. Left-wing guerrilla group

Founded.   1974

History.   The OPM (which is also known as the Organización Primero de Marzo, March 1 Organization) was formed as an alliance between radical students and peasants. The group, which advocated armed resistance to the regime, was infiltrated by government agents and suppressed in a wave of repression culminating in the arrest of 2,000 peasants and 200 students in April and May 1976. Among the 20 members of the OPM who died in police custody were two of its leaders, Juan Carlos da Costa and Mario Schaerer. Many others fled into exile.

According to a statement in May 1976 by the Paraguayan Minister of the Interior, the group had links with Argentinian guerrilla organizations and had as one of its leaders a Spanish Jesuit priest, Fr Miguel Sanmartí García. One French and six Spanish Jesuits were expelled from Paraguay in April 1976 for allegedly spreading Marxist propaganda and supporting OPM guerrilla activities; the police appealed for help in locating Fr Sanmartí, but his Jesuit superior stated that he had been in Spain for the five months prior to the allegations against him.

On Dec. 18, 1977, 19 trade unionists mainly associated with the Confederación Cristiana de Trabajadores (Christian Confederation of Workers) and the Liga Agraria Cristiana (Christian Agrarian League) were arrested at Ypacarai (near Asunción) and charged with reorganizing the OPM. Nine of them were released in February 1978.

With most of its known leaders dead or in exile, it is unlikely that the OPM still has a presence in Paraguay; however, the regime has from time to time invoked its name to justify detentions of political opponents.

Organización Primero de Marzo (OPM)

See Organización Político–Militar (above).

Partido Colorado

See ANR-PC (above).

Partido Colorado en el Exilio

See ANR-PC en el Exilio (above).

Partido Comunista Paraguayo (PCP)
Paraguayan Communist Party (Creydt faction)

Leadership.   Oscar Creydt (leader)

Orientation.   Maoist

Founded.   1967

History.   This party, which like the Maidana faction (see below) claims to be the historic representative of the Paraguayan communist movement, was formed after the abortive guerrilla warfare of the early 1960s. When the communist guerrillas were finally defeated in 1965 the then general secretary of the sole Paraguayan Communist Party, Oscar Creydt, was expelled by the pro-Soviet majority faction; he took about 50 members with him and founded an alternative party aligned with Peking.

In March 1982, 31 alleged members of this party were displayed to the Paraguayan press by police authorities. The prisoners were mostly peasant activists arrested during the previous month; there was no substantial evidence of their involvement with the party.

Policies.   The party combines Marxist–Leninist theory with an intense patriotism; it advocates revolutionary change and looks in particular to the peasantry to take up arms against the regime. Much of its rhetoric is concerned with condemning the other PCP and "Soviet imperialism".

Publications. *Adelante*, party organ; various pamphlets

Partido Comunista Paraguayo (PCP)
Paraguayan Communist Party (Maidana faction)

Leadership. Antonio Maidana (last general secretary, possibly deceased)

Orientation. Orthodox communist

Founded. Feb. 19, 1929

History. A small group of communists existed in Paraguay in the early 1920s but the party was not formally constituted until 1929. On Feb. 20, 1931, Obdulio Barthe, later to become an important figure in the party, led an uprising in Paraguay's second city, Encarnación. The "revolutionary commune" which was established was rapidly crushed and the leaders fled. In its early days the PCP competed with the anarchist movement, which was quite influential in the trade unions. By the early 1930s the PCP had a significant presence among railway workers and in other parts of the labour movement through its Comité Sindical de Unidad Clasista (Trade Union Committee for Class Unity). The Central Obrero Regional (Regional Workers' Centre) also passed into communist control before its collapse in 1934, and the party led the Confederación Nacional de Trabajadores (CNT – National Workers' Confederation) on its establishment in 1936.

The PCP held its first congress in 1934, when it had about 500 active members. It opposed the Chaco War against Bolivia and consequently its leaders, including Barthe and Oscar Creydt, were imprisoned. The party supported the Febrerista coup of 1936 and was legalized by the Franco government, only to be outlawed again after 15 days, together with all other political parties. Its activities were nevertheless tolerated and many communists returned from exile during the 18 months of the regime.

The PCP was the main force behind the Primer Congreso Obrero del Paraguay (First Workers' Congress of Paraguay) formed in 1939; it organized a number of strikes under the Morínigo regime but several of its leaders were arrested. In June 1946 it was again legalized; exiled members returned and the party claimed 10,000 members. After a change of regime in January 1947 it was banned yet again and its leaders imprisoned. It took part in the abortive rebellion of August 1947, following which many communists were arrested including the party's general secretary, Alberto Candía, who died in custody.

The exiled PCP leadership subsequently concentrated on organizing in urban areas. It was involved in the general strike of August 1958, when three prominent members, Julio Rojas, Dr Antonio Maidana and Alfredo Alcorta, were arrested; they spent the following 20 years in prison. The defeat of the strike led the party to adopt a military strategy in 1959. Small guerrilla columns operated in Paraguay from 1960, but suffered infiltration, betrayal and severe losses until their final defeat in 1965.

Discontent over the direction of the guerrilla campaign by the general secretary, Creydt, led to the formation of the Partido Comunista Leninista Paraguayo in 1963, under the leadership of Barthe. In 1965 this group became the Comité para la Defensa y Reorganización del PCP; it received the recognition of the Soviet Communist Party and in 1967 announced the reconstitution of the party and the expulsion of Creydt, whose supporters, also claiming the name PCP, followed a pro-Chinese line.

The "Soviet line" PCP continued to operate clandestinely in Paraguay and in 1971 held a congress and elected a new central committee. In

November 1975 some party organizations were discovered by the police. By mid-January 1976 about 70 people had been arrested; it was reported that they included elderly people, children and pregnant women, and that several – including the general secretary, Miguel Angel Soler, and central committee members Derliz Villagra and Rubén Octavio González – died under torture. In February 1977 Maidana, Roa and Alcorta were released from prison, and later Gilberta Verdún, imprisoned in 1968, was also freed. Maidana became the party's general secretary. Together with central committee member Emilio Roa, he disappeared in Argentina in 1980; it was reported that he was handed over to Paraguay, but the authorities have never confirmed this.

Policies. The PCP is an internationalist Marxist–Leninist party. It advocates a democratic broad front strategy combined with international pressure on the Stroessner regime to produce improvements in the human rights situation and the removal of repressive legislation.

Publications. *Adelante*, party organ, and pamphlets, mainly published in exile

International affiliations. This party is recognized by the Soviet Communist Party and its allies.

Partido Demócrata Cristiano (PDC)
Christian Democratic Party

Address. Colón 871, casi Pirebebuy, Casilla 1318, Asunción

Leadership. Luis Alfonso Resck (leader, in exile); Alfredo Rojas León (president); Florencio Riveros Vásquez, Juan Descalzo Buongermini (vice-presidents); Jorge Darío Cristaldo (secretary)

Orientation. Centrist, anti-*Stronista*

Founded. May 1960

History. The PDC has been refused legal status on the grounds that it has urged its supporters to abstain in elections. In 1978 it joined the Acuerdo Nacional (see above). Resck was arrested, allegedly tortured, went on hunger strike and was deported from Paraguay for alleged subversive activities in July 1981; he remains in exile in late 1985.

Policies. The PDC has demanded the lifting of the state of siege, the release of political prisoners and the return of exiles. In the longer term it seeks the "transformation of the existing political structure into a true democracy" and economic development on the basis of private ownership and free enterprise.

Structure. The party is organized in districts and regions and has separate sections for youth, labour, farmers and women; it has a national committee appointed by its highest authority, the national convention.

Membership. 38,000

Publications. *DC-CE*, party organ, circulation 10,000; *Revolución*, youth branch organ, circulation 5,000

International affiliations. The PDC belongs to the Christian Democratic International and the Christian Democratic Organization of America.

Partido Liberal (PL)
Liberal Party

Leadership. Dr Hugo Fulvio Celauro (leader)

Orientation. Centre-right

Founded. 1961

History. The PL is one of various factions derived from the original Partido Liberal which was organized by pro-Argentinian interests in 1887 and was continually in power, although competing with the Colorados, until 1940 (apart from the Febrerista interlude – see PRF, below). In 1940 the then leader of the liberals, the Chaco war leader Marshal Estigarribia, was killed in an air crash; his successor, Gen. Higinio Morínigo, eventually aligned himself with the Colorados and dissolved the Partido Liberal for "subversive activities" in April 1942.

Dissident liberals joined Febreristas and communists in an unsuccessful uprising against Morínigo in 1947. Exiled liberal students and intellectuals led by Vargas Peña formed the 14 de Mayo guerrilla movement in 1959; a column led by a young poet, Juan José Rotela, crossed into Paraguay on Dec. 12, but was crushed by the army. Other raids were made by the movement in 1960 but in 1961, having suffered tremendous casualties, the liberals gave up the strategy of armed resistance.

The liberal movement regrouped in 1961 as the PL, from which the PLR and the PLT (see below) subsequently split. The rump of the PL achieved official recognition as a political party and in 1963 (as the Movimiento Renovación, Renewal Movement) stood unsuccessfully against President Stroessner; it lost other presidential and congressional elections in 1968, 1973 and 1978 (although in 1977 it boycotted the elections to a constitutional convention). A further split in 1977 gave rise to the PLU (see below).

The PL candidate in the 1983 presidential election, Celauro, obtained only 3.2 per cent of the vote according to the official count. The party was allocated seven seats in the Chamber and four in the Senate.

Policies. The PL stands for democratization and free enterprise; it is strongly anti-communist.

Partido Liberal Radical (PLR)
Radical Liberal Party

Address. Yegros y Manuel Domínguez, Asunción

Leadership. Justo Pastor Benítez (leader); Persio Franco (president)

Orientation. Centre-right

Founded. 1961

History. The PLR is one of few opposition groups recognized by the government as a political party. It was formed by a majority faction of Partido Liberal (see above). In 1967, as the principal opposition party, it gained 28 (out of 109) seats in a national constituent convention, and in 1968 and 1973 it won 16 (out of 60) seats in the Chamber of Deputies. In 1977 the majority of its members, including the party president, Domingo Laíno, joined the majority of the PL to form the PLU (see below). The PLR boycotted the 1977 elections to a constitutional convention and unsuccessfully opposed Stroessner in the 1978 presidential election.

In 1983 its presidential candidate, Dr Enzo Doldán, received only 5.7 per cent of the vote, according to the official count. It was given 13 seats in the Chamber and six in the Senate, making it the second-largest party bloc. The January 1985 party convention replaced Doldán as party president with Franco; in the same convention members of the MILR (see above) announced their departure from the PLR.

Publications. *El Radical*, weekly

Partido Liberal Radical Auténtico (PLRA)
Authentic Radical Liberal Party

Leadership. Dr Domingo Laíno (leader, deported in 1982); Miguel

Angel Martínez Yaryef (president); Dr Juan Manuel Benítez Florentín, Hermes Rafael Saguier (deputy leaders); Miguel Abdón Saguier (general secretary)

Orientation.   Centre-left

Founded.   1978

History.   The PLRA broke away from the PLU (see below), its founding members including Laíno (who had led the PLR in 1974–77), Carlos Alberto González and Miguel Angel Saguier. It is now probably the largest of the liberal factions but has been refused legal status. It is the leading member of the Acuerdo Nacional (see above). Laíno was arrested on July 7, 1978, on his return from a US trip when he testified against the regime to the Organization of American States. He was charged with subversion and association with left-wing extremists, but was released on Aug. 8. He was again detained in 1979 and in 1980, and during 1981 he visited Brazil where he held talks with the exiled leadership of the Mopoco (see above) and with the Brazilian opposition. He was deported from Paraguay in December 1982 after making statements construed as insulting to the memory of the former Nicaraguan dictator, Anastasio Somoza, who had been assassinated in Asunción in 1980.

Laíno has attempted to return to Paraguay on at least three occasions, most recently in March 1985, but has been turned back. From May 1984 to February 1985 many PLRA supporters were detained in separate incidents, including 14 arrested for attending a PLRA meeting in Itapúa in January 1985. Six of those, including a young girl, were reported to have been tortured. The PLRA deputy leader, Benítez, was also detained briefly in December 1984 (with three members of the party's youth wing) and in January 1985. A warrant was issued in Paraguay for Laíno's arrest following a mass demonstration against the Stroessner regime, held in Posadas, Argentina, on Dec. 1, 1984. Laíno, who was not at the meeting, attempted to return to Paraguay to answer the charges against him but was instantly expelled. A PLRA press statement in February condemned the death in police custody of PLRA peasant activist Pablo Martínez, saying that "constitutional guarantees are being violated unscrupulously and systematically" and that "the ruling despotic regime uses power as its favourite tool to repress the opposition through police brutality". Abdón Saguier was arrested in September 1985 after assuming sole responsibility for the calling of an unauthorized political meeting raided by the police in Itapúa.

Policies.   The PLRA has maintained a policy of boycotting polls held by the Stroessner regime. It calls for democratization, the lifting of the state of siege and respect for human rights.

Associated organizations.   See Acuerdo Nacional (above). The party has a trade union affiliate, the Movimiento Obrero Liberal Radical Auténtico (MOLRA – Authentic Radical Liberal Workers' Movement) and a youth wing, the Juventud Liberal Radical Auténtico.

International affiliations.   Neither the PLRA, nor any of the smaller groupings, is recognized by the Liberal International, although in 1985 the International decided to accept the affiliation of one individual – whose identity is confidential – as a representative of Paraguayan liberalism.

Partido Liberal Teeté (PLT)
Teeté Liberal Party

Leadership.   Carlos A. Levi Ruffinelli (president); Fernando Levi Ruffinelli

Orientation. Centre-right

Founded. 1977

History. The PLT is recognized by the government as a political party. It is among the smallest of the factions derived from the Partido Liberal (see above). In the 1978 general elections it was given four seats in each chamber of Congress; it did not contest the 1983 elections.

Policies. The PLT is a right-wing liberal formation advocating laissez-faire capitalism.

Partido Liberal Unificado (PLU)
Unified Liberal Party

Orientation. Centrist

Founded. 1977

History. The PLU is an unrecognized faction of the liberal movement, and was formed by the majorities of the PL and the PLR (see above). Most of its members went on to form the PLRA (see above). Most of its members its members went on to form the PLRA (see above). It has never taken part in elections and has not recently been reported as active.

Partido Revolucionario Febrerista (PRF)
February Revolutionary Party

Address. Manduvirá 552, Asunción

Leadership. Dr Euclides Acevedo (president); Ricardo Lugo Rodríguez (general secretary)

Orientation. Left-wing social democratic

Founded. 1936

History. The PRF derives its name from the coup of Feb. 17, 1936, and was founded by the leader of the resulting radical nationalist government, Col. Rafael Franco. The Franco regime, supported by Chaco War veterans, communists and others, enacted extensive land reform. It was deposed by a counter-coup on Aug. 13, 1937, and the party was banned until the liberalization of the Morínigo regime led to the formation in August 1946 of a Febrerista–Colorado coalition government. After a rare period of political freedom, marked by occasionally rowdy demonstrations and an unsuccessful Febrerista coup attempt, right-wing Colorados took power and removed the PRF from government in Jan. 13, 1947. Many Febreristas fled to the north of the country where they combined with communist and liberal dissidents to seize the city of Concepción on March 8, but the uprising, again led by Franco, was completely defeated, and its leaders killed, imprisoned or exiled, by late August. The exiled leadership, dominated by moderates, purged the party of communists and other left-wingers.

The PRF and the Partido Liberal were banned in Paraguay, but continued to operate in exile, and in 1959 established an Unión Nacional (National Union) to co-ordinate opposition forces and organize a boycott of the 1960 presidential election. Also in 1959, a group of young members formed the Vanguardia Febrerista (Febrerista Vanguard) guerrilla column which was quickly defeated by the Paraguayan army; some joined the communist guerrilla columns, but this was the last attempt by Febreristas to engage in armed rebellion.

The PRF regained legal status and in 1967–68 dropped its policy of boycotting elections, gaining three seats in a constituent convention and one in the Chamber of Deputies. It has boycotted subsequent elections, since

1978 as a member of the Acuerdo Nacional (see above), and is the sole party with legal status not to be represented in Congress. It is currently divided between the majority radical faction, whose leader, Acevedo, was elected party president in November 1983, and a right-wing faction led by Alarico Quiñónez.

On Feb. 17, 1984, the PRF held the first anti-government demonstration to take place in over 20 years, attracting more than 2,000 people. Another demonstration, with the slogan "Resistance, Peace and Change", was attended by 5,000 people on Feb. 16, 1985.

Publications. *El Pueblo*, weekly; *El Progreso*

Associated organizations. See Acuerdo Nacional (above).

International affiliations. The PRF is affiliated to the Socialist International.

Peru

Capital: Lima   **Population: 19,500,000**

Peru gained independence from Spain in 1826. Its recent political history has been dominated by a tradition of hostility between the armed forces and the Alianza Popular Revolucionaria (APRA), a party founded in the 1920s by Dr Víctor Raúl Haya de la Torre. APRA was banned between 1931 and 1956 with the exception of the years 1945–48, when it was the largest party in Congress. Gen. Manuel Odría led a bloodless coup in 1948 and ruled until 1956, when Dr Manuel Prado y Ugartache was elected President. Prado legalized APRA and permitted the return from exile of Haya de la Torre.

By the 1962 presidential and congressional elections APRA had become a moderate left-wing party. Haya de la Torre polled the highest number of votes in the presidential election, although narrowly failing to secure the one-third of the total vote needed for election. The Constitution stipulated that in such circumstances Congress should choose the President, but the armed forces – alleging widespread electoral irregularities – seized power, annulled the elections and set up a military government. In fresh elections in 1963 the APRA leader lost to Fernando Belaúnde Terry, the leader of the Acción Popular (AP), which he had founded in 1956. APRA's greater strength in the Chamber of Deputies caused instability during Belaúnde's presidency, which was ended in 1968 by a coup led by the radical Gen. Juan Velasco Alvarado; he was himself overthrown in August 1975 by the more conservative Gen. Francisco Morales Bermúdez.

Elections to a Constituent Assembly were held in June 1978 and APRA emerged as the largest party, winning 37 of the 100 seats. A new Constitution came into force in 1980, when presidential and

217

congressional elections were held; Belaúnde was elected President with 45.4 per cent of the vote, thereby ending 12 years of military rule.

The Maoist Sendero Luminoso guerrilla group – one of a number of *indigenista* political movements to emerge in the 1970s – began an armed campaign in 1980, centred on the Ayacucho region (in the south-east of the country). Numerous attacks on the security forces and local officials, as well as the sabotage of electricity pylons, transport infrastructure and other targets, were attributed to the group. (Most other *indigenista* groups are now involved in cultural and consciousness-raising work, and participate in mainstream politics, if at all, through the medium of the established parties of the centre and left.) The armed forces, given nationwide responsibility for all counter-insurgency operations in July 1984, were alleged to have committed numerous violations of human rights in the course of their campaign against the group.

The April 1985 elections produced a clear victory for APRA, which won the presidency – for the 36-year-old Alan García Pérez – and a majority in both congressional chambers.

Constitutional background. The 1980 Constitution provided for a bicameral National Congress consisting of a 180-member Chamber of Deputies chosen according to a system of proportional representation, and a Senate consisting of 60 members elected on a regional basis and, in addition, the former Presidents of constitutional governments as life senators. The Congress, the President and two Vice-Presidents are elected by universal suffrage of citizens over the age of 18, for five-year terms. In all elections after 1980 a presidential candidate required an absolute majority, with a second round of voting between the two leading candidates if necessary. The President has powers to submit draft bills, to review laws prepared by Congress, and, if so authorized by Congress, to legislate by decree.

Recent election results. A presidential election on April 14, 1985, was won by Alan García Pérez of the APRA, with 45.7 per cent of the total valid votes. The second-placed candidate, Dr Alfonso Barrantes Lingán of the Izquierda Unida (IU) coalition, won 21.3 per cent, but withdrew, so obviating the need for a second round. The third major candidate, Dr Luis Bedoya Reyes of the Convergencia Democrática, won 9.7 per cent, and the fourth, Dr Javier Alva Orlandini of the AP, won 6.3 per cent, the remainder being shared by five minor contenders. García assumed office in late July. Seats in the Chamber of Deputies were distributed as follows: APRA 107, IU 48, Convergencia Democrática 12, AP 10, Izquierda Nacionalista 1, independents 2; in the Senate, the APRA had 32 seats, IU 15, Convergencia Democrática 7, AP 5 and Izquierda Nacionalista 1.

Acción Política Socialista (APS)
Socialist Political Action

Leadership. Gustavo Mohme (leader)

Orientation. Socialist

History. This small group was reportedly active in the early 1980s.

Acción Popular (AP)
Popular Action

Address. Paseo Colón 218, Lima

Telephone. 234177

Leadership. Dr Javier Alva Orlandi (general secretary)

Orientation. Centre-right

Founded. 1956

History. In the presidential election of 1956 the party's leader, Fernando Belaúnde Terry, came second, and he was again defeated in 1962, but by a narrow margin. After the annulment of that election he was in June 1963 elected President as the joint candidate of the AP and the PDC (see below), but was overthrown in a military coup in 1968 and went into exile. The military regime suspended Congress, in which the AP had in 1963 won 56 seats in the Chamber of Deputies and 19 in the Senate. After the coup the AP split into a pro-military faction led by the former Vice-President of Peru, Edgardo Seoane Corrales, and a pro-Belaúnde faction which was outlawed in 1974. Although the ban was lifted and Belaúnde allowed to return to Peru in January 1976, the party refused to participate in the 1978 elections of a Constituent Assembly.

In May 1980 Belaúnde was again elected President, winning 45.4 per cent of the vote, and the AP gained 98 of the 180 seats in the Chamber of Deputies. In July the AP formed a government with the participation of the PPC (see below), pursuing conservative policies. The party suffered a setback in municipal elections held on Nov. 13, 1983, when it obtained only 12 per cent of the vote in Lima against 35 per cent in 1980. New AP governments were formed in April and October 1984, without the assistance of the PPC. The party experienced a dramatic decline in popularity during Belaúnde's presidency, and returned to opposition after the 1985 elections, in which it gained only 10 seats in the Chamber and five in the Senate.

Policies. The AP defines itself as democratic, nationalist and revolutionary, seeking to defend the interests of the working class. It is generally regarded, however, as conservative and pro-United States.

Structure. The party has a 70-member national plenum and various national, departmental, provincial and district committees.

Membership. 900,000

Publications. *Adelante*, circulation 50,000

Acción Socialista Revolucionaria (ASR)
Revolutionary Socialist Action

Orientation. Marxist

History. This group was reportedly active in 1984.

Alianza Popular Revolucionaria Americana (APRA)
American Popular Revolutionary Alliance

Address. Avenida Alfonso Ugarte 1016, Lima 5; Apartado 1815, Lima 100

Telephone. 247479; 236792

Leadership. Alan García Pérez (President of Peru and of the party); Armando Villanueva del Campo (former president of the party, leader of left wing, alternate general secretary); Luis Alberto Sánchez (congressional leader); Luis Negreiros (alternate general secretary); Carlos López Cano (international secretary)

Orientation. Centre-left

Founded. 1924; in Peru, 1930

History. The APRA was originally envisaged as a continent-wide movement; it was founded in Mexico in 1924 by a Peruvian exile, Dr Víctor Raúl Haya de la Torre, and attracted a limited following in other Latin American countries. It was not established in Peru until 1930, when Haya de la Torre returned from exile. He contested the 1931 presidential election for the party, which was then a radical Marxist group. He was imprisoned in 1932–33; a refugee at the Colombian embassy in Lima in 1948–53; and in exile again in 1954–56 and 1968–69. The party, which was also known as the Partido Aprista Peruano (PAP), was accorded legal status in 1945, outlawed in 1948 and legalized again by the Prado regime in 1956.

In presidential elections in 1962, by which time APRA had moved to a social democratic position, Haya de la Torre obtained the largest number of votes but not the one-third required for election, so that it was for Congress to decide on the winner. The APRA leader withdrew his candidature in favour of Gen. Odría but a military coup intervened. Fresh elections in 1963 gave Haya de la Torre second place with 34.3 per cent of the vote, while APRA became the largest party in the Chamber of Deputies with 58 of the 140 seats. The party nevertheless remained in opposition.

From 1969 the military government received the qualified support of APRA, despite friction resulting from Aprista trade union activities in 1970–76. It emerged the leader in the 1978 elections to a Constituent Assembly with 35 per cent of the vote. Haya de la Torre died in August 1979 at the age of 84.

A right–left split weakened the party in 1980–81, with many of its members leaving to form the MBH (see below) after the expulsion of the former leader, Andrés Townsend. In the 1980 general elections it was relegated to second place with 27.4 per cent of the presidential vote and 58 of the 180 seats in the Chamber. Alan García, since 1982 the general secretary of the party, won the presidency in the 1985 elections, when the party also won 107 seats in the Chamber and 32 in the Senate.

García strengthened his control over the party when at its 15th national congress, on July 12–14, 1985, he was elected as the first-ever president of the party as well as gaining the traditional leadership post of president of the political commission.

Policies. The APRA sees itself as a popular democratic left-wing party. It was founded as a nationalist revolutionary movement to fight imperialism, to attain political unity in Latin America, to achieve international control of the Panama Canal and to establish social control over land and industry. The policies which it has actually pursued in recent years have been somewhat less radical and more pragmatic.

Structure. The supreme organ of the party is the national congress, which meets infrequently; the congress elects a political commission and, from 1985, a party president.

Membership. 700,000

Associated organizations. The APRA is linked with one of the main trade union organizations, the Confederación de Trabajadores Peruanos (CTP – Confederation of Peruvian Workers).

International affiliations. The APRA is a consultative member of the Socialist International.

Comandos Revolucionarios del Pueblo (CRP)
People's Revolutionary Commandos

Orientation. Left-wing guerrilla group

Founded. 1985

History. This group seized a radio station on July 18, 1985, and broadcast a message to the effect that it was adopting a "vigilant" attitude towards the new García government and opposed the "unjust social order" in Peru.

Comité Comunista Unificado Marxista–Leninista (CCUML)
Unified Marxist–Leninist Communist Committee

Orientation. Maoist guerrilla movement

History. The CCUML was active in the early 1980s

Membership. It is a coalition of ultra-left movements advocating guerrilla warfare, including the MIR-El Militante, the Pasache faction of the PCP-Patria Roja and VRPC (see below).

Convergencia Democrática
Democratic Convergence

Orientation. Centrist

Founded. 1984

History. This alliance of centrist parties was formed to contest the 1985 general elections, in which its candidates won 12 seats in the Chamber of Deputies and seven in the Senate. Its presidential candidate, however, received a very small number of votes.

Membership. The parties constituting the alliance were the MGH and the PPC (see below)

Coordinadora Nacional de Derechos Humanos
National Human Rights Co-ordinating Body

Orientation. Civil rights coalition

History. The Coordinadora was created in the early 1980s to develop a joint strategy and information centre for numerous groups working to document, publicize and resist violations of human rights; it has concentrated on the activities of counter-insurgency troops in the military-controlled zones, where it alleges that more than 1,000 people disappeared in 1983–85.

Membership. In mid-1985 the Coordinadora represented at least 13 departmental and national human rights organizations.

Ejército de Liberación Nacional (ELN)
National Liberation Army

Leadership. Juan Pablo Chang Navarro (leader)

Orientation. Marxist–Leninist guerrilla movement

Founded. 1962

History. The ELN was one of several guerrilla movements active in Peru in the 1960s, but its operations, in the Ayacucho area, were suppressed by the Army in the last months of 1965, the surviving guerrillas withdrawing to Ecuador. A reorganized ELN appeared in September 1980 under the leadership of Chang Navarro, but it has had little impact.

Policies. The original ELN issued a manifesto in 1965 calling for both an armed struggle and a "policy of unity" for the liberation of the workers and peasantry.

Membership. The current strength of the ELN has been estimated at less than 20 members.

Frente Democrático de Unidad Nacional
Democratic Front for National Unity

Orientation. Centrist

Founded. 1985

History. This small grouping contested the 1985 presidential elections, but polled insignificantly.

Frente de Liberación Nacional (FLN)
National Liberation Front

Address. Emancipación 412, Oficina 203, Lima 1

Leadership. Dr Angel Castro Lavallero (president)

Orientation. Revolutionary left

History. The FLN is a member of the UNIR alliance (see below), for which its leader has sat in the Senate, and through the UNIR is part of the Izquierda Unida coalition (see below).

Frente de Liberación Tawantinsuyo
Tawantinsuyo Liberation Front

Leadership. Aureliano Turpo Choquehuanca (leader)

Orientation. *Indigenista*

Founded. Sept. 15, 1981

History. This Front was established at a meeting on the shores of Lake Titicaca by representatives of indigenous groups from Bolivia, Ecuador and Peru. It was named after the region of the former Inca empire centred on Peru.

Policies. The Front aimed to restore the sovereignty of that region which it regarded as having been artificially fragmented by the borders of the Andean nation-states. (The indigenous population of Bolivia comprised about 59 per cent of its total population; that of Peru, 37 per cent, and that of Ecuador, 34 per cent.)

Frente Nacional de Trabajadores y Campesinos (Frenatraca or FNTC)
National Workers' and Peasants' Front

Address. Avenida Colonial 105, Lima 1

Telephone. 272868

Leadership. Dr Róger Cáceres Velásquez (president); Dr Edmundo Huanqui Medina (general secretary)

Orientation. Leftist

Founded. May 12, 1968

History. The party has its origins in the Frente Departamental de Trabajadores y Campesinos which was successful in municipal elections in the department of Puno in 1963 and 1966, and which in 1963 sent three members to Congress. After 10 years of military rule the FNTC re-emerged at the end of 1977 and was again successful in municipal elections in Puno. It gained four seats in the Constituent Assembly elected in June 1978, and in May 1980 it won four seats in the Chamber of Deputies and one in the Senate.

Policies. The FNTC is a left-wing nationalist group, which draws on the tenets of ancient Peru (*Tahuantisuyo*).

Structure. The highest organ of the Front is the national congress, meeting every two or three years and electing a 17-member national executive committee.

Frente Obrero, Campesino, Estudiantil y Popular (FOCEP)
Worker, Peasant and Student Popular Front

Address. Jirón de la Unión 706, Oficina 220, Lima 1

Telephone. 279270

Leadership. Dr Genaro Ledesma Izquieta (president)

Orientation. Trotskyist

Founded. 1962

History. The FOCEP was granted legal status in 1978, when it came third in elections to a Constituent Assembly by winning 12 of the 100 seats. It was reduced to one representative in the Senate (Dr Ledesma) in the 1980 elections.

Associated organizations. The Front contested the 1983 municipal elections as a member of the IU coalition (see below).

Izquierda Nacionalista
Nationalist Left

Orientation. Centre-left

Founded. 1984

History. This small formation contested the 1985 congressional elections, winning one seat in each chamber.

Izquierda Unida (IU)
United Left

Address. Avenida Grau 184, Lima 23

Telephone. 278340

Leadership. Dr Alfonso Barrantes Lingán (president)

Orientation. Left-wing alliance

Founded. 1980

History. This alliance gained two seats in each chamber in the 1980 elections. In the same year it gained 27 per cent of the national vote in municipal elections, and in 1983 it won 33 per cent of the vote in the Lima municipal elections and installed Barrantes as mayor. The IU contested the

1985 general election, winning 21.3 per cent of the vote and second place for its presidential candidate – Barrantes – and 48 seats in the Chamber. It also won 15 of the Senate seats, becoming the second-largest party in both chambers. The party decided not to force a second round of the presidential election and has offered critical support to the social democratic APRA government.

Membership. The IU is an alliance of communist, socialist and other leftist parties. The founding members were the PCP, the PCR, the PSR and the UDP (see below). Subsequent adherents were the FOCEP (see above), the PADIN and the UNIR (see below).

Movimiento de Bases Hayistas (MBH)
Hayista Groups Movement

Address. Pasaje Velarde 180, Lima

Leadership. Dr Andrés Townsend Ezcurra (leader)

Orientation. Reformist

Founded. 1981

History. The MBH resulted from a split in the APRA (see above) caused by the expulsion of the former APRA leader, Townsend, who had argued (against his successor, Villanueva del Campo) that the party should reject alliances with centre-left parties.

Policies. The MBH advocates reformist and anti-imperialist policies which it sees as derived from the ideas of Haya de la Torre, the founder of *aprismo.*

Associated organizations. The party contested the 1985 presidential and congressional elections as part of the Convergencia Democrática alliance (see above).

Movimiento Cívico Nacional 7 de Junio
June 7 National Civic Movement

Orientation. Right-wing

Founded. 1984

History. This very small group presented a candidate in the 1985 presidential election, but received an insignificant number of votes.

Movimiento Democrático Peruano (MDP)
Peruvian Democratic Movement

Orientation. Right-wing

History. This movement took part in the 1978 elections to a Constituent Assembly but gained only 20,000 votes and no seats.

Movimiento de Izquierda Revolucionaria (MIR)
Revolutionary Left Movement (Tapia faction)

Leadership. Carlos Tapia (general secretary)

Orientation. Left-wing

Founded. 1959

History. The MIR was formed as an offshoot of the APRA (see above) by Luis de la Puente, who in 1968 led the group in guerrilla warfare against the military regime. In 1978 this faction of the MIR joined the UDP (see below).

Movimiento de Izquierda Revolucionaria – El Militante (MIR-El Militante)

See PSR-ML/MIR-El Militante (below).

Movimiento de Izquierda Revolucionaria del Perú (MIR Perú)
Revolutionary Left Movement of Peru

Leadership.   Dr Gonzalo Fernández Gasco (leader)

Orientation.   Left revolutionary

Founded.   1959

History.   This faction of the MIR, whose leader was involved in the guerrilla campaigns of the 1960s, is now a member of the UNIR alliance (see below), and through the UNIR is part of the Izquierda Unida coalition (see above).

Movimiento Revolucionario Tupac Amaru (MRTA)
Tupac Amaru Revolutionary Movement

Leadership.   Marco Turkowsky (leader)

Orientation.   Marxist–Leninist guerrilla movement

Founded.   1984

History.   This group came to public notice after claiming responsibility for a series of bombings of US and other targets in Lima in September 1984. On Sept. 29 members of the group forced staff at two US press agencies to transmit a manifesto condemning "yankee imperialism". Nine alleged members of the MRTA were arrested in Cuzco on Nov. 27; two journalists were later kidnapped to ensure the publication of an MRTA protest against the alleged torture of the detainees. The home of the labour minister was bombed on March 19, 1985; that of the US ambassador on May 16; and two car-bombs exploded outside the presidential palace on June 8, during the state visit by President Alfonsín of Argentina. Members of the movement burnt down three Kentucky Fried Chicken franchises during March. The MRTA may have been responsible for some of the other bombings and shootings carried out in 1985, most of which were attributed by the media to Sendero Luminoso (see below). In mid-August it was reported to have offered a truce to encourage the García government to proceed with planned reforms. The group's name derived from an 18th-century indigenous rebel leader.

Policies.   There has been speculation that the MRTA is linked with army officers sympathetic to the ideals of Gen. Velasco's radical regime (see introduction). The group's insignia bears the motto "For the cause of the poor, with the masses, up in arms".

Núcleos Marxistas–Leninistas
Marxist–Leninist Nuclei

Orientation.   Marxist–Leninist guerrilla movement

Founded.   1974

History.   This movement was formed after a split in the PCP-Bandera Roja (see below). It has its main strength in the Chimbote area.

Partido Avanzada Nacional
National Advance Party

Orientation.   Right-wing

Founded.   1984

History. This minor group contested the 1985 presidential election, but did not win significant support.

Partido Comunista del Perú – Bandera Roja (PCP-Bandera Roja)
Communist Party of Peru – Red Flag

Orientation. Maoist

Founded. 1963

History. The PCP-Bandera Roja, a Maoist offshoot of the main Peruvian communist movement, suffered a split in 1969 when pro-Chinese elements established the PCP-Patria Roja (see below), and another in 1974 leading to the formation of the Núcleos Marxistas–Leninistas (see above).

Policies. The party has adopted a staunchly pro-Albanian line, regarding the Chinese and the Soviet versions of communism as deviations.

Partido Comunista del Perú – Patria Roja (PCP-Patria Roja or Patria Roja)
Communist Party of Peru – Red Homeland (Breña faction)

Address. Apartado 51, Lima 100

Leadership. Rolando Breña Pantoja (leader); Alberto Moreno (general secretary)

Orientation. Maoist

Founded. 1969

History. The PCP-Patria Roja was formed after a split in the PCP-Bandera Roja (see above) between those favouring respectively the Chinese and the Albanian versions of communist theory. It has itself split between this (majority) faction favouring participation in the parliamentary process, and a guerrilla faction led by Jerónimo Pasache (see below). Breña has been elected to the Senate on the UNIR list.

Policies. The party has followed the lead of the Chinese Communist Party on foreign policy issues.

Associated organizations. The majority group of Patria Roja is a member of the UNIR alliance (see below), through which it is part of the Izquierda Unida coalition (see above).

Partido Comunista del Perú – Patria Roja (PCP-Patria Roja or Patria Roja)
Communist Party of Peru – Red Homeland (Pasache faction)

Leadership. Jerónimo Pasache (leader)

Orientation. Maoist guerrilla movement

History. The Pasache faction split from the main body of Patria Roja (see above) in disagreement with the latter's adoption of a parliamentary strategy.

Policies. This group advocates immediate armed insurrection.

Associated organizations. It has associated with similar Maoist groups in the CCUML (see above).

Partido Comunista Peruano (PCP)
Peruvian Communist Party

Address. Jirón Lampa 774, Lima 1

Leadership. Jorge del Prado (general secretary)

Orientation. Communist

Founded. October 1928, as Partido Socialista del Perú (PSP – Socialist Party of Peru)

History. The PCP was founded by José Carlos Mariátegui, a former associate of Raúl Haya de la Torre (see APRA, above). It adopted its present name in 1930. It was excluded from participation in elections by the 1933 Constitution, and was refused legal status.

The party has suffered a number of splits resulting from policy differences and from the Chinese–Albanian–Soviet disputes, with this majority faction being close to the Soviet line until recently; among the groups to arise from the splits are the PCP-Bandera Roja, the PCP-Patria Roja and the PCP-Mayoría.

In October 1968 the PCP decided to support the "anti-imperialist and anti-oligarchic transformations" promised by the new military regime. The party was active in reorganizing the labour movement. In 1978 it contested the Constituent Assembly elections as the PCP-Unidad, the suffix (Unity) distinguishing it from the other PCP factions; it emerged as the fifth strongest party. Since 1980 it has advocated the unification of left-wing parties.

Policies. Originally regarded as pro-Soviet, the PCP has in recent years followed an independent foreign policy with an emphasis on Third World solidarity.

Structure. The party's organizational principle is democratic centralism; between national congresses the supreme organ is the central committee.

Publications. *Unidad*, weekly

Associated organizations. Since the congressional elections of 1980 the party has been a member of the Izquierda Unida coalition (see above). The party also has close connections with the trade union movement, particularly through the Confederación General de Trabajadores del Perú (CGTP – General Confederation of Workers of Peru), which gained legal recognition in 1971.

Partido Comunista Peruano – Mayoría (PCP-Mayoría)
Peruvian Communist Party – Majority

Orientation. Orthodox communist

History. The PCP-Mayoría broke away from the main PCP (see above) in the early 1980s.

Policies. This faction adopted a strongly pro-Soviet stance.

Partido Comunista Revolucionaro (PCR)
Revolutionary Communist Party

Address. Plaza 2 de Mayo 70, Lima 1

Telephone. 233149

Leadership. Manuel Dammert (general secretary)

Orientation. Left-wing communist

Founded. 1974

History. The PCR contested elections after 1980 as part of the IU coalition (see above).

Partido Demócrata Cristiano (PDC)
Christian Democratic Party

Address. Avenida España 321, Apartado 4682, Lima 1

Leadership. Carlos Blancas (president)

Orientation. Christian democrat

Founded. January 1956

History. One of Peru's many Christian democratic groupings, the PDC won 12 seats in the Chamber of Deputies and five in the Senate in the elections of 1963. It was the minor partner in a coalition government with the AP (see above) in 1963–66. The party suffered a major split in 1966, leading to the formation of the PPC (see below), and has not subsequently regained parliamentary representation.

Policies. The PDC regards the state as existing for the service of society; it advocates a system in which labour will prevail over capital and the social interest over that of the individual.

Structure. The supreme organ of the PDC is the national executive committee, which, with the departments of organization, propaganda, ideology and administration, forms the national secretariat. There are women's, youth and labour sections. The party has committees at departmental, provincial and district level.

Membership. 95,000

International affiliations. The party belongs to the Christian Democratic International and the Christian Democratic Organization of America.

Partido de Integración Nacional (PADIN)
National Integration Party

Address. Avenida Petit Thouars 4469, Apartado 3073, Lima 1

Telephone. 453813

Leadership. Miguel Angel Mufarech (general secretary)

Orientation. Centre-left

Founded. January 1982

History. The PADIN was founded by former members of the PPC (see below) who were opposed to that party's support for Acción Popular (see above).

Associated organizations. The PADIN is a member of the IU coalition (see above).

Partido Obrero Revolucionario Marxista – Partido Socialista de los Trabajadores (PORM-PST)
Revolutionary Marxist Workers' Party – Socialist Workers' Party

Address. Jirón Apurimac 465, Lima 1

Telephone. 280443

Leadership. Ricardo Napurí, Enrique Fernández Chacón (leaders)

Orientation. Trotskyist

Founded. 1971 (PORM), 1974 (PST)

History. The PORM-PST was established in 1982 by the fusion of two Trotskyist parties formed in the early 1970s (PORM having resulted from a split in the FOCEP – see above). It has gained a limited congressional representation. It contested the 1985 presidential election (as the PST), but gained a very small number of votes.

Partido Popular Cristiano (PPC)
Popular Christian Party

Address. Avenida Alfonso Ugarte 1406, Lima

Telephone. 233120

Leadership. Dr Luis Bedoya Reyes (leader and national political secretary)

Orientation. Conservative Christian democrat

Founded. December 1966

History. The PPC was formed after a split in the PDC (see above) and has since overtaken the parent party in both membership and electoral performance. It came second in the 1978 Constituent Assembly elections, winning 25 of the 100 seats, but in 1980 it elected only 10 deputies out of 200 (and 18 senators). It was represented in Cabinets led by Acción Popular (see above) until April 1984, when it relinquished its two portfolios but indicated that it would continue to support AP (despite dissent among the membership which had led to the formation of the PADIN in 1982 – see above). Its leader contested the 1985 presidential election, securing third place with 9.7 per cent of the vote.

Structure. The party has a 15-member national political committee, a 21-member national executive committee and eight national secretariats overseeing various areas of the party's work. It is organized in 24 departmental, 152 provincial, 1,630 district and 514 zonal secretariats.

Membership. 120,000

Associated organizations. The PPC has influence in the trade union movement through the Confederación Nacional de Trabajadores (CNT – National Confederation of Workers). It contested the 1985 election as part of the Convergencia Democrática alliance.

Partido Revolucionario de los Trabajadores (PRT)
Revolutionary Workers' Party

Address. Plaza 2 de Mayo 38, Apartado 2449, Lima 100

Leadership. Collective leadership; Hugo Blanco (spokesperson)

Orientation. Trotskyist

Founded. Oct. 8, 1978

History. The main representative of this movement, Hugo Blanco, was a well-known guerrilla leader in the La Convención area in 1959–63. The PRT was part of FOCEP (see above) until 1979, and drew much of its membership from small groups leaving FOCEP and the UDP (see below). It was legalized in 1980 when it produced the signatures of 90,000 supporters. In the 1980 general elections it obtained 5 per cent of the vote, giving it three deputies and one senator. In the municipal elections of 1980 it gave "critical support" to the IU parties (see above).

A number of PRT activists were subsequently imprisoned and Blanco was suspended from membership of the Chamber of Deputies. The party obtained less than 1 per cent of the vote in the November 1983 municipal elections.

Membership. 5,000 (1980)

Publications. *Combate Socialista*, circulation 2,500

Associated organizations. The PRT applied in 1984 for admission to the Izquierda Unida coalition (see above).

International affiliations. The party is the Peruvian section of the Fourth International.

Partido Socialista del Perú (PSP)
Socialist Party of Peru

Address. Jirón Azángaro 105, Lima 1

Leadership. Dr María Cabredo de Castillo (leader)

Orientation. Socialist

Founded. 1930

History. The PSP remained in existence in the early 1980s, but had made no significant electoral impact.

Partido Socialista Revolucionaria (PSR)
Revolutionary Socialist Party

Address. Plaza Bolognesi 123, Lima

Leadership. Gen. Leonidas Rodríguez Figueroa (president); Enrique Bernales (general secretary)

Orientation. Socialist

Founded. November 1976

History. The PSR evolved from an earlier Movimiento de la Revolución Peruana (Movement of the Peruvian Revolution), and Gen. Rodríguez had been one of the leaders of the 1968 military coup. In January 1977 he was deported from Peru together with three other prominent members of the party, but they returned under an amnesty decreed in March 1978. In the 1978 elections to a Constituent Assembly the PSR won six of the 100 seats, making it the fourth-strongest party. It contested the 1980 general elections as part of Izquierda Unida (see above). The party lost an element of its left wing with the formation of MIR-El Militante (see above).

Policies. The PSR called, at its formation, for "the defence, deepening and consolidation of the reforms already begun and those still needed to take the country out of the capitalist system and build Peruvian socialism".

Associated organizations. The party is a member of the IU coalition (see above).

Partido Socialista Revolucionario Marxista–Leninista/Movimiento de Izquierda Revolucionaria – El Militante (PSR-ML/MIR-El Militante)

Revolutionary Socialist Party (Marxist–Leninist)/Movement of the Revolutionary Left – El Militante

Orientation. Marxist–Leninist

History. The MIR-El Militante (which derives its name from the periodical around which it organized) was founded by former members of the PSR (see above) who were opposed to that party's participation in parliamentary politics. It has since united with another dissident PSR faction.

Associated organizations. It has associated with other ultra-left groups favouring a guerrilla struggle in the CCUML (see above).

Partido Socialista de los Trabajadores (PST)

See PORM-PST (above).

Puka Llatka
Red Homeland

Orientation. Maoist *indigenista* guerrilla movement

History. This movement is strongest in the Cerro de Pasco, Mantaro and La Oroya areas.

Policies. It is ideologically similar to the PCP-Patria Roja group and the

CCUML groups (see above), with an emphasis on protecting the rights and culture of the indigenous peasantry.

Rondas Campesinas
Peasant Patrols

Orientation. Peasant land rights movements

Founded. 1970s

History. These groups were active during the 1970s in the illicit occupation of lands in the Andes. Their request for legalization was rejected by the civilian government installed in 1980, and the groups responded by declaring the "independence" of the province of Chota (in the department of Cajamarca). Although they have continued their agitation for land redistribution they have not posed a serious challenge to the central government.

Sendero Luminoso
Shining Path

Leadership. Antonio Díaz Martínez (last known leader; under arrest since 1983)

Orientation. Radical Maoist

Founded. 1970

History. Sendero Luminoso is an illegal guerrilla organization centred on the extremely poor Ayacucho region and drawing its strength from the peasantry. It was founded by Maoists who left the PCP-Bandera Roja (see above) in 1970, and remained faithful to radical Maoist ideas after the death of Mao Zedong and the discrediting of the radical "Gang of Four" in China. The name of the organization was taken from the title of one of its first pamphlets, *The Shining Path of José Carlos Mariategui*, on the "Peruvian socialism" espoused by the founder of the country's communist movement (see PCP, above).

Sendero Luminoso, led by its founder, Dr Abimael Guzmán Renoso – a former philosophy lecturer – went underground in 1977 and took up arms against the Peruvian state in 1980. The first stage of its campaign was a series of sabotage acts designed to publicize the group's existence; the second consisted of fund-raising by attacks on banks and businesses, and the third involved attacks on remote police posts with the aim of seizing weapons and forcing the withdrawal of the police. The strategy aimed at the establishment of substantial "liberated zones" in which the movement could operate freely, and eventually at the overthrow of the state.

The movement has attempted to broaden its base among the peasantry. One of its early tactics was the organization of summary trials by "people's courts" and subsequent killings of mayors and other "enemies of the people".

By mid-1982 the movement claimed to have carried out 2,900 guerrilla actions in two years. Among other actions in 1982, Sendero Luminoso was reportedly responsible for an assault by about 200 guerrillas on a prison in Ayacucho on March 3, when seven of the attackers, three policemen and four inmates were killed and about 250 prisoners, including about 80 guerrillas, escaped; the Supreme Court building in La Libertad department was simultaneously bombed. (Both these attacks were also claimed at the time by the PCP-Patria Roja – see above). The US embassy and other targets in Lima and Ayacucho were bombed in July. A 140-member commando of Sendero Luminoso caused damage estimated at US$1,400,000 to buildings of the University of Ayacucho on Aug. 3. The group succeeded in temporarily cutting off electricity supplies to Ayacucho, to Lima and to eight other cities on Aug. 20, and again to Lima on Dec. 3. Some 200 guerrillas attacked an Ayacucho police station on Aug. 22, killing five policemen and losing 20 of their own number in a four-hour gun-battle. Between August and October about 34,000 people were arrested in Lima and the nearby port of Callao, but only 33 were held as suspected guerrillas. On Dec. 2 about 300 guerrillas took control of five villages in Ayacucho and carried out 22 summary trials. President Belaúnde claimed on Dec. 26 that the movement had been responsible for the deaths of 150 people in 1982 and, after appealing for the unconditional surrender of the guerrillas, on Dec. 29 he ordered an all-out assault on the movement.

As the Sendero Luminoso guerrillas had extended their activities to new areas, the President had by Jan. 18, 1983, placed eight provinces under military control. There were reports that more than 100 members of the movement were killed in clashes with the security forces and peasant militias in the first two months of 1983. Further clashes in the Ayacucho area during April were said to have been the heaviest to date; by the end of the month the death toll since the beginning of the year was put at 370. Bombings in Lima on May 27 caused US$100,000,000 worth of damage to electrical, industrial and transport infrastructure; about 500 people were arrested by the security forces in Lima and Ayacucho in the latter part of May. On May 30, Sendero Luminoso made its first attack north of Lima, with the bombing of several power lines 160km from the capital. The Lima offices of the ruling AP party were attacked on July 11, when three people were killed, and on July 25 the police headquarters were bombed. Bombings in Ayacucho and Huancavelica killed about 22 people during the municipal elections in November. The Sendero leadership was reported on Dec. 20 to have offered a two-year truce, but subsequent attacks – including one on the Chinese embassy on Dec. 26 – were attributed to the group, raising the possibility of a split within it.

The movement attacked a military base at Las Borbones in January 1984, resumed its bombing campaign in Lima in April, and launched a major new offensive, including activities in the north-eastern jungle area, on June 22. As the situation became more serious the armed forces were given extensive powers in the zone covered by emergency decrees, then amounting to 13 provinces. Some 160 people died in clashes with the security forces in the first half of July, and there were frequent allegations of atrocities on both sides and abuses of human rights. Bombings in Lima led to some 2,000 arrests in September.

The movement called for abstention in the 1985 elections, and in April attempted to kill the head of the electoral commission. During a visit to Peru by Pope John Paul II in February the movement cut the power supply to the capital; later in the month two banks and two party offices were bombed by the group, two of whose members were killed in a subsequent confrontation with the police. About 2,000 people were arrested in May after the shooting of two policemen in Lima. On June 7, during a state visit by President Alfonsín of Argentina, it was held responsible for another power cut and for bombings at the Supreme Court, the presidential palace and 10 department stores. There were other bombings and shootings in Lima on July 14 and July 27 – the day before the inauguration of President García – and in Callao and Lima on Aug. 8 and 27, leading to more than 1,400 arrests. About 27 members of the group were reportedly killed by the police in two clashes in Ayacucho in early August. Four policemen and a civilian were shot dead by alleged *senderistas* on Aug. 29, and a car-bomb which exploded in Callao on Aug. 30 was reportedly the sixth such attack in three months.

The number of deaths attributed to the campaigns of Sendero Luminoso and other guerrilla groups, and to state counter-measures, between 1980 and mid-September 1985, was 5,400, including 220 members of the security forces, 72 officials, 2,500 civilians and 2,600 people described by the authorities as "subversive delinquents". About 2,000 others were listed as "disappeared". By August 1985 emergency regulations had been applied to 27 provinces.

Policies. In a pamphlet published in July 1982, Sendero Luminoso described itself as "a new type of Marxist–Leninist–Maoist party" waging a "people's war" from the countryside with the aim of carrying it into the cities; it would pursue "total war" until the government was overthrown. From 1979 it regarded the Chinese Communist Party leadership as "traitors"; it also condemned the "revisionism" of the Cuban and Soviet parties. Its members are devoted to the reputation of its founder, Guzmán, whom they call "the fourth sword of the world revolution", the first, second and third swords being respectively Marx, Lenin and Mao. Some sociologists regard it as a millenarian movement, pointing out its similarities with various Andean utopian groups of the recent past. The group's policy and strategy are rejected by all legal left-wing groups in Peru.

Membership. The strength of the Sendero "army" is often estimated at 3,000 members.

Unidad Democrática Popular (UDP)
Popular Democratic Unity

Address. Plaza 2 de Mayo 46, Lima 1

Telephone. 230309

Leadership. Dr Alfonso Barrantes Lingán (leader)

Orientation. Left-wing socialist

Founded. 1978

History. The UDP was formed as a coalition of the Tapia faction of the MIR (see above) and the Vanguardia Revolucionaria (see below). It held four seats in the 1978 Constituent Assembly, and in 1980 won three seats in the Chamber and two in the Senate.

Associated organizations. It is a prominent member of the IU coalition (see above) of which Barrantes is president.

Unión de Izquierda Revolucionaria (UNIR)
Union of the Revolutionary Left

Address. Jirón Puno 258, Apartado 1165, Lima 100

Telephone. 274072

Leadership. Rolando Breña Pantoja (president); Jorge Hurtado (general secretary)

Orientation. Left-wing alliance

Founded. 1979

History. The UNIR is a coalition of three parties and is a member of the IU coalition (see above). It won two seats in each chamber in the 1980 congressional elections. It held its first national congress on Nov. 25–27, 1983.

Membership. The constituent parties of UNIR are the FLN, MIR Perú and Breña's faction of the PCP-Patria Roja (see above). It claims 50,000 individual members.

Publications. *El Unirista*, circulation 10,000

Associated organizations. See IU (above).

Unión Nacional Odríista (UNO)
National Odríista Union

Leadership. Fernando Noriega (leader)

Orientation. Right-wing

History. The founder of the UNO, Gen. Manuel A. Odría, was head of the ruling junta in 1948–50 and President of Peru in 1948–56, during which period he banned the APRA (see above). In inconclusive presidential elections in June 1962 he came third, but the second-placed candidate, the APRA leader, withdrew in his favour; before the issue could be decided by Congress there was a military coup in July and Odría went underground. However, in June 1963 the party was allowed to take part in presidential elections and its leader again came third, on this occasion gaining 25.6 per cent of the vote. Following his death in 1974 the party's influence declined, and it gained only two seats in the Constituent Assembly elected in 1978 and none in the 1983 general elections.

Vanguardia Revolucionaria (VR)
Revolutionary Vanguard

Leadership. Javier Díaz Canseco (general secretary)

Orientation. Very left-wing

Founded. 1965

History. The VR was held responsible for numerous guerrilla actions in 1971–72, including bank robberies and the killing of policemen. In 1976 it controlled the Confederación Campesina del Perú (CCP – Peruvian Peasants' Confederation), which organized land seizures in protest at the slow progress of the government's land reform. In 1978 the VR joined with a faction of the MIR to form the UDP (see above).

Vanguardia Revolucionaria Proletario–Campesino (VRPC)
Proletarian–Peasant Revolutionary Vanguard

Leadership. Julio Mezzich (leader)

Orientation. Marxist–Leninist guerrilla movement

History. The VRPC has linked with other ultra-left groups favouring a guerrilla struggle in the CCUML (see above).

Victoria Navarro

Orientation. Left-wing guerrilla movement

History. This group is the result of a split in the MIR Perú (see above); it is strongest in the Chosica region.

Victoriano Esparraga Cumbi

Orientation. Left-wing guerrilla movement

History. This group was also formed after a split in the MIR Perú (see above); it is based in the Cajamarca, La Libertad and Piura regions.

Membership. Its strength has been estimated at 50 to 100 members.

Puerto Rico

Capital: San Juan   **Population: 3,281,000**

After three centuries as a colony of Spain, Puerto Rico became a US possession in 1898. It was administered as an unincorporated territory of the United States by an appointed Governor until 1947 and by an elective Governor thereafter. In 1952 it became the Commonwealth of Puerto Rico, "a free state in association with the United States". Political debate in Puerto Rico has subsequently been conducted within and between, on the one hand, those groups which seek a weakening or termination of the association with the United States and, on the other hand, those who seek a strengthening of the commonwealth relationship or even the absorption of Puerto Rico into the Union by the granting of statehood. A referendum on the issue was held on July 23, 1967, when 60.5 per cent of those voting supported the retention of the commonwealth system, 38.9 per cent favoured statehood and fewer than 1 per cent favoured independence. The political parties representing the two most favoured options are currently the pro-commonwealth Partido Popular Democrático (PPD) and the pro-statehood Partido Nuevo Progresista (PNP), founded in 1939 and 1967 respectively.

The PNP won the gubernatorial elections of 1968, 1976 and 1980 – the last by a very narrow margin – while the PPD won those of 1972 and 1984. Control of the legislature went to the party winning the governorship, except in the 1980 election.

Independence movement. Political violence in Puerto Rico has come mainly from left-wing groups advocating the "decolonization" and independence of Puerto Rico. Such violence has not been confined to the islands; much of it has occurred in the United States, which has a substantial minority population of Puerto Rican origin.

The Partido Nacionalista Puertorriqueño (Puerto Rican Nationalist Party) was for many years the leading political-military organization campaigning for Puerto Rican independence. It was founded in 1928 by Dr Pedro Albizu Campos; it received very little support in the elections of 1932 and thereafter did not take part in elections. Dr Albizu and other party members were convicted of conspiracy to overthrow the US government in Puerto Rico and served prison sentences in 1937–43. After some years on parole in New York they were permitted to return to Puerto Rico in 1948. In an insurrection led by the party on Oct. 30, 1950, some 27 people were killed, 51 injured and several hundred arrested. Dr Albizu was subsequently sentenced to long terms of imprisonment; 21 other party members, convicted of killing a policeman, were each given life sentences on May 21, 1951.

A member of the party was sentenced to death on April 1, 1951, for an attempt on the life of US President Harry S. Truman on Nov. 1, 1950. A White House guard was killed during the attempt. The sentence was later commuted to life imprisonment.

On March 1, 1954, three members of the party shot and wounded five US Congressmen in Washington; on July 8 the three were given prison sentences of up to 75 years. Numerous other party members were arrested in Puerto Rico and in the USA in March and May of 1954 and 13 of these were on Oct. 26 sentenced to six years in prison for "seditious conspiracy" against the US government.

The release of the four sentenced in April 1951 and July 1954 became a major demand of legal and illegal nationalist groups in the 1960s and 1970s. On Sept. 6, 1979, the four were granted clemency by President Jimmy Carter and were released. They indicated their intention to continue the struggle for Puerto Rican independence.

Statistics produced by the US Federal Bureau of Investigation (FBI) claimed that in 1982 there were 51 "acts of terrorism" in the United States, 25 of which were ascribed to Puerto Rican independence organizations.

Constitutional background. The 1952 constitution, adopted by referendum in Puerto Rico and by Act of Congress in the United States, defined the political and economic parameters of the Commonwealth association and established a system of government by an Executive appointed by a directly-elected Governor. There is an elected bicameral Legislative Assembly consisting of a 27-member Senate and a 51-member House of Representatives, the term of office in both chambers being four years. Of the members of the House of Representatives, 40 are elected in the 40 representative districts and 11 are elected "at large", having no specific local constituency. If any party wins two-thirds or more of the seats in either chamber, additional seats numbering up to one-third of the total are created and are reserved for minority parties.

In order to obtain official registration a new party, or one which has secured less than 5 per cent of the votes in the previous election, must deposit a list of signatures from at least three-quarters of the electoral districts and exceeding 5 per cent of the total votes cast in the previous gubernatorial election. Established parties are subsidized from public funds, while new parties receive subsidies in proportion to the number of votes which they win.

Recent election results. In elections held on Nov. 6, 1984, 33 seats in the House of Representatives and 18 in the Senate were gained by the PPD, 17 House seats and eight Senate seats by the PNP, and one seat in each chamber by the Partido Independentista Puertorriqueño (PIP). On the same day the PPD candidate, Rafael Hernández Colón, was elected Governor with 47.6 per cent of the votes cast, with 44.5 per cent going to the PNP, 4 per cent to the Partido de Renovación Puertorriqueño and 3.8 per cent to the PIP.

Comandos Armados de Liberación (CAL)
Armed Liberation Commandos

Orientation. Left-wing pro-independence guerrilla group

History. This group was reported to have been active in August 1981.

Ejército Popular Boricua (EPB)
Puerto Rican People's Army

Leadership. Victor Manuel Gerena (presumed leader)

Orientation. Left-wing pro-independence guerrilla group

History. This clandestine group, also known as Los Macheteros (The Cane-Cutters), claimed responsibility for attacks on 10 US Air National Guard planes in Puerto Rico in January 1981, and for the bombing of a power station at San Juan on Nov. 27, 1981. It was also held responsible for the fatal shooting of a number of US military personnel in Puerto Rico and in October 1984 claimed that it had carried out a $7,000,000 armed robbery in Connecticut in 1983. Agents of the FBI arrested 14 Puerto Ricans in August 1985 in connection with that robbery, and were seeking Gerena, who had, according to some reports, been granted asylum in Cuba.

Fuerzas Armadas de Liberación Nacional (FALN)
Armed Forces for National Liberation

Leadership. Carlos Alberto Torres (leader)

Orientation. Socialist, pro-independence guerrilla group

History. This organization has been involved in acts of violence in Puerto Rico and in various parts of the United States since 1972. By early 1979 it had been held responsible for more than 100 bombing incidents, including one in New York in 1975 which killed four people and injured 60. On July 3, 1978, two Puerto Rican nationalists attacked and occupied the Chilean consulate in San Juan in support of their demand for the release of nationalists imprisoned in the 1950s (see introduction, above) but they surrendered on the following day without their demand being met.

On April 11, 1979, a FALN member was sentenced in New York to 10 years in prison for unlawful possession of bombs and weapons. An alleged FALN member serving an 89-year sentence for bombings escaped from custody in New York in May of that year, and it was not until May 1983 that he was recaptured after a gun-battle with Mexican police in which two of his companions were killed. In 1980 FALN members attacked both Republican and Democratic party offices during the presidential election campaign. On Aug. 4, 1980, two FALN members were each sentenced in Chicago to 30 years in prison for conspiracy and illegal possession of arms. In March 1981 the FALN was reported to have issued threats against US Army recruiting officers. Later in 1981 10 FALN members were given lengthy sentences for bombings in the Chicago area.

The FALN claimed responsibility for four bomb explosions in New York's Wall Street area on Feb. 28, 1982. Five alleged FALN members arrested in New York refused to testify to a Federal Grand Jury on Sept. 28, 1982, on the grounds that they would not "collaborate with a tool of coercion aimed at all advocates of Puerto Rican independence". All were later convicted of contempt of court and gave themselves up in April 1984 to serve three-year sentences. On Dec. 31, 1982, four explosions in New York, which injured three policemen, were stated in a telephone call to be the work of the FALN. The FALN was held responsible for 10 "terrorist acts" of the 25 attributed by the FBI to Puerto Rican nationalists in 1982.

Among other actions in the course of 1983 the FALN bombed a marine recruiting office in Washington on Aug. 18. Four alleged FALN members were brought to trial in New York in January 1984, charged with planning to bomb military installations. Related contempt-of-court proceedings resulted in the imprisonment in 1984–85 of at least 10 people who had refused to co-operate with a grand jury investigation.

Policies. The FALN advocates revolutionary violence as a means to achieve independence from the United States, and to gain the release of their members and supporters imprisoned by the US authorities.

Associated organizations. The FALN is ideologically close to the PSP (see below).

International affiliations. The independence movement is supported in the United States by a New Movement in Solidarity with Puerto Rican Independence and Socialism and various other groups.

Federación Universitaria Pro-Independentista (FUPI)
Pro-Independence University Federation

Leadership. Juan Otero Garabís (president)

Orientation. Left-wing pro-independence group

History. This student group was reported to have been active in March 1985.

Policies. The group opposes the US presence in Puerto Rico and in particular what it sees as the militarization of the island. It also advocates the autonomy and democratization of the university system.

Grupo Amplio de Reflexión sobre Puerto Rico
Broad Group for Reflection on Puerto Rico

Leadership. Sarah Sosa (spokesperson)

Orientation. Catholic pro-independence group

History. This group, based in San Juan, was reported to have issued a statement in August 1981 calling for the ending of Puerto Rico's status as a "US colony" and for "full transfer of power to the people".

Los Macheteros

See Ejército Popular Boricua (above).

Movimiento Independentista Armado (MIRA)
Armed Pro-Independence Movement

Orientation. Left-wing pro-independence guerrilla group

History. This group was reported to have been active in 1981.

Movimiento de Liberación
Liberation Movement

Orientation. Left-wing pro-independence guerrilla group

History. This group claimed responsibility for an attack in which several shots were fired at a US Army base outside San Juan on Nov. 28, 1981.

Movimiento de Resistencia Armada Puertorriqueña (MRAP)
Puerto Rican Armed Resistance Movement

Orientation. Left-wing pro-independence guerrilla group

History. This group, an offshoot of the FALN (see above), has claimed responsibility for numerous bomb attacks in recent years, including those at Kennedy Airport, New York, on May 16–17, 1981, in which an airport employee died. In a communiqué issued in 1981 the group threatened further actions against US, Argentinian, Guatemalan and Honduran targets.

Movimiento Revolucionario Armado
Armed Revolutionary Movement

Orientation.   Left-wing pro-independence guerrilla group

History.   Two of the five members of this movement were killed by Puerto Rican police on July 25, 1978, in circumstances which led to considerable controversy and to the conviction on March 28, 1985, of 10 police officers on murder and perjury charges.

National Association for Statehood

Leadership.   Eliseo Casillas Galarza (president)

Orientation.   Pro-statehood

History.   This association was one of a number of Puerto Rican groups to take part in hearings of the United Nations Committee on Decolonization during 1981.

Policies.   The group seeks the integration of Puerto Rico with the United States as the 51st state of the Union.

Organización de Voluntarios para la Revolución Puertorriqueña (OVRP)
Organization of Volunteers for the Puerto Rican Revolution

Orientation.   Left-wing pro-independence guerrilla group

History.   This small group claimed responsibility for several bomb attacks in 1979–80, including an attack on communications installations on July 14, 1980. It was active again in 1984, claiming responsibility for at least two of four bombings of military and other targets in various Puerto Rican cities on Dec. 9–10.

Partido Comunista Puertorriqueño (PCP)
Puerto Rican Communist Party

Leadership.   Franklin Irrizarry (general secretary)

Orientation.   Communist, pro-independence

Founded.   September 1934

History.   In the 1950s PCP party workers were prosecuted under US laws in the same way as active members of the US Communist Party. The PCP's present programme was agreed upon in 1954.

Policies.   The PCP is opposed to the US military and political presence in Puerto Rico and calls for immediate independence. Its foreign policies are similar to those of the Soviet Communist Party.

Structure.   The PCP is organized on the basis of residential area and workplace groups. Its highest organ is the congress, held every five years, and between congresses a central committee which is elected by congress and which appoints a political commission.

Publications.   *El Pueblo*, monthly, circulation 3,000

International affiliations.   The PCP is recognized by the Communist Party of the Soviet Union and its allied parties.

Partido Independentista Puertorriqueño (PIP)
Puerto Rican Independence Party

Address. Avenida Roosevelt 963, Puerto Neuvo, San Juan, 00920

Leadership. Rubén Berríos Martínez (president); Fernando Martín García (vice-president; 1984 gubernatorial candidate)

Orientation. Social democratic, pro-independence

Founded. 1946

History. The party has worked since its formation for the full independence of Puerto Rico, and was particularly active in the campaign leading up to the plebiscite held in July 1967. At that time, fewer than 1 per cent of the voters backed independence; however, the vote was widely regarded as unrepresentative, and in 1978 a Democratic member of the US House of Representatives said that the result had been "deformed" by the harassment of PIP activists by agents of the US Federal Bureau of Investigation.

In the 1972 gubernatorial election the PIP's leader obtained third place, and in the 1976 elections to the Puerto Rican House of Representatives the PIP gained 76,000 votes, or 5.4 per cent of the total. In the gubernatorial election of 1980 Berríos Martínez polled 87,000 votes, while in that of 1984 Martín polled 66,000 votes. The party won one Senate seat (for Berríos) and one House seat in 1984, giving it its first parliamentary representation.

Policies. The PIP calls for immediate independence and the establishment of a Puerto Rican republic under democratic socialist principles. It also advocates the designation of the island as a nuclear-free zone.

Membership. 6,000

International affiliations. The PIP is a consultative member of the Socialist International.

Partido Nuevo Progresista (PNP)
New Progressive Party

Address. PO Box 5192, Puerta de Tierra Station, San Juan, 00906

Leadership. Presidency vacant in September 1985; Rafael Rodríguez Aguayo (secretary)

Orientation. Pro-statehood

Founded. August 1967

History. The PNP, which gained much of its initial strength from a split in the PPD (see below), won control of the Puerto Rican House of Representatives in the 1968 elections. It was ousted by the PPD in 1972, but, following a reorganization of the party during 1976, gained a majority in both chambers in the November 1976 elections. In November 1980 the PNP and the PPD each won 25 of seats in the House, the remaining seat being filled later by the PPD. The PNP, which had narrowly won the 1980 gubernatorial election, lost both the gubernatorial and the legislative elections of 1984; the former governor, Carlos Romero Barceló, resigned the party presidency in September 1985 in order to facilitate a reorganization. A split in the PNP led to the formation in 1983 of the PRP (see below).

Policies. The PNP advocates a more equitable distribution of wealth and the assimilation of Puerto Rico into the United States through the granting of statehood.

Structure. The highest authority in the party is the general assembly, consisting of delegates directly elected by the membership. Between assemblies the supreme organ is the central board, composed of senators, representatives, mayors and other leading figures in the party.

Membership. 225,000

Publications. *Camino al 80,* monthly, circulation 25,000

Partido Popular Democrático (PPD)
Popular Democratic Party

Address. Avenida Ponce de León 403, PO Box 5788, Puerta de Tierra Station, San Juan, 00906

Telephone. (809) 724 1984

Telex. ITT 0601

Leadership. Rafael Hernández Colón (president)

Orientation. Liberal, pro-Commonwealth

Founded. March 1939

History. In elections held in 1940 the PPD gained control of the Puerto Rican Senate; it also won control of the House of Representatives before the 1944 elections and held power thereafter until a split in the party in 1968 gave a majority to the PNP (see above). It regained control in 1972 but lost it again in the 1976 elections. In 1980, however, it won a close election and a majority in both chambers, though the governorship remained with the PNP; the PPD won the governorship and retained its legislative control in 1984 (see introduction). In 1985 the PPD controlled 57 of the 78 municipalities and its candidate was elected as Puerto Rico's (non-voting) delegate to the US House of Representatives.

The PPD was responsible, with the US Congress, for the creation of Puerto Rico's Commonwealth status in 1950–52.

Policies. The PPD is in favour of the retention and improvement of Commonwealth status. It also advocates "a more just society with particular emphasis on helping the poor, educating the masses and creating jobs through private enterprise".

Structure. The PPD has a 19-member board of governors, a general assembly, senatorial district boards and a council of founders.

Membership. 660,000

Publications. *El Yunque,* monthly, circulation 50,000

Partido de Renovación Puertorriqueño (PRP)
Puerto Rican Renewal Party

Leadership. Hernán Padilla Ramírez (leader)

Founded. July 1983

History. The PRP was founded as a result of a split in the PNP (see above). Its leader, then PNP mayor of San Juan, broke with the parent party while contesting the 1984 gubernatorial nomination and ran instead as a PRP candidate. He secured 4 per cent of the vote. The party is as yet unrepresented in either chamber of the Legislative Assembly.

Partido Socialista Puertorriqueño (PSP)
Puerto Rican Socialist Party

Address. Padre Colón 256, Río Piedras, San Juan, 00925

Leadership. Juan Mari Bras (leader, general secretary); Carlos Gallisá (president)

Orientation. Socialist, pro-independence

Founded. 1959, as Movimiento Pro-Independentista (MPI – Pro-Independence Movement)

History. The PSP came into being in November 1971 as a result of a decision to convert its predecessor, the MPI, into a political party. The MPI, originally a nationalist movement without clear ideology, had in 1968 embraced Leninism in the conviction that "independence will be reached together with socialism" and that "the social class capable of achieving this transformation is the working class".

In 1974–76 the party had the support of one member of the Puerto Rican House of Representatives. The party first took part in elections in 1976, when it gained less than 1 per cent of the vote. It obtained the same level of support in 1980 and did not contest the 1984 gubernatorial election.

Policies. The PSP advocates complete independence from the United States and the establishment of a socialist republic.

Structure. The party congress elects a central committee which appoints a political bureau and bureaux of political education, of democratic socialism and of organization.

Membership. 6,000

Publications. *Claridad*, weekly; *Tribuna Roja* and *Nueva Lucha*, bimonthly ideological magazines

Uruguay

Capital: Montevideo   **Population: 3,000,000**

The independence of Uruguay was recognized in 1828, after a period in which its territory was the subject of a dispute between Argentina and Brazil. Internal affairs have since been dominated by the struggle between the liberal Colorado (red) movement and the conservative Blancos (whites), giving rise to several outbreaks of civil war in the 19th century. The Colorados held power continuously from 1865 to 1958 and introduced an advanced social welfare system early in the present century. A plebiscite in 1951 replaced the executive presidency with a nine-member collective leadership, but in 1966 the presidential system was reintroduced after an election which also ended the eight years of Blanco government.

Under Jorge Pacheco Areco, who took office in December 1967, Uruguay became increasingly unstable; economic difficulties resulted in labour unrest and student activism. A serious threat to the established through a Council of State. Left-wing organizations were movement, the Tupamaros, and a ruthless counterinsurgency campaign, begun in 1971, was intensified under the next Colorado President, Juan María Bordaberry, who took office in March 1972. An "internal war" crushed the guerrilla movement by the end of 1973; congress was dissolved and effective military rule was established through a Council a State. Left-wing organizations were banned, press censorship and other repressive measures were introduced, and there were frequent reports of serious violations of human rights.

In 1976 Bordaberry was ousted; the military regime which replaced him attempted by means of successive Institutional Acts to restore stability by restructuring political institutions, depriving the judiciary of its independence, banning certain politicians from public activity and reorganizing the welfare system. A new constitution, designed to guarantee a continuing role for the armed forces in national decision-making, was rejected by the electorate in November 1980, and the military began a process of returning the country, then experiencing very severe economic difficulties, to civilian rule. By mid-1981 Uruguay was thought to have about 7,000 political prisoners, then the highest proportion of the population in any country. In November 1982 the three officially-permitted parties held internal elections resulting in victories for anti-military candidates; the subsequent intensification of repression failed to silence trade union and political opposition, and in August 1984 agreement was reached between the parties and the regime on the conditions for a transition to democracy, including the establishment of an advisory National Defence Council.

Elections in November 1984 were won by the Colorados, whose leader, Julio Sanguinetti, took office as President in March 1985. Press censorship, political detention and party proscriptions were ended and the Colorado government sought to establish a consensus approach to major economic and political issues.

Constitutional background. At the time of writing, there are plans for the revision of the 1966 Constitution, which defines Uruguay as a republic with an executive President and a bicameral congress, both elected by universal adult suffrage on a national party and faction list system for five-year terms. There are 99 seats in the Chamber of Deputies and 30 in the Senate.

Recent election results. In the elections of Nov. 25, 1984, the various lists of the Partido Colorado won 38.6 per cent of the vote, giving it the presidency, 41 seats in the Chamber and 13 seats in the Senate; the Partido Blanco won 32.9 per cent (35 and 11), the left-wing Frente Amplio 20.4 per cent (21 and 6) and the Christian democratic Unión Cívica 2.3 per cent (2 and none). The Colorados won local elections in 12 departments, including the capital, and the Blancos the other seven.

Agrupación Batllista Pregón "Julio César Grauert"

See Grupo Pregón (below).

Alianza Principista

See Batllismo Radical – Alianza Principista (below).

Batllismo Radical – Alianza Principista
Radical Batllismo – Principista Alliance

Leadership. Manuel Flores Mora (leader)
Orientation. Centre-left

History. This movement was formed by the uniting of two centre-left tendencies within the Partido Colorado (see below).

Consejo Nacional Herrerista
National Herrerista Council
Leadership. Luis Alberto Lancalle, Francisco Ubilles (leaders)

Orientation. Conservative

History. The Consejo is one of a number of contending factions in the Partido Blanco (see below).

Convergencia Socialista
Socialist Convergence
Leadership. Carlos Cerroti Frioni (leader)

Orientation. Left-wing

History. This small group participated in the 1984 elections with Cerroti as its unsuccessful presidential candidate.

Corriente Batllista Independiente
Independent Battlista Tendency
Leadership. Manuel Flores Silva (leader)

Orientation. Liberal

History. This movement is the smallest of five factions within the Partido Colorado (see below).

Corriente Popular Nacionalista
See Por la Patria (below).

Democracia Avanzada
See PCU (below).

Divisa Blanca
White Badge
Leadership. Eduardo Pons Etcheverry (leader)

Orientation. Conservative

History. The Divisa Blanca is one of the smaller factions within the Partido Blanco (see below).

Frente Amplio
Broad Front
Leadership. Gen. Líber Seregni Mosquera (leader)

Orientation. Left-wing

Founded. 1971

History. The Frente was formed as a left-wing electoral alliance by 17 groups ranging from communists to Christian democrats, and including dissident factions of both the Blanco and the Colorado parties. It won almost 19 per cent of the valid vote in the 1971 general elections, with Seregni – a former Colorado – as its presidential candidate, so becoming the third largest political force; no non-traditional party had previously won more than 6 per cent. The Frente was banned in 1973; many of its activists, including Seregni, were arrested and others, including a leading member, Zelmar Michelini, were killed. Seregni was released in late 1974 but rearrested in early 1976 and sentenced in May 1978 to 14 years in prison; although he was released in March 1984, he was proscribed from political activity until after the November elections. The Frente was involved in discussions with the military regime concerning the restoration of democracy, and was permitted to resume activities in August 1984. In November it was narrowly defeated in the Montevideo local government elections – the main focus of its campaign – and its presidential candidate, Dr Juan José Crottogini, was accorded 393,949 votes (20.4 per cent).

Membership. The Frente Amplio is a coalition of opposition groupings, with 13 members in 1985, including the Frente Izquierda de Liberación, the Grupo Pregón, the GAU, the Lista 99, the MAN, the MBPP, the Movimiento Socialista, the Movimiento 26 de Marzo, the Núcleos de Base Frenteamplista, the Partido Comunista (operating in the Frente Amplio as Democracia Avanzada), the Partido Demócrata Cristiano, the Partido Socialista Uruguayo and the Unión Popular (see below).

Policies. The Frente Amplio advocates radical land reform, the nationalization of the financial sector, state control of the export trade and a more active state participation in the economy. During the period of military rule it strongly supported the amnestying of political prisoners and opposed violations of human rights.

Frente Izquierda de Liberación (Fidel)
Left Liberation Front

Leadership. Adolfo Aguirre González (leader)

Orientation. Socialist

Founded. 1962

History. This organization, which was formed with the support of several left-wing groups including the PCU (see below), won a seat in the Senate and three in the Chamber in 1962, and five in the Chamber in 1966. It was a founding member of the Frente Amplio (see above) in 1971, and was banned with other leftist parties during the period of military rule.

Grupo Pregón
Pregón Group

Leadership. Sergio Previtali, Enrique Moras (leaders)

Orientation. Left-wing liberal

History. This organization, formally known as the Agrupación Batllista Pregón "Julio César Grauert", was formed as a faction of the Partido Colorado (see below) and joined the Frente Amplio in 1971. After a period of proscription it was permitted to reorganize in July 1984.

Grupos de Acción Unificadora (GAU)
Unification Action Groups

Leadership. Héctor Rodríguez (leader)

Orientation. Left-wing

Founded. February 1980

History. This organization, supported mainly by intellectuals and with influence in the trade union movement, was established within the Frente Amplio (see above).

Iglesia de Unificación
Unification Church ("Moonies")

Leadership. Sun Myung Moon (leader)

Orientation. Anti-communist religious cult

245

History. The Unification Church, widely known as the "Moonies" after its South Korean founder, is an international cult which has recently built up a presence in Uruguay. It uses its considerable resources to support various right-wing and anti-communist causes around the world, partly through its control of certain newspapers and publishing companies.

Publications. *Ultimas Noticias,* daily, circulation 19,000

Associated organizations. The Church owns Editorial Polo, a publishing company.

Libertad y Cambio
Liberty and Change

Address. Vásquez 1271, Montevideo

Leadership. Enrique E. Tarigo (leader)

Orientation. Left-wing liberal

History. This movement is allied with Unidad y Reforma (see below), forming the dominant tendency within the Partido Colorado (see below), of which its leader is general secretary.

Publications. *Opinar,* circulation 10,000

Lista 15

See Unidad y Reforma (below).

Lista 99
List 99

Leadership. Hugo Batalla (leader)

Orientation. Left-wing

Founded. 1962

History. This organization, also known as the Movimiento por el Gobierno del Pueblo (Movement for a People's Government), was originally a left-wing liberal grouping within the Partido Colorado (see below). It left the party in December 1970 and helped to found the Frente Amplio (see above), of which it is still an important member. Its then leader, Zelmar Michelini, was assassinated in Buenos Aires in May 1976.

Movimiento de Acción Nacionalista (MAN)
Nationalist Action Movement

Leadership. Jorge Durán Matos (leader)

Orientation. Left-wing nationalist

History. This organization was originally a progressive conservative tendency within the Partido Blanco (see below). In 1970 it became a founding member of the Frente Amplio (see above).

Movimiento Blanco Popular y Progresista (MBPP)
Popular Progressive Blanco Movement

Leadership. A. Francisco Rodríguez Camusso (leader)

Orientation. Moderate left-wing

History. This organization was originally a progressive tendency within the Partido Blanco (see below). It left the party in December 1970 and became a founding member of the Frente Amplio (see above).

Movimiento por el Gobierno del Pueblo

See Lista 99 (above).

Movimiento de Independientes 26 de Marzo

See Movimiento 26 de Marzo (below).

Movimiento de Liberación Nacional
National Liberation Movement

Leadership.   Raúl Sendic Antonaccio (leader)

Orientation.   Radical socialist

Founded.   1962

History.   This movement, popularly known as the Tupamaros (after Tupac Amaru, a Peruvian Indian rebel leader of the 18th century) was organized initially among sugar workers in the north of Uruguay. From 1963 it conducted a campaign of urban guerrilla warfare based on the strategy devised by Abraham Guillén, of Spain, including hit-and-run tactics aimed at obliging the government forces to surrender terrain and the organization of semi-autonomous guerrilla cells which could act without reference to a higher command. This strategy was reinforced by political work aimed at gaining mass support.

By mid-1972 the Tupamaros were said to number about 6,000, recruited mainly from among left-wing students and teachers. Their early actions included robberies, the proceeds of which they distributed among the poor, and later they engaged in kidnappings, assassinations, shootings and bombings with the aim of weakening the country's political leadership which they held responsible for the economic crisis. Notable victims of Tupamaro action were Dan A. Mitrione, a US adviser to the Uruguayan police force, kidnapped and killed in August 1970; Geoffrey Jackson, British ambassador in Montevideo, kidnapped in January 1971 and held until September; and Col. Artigas Alvarez, chief of the civil defence force, assassinated in July 1972.

The Tupamaros posed a substantial threat to the government by 1971, but in that year a counter-insurgency campaign was undertaken, and in 1972, under a new government, the army was given free rein and pursued the campaign with extreme rigour. The movement was effectively crushed by the end of 1973, and leading members either went into exile or, like Sendic, were imprisoned and treated with great severity.

In March 1985 the Supreme Court conducted a review of the cases of remaining Tupamaro prisoners and ordered their release. A statement released by the movement on Sept. 4, 1985, announced the permanent abandonment of armed struggle and the intention of the Tupamaro leadership to bring the movement into the Frente Amplio coalition (see above). It also announced the fusion of the movement with the Movimiento 26 de Marzo (see below).

Policies.   Since his release in March 1985, Sendic has indicated that the Tupamaro movement would reorganize not as a guerrilla group but as a political party with a programme including the nationalization of banks, land reform and the abrogation of all foreign debts contracted by the military regime.

Movimiento de Rocha

See Por la Patria (below).

Movimiento Socialista
Socialist Movement

Leadership.   Eduardo Jaurena, Jorge Andrade Ambrosoni (leaders)

Orientation.   Socialist

History. This organization was formed as a faction of the PSU (see below). It presented its own list in the general elections of 1966 and subsequently became a founding member of the Frente Amplio (see above).

Movimiento 26 de Marzo
March 26 Movement

Orientation. Socialist

History. The movement (formally known as the Movimiento de Independientes 26 de Marzo) was formed during the "internal war" against the Tupamaro guerrilla movement (which was itself formally known as the Movimiento de Liberación Nacional – National Liberation Movement). It joined the Frente Amplio coalition as one of its more left-wing components, and was banned with the other Frente parties in 1973. It remained proscribed until March 1985, and encouraged its followers to support the Frente Amplio candidates in the November 1984 general election. On Sept. 4, 1985, it announced the fusion of the movement with the Movimiento de Liberación Nacional (see above).

Policies. The Movement is ideologically identical with the Tupamaro guerrilla organization, with which it maintained contact during its years in clandestinity.

Núcleos de Base Frenteamplista
Broad Front Local Groups

Leadership. Danilo Astori (leader)

Orientation. Socialist

History. This organization is a member of the Frente Amplio (see above).

Partido Blanco
Blanco (White) Party

Address. 18 de Julio 2338, Montevideo

Telephone. 903355

Leadership. Wilson Ferreira Aldunate (party president); Carlos Julio Pereyra (president of national executive)

Orientation. Conservative

Founded. 1836

History. The Partido Blanco (formally known as the Partido Nacional) derives its popular name from the white flag which was used by the conservative side in the civil war of 1836–38. It was excluded from power until 1958, when it won elections to secure six of the nine seats on the national executive council, a form of collective presidency. It maintained this position after the 1962 general elections, but lost the November 1966 presidential and congressional elections and returned to opposition. In 1971 one of its main leaders, Ferreira Aldunate, narrowly failed to win election to the presidency. After the dissolution of congress in 1973 he left the country, and on his return in June 1984 he was arrested, and was not released until after the November elections in which the leading Blanco candidate, Alberto Sáenz de Zumarán, was accorded 634,166 votes (32.9 per cent). After the elections the party remained the largest opposition formation.

It is currently divided into various tendencies or *sublemas*, including the Consejo Nacional Herrerista and the Divisa Blanca (see above); the Partido Nacional–ACF, the Partido Nacional–Barrán, the Por la Patria–

Movimiento de Rocha–Corriente Popular Nacionalista alliance (see below) and a right-wing grouping led by Alberto Gallinal Héber.

Policies. The Blancos have traditionally been a rural conservative movement, but under Ferreira Aldunate the party has shifted to the left, the leader's policies including land reform and the nationalization of private banks.

Publications. *La Democracia*, party weekly, circulation 17,000; the most important daily newspaper supporting the Blancos is *El País*, circulation 130,000.

Partido Colorado
Colorado (Red) Party

Address. Vásquez 1271, Montevideo

Telephone. 490180

Leadership. Dr Julio María Sanguinetti Cairolo (President of the Republic, effective leader); Enrique E. Tarigo (Vice-President of the Republic; general secretary)

Orientation. Liberal

Founded. 1836

History. The party derives its name from the red flag used by the liberal faction in the civil war of 1836–38. It was in government from 1865 to 1958, and returned to power after the 1966 elections in which one of its two candidates was elected President and it gained 50 of the 99 seats in the Chamber of Deputies. In 1971 it lost its absolute majority but remained the largest party, with 41 seats, and its candidate, Juan María Bordaberry, was elected President. The party continued to govern until the military intervention of 1973 which led, in 1976, to the dismissal of Bordaberry. In the 1984 elections, ending the period of military rule, the Partido Colorado won the presidency for Julio María Sanguinetti with 744,999 votes (38.6 per cent) and became the strongest party in congress, but failed to secure an absolute majority in either chamber.

It is currently composed of five distinct tendencies or *sublemas*, each of which may put up its own list of candidates in elections; there are Batllismo Radical–Alianza Principista, the Corriente Batllista Independiente and Libertad y Cambio (see above); Unidad y Reforma and the Unión Colorado Batllista (see below).

Policies. The Partido Colorado is a mass party, attracting most of its support from the urban middle and working classes. Its domestic policies have favoured the urban sector of society, promoting state participation in the economy and the maintenance of a strong welfare system.

Publications. A number of newspapers and periodicals are loosely identified with factions of the party; the most important Colorado daily is *El Día*, circulation 100,000.

Partido Comunista Revolucionario (PCR)
Revolutionary Communist Party

Orientation. Maoist

History. This small party was active in 1985.

Partido Comunista del Uruguay (PCU)
Communist Party of Uruguay

Leadership. Rodney Arismendi (general secretary); Enrique Rodríguez, Alberto Altesor, Germán Araujo

Orientation.   Orthodox communist

Founded.   1920

History.   The PCU adopted its present name in 1921, but was in effect formed by the decision in 1920 of the left-wing majority of the Partido Socialista Uruguayo to affiliate that party to the Communist International. The party was legal for the first 52 years of its history. In recent decades it has followed a popular front strategy, supporting the formation of coalitions such as the Frente Izquierda de Liberación (see above) in 1962 and the Frente Amplio (see above) in 1971. It was made illegal in 1973 and severely repressed, its leaders being imprisoned or exiled.

The party's leader, Arismendi, who was deported in 1975, returned to Uruguay in November 1984, but the party was not legalized until March 1985. Although not permitted to take part as such in the November 1984 elections, the PCU campaigned actively within the Frente Amplio under the name Democracia Avanzada (Advanced Democracy), winning 6 per cent of the vote in 1984.

Policies.   As an orthodox "Moscow line" party, with a strong trade union presence (particularly in the Convención Nacional de Trabajadores – National Workers' Convention), the PCU condemned revolutionary guerrilla warfare as advocated by the Tupamaros; after the return to civilian government it announced that its priority was to assist in the consolidation of democratic institutions.

Membership.   7,500

International affiliations.   The PCU is recognized by the Soviet Communist Party and its allies.

Partido Demócrata Cristiano
Christian Democratic Party

Leadership.   Juan Guillermo Young (president)

Orientation.   Left-wing Christian democrat

Founded.   1872

History.   The party is directly descended from the Unión Cívica del Uruguay, founded in 1872, but adopted its present name in 1962. The original name was revived by the right-wing faction which split from the party in 1971 (see below). The party joined the Frente Amplio coalition (see above), was banned in 1973 and was legalized in July 1984.

Partido Laborista
Labour Party

Orientation.   Right-wing

Founded.   1984

History.   This group allied itself for the 1984 general elections with the Unión Patriótica (see below), but the joint presidential candidate, the leader of the Unión, died before election day.

Partido Nacional

See Partido Blanco (above).

Partido Nacional – ACF
National Party – ACF

Address.   Canelones 1055, Esc. 503, Montevideo

Leadership.   Horacio Muñiz Durand (director of *ACF* magazine)

Orientation.   Conservative

Founded. 1983 (*ACF* magazine)

History. The ACF faction is one of a number within the Partido Blanco (see above).

Publications. *ACF*, weekly

Partido Nacional – Barrán
National Party – Bernardo Barrán tendency

Orientation. Conservative

History. This is one of a number of contending factions in the Partido Blanco (see above).

Partido Obrero Revolucionario Trotskista (PORT)
Workers' Revolutionary Party, Trotskyist

Orientation. Trotskyist

Founded. 1937, as Liga Obrera Revolucionaria (Workers' Revolutionary League)

History. The party in 1963 supported the faction of the Fourth International led by Juan Posadas, who established his headquarters in Montevideo, and changed its name from Partido Obrero Revolucionaria, 4a Internacional, to the present form. Most of its leaders were arrested in 1968 on suspicion of complicity with the Tupamaros, and Posadas was deported.

International affiliations. Posadist Fourth International

Partido Socialista Uruguayo (PSU)
Uruguayan Socialist Party

Leadership. José Pedro Cardozo (general secretary); Hugo Rodríguez Filippini

Orientation. Socialist

Founded. 1910; reorganized 1921

History. The PSU was the first social democratic party in Uruguay, and gave rise to the PCU (see above) which was formed by a majority of PSU members in 1920–21. From 1959 the party adopted a more left-wing stance; it joined the Frente Amplio coalition (see above) in 1971.

Partido Revolucionario de los Trabajadores (PRT)
Workers' Revolutionary Party

Orientation. Trotskyist

Founded. 1969

History. The PRT was banned in 1973 but had its legal status restored in 1985.

International affiliations. Fourth International, United Secretariat

Partido de los Trabajadores
Workers' Party

Leadership. Juan Carlos Andrade (leader)

Orientation. Left-wing

Founded. 1984

History. This small formation contested the November 1984 elections, with Andrade as its presidential candidate, but failed to win representation.

Partido por la Victoria del Pueblo (PVP)
Party for the Victory of the People
Orientation. Revolutionary socialist

History. The PVP was formed as the Resistencia Obrero Estudiantil (ROE – Student and Worker Resistance), an independent opposition grouping outside the Frente Amplio. It suffered severe repression under the military regime, with an extensive series of arrests in 1976. The PVP remained proscribed during the November 1984 elections, but its legal status was restored with the return to civilian government in March 1985.

Por la Patria – Movimiento de Rocha – Corriente Popular Nacionalista
For the Homeland – Rocha Movement – Popular Nationalist Current
Leadership. Wilson Ferreira Aldunate, Carlos Julio Pereyra, Juan Raúl Ferreira, Juan Pivel Devoto (leaders)

Orientation. Centrist conservative

History. This coalition consists of three anti-military factions of the Partido Blanco (see above).

Servicio Paz y Justicia (Serpaj)
Peace and Justice Service
Leadership. Francisco Bustamante, Luis Pérez (spokespersons)

Orientation. Human rights concerns

History. This organization, the leading human rights pressure group in Uruguay, was formed with the support of the Argentinian organization of the same name which is directed by the Nobel Peace Prize winner, Adolfo Pérez Esquivel.

Tupamaros
See Movimiento de Liberación Nacional (above).

Unidad y Reforma
Unity and Reform
Leadership. Jorge Batlle Ibáñez, Dr Julio María Sanguinetti (leaders)

Orientation. Centrist liberal

History. This movement, also known as the Lista 15 (electoral list 15), is one of five factions within the Partido Colorado (see above); it is allied with the Libertad y Cambio group (see above).

Publications. Sanguinetti is one of two directors of the political weekly *Correo de los Viernes*, circulation 8,000.

Unión Cívica
Civic Union
Address. Río Branco 1486, Montevideo

Telephone. 905535

Leadership. Juan Vicente Chiarino (leader)

Orientation. Right-wing Christian democrat

Founded. 1971

History. The Unión Cívica del Uruguay was founded in 1872, but the present user of the name is a right-wing faction which broke away from what had become the PDC (see above) in 1971. It was banned under the military regime, but was revived as a right-wing Catholic party in 1981; it was one of the three parties permitted to hold internal elections in 1982, and in 1983–84 it was involved in the negotiations leading to a return to civilian rule. In the November 1984 general elections it secured only two seats in the lower chamber.

Unión Colorado Batllista
Batllista Colorado Union

Leadership. Jorge Pacheco Areco (leader)

Orientation. Right-wing liberal

History. This movement, also known as the Pachequista tendency after its leader, represents the pro-military right wing within the Partido Colorado (see above). Its leader was President of Uruguay from 1967 to 1972.

Unión Patriótica
Patriotic Union

Orientation. Right-wing

Founded. September 1982

History. This pro-military grouping (also known as the Unión Patriótica Salvadora de la Democracia – Patriotic Union for the Salvation of Democracy) was formed by Col. (retd) Néstor Bolentini, who was Minister of the Interior in 1973–74. In the run-up to the November 1984 elections it co-operated with the Partido Laborista, with Bolentini as the presidential candidate, but his death shortly before the election left the future of the party uncertain.

Unión Popular
Popular Union

Leadership. Enrique René Erro (leader)

Orientation. Progressive

Founded. 1962

History. Originally a faction of the Partido Blanco (see above), the Unión Popular joined the Frente Amplio (see above) in 1971. Its leader sought asylum in Argentina after the 1973 military takeover in Uruguay, but he was arrested in Buenos Aires in April 1976.

Venezuela

Capital: Caracas   **Population: 17,200,000**

The Republic of Venezuela achieved separate independence in 1830, and did not have a democratically-elected government until the centre-left Acción Democrática (AD) regime of Rómulo Gallegos was installed in 1947. Gallegos was ousted by a military coup in 1948, but the ensuing dictatorship was itself overthrown by a popular revolt in January 1958. After a period of rule by a revolutionary junta, Rómulo Betancourt of the AD was elected President in December, served a complete term of office – the first in the country's history – and was replaced in December 1963 by Raúl Leoni, also of the AD.

Extra-parliamentary protest activities, organized by left-wing groups most of which had broken away from the AD, began in 1960, and in 1962 the Fuerzas Armadas de Liberación Nacional (FALN) began a guerrilla campaign. Together with the Movimiento de la Izquierda Revolucionaria it attempted to disrupt the 1963 elections. Urban guerrilla warfare continued until the mid-70s although by 1967 divisions had arisen within and between the combatant groups. That year the Partido Comunista de Venezuela declared a "democratic peace" and renounced violence; in 1969 it was legalized. A right-wing military coup was foiled in 1966. By 1975 the FALN had been more or less defeated and its leader, Douglas Bravo, accepted an amnesty in 1979. The left-wing Bandera Roja movement, which had been involved in violent incidents in the early 1970s, was again involved in kidnappings, robberies and hijackings in the late '70s and early '80s, but the athorities claimed to have broken up the group by mid-1983.

Dr Rafael Caldera Rodríguez, the candidate of the Partido Social Cristiano (COPEI), was elected President in 1968; he was succeeded by Carlos Andrés Pérez of the AD in the elections of 1973 and by Luis Herrera Campíns of the COPEI in those of 1978. Jaime Lusinchi of the AD was elected in 1983, his term of office commencing on Feb. 2, 1984.

Constitutional background. Under the 1961 Constitution executive power is vested in the President, who appoints a Council of Ministers; legislative power is exercised by a bicameral Congress, the Senate having 44 elected members and as life members the ex-presidents of constitutional governments, and the Chamber of Deputies having 199 members. The President and Congress are elected for concurrent five-year terms by universal and compulsory adult suffrage. The Republic is a confederation of 20 states, each with

254

an appointed Governor and an elected legislature, two federal territories and a federal capital district.

Recent election results. In the elections of Dec. 4, 1983, Jaime Lusinchi of the AD received 56.8 per cent of the vote; ex-President Caldera of the COPEI received 34.6 per cent, Teodoro Petkoff of the MAS received 4.2 per cent and the remainder was shared by 10 other candidates. The AD won 109 seats in the Chamber, the COPEI 60, the MAS 10, the URD 8, Opina 3, the PCV 2, the MIN 2 and the NA 1. In the Senate, seats were distributed as follows: AD 27, COPEI 16, MAS 2 and URD 2. Municipal elections took place in May 1984, the AD winning 52.6 per cent of the vote, the COPEI 21.7 per cent and the MAS 7.2 per cent, the rest being shared by 121 parties, mostly local formations.

Acción Democrática (AD)
Democratic Action

Address. Calle Los Cedros, La Flórida, Caracas 1050

Leadership. Dr Gonzalo Barrios (president); Manuel Peñalver (general secretary); Enrique Tejera Paris (international secretary)

Orientation. Social democratic

Founded. 1936, as Partido Democrático Nacional (National Democratic Party)

History. The party obtained legal status and adopted its present name in 1941, declaring itself to be democratic, socialist, nationalist, revolutionary, anti-feudal and anti-imperialist. It had supporters among all classes of the population but was based on the organized workers and came to control most of the trade unions.

The AD was in power in 1945–47 when its founder, Rómulo Betancourt, headed a revolutionary junta, but its first elected President, Rómulo Gallegos – installed in 1947 – was overthrown in 1952 by a military coup and the ensuing dictatorship was not itself overthrown until 1958. The party's candidates were elected to the presidency for 1959–64 (Betancourt), 1964–69 (Raúl Leóni) and 1974–79 (Carlos Andrés Pérez). These years were marked by land reform, the nationalization of oil and iron ore resources and rapid agricultural and industrial development.

The AD lost the elections of 1978 but returned to power after the general elections of Dec. 4, 1983, when its presidential candidate, Dr Jaime Lusinchi, obtained 56.8 per cent of the votes cast, and its congressional candidates 50 per cent. It gained 109 seats in the Chamber of Deputies and 27 in the Senate. The party is currently divided into two factions, one loyal to Lusinchi and the other supporting ex-President Pérez.

Policies. The AD is a social democratic movement with the aim of political, economic and social equality for all Venezuelans. On the international front it promotes North–South and South–South co-operation.

Membership. 1,450,000

Associated organizations. The party has a very substantial influence in the trade union movement through its affiliate, the Confederación de Trabajadores de Venezuela (CTV – Workers' Confederation of Venezuela), which represents 1,500,000 workers.

International affiliations. The AD is a member of the Socialist International, of which Barrios is an honorary president.

Bandera Roja
Red Flag

Leadership. Juan Pablo Miranda Herrera (alleged leader; in custody)

Orientation. Marxist–Leninist guerrilla group

Founded. 1968

History. This small group broke away from the FALN (see PRV, below) and was engaged in various guerrilla activities until 1978. Its leaders, the brothers Carlos and Argenis Betancourt, were both arrested in 1977. The group, however, was again active in September 1980, when it seized weapons and the equivalent of US$2,000,000 in a raid in Valencia, east of Caracas.

The then leader, Gabriel Puerte Aponte, and 10 other members were captured in Caracas on May 6, and four members of the group and two policemen were killed in a clash some 200 miles east of Caracas on May 12. By June 1983 the Venezuelan authorities were claiming that the group had been destroyed, but it claimed responsibility for the bombing of a radio station and a newspaper office on Sept. 16, 1984. Miranda Herrera, a Chilean, was among 24 suspected members of the group arrested in June 1983.

Associated organizations. Reports in 1982 described the Frente Américo Silva and the Comandos Internacionales Manuel Rojas Luzardo (see below) as linked to the Bandera Roja Group. (See also Colombian ELN.)

Causa R
Cause R

Orientation. Left-wing

History. This group, originally known as Causa Radical (Radical Cause), supported the NA coalition (see below) in the 1983 elections. Some of its members went on to join the MPS (see below).

Comando Ramón Emeterio Betance
Ramón Emeterio Betance Commando

Orientation. Left-wing guerrilla group

History. This group, which is probably extinct, was named after a 19th-century Puerta Rican nationalist. On Dec. 7, 1981, it claimed responsibility for the hijacking to Cuba of three Venezuelan airliners. The hijackers demanded the release of 23 alleged political prisoners in Venezuela and the payment of a cash ransom; they also appealed for solidarity with the guerrillas of El Salvador and distributed leaflets on behalf of the Comandos Internacionales Manuel Rojas Luzardo (see below). All the hijackers were arrested in Cuba on Dec. 8.

Comando Revolucionario Armigiro Gabaldón
Armigiro Gabaldón Revolutionary Commando

Orientation. Left-wing guerrilla group

History. This group, which may now be defunct, was responsible for the kidnapping on Feb. 27, 1976, of a US businessman working in Caracas. The group secured as part of a ransom deal the publication in three international newspapers of a communiqué attacking the role of transnational corporations in the Venezuelan economic and political system.

In an effort to prevent the payment of the cash element of the ransom the Venezuelan authorities arrested a number of persons including two opposition deputies and the general secretary of the Liga Socialista (see below); the latter was killed by four policemen reportedly acting without orders. The kidnapped executive was released on June 30, 1979, near Ciudad Bolívar; accounts differed on whether he was freed by police after a shootout in which two guerrillas were killed, or whether the release resulted from negotiations conducted by the government as part of its "pacification policy" (see PRV, below).

Comandos Internacionales Manuel Rojas Luzardo
Manuel Rojas Luzardo International Commandos

Orientation. Left-wing guerrilla group

History. This group, which was active in the early 1980s, was described in some reports as linked with the Bandera Roja movement (see above). Its leaflets were distributed during a 1981 hijack attributed to the Comando Ramón Emeterio Betance (see above).

Comité de Organización Política Electoral Independiente (COPEI)

See Partido Social Cristiano (below)

Constancia Gremial
Union Steadfastness

Orientation. Left-wing labour group

History. This organization was reportedly active in 1984.

Associated organizations. Constancia Gremial is one of the members of the NA left coalition (see below).

Coordinadora Nacional de la Izquierda
National Left Co-ordinating Committee

Orientation. Broad left front

History. This body was established by the main left-wing parties in response to the poor showing of the left in the 1978 elections. In January 1981 it established a commission to explore the possibility of a single left-wing candidature in the 1983 presidential election, but the project foundered on the differences arising between the Rangel and Petkoff factions of the largest constituent group, the MAS (see below). Most of the Coordinadora followed the Rangel group into the Nueva Alternativa coalition (see below).

Frente Américo Silva
Américo Silva Front

Orientation. Left-wing guerrilla group

History. Army and police units clashed on Oct. 4, 1982, with a guerrilla group at Cantuaura, 150 miles south-east of Caracas. One policeman and 27 others were killed. It was reported that the guerrillas belonged to the Américo Silva Front, which was described as the armed wing of the Bandera Roja movement (see above).

Fuerzas Armadas de Liberación Nacional (FALN)

See PRV (below).

Grupo de Acción Revolucionaria (GAR)
Revolutionary Action Group

Orientation. Left-wing

History. This group gave its support to the NA alliance (see below) in the 1983 presidential election. Some of its members were later involved in the MPS (see below).

Liga Socialista
Socialist League

Leadership. Carmelo Laborit (president)

Orientation. Trotskyist

Founded. 1974

History. The League succeeded the Partido Socialista de los Trabajadores (Workers' Socialist Party, founded in 1972) and the Organización de Revolucionarios (OR – Organization of Revolutionaries). In 1976 it was suspected of involvement in a kidnapping, and its general secretary, Jorge Rodríguez, was tortured to death by policemen (see Comando Revolucionario Armigiro Gabaldón, above). The League was the smallest party to gain a seat in the 1978 elections to the Chamber of Deputies, when it gained 0.6 per cent of the vote. In March 1979 its then leader, David Nieves, was released from prison by the newly-inaugurated President Luis Herrera Campins of the COPEI. He assumed the party's seat and retained it in the 1983 elections.

International affiliations. Fourth International, United Secretariat

M-28

Orientation. Left-wing guerrilla group

History. Members of this small group were sought by the police and army in operations conducted in August 1980 near Valencia, east of Caracas.

Movimiento Electoral del Pueblo (MEP)
People's Electoral Movement

Address. Quinta La Trinidad, Calle Bolívar, Urbanización Washington, Caracas

Leadership. Dr Luis Beltrán Prieto Figueroa (president); Dr Jesús Angel Paz Galarraga (general secretary)

Orientation. Left-wing social democratic

Founded. December 1967

History. The MEP was founded as a result of a split in the AD (see above), partly over the question of the AD candidature in the 1968 presidential election. The MEP presented its own candidate, securing fourth place with 19.3 per cent of the vote; in simultaneous elections to the Chamber of Deputies, the MEP became the third strongest party with 26 of the 188 seats. In the 1973 elections, however, it was reduced to eight seats out of 203. Paz Gallarga was the 1973 presidential candidate of the Fuerza Nueva (New Force) coalition, comprising the MEP and the PCV (see below), and came third with 5.1 per cent of the vote; in 1978 Beltrán stood for the MEP and obtained only 1.1 per cent.

In the 1983 presidential election the MEP supported the candidature of José Vicente Rangel (see Nueva Alternativa, below), and in the congressional elections held at the same time it secured 2 per cent of the vote.

Membership. 100,000

International affiliations. The MEP is a consultative member of the Socialist International.

Movimiento de Integración Nacional (MIN)
National Integration Movement

Address. Edificio José María Vargas 1°, esq. Pajaritos, Caracas

Leadership. Gonzalo Pérez Hernández (general secretary)

Founded. 1977

History. This group won a single seat in the 1983 elections to the Chamber of Deputies.

Movimiento Internacional del Proletariado
International Movement of the Proletariat

Orientation. Left-wing guerrilla group

History. Two members of this group hijacked a Venezuelan airliner, with 55 passengers, to Cuba on Nov. 6, 1980, in protest at the acquittal by a Venezuelan court of four men accused of the killing of 73 people on a Cuban airliner bombed in 1976 (see El Condor, in the Cuban section). The group has not been active recently and may be extinct.

Movimiento de Izquierda Revolucionaria (MIR)
Revolutionary Left Movement

Leadership. Moisés Moleiro (general secretary)

Orientation. Marxist–Leninist

Founded. 1960

History. The MIR was founded by left-wing members of AD (see above). It pursued a strategy of urban guerrilla warfare in 1962–64 and operated from rural bases thereafter. It was banned in 1962 but legalized in 1969 after it adopted a parliamentary strategy. It supported the MAS (see below) in the 1973 presidential elections and gained one seat in simultaneous elections to the Chamber of Deputies. In 1978 it increased its representation to four seats, and presented its own presidential candidate, Américo Martín, who gained less than 1 per cent of the vote and subsequently led a breakaway group into the Vanguardia Unitaria (see below). In the 1983 general elections, the MIR again supported the MAS; it gained two seats in the Chamber (and the MAS 10).

Movimiento Patria Socialista (MPS)
Socialist Homeland Movement

Orientation. Left-wing

Founded. May 1983

History. The MPS was founded by dissident left-wing members of the MAS (see below), and attracted members of other leftist groups including Causa R and the GAR (see above) and Vanguardia Unitaria (see below). It supported the Nueva Alternativa candidate in the 1983 presidential election.

Associated organizations. The MPS has joined the NA left coalition (see below).

Movimiento Revolucionario Popular (MRP)
Popular Revolutionary Movement

Orientation. Very left-wing

History. The MRP was reported to be active in 1984.

Associated organizations. It is a member of the NA left coalition (see below).

Movimiento al Socialismo (MAS)
Movement towards Socialism

Address. Quinta Alemas, Avenida Valencia, Urbanización Las Palmas, Caracas

Leadership. Teodoro Petkoff (president); Pompeyo Márquez (general secretary)

Orientation. "Eurocommunist"

Founded. January 1971

History. The MAS was formed after a split in the PCV (see below) over questions such as the interpretation of Marxism, the Czechoslovakian crisis, the form of socialism to be established, the role of the party and the analysis of society. In the 1973 elections it won some 275,000 votes and nine of the 203 seats in the Chamber of Deputies; it also secured two of the 49 seats in the Senate. In December 1978 its presidential candidate, José Vicente Rangel, came third with 5.1 per cent of the vote, while it increased its congressional vote to 350,000; in the June 1979 municipal elections it took 500,000 votes or 12 per cent of the total.

The movement split in the early 1980s between factions led by Petkoff, who favoured the presentation of a MAS candidate in the 1983 presidential election, and Rangel, who brought the movement into the Coordinadora coalition (see above) in an unsuccessful effort to find a "broad left" candidate. The Rangel faction went on to join the Vanguardia Unitaria and the Nueva Alternativa coalition (see below), while the MAS under Petkoff was allied only with the Moleira faction of the MIR (see above). In the 1983 presidential election Petkoff obtained 4.2 per cent, while in the congressional elections the party obtained 5.8 per cent, giving it 10 seats in the Chamber and two in the Senate. The MAS has suffered other factional splits, including that leading to the formation in 1983 of the MPS (see above).

Policies. The MAS promotes a form of socialism particular to the historical experience and needs of Venezuela.

Structure. The party consists of cells, zonal and regional committees, a representative national leadership and a national bureau.

Membership. 180,000

Publications. *Reflexiones*; *Boletín Nacional*; *Boletín Fracción Socialista*; *SDL*; *Punto*

Nueva Alternativa (NA)
New Alternative

Address. Edificio José María Vargas 2°, esq. Pajaritos, Caracas 1010; Apartado 20193, San Martín, Caracas

Leadership. Guillermo García Ponce, Américo Martín, Estanislao González, Luis Miquelena, Dr José Vicente Rangel (members of national co-ordinating committee)

Orientation. Left-wing

Founded. July 24, 1982

History. Nueva Alternativa was established as an electoral coalition including, or supported by, 12 left-wing groups which retained their separate identities; the leading groups were Vanguardia Unitaria (see below) and the MRP (see above). For the 1983 presidential elections the coalition nominated Rangel (formerly of the MAS – see above) and secured the support of various other left-wing parties and groups, including the PCV (see below). Rangel obtained 219,368 votes – 3.3 per cent – and the coalition secured one seat in the Chamber of Deputies and several in two state legislatures, as well as some on municipal councils.

Policies. The alliance favours fundamental economic reforms to equalize the distribution of wealth and end the power of monopolistic groups.

Structure. The supreme organ of the alliance is its 140-member national directorate, which elects a 21-member national political committee. A small national co-ordinating committee, or general secretariat, deals with day-to-day political and organizational tasks.

Membership. The principal members of the NA coalition are Constancia Gremial, the MPS and the MRP (see above) and Vanguardia Unitaria (see below).

Publications. *Década 80* and *Nueva Alternativa*, circulation of both 15,000

Associated organizations. Groups which supported the 1983 presidential campaign of the coalition included Causa R, the GAR and the MEP (see above); the PCV and the URD (see below).

Nueva Generación
New Generation

Leadership. Gen. (retd) Arnaldo Castro Hurtado (leader)

Orientation. Right-wing

Founded. 1979

History. Nueva Generación presented Castro as its candidate in the 1983 presidential election, but he polled only a negligible number of votes.

Opinión Nacional (Opina)
National Opinion

Address. Pájaro a Curamichate 92, 2°, Caracas 101

Leadership. Dr Pedro Luis Blanco Peñalver (president); Amado Corneilles (general secretary)

Orientation. Centre-right

Founded. March 1961

History. Opina has repeatedly been represented in Congress, and in the December 1978 general elections it won one seat in the Chamber of Deputies. In the 1978 presidential election it supported the successful candidate of the COPEI (see Partido Social Cristiano, below), but in 1983 it nominated its own candidate, Jorge Olavarría, who obtained only 0.5 per cent of the vote. In the 1983 congressional elections the party obtained 2 per cent of the votes and three seats in the Chamber.

Policies. The party expounds its own philosophy of "collective integralism".

Structure. The party has a national congress, a supreme federal council, a central committee and a national disciplinary council. It is organized at state, district and communal level.

Membership. 22,000

Publications. *Opina*, monthly; Olavarría is the publisher of the weekly news magazine *Resumen*, circulation 65,000

Partido Comunista de Venezuela (PCV)
Communist Party of Venezuela

Address. Edificio Cantaclaro, esq. San Pedro, San Juan, Caracas

261

Leadership.   Jesús Faría (general secretary)

Orientation.   Communist

Founded.   1931

History.   The PCV operated clandestinely until 1945, when it was granted legal status by an AD government. In 1946 it contested the Constituent Assembly elections, winning two of the 160 seats. It unsuccessfully contested the December 1948 presidential election. It was again banned between May 1950 and January 1958, but was briefly in government as one of four parties which formed a Patriotic Junta in the latter month. It won two Senate seats and seven in the Chamber in 1958.

In May 1962 the PCV was banned on the grounds of its participation in guerrilla activities. The party leadership abandoned the guerrilla strategy in 1967 in favour of an electoral strategy based on the construction of a "broad popular movement for progressive democratic change". The PCV regained legal status in 1969 and subsequently held five seats in the Chamber of Deputies until 1973, and two until 1978. In 1978 its presidential candidate secured less than 1 per cent of the vote, and in 1983 it supported the unsuccessful candidature of Dr Rangel of Nueva Alternativa (see above). The party won two seats in the Chamber of Deputies.

The history of the PCV has been marked by a number of splits, purges and expulsions, including those leading to the formation of the MAS (see above) and of Vanguardia Unitaria (see below). A leading member of the party, Hemmy Croes – president of the Confederación Unitaria de Trabajadores de Venezuela (CUTV – Unified Confederation of Venezuelan Workers) – was assassinated by unidentified gunmen on March 4, 1985.

Policies.   In 1971 the party congress proclaimed the PCV's "loyalty to Marxism–Leninism and uncompromising struggle against opportunism". The foreign policies of the PCV are in sympathy with those of the Soviet Communist Party (although in 1960 it had supported the Chinese party).

Structure.   The supreme organ of the PCV is the congress, which elects a central committee.

Membership.   22,000

Publications.   *Tribuna Popular*, weekly newspaper; *Ideología*, theoretical journal

Associated organizations.   The party has a presence in the trade union movement, being the leading force in the Central General de Trabajadores (General Congress of Workers).

International affiliations.   The PCV is recognized by the Communist Party of the Soviet Union and its allied parties.

Partido de la Revolución Venezolana (PRV)
Party of the Venezuelan Revolution

Leadership.   Douglas Bravo (leader)

Orientation.   Marxist

History.   The leader of the PRV was previously better known as the commander of a guerrilla movement, the Fuerzas Armadas de Liberación Nacional (FALN – Armed Forces of National Liberation). The FALN, which started its campaign with the bombing of oilfield installations in 1962, carried out numerous and spectacular actions in the 1960s and early 70s, but was largely subdued by the security forces by 1975. The FALN leadership took advantage of a "pacification policy" pursued by the COPEI government elected in 1978 to establish a ceasefire, emerge from clandestinity and enter electoral politics. Bravo received an amnesty in September 1979, and established the PRV in the early 1980s.

Partido Social Cristiano – Comité de Organización Política Electoral Independiente (COPEI)

Social Christian Party – Independent Electoral Political Organizing Committee

Address. Avenida Panteón esq. Fuerzas Armadas, San Bernardino, Caracas 1011

Leadership. Dr Rafael Caldera Rodríguez (President of Venezuela 1968–73); Dr Luis Herrera Campíns (President of Venezuela 1979–83); Dr Pedro Pablo Aguilar, Dr Godofredo González (other leaders); Dr Eduardo Fernández (general secretary)

Orientation. Social Christian

Founded. 1946

History. The party, which is universally known as COPEI, won 19 of the 160 seats in the Constituent Assembly elected in 1946. Its presidential candidate in 1943, Dr Caldera, lost overwhelmingly to AD. The party gained 14 of the 104 seats in the Constituent Assembly elected in 1952. Together with AD, the PCV and the Partido Demócrata Republicano, it was in the Patriotic Junta which overthrew the Pérez Jimnez regime in January 1958, and the same parties, with the exclusion of the PCV, subsequently allied as the Frente Cívico (Civic Front). In December the COPEI won 19 of the 133 seats in the Chamber of Deputies, securing 14.4 per cent of the vote, and for the following five years it governed in coalition with AD.

In 1963 the COPEI won 40 seats and Dr Caldera came second in the presidential election, with 20.2 per cent of the vote. In 1968 he obtained 29.1 per cent and was elected President, while the party secured 50 of the 188 seats in the Chamber. The COPEI formed its first government with the support of independent deputies.

In 1973 it increased its representation to 64 seats out of 188, and its presidential candidate gained 36.8 per cent but came second. The AD returned to government until 1978, when a COPEI President, Dr Herrera Campíns, was elected with 46.6 per cent of the vote. In 1979 the party gained an absolute majority of the votes cast in municipal elections, but then began to decline in popularity.

In December 1983 Dr Caldera was again the COPEI candidate for the presidency. He lost with 34.6 per cent of the vote, while the party's congressional candidates obtained only 28.7 per cent. The party gained 60 seats in the Chamber and 16 in the Senate.

Policies. The party advocates a centrist form of Christian democracy.

Structure. The supreme authority is the national convention, meeting ordinarily every 2½ years. There is a national directorate, meeting at least annually; a national committee, elected at alternate conventions; a national disciplinary tribunal and other bodies at national, regional, district, municipal and branch levels.

Membership. Estimated variously at 400,000–800,000

Associated organizations. The party has a trade union affiliate, the Confederación de Sindicatos Autónomos de Venezuela (Codesa – Venezuelan Confederation of Autonomous Trade Unions).

International affiliations. The COPEI is an active member of the Christian Democratic International and of the Christian Democratic Organization of America.

Punto Cero
Zero Point

Orientation. Marxist guerrilla group

Founded. 1975

History. This small urban guerrilla group was active in the late 1970s; it rejected a presidential amnesty offer in December 1979 and was again reported active in 1981.

Rescate Nacional
National Rescue

Leadership. Gen. (retd) Luis Enrique Rangel Bourgoin (leader)

Orientation. Right-wing

History. The party leader, who had been Minister of Defence in 1979–80, stood as an independent candidate in the 1983 presidential election but polled negligibly.

Tradición, Familia y Propiedad (TFP)
Tradition, Family and Property

Orientation. Catholic traditionalist, anti-communist

Founded. 1960

History. This international anti-communist organization, founded in Brazil by Plínio Correa de Oliveira, established a branch in Venezuela in the 1970s. It was banned by the AD goverment late in 1984 on the grounds that it was engaging in subversive activities.

Policies. The aim of the TFP is "to combat the penetration of socialism and communism"; its branches in various Western countries have been responsible for the placement of full-page advertisements in major newspapers attacking, for example, the Mitterrand regime in France.

Unión Republicana Demócrata (URD)
Democratic Republican Union

Address. Quinta Amalia, Avenida Páez, El Paraíso, Caracas

Leadership. Dr Jóvito Villalba (leader)

Orientation. Centre-left

Founded. 1946

History. The URD contested the 1952 Constituent Assembly elections with the support of AD (see above), which was then illegal. It became the second-largest party with 29 of the 104 seats. With other parties, it was suppressed by the Pérez Jiménez dictatorship, but contributed to the overthrow of the regime in January 1958 as part of the Patriotic Junta.

The URD parliamentary representation subsequently declined in numbers as the number of seats in the Chamber of Deputies increased; it won 34 out of 133 seats in 1958, 29 of 179 in 1963, 14 of 188 in 1968, and five of 203 in 1973. In 1978 it was reduced to three deputies, who sat with the COPEI bloc, and in 1983 it won eight seats in the Chamber and two in the Senate. It has been unsuccessful in presidential elections, whether with its own candidates or in alliances, most recently in 1983 when it supported the candidate of Nueva Alternativa (see above). It has suffered from a number of defections and splits.

Vanguardia Unitaria
Unity Vanguard

Address. Apartado 20193, San Martín, Caracas

Leadership. Eduardo Machado (president); Guillermo García Ponce (general secretary)

Orientation. Marxist

Founded. November 1974

History. The Vanguardia Unitaria was founded as a result of the withdrawal from the PCV (see above) of a group which had unsuccessfully demanded the "democratization" of the party apparatus. In 1978 it supported the losing presidential candidate of the MAS (see above), José Vicente Rangel, and in June 1979 fought the municipal elections as part of a six-party left alliance. It drew additional strength from a split in the MIR (see above); a moderate faction led by Américo Martín split from the tendency led by Moisés Moleiro in the early 1980s, the principal strategic difference being on the question of support for the MAS (see above) and its prospective 1983 presidential candidate, Teodoro Petkoff (supported by Moleiro), or for a broad front of leftist parties with a common candidate, as advocated by Martín (who had been the MIR candidate in 1978). The Martín faction joined the Vanguardia and Martín became for a time its leader. In 1982 the Vanguardia was a founding member of the Nueva Alternativa left coalition (see above), supporting the NA candidate – again Dr Rangel – in the 1983 presidential election.

Policies. Advocating an "undogmatic" Marxism adapted to the realities and needs of Venezuela, the party seeks the establishment of a government of advanced democracy.

Index of Names

Names are listed according to their English-language alphabetical sequence, i.e. treating ll and ch as two letters each, and ignoring accentuation.

267